DATE DUE

DEC 5 1973	OCT 3 1 1986
MAR 2 0 1979	1 4 DEC 2005
NOV 2 1983 1984	
FEB 2 2 1984	
NOV. 15 1984	
MAR 1 9 1986	
FEB 1 8 1997	

CANADIAN LABOUR IN TRANSITION

CANADIAN LABOUR
IN
TRANSITION

Edited by

Richard Ulric Miller

Associate Director
Industrial Relations Research Institute
The University of Wisconsin

and

Fraser Isbester

Faculty of Business
McMaster University

P
PRENTICE-HALL ✦ OF CANADA, LTD.
h

Scarborough, Ontario

PRENTICE-HALL, INC., ENGLEWOOD CLIFFS, NEW JERSEY
PRENTICE-HALL INTERNATIONAL, INC., LONDON
PRENTICE-HALL OF AUSTRALIA, PTY., LTD., SYDNEY
PRENTICE-HALL OF INDIA PVT., LTD., NEW DELHI
PRENTICE-HALL OF JAPAN, INC., TOKYO

Library of Congress Catalog Card No. 72-134453

0-13-113258-X (pa)
0-13-113266-0 (cl)
1 2 3 4 5 75 74 73 72 71

PRINTED IN CANADA

To

Louise

and

Jackie

CONTENTS

Preface
ix

The Contributors
xi

The Essays
xiii

Introduction
Richard Ulric Miller and Fraser Isbester
1

1
The Canadian Labour Market
Sylvia Ostry
11

2
Federal Manpower Policies
Gerald G. Somers
56

PREFACE

As Canada approached its centennial in the mid-1960's, social and economic events bore heavily upon the political integrity and future of the Dominion. The realization that an extensive transformation of traditional institutions was then underway led us to consider these changes as they might affect the set of social relationships encompassed by the Canadian system of industrial relations. It seemed to us that the future development of the industrial relations system and the new forms of its components, particularly the labour movement, were obscured by the magnitude and complexity of these changes. It seemed appropriate that a study be initiated to clarify these new directions and forms; six industrial relations scholars, therefore, were invited to join us in such a study. It was our intention that each contributor would go beyond merely imparting information to present a particular point of view. We hope that any disagreement thereby provoked will stimulate further analysis and discussion of the current and future status of Canadian labour problems.

In a venture of this kind, the issues are obviously diverse and manifold. Although we have attempted to select those topics that reflect the influence of change, it must be admitted that our choice was arbitrary.

The authors wish to acknowledge the following persons whose encouragement and assistance have contributed to the completion of this volume: Mr. Gerard Halpin of Prentice-Hall of Canada, Ltd. for his patience and confidence; Miss Joyce Clifton and Miss Sandra Castle, who assisted in the preparation of the final manuscript; and Mrs. Clare McKeon, our production editor, for her diligence and attention to detail.

R.U.M.

F.I.

THE CONTRIBUTORS

Syed M. A. Hameed is an Associate Professor of Industrial Relations and the Chairman of the Behavioral Science Group in the Faculty of Business Administration and Commerce, University of Alberta, Edmonton, Alberta. He was a senior research economist with the Canada Department of Labour in Ottawa, 1964-68. His publications include *Economic Development and Manpower Utilization in Pakistan* and articles contributed to the *British Journal of Industrial Relations* and the *Journal of Economic Studies.*

Fraser Isbester is an Associate Professor of Industrial Relations in the Faculty of Business, McMaster University, Hamilton, Ontario. He holds his doctorate from Cornell University, New York, and has earned other degrees at Queen's University in Kingston, University of Western Ontario in London, and Bishop's University in Quebec. The editor of two books on labour (with D. Coates and C. B. Williams), *Industrial and Labour Relations in Canada: A Selected Bibliography* and *Industrial and Labour Relations: New Perspectives,* he is presently engaged in research concerning organization for collective bargaining of white-collar and professional workers in Canada.

Aranka E. Kovacs is a Professor of Economics at the University of Windsor, Ontario. A Ph.D. from Bryn Mawr College in Pennsylvania, she also holds degrees from McMaster University, Hamilton, and the University of Toronto, Ontario. Her collection, *Readings in Canadian Labour Economics,* published in 1961, is still widely used in the classroom and she has become well known for her published work on the philosophy of Canadian Labour.

Arthur M. Kruger is a Professor of Political Economy and the Chairman of the Division of Social Sciences, Scarborough College, University of Toronto, Ontario. He holds his doctorate in economics from Massachusetts Institute of Technology, Massachusetts, and is also a graduate of the University of Toronto and the Wharton School of Finance, University of Pennsylvania, Pittsburgh. He is the author of *International Unions and Canadian American Relations* and a co-author of *The Canadian Labour Market.*

Richard U. Miller is an Associate Professor, Graduate School of Business, University of Wisconsin, Madison, Wisconsin and the Associate Director of that University's Industrial Relations Research Institute. He holds a Ph.D. from Cornell University. He has published extensively on problems of labour and economic development in Latin America and on arbitration practices in the United States.

Sylvia Ostry is the Associate Director of the Economic Council of Canada. Prior to this appointment, she was Director of the Special Manpower Studies and Consultation Branch of the Dominion Bureau of Statistics. She earned her doctorate at Cambridge and McGill Universities and she also studied at the University of Manitoba in Winnipeg. She is especially well known for her many statistical studies of the Canadian labour force and as co-author (with H. D. Woods) of *Labour Policy and Labour Economics in Canada.*

Gerald G. Somers is a Professor and the Chairman of the Department of Economics at the University of Wisconsin. He holds his Ph.D. from the University of California (Berkeley) and other degrees from the University of Toronto. The author of numerous works on manpower retraining and relocating, his most recent studies include *Retraining the Unemployed,* and "Evaluation of Manpower Policies," a paper prepared for the Joint Economic Committee of the United States Congress.

C. Brian Williams is the Associate Dean and an Associate Professor in the Faculty of Business, University of Alberta, Edmonton, Alberta. He holds a Ph.D. from Cornell University, and other degrees from the University of British Columbia, in Vancouver and the University of Washington, in Seattle. He prepared a study of Canadian labour philosophy for the Task Force on labour and is the author of several essays on international unionism in Canada.

THE ESSAYS

1 The Canadian Labour Market

It is appropriate to begin our consideration of the relationship between social change and industrial relations in Canada with a discussion of the Canadian labour market. Manpower allocation and pricing functions reflect significantly even small modifications in population, technology, values, enterprise structure and governmental activities. In addressing herself to the Canadian labour market, Mrs. Ostry first describes the historical growth and change that has marked the quantitative and qualitative supply of labour, including population, labour force, and participation rates as well as such factors as age and sex, geographic distribution and urbanization.

The subsequent section, in review of the demand for labour, investigates two main variables — the postwar growth record of the Canadian economy and the impact of technology. Against this background, the essay briefly evaluates two major labour market issues, the "structuralist" unemployment controversy, and the interrelationships of wages, prices, and employment. Regarding the former, the author concludes that the debate is over since the reduction of general employment that occurred during the prosperity of the 1960's proved the aggregate demand hypothesis. The debate has now shifted to differences in manpower utilization as the means of "explaining the distressingly high interregional differences in per capita earned income in Canada and shaping the regional 'profile of poverty' in Canada." Structure is consequently not entirely discarded as an explanation of unemployment, particularly where the aged and teen worker are concerned; instead, it is to be recast as a determinant of "poverty proneness."

The debate over the latter manpower issue, the wages, prices and employment adjustment mechanism, is not ended, however; it continues over measurement problems and "trade-off" effects. Given the constraints imposed by the structure of both the Canadian economy and government, the result may be an inability to design effective manpower policies to attain appropriate employment and price trade-offs, or, succeeding in this, an inability to implement the policies provincially.

2 Federal Manpower Policies

The 1960's witnessed an explosion of manpower programmes founded on the structural unemployment thesis and aimed at reducing the relatively high levels of unemployment characterizing the 1950's. Ranging over such activities as adult training, vocational rehabilitation, area development, and labour market counselling and information, the programmes prompted the complete reorganization of the Department of Labour and the creation of six manpower agencies under the supervision of the new Department of Manpower and Immigration. The new programmes focused on training and mobility and came to represent a very sizeable federal investment.

Although neither critics nor proponents could agree on the theoretical results to be obtained from investments in manpower programmes, Somers points out that little effort was made to obtain the empirical data that could resolve the controversy. For example, the effects of expansionist fiscal and monetary policy could not be disentangled from those produced by the manpower programmes themselves. This issue may be academic however, for of greater importance is the conclusion that "even if it could be theoretically established that government training programmes could create jobs and/or reduce unemployment, the scale of the federal training and retraining programmes in Canada and the United States in the 1960's, it is argued, has not been sufficiently large to bring about any significant results."

The effectiveness of Canadian manpower policies and the provision of sufficient operating funds were matters of faith as the sixties ended. Somers believes that the tendency of legislators to accept manpower policies on this basis is coming to an end. This fact, coupled with Mrs. Ostry's concern with the complexity of formulating manpower policies for a situation in which 90 per cent of the labour force is covered by provincial jurisdiction, raises apparent obstacles to the continuation into the 1970's of the programme expansion initiated in the previous decade.

3 The Direction of Unionism in Canada

Professor Kruger's essay traces the evolution of the labour movement as it was affected by the environmental determinants identified in the introduction and discussed in part by Ostry. Of specific concern is the membership and structure of Canadian labour today. After a relative decline in the early 1960's, union membership has increased and now constitutes over 33 per cent of the non-agricultural labour force. According to Kruger, "the rate of growth of labour organization has largely followed the growth of the Canadian population and labour force. The composition of our union movement, to a considerable degree, has reflected the distribution of employment, which itself is largely determined by the composition of our Gross National Product." Of further importance is a marked tendency toward a large number of unions, many of which are small in size. This fragmented structure reflects in part the dominance in

Canada of the United States-based international unions with which some two-thirds of Canadian unionists have affiliated.

Kruger maintains that changes in population, labour, technology and related environmental factors are significantly transforming union membership and structure. He predicts, for example, the emergence of new, professionally oriented associations, unaffiliated with the former labour centres or trade unions. Traditional unions will decline or disappear, to be replaced not only by professional associations but also by larger, merger-created, blue-collar labour organizations.

Perhaps the most revolutionary structural change the author foresees is the loosening of ties with the American internationals. "Canadian nationalism and French Canadian separatism are in the ascendancy" and as a result this "means that few internationals will survive in [Quebec]. Furthermore, it would seem that even in other parts of the country, Canadian workers will seek greater independence, even at some sacrifice in bargaining power."

4   The Philosophy of the Canadian Labour Movement

In Williams' essay, the status of the international union will be more fully discussed. First, however, the related issue of the philosophy of Canadian labour must be considered.

Just as labour force and technology have a demonstrated impact on the size and composition of the membership and on the structure of the unions, the attitudes and goals that the members bring into their organization produce similar effects. Accordingly, Professor Kovacs undertakes a review of philosophy as it has motivated Canadian labour from its inception. The evolution of unionism is seen as a three-stage process in which the establishment stage represents midpoint on a continuum that carries labour from the initial formative stage to the culminating power stage. The philosophy of labour in this middle period is pragmatic, in contrast to a greater idealism and social orientation that characterizes both the formative and power stages. The distinctive feature of the final stage is the channeling of protest into structured institutions, formal grievance procedures for example, and the substitution of the traditional view of labour as producer with that of labour as consumer. To the charge that labour has outlived its usefulness and can look forward now only to declining years on the margin of society, Kovacs counters that, sustained by the philosophy of its power stage and the collective bargaining tools of the establishment period, Canadian labour will strengthen its position, exerting a strong economic and social influence over society.

Of less certainity is the trade union's political influence. In Kovacs' view, direct political action must supplement collective bargaining but a hesitant labour movement seems unable to make the necessary step. The Miller essay on labour and politics may assist in unraveling this puzzle.

5   Trade Union Structure and Philosophy: Need for a Reappraisal

If one were to draw up a balance sheet of Canadian labour's contributions, would labour's net valuation be an asset or a liability? Williams considers this question essential in assessing, among other things, the compatibility of labour's structure and philosophy with the social and economic climate within which it must operate. His conclusion, unlike the one reached by Kovacs, is largely negative: ". . . it does appear that labour is no longer able to define for itself an accommodative role in contemporary economic and social affairs. It is as though it were living in the past, completely unaware of changes that have taken place around it. Its structure and philosophy is obsolete and its image is riddled with criticism." The author lays the blame for this state of affairs at the door of international unionism. It is not that freedom of Canadian locals is internationally restricted, but rather that "national needs, aspirations, and conditions are not sufficiently stressed in the formulation of the collective bargaining policies to be followed by the branches of the internationals operating in Canada."

Canadian unionism, Williams asserts, having no forum of its own and being forced to adapt a much too narrow, self-centered — self-help philosophy cannot meet the challenges that social change in Canada is creating. Recasting the structure and reorienting the philosophy is improbable under present circumstances. The future of Canadian labour is therefore much less promising in Williams' view than it is for either Kovacs or Kruger.

6   Canadian Collective Bargaining: Analysis and Prospects

The environmental factors around which Professor Hameed structures his essay on collective bargaining in Canada are: the expansion of markets; management maximizing or satisficing functions; the legal foundations of conflict resolution; and power as a basis for negotiation. These four factors provide an analytical framework from which to view degrees of unionization, management resistance to unions, the process of conflict resolution, and the contents of collective bargaining agreements as resultants of the functioning of the Canadian system of industrial relations. Hameed's framework enables us to identify the part that market expansion is now playing in the emergence of white-collar unions, in the centralization of bargaining, and in the amalgamation of smaller unions into larger labour organizations. In this respect, therefore, his conclusions would parallel those of Kruger.

Concentrating on bargaining behaviour more closely than do the other authors of this volume, Hameed concludes that, given the likelihood of increased management resistance, the growth of both business organizations and unions will contribute to a pattern of rugged labour relations in the 1970's: "union militancy matched by management hard line." That the government increasingly interjects itself as a third party at the bargaining table will be the controlling factor in determining whether this labour management disharmony will result in open conflict.

Government, particularly at the provincial level, is disinclined to tolerate a disruption in the bargaining relationships and is turning, therefore, with greater enthusiasm to legislated systems that leave the possibility of imposed settlements open. Cited as illustrative of the trend are the new dispute settlement laws of British Columbia, Nova Scotia and Quebec, among others.

Hameed closes his essay by asking what lies ahead — an age of compulsory arbitration? political action by unions? As the following essay by Miller will indicate, the answer to the query concerning compulsory arbitration is less clear than that regarding increased political action.

7 Organized Labour and Politics in Canada

Two of the essayists introduced previously in this section, Kovacs and Hameed, foresee increased political action by trade unions as a response to the new rules and status that society is pressing upon the labour movement. Professor Richard Miller confronts the question directly. He notes that, in Canada, labour has been pulled in opposing philosophical directions; on one hand, there is the influence of its British union counterparts and the tradition of a parliamentary political system, while on the other, are the non-partisan political beliefs of the exogenous parent international unions.

Throughout the history of Canadian labour, political action has been a part of the trade union's arsenal. For most of this time the advocates of non-partisan, legislative action have held a dominant place, although partisan political alliances have been formed on occasion, with such parties as the Canadian Labour Party at the end of World War I, the Canadian Commonwealth Confederation in the 1940's, and currently with the New Democratic Party.

The bulk of the Canadian union movement has steadfastly refrained from identification with any single "labour party," preferring to support the Liberals or Conservatives on the federal level and regional parties such as the Union Nationale or Social Credit in provincial politics as individual consciences and beliefs dictate. This factor, more than impediments posed by union constitutional bars or other obstacles, has limited the success of the labour centres' campaigns to generate concrete union support for the New Democratic Party.

Collective bargaining, supplemented by non-partisan, legislative action, is now the major union weapon for Canadian labour. Miller concludes that if labour is to alter its priorities of economic and political action, significant changes in structure and philosophy would be required. With Williams, he foresees no prospect for this and, therefore, no change in the coming decades.

8 Quebec Labour in Perspective: 1949-1969

In certain respects, Quebec is a microcosm of Canada in which the tensions of social change have been magnified many times. For this province, aspirations of nationalism, economic independence and political autonomy are not novel; neither are the complexities of urban change, poverty, and social disintegration. The issues seem more sharply defined in Quebec and thus the challenges to the industrial relations system seem more exaggerated.

In this examination of Quebec labour, Isbester illustrates how changes since 1949 has altered both the structure and the leadership of the CNTU, have heightened its conflicts with the CLC and international unions, and have thrown its philosophy into some disarray. Paradoxes that defy resolution centre on questions of inter-union cooperation or rivalry, economic or political action, and class militancy or cooperation, to name but a few. The consequent dysfunctions have been enormous although somewhat obscured by successes in bringing workers into the union fold.

If the union movement is to be effective in Quebec (in the face of a strong government), argues Isbester, the warfare between QFL and CNTU must be ended. The future of these industrial relations institutions is uncertain; therefore, the future of Quebec labour itself is equally uncertain. To know what lies ahead in Quebec, however, may very well provide an insight into the future of all Canadian labour.

CANADIAN LABOUR IN TRANSITION

INTRODUCTION

Richard Ulric Miller and Fraser Isbester

In the more than one-hundred years since the enactment of the British North America Act in 1867, an industrial and commercial transformation has occurred in Canada, touching all facets of Canadian working life. The once prominent agricultural worker today constitutes only nine per cent of the labour force, having been displaced many years ago by a multitude of industrial and service employees. Canada closely resembles the United Kingdom and the United States in this respect, a resemblance that extends to its standard of living and level of income. Whether one considers industrial output, value of exports, or per capita national income, Canada has attained a position in the top ranks of the world's economically advanced nations.

Industrialization, however, has not been without serious costs. The wastage of resources and their international control along with the almost intransigent problems of pollution and urban decay are well documented negative products, requiring no detailed discussion here. The haste of industrialization has also left an uncertain economic legacy — poverty, which for its pertinence to industrial relations does merit our attention. Despite the accumulation of considerable wealth, its creation and distribution have been very uneven. Geographical regions such as the Maritimes and ethnic groups including the Indians, Eskimos, and Métis still await the receipt of industrial affluence so visibly available to others. Confronting the issue directly, the Economic Council of Canada asserted:

Poverty in Canada is real. Its numbers are not in the thousands, but the millions. There is more of it than our society can afford, and far more than existing measures and efforts can cope with. Its persistence, at a time when the bulk of Canadians enjoy one of the highest standards of living in the world, is a disgrace.[1]

[1] Economic Council of Canada, *The Challenge of Growth and Change,* Fifth Annual Review (Ottawa: Queen's Printer, September 1968), p. 103.

1

Industrial change has not only been a source of new products, both good and bad, but also a source of new patterns of social interaction.[2] Institutions have been created and existing relationships altered in response to the needs of a society no longer oriented to rural living or agricultural pursuits. On one plane, for example, a political party suited to the ideals of a small group of "agrarian radicals" loses its relevancy as urban industrial workers displace farmers in the country's labour force. On another, governmental agencies such as the old Federal Department of Labour, facing an unmanageable set of manpower problems with an obsolete organizational structure, must be transformed, amoeba-like, into several new portfolios — one bearing the old name, but with modified functions, and one entirely new in name and function: Manpower and Immigration.

The strains on established institutional structures are both intensive in strength and extensive in scope, calling very basic patterns of social interaction seriously into question. Words now widely adopted into daily conversation — separatism, federalism, bilingualism, and economic nationalism — suggest the magnitude of the economic, social, and political challenges (or threats) confronting contemporary Canadian society.

CANADIAN INDUSTRIAL RELATIONS: OLD BEFORE ITS TIME?

As Dunlop observed more than a decade ago, the initial consequence of industrialization is the creation of managers and workers as distinct groups in a society.[3] By the nature of their contrasting concerns — management with efficiency and workers with security — the interdependence of the two groups requires that they structure their interaction in some fashion, unilaterally or jointly devising rules that will shape and control the relationships at the workplace.[4] An industrial relations system thus is born whose primary function consists of "defining the power and authority relationships among managers, labour organizations, and government agencies; of controlling or channeling worker protest; and of establishing substantive rules."[5]

An industrial relations system is not a static structure with patterns of interaction and relationships once laid down at the onset of industrialization thereafter remaining fixed. Such a system exists primarily to fulfill the needs and goals of the specialized community it serves. The industrial relations system is linked horizontally to the economic and political systems and vertically to the general social system of the broader community. Thus, as needs and goals evolve and as the other systems change, the pressures for an adaptive response from the industrial relations system intensify.

The central question for us is: Can the institutions that comprise the Canadian industrial relations system accommodate the change and respond adaptively? Current widespread concern, amounting, as the Prime Minister's Task Force on Labour points out, "to a crisis of confidence" seems to leave a positive answer in doubt.[6] Critics accuse the system's labour and management practitioners as shortsighted in outlook, unresponsive to public needs, and wedded to unnecessary applications of force. Thus, as work stoppages of teachers, fire-fighters and postal workers increasingly disrupt hitherto inviolate community services and contract settlements accelerate the upward spiral of prices, the clamour grows from all sides for intervention, regulation and suppression. The Task Force report concluded:

> . . . *collective bargaining must be judged by its function. It is a strategy in a mixed enterprise economy for the protection of the interests of labour. As such it is a means to an end, not an end in itself. If the system of collective bargaining should be weighed and found wanting because of limitations inherent in the system or because of defects that have too long gone uncorrected, society may reject the system as unsuitable for its purpose.*[7]

Collective bargaining is the "linch-pin" of industrial relations and criticisms of it therefore devolve onto its practices and constituent parts. Illustrative are such statements as that of Judge Ivan C. Rand who characterized the strike as "a residual of the primordial struggle" and recommended its strict regulation.[8]

Labour organizations, as well, have been the object of faultfinding by those who question whether traditional trade union structures and philosophy are relevant to social needs and economic problems. Conventional approaches, it is argued, produce an inequitable distribution of gains and losses between workers, employers, and consumers. As a consequence, one observer predicts that "organized labour cannot count on an illustrious future unless it is prepared to adapt to the needs of the times."[9]

While the critics do not always agree on the severity of the problem or its most appropriate resolution, almost unanimously they agree on its roots: the accumulated effects of the historical transformation of Canadian Society. In this regard the Task Force Report noted:

---

[2] See Hugh G. J. Aitken, "Canada's Industrial Society," in *Canada: 1867-1967,* (Ottawa: Dominion Bureau of Statistics, 1968), pp. 330-336.

[3] John T. Dunlop, *Industrial Relations Systems* (New York: Henry Holt and Company, 1958), p. 5.

[4] *Ibid.,* p. 4. See also Alton W. Craig, "A Model for the Analysis of Industrial Relations Systems," paper presented to the annual meeting of the Canadian Political Science Association, June 1967, p. 2.

[5] Clark Kerr et al., *Industrialism and Industrial Man* (Boston: Harvard University Press, 1960), p. 192. By permission of Harvard University Press and Heinemann Educational Books Limited, London, England.

[6] *Canadian Industrial Relations: The Report of the Task Force on Labour Relations,* Privy Council Office (Ottawa: Queen's Printer, December 1968), p. 3.

[7] *Ibid.,* p. 38.

[8] *Report of the Royal Commission Inquiry into Labour Disputes,* The Honourable Ivan C. Rand, Commissioner (Toronto: Queen's Printer, August 1968), p. 42.

[9] John H. G. Crispo, "Looking Backwards and Forwards in Industrial Relations," *Relations Industrielles,* October 1965, p. 700.

In the normal course of social and economic growth in North America, change is pervasive and the rate of change is accelerating in technology, organization, administration, urban development, communication, education, and endless other areas. ... These changes may well work a transformation in the nature and the role of employment, trade unionism and collective bargaining, and particularly in decision making.[10]

If obsolescence in the face of social change is therefore the charge placed against the Canadian industrial relations system, it is appropriate to identify those aspects of change responsible, the nature of the response the system is making, and finally the results one might thereby expect.

FORCES FOR CHANGE IN INDUSTRIAL RELATIONS

Challenges to the *status quo* confront the system of industrial relations at any one of several points: the values, goals, and power of the labour, management, and government actors; the collective bargaining mechanism for rule making; the organizations created by the actors; or the scarcity or abundance of rewards to distribute. It is the environmental contexts of the system itself, however, that initiate the pressure to change. The following factors seem to be particularly relevant for Canadian industrial relations: population growth and change, the general value system, technology, enterprise structure and administration, and governmental structure and administration.

POPULATION.   An enormous transformation in the population and labour force has occurred in recent years. As the population has evolved, labour force participation rates of young and old, and males and females, have been dramatically altered. In addition, immigration to Canada from eastern Europe, India, and the West Indies has modified the former predominance in the labour force of individuals of United Kingdom and northern European descent. Clearly discernible also is a radical shift in the location of the Canadian population, flowing from the long standing but now accelerating process of urbanization. At the onset of World War II, 50 per cent of the Canadian population resided in an urban area. By 1966 the degree of urbanization had risen to 74 per cent, and recent projections by the Economic Council of Canada indicate that by the 1980's it is likely that 80 per cent of the Canadian population will be living in an urban setting.

The population and labour force changes are coincident with changes in occupational and industrial employment. Blue-collar workers once outnumbered their white-collar counterparts; the reverse is now true. As the shift away from primary and secondary employment to tertiary or services continues (the latter now constitutes 57 per cent of all employment), the numerical superiority of white-collar employees will undoubtedly increase.

Qualitatively the labour force is changing as well. The increasing attention to the health programmes, the modernization of traditional welfare concepts, and the expansion and upgrading of educational institutions are being reflected in the attributes of the average worker. His life has been significantly lengthened, his skills and technical training have been greatly improved, and his education has been raised well above that of his forebears just a few generations back.

A predominance of younger, better educated, white-collar and professional workers being generated by qualitative and quantitative population changes is not conducive to the continuance of a blue-collar, manual worker constructed *status quo*. As will be explored more fully in the next section, these workers tend to look skeptically on established union traditions as well as to act independently of labour leadership and authority.

Paralleling labour force changes involving younger workers is an increase in the participation rate of females. Women now constitute one-third of the labour force and in certain occupations and professions account for even greater proportions. It is often argued that women look at their employment as only temporary, that their turnover rates are high and that they are therefore hard to organize.[11] While the immediate consequence of this may be a further reduction in union growth, the long-term consequence is more likely to be a shift in bargaining demands to subjects more relevant to females (child care, pre-natal care, post-natal leaves, and the like) and perhaps a decline in militancy.

CANADIAN VALUES. It is not surprising that the transformation in the population has been accompanied by an equally thoroughgoing alteration in Canadian values and attitudes. The now not so "quiet revolution" in Quebec indicates the differing priorities by which Canadian and Canadienne have come to order their goals, to govern their interaction with each other, and to affect the institutions through which achievement of diverse social, political, or economic goals is sought. Most notable in this regard is the advent of national, regional, and ethnic particularism, which stresses the unique as opposed to the universal, the diffusion and decentralization of authority, and a general resistance to perceived threats to local customs, values and organizations. The resultant tendencies pit not only French Canadian against Anglo Canadian but also Easterner against Westerner, provincial against federal government, prairie wheat farmer against urban factory worker, and Canadian against American.

In the realm of industrial relations, the issues that arise from nationalism, regionalism, and ethnicism are often the hardest to confront successfully. The Canadian Labour Congress, for example, must walk a perilously narrow line, simultaneously decrying the "threat" of American capital and justifying international unionism. Bargaining tactics and structure must accommodate the artificial division of labour and product markets along federal-provincial jurisdictional lines. Within provinces, disparate goals and attitudes have heightened old jurisdictional rivalries

---

[10] *The Report of the Task Force on Labour Relations*, p. 38.
[11] See Wilfred List, "Women at Work Pose Problems for Unions," *Globe and Mail* (Toronto: December 28, 1967).

long endemic between craft and industrial or national and international unions, as well as crystalizing latent conflicts marking Anglo and French Canadian labour relations.

The increasing influx of young workers into the labour movement presents a further challenge as the proportion of trade unionists below the age of thirty is now larger than ever before. These young workers, better educated and more mature, are the product of a social and economic environment far different from that governing their predecessors.[12] As Vallée so aptly points out in this regard, the under-thirty worker "was not shaped by war but rather by the television set; he is more interested in looking into the future than the past."[13] The consequence is a new breed of union member, unaffected by old union glories and past achievements, feeling little loyalty or gratitude to the union, and having no hesitancy about either striking or changing jobs if circumstances seem to require such action.[14] Indeed, the widespread restlessness of today's worker seems attributable in no small part to the generation gap separating youthful rank-and-file members from their more senior officers.[15]

From the standpoint of trade-unionism, it is more than just a matter of being affected by community values or responding to the new mechanisms established for their attainment. In the long run, self-preservation dictates that unions assert some minimal level of influence on the selection and achievement of these values and mechanisms. The economic institutions created by labour are poorly suited to deal with the political issues that such goal or policy formulation requires. Illustrative of the structural and strategic dilemma created is Waisglass and Craig's query concerning the issue of federal prices and incomes policy:

What functions can and will labour organizations play in setting the precise goals for this policy and assisting in its implementation? Assuming that the central labour bodies, along with management and government, can agree upon a policy, do the central labour bodies have sufficient authority over their affiliates and the thousands of local unions across Canada to implement such a policy? [16]

TECHNOLOGY.   Marx to the contrary, it was technology and not capitalism that originally divided the ranks of the labour force into manager and managed, and it is continuing technological change that provides its own permanent challenge to the industrial relations *status quo*. Industries, occupations and jobs are created that stimulate new manpower demands in their wake. As with all change, the blessings are mixed and as certain manpower demands occur others slacken or shift, reducing employment and diluting required skills.

The impact of technology has been felt all across the Canadian labour market, covering white-collar and services vocations, as well as the blue-collar occupations characterizing primary and manufacturing employment. To point to the textile weavers, railroad firemen, or miners as examples of groups hard hit by technology is to obscure the information systems revolution in clerical employment and the innovations in material handling in wholesale and retail trades.[17] Further, although aggregate employment has risen in recent years, it has also declined in particular industries such as agriculture, mining, forestry, construction and transportation while remaining relatively stable in manufacturing. In fact, the comparatively high rates of unemployment Canada has continued to experience despite prosperity is felt by some to be structural in nature. That is, workers are unemployed because there is no demand for the skills or knowledge they possess.

As one might expect, bargaining issues soon come to reflect concerns over job security, income protection, control of machinery, and production standards. Equally important, however, is the erosion of membership and the subsequent need to shift organizational efforts to the workers of the emerging industries. While this will be discussed at greater length in Chapter 3 of this volume, suffice to say that the lack of observable growth in union membership since the 1950's is directly attributable to the declining industrial organizational base and an inability to unionize the expanding white-collar and service industries.

Coping with technological change under these conditions and by means of traditional industrial relations devices therefore constitutes a nearly unmanageable problem. Writing recently in the journal of the Canadian Labour Congress, John L. Fryer concluded:

Collective bargaining alone, however imaginative, cannot solve all the problems of adjustment inherent in a technological age. The search for the correct mix of public and private policies is a matter of urgent consideration and hopefully it will occupy much of our time in the next decade.[18]

ENTERPRISE MANAGEMENT AND STRUCTURE. In many ways, enterprise practices and structure mirror technological change. Roots of organizational change often are scientific in origin and efficiency-oriented. Moreover the consequences of each type of change often are parallel, as witnessed by Marx, Durkheim, Weber and Merton in their writings on anomie, alienation and bureaucratic pathology. One could argue that although technology created the respective roles of workers and managers,

---

[12] Emil Vallée, "A View from Under Thirty," *Canadian Labour*, March 1969, p. 15.

[13] *Ibid.*

[14] *Ibid.* See also Morden Lazarus, "A View from Over Thirty," *Canadian Labour*, March 1969, p. 19. Lazarus concludes that the attitude of students toward unions is basically negative: "They usually attend one union meeting and never return. They find the proceedings boring and confusing. Young people regard the union as an agency they pay to provide them with more benefits."

[15] See John L. Fryer, "Labour's Changing Role," *Canadian Labour*, June 1968, pp. 15-17, 71-72.

[16] H. J. Waisglass and A. W. J. Craig, "Collective Bargaining Perspective," *Labour Gazette*, October 1968, pp. 576-582.

[17] Economic Council of Canada, *Economic Goals for Canada to 1970*, First Annual Review (Ottawa: Queen's Printer, December, 1964), pp. 152-157.

[18] *Canadian Labour*, June 1968, p. 16.

it is the bureaucratic structuring of their relationship that in turn motivates the will to unionize.

Recent changes in enterprises give rise to doubts, however, concerning the current utility of unionization as an expression of worker discontent. A first consideration is the arrival of the human relations specialists or their lineal descendants, the organizational behaviorists, providing the manager with the means of assessing worker goals and motivation and arguing that an enlightened enterprise no longer requires a union watchdog to ensure industrial justice. A second consideration is the structural development of the corporate conglomerate with its vast resources and diffused authority. Cutting across established industrial and occupational lines as well as political boundaries, the conglomerate, by virtue of its diversified holdings and multiplicity of firms, de-emphasizes the importance of any single organizational unit. In this respect, it is unlike its corporate antecedents whose growth proceeded by means of vertical or horizontal integration aimed at controlling supplies and distributors or monopolizing markets.[19]

For Canadian industrial relations institutions, the multinational nature of the conglomerates introduces a political facet to the already existing economic complexities. The "Watkins Report" prepared for the Gordon Commission revealed that by the late 1960's approximately $33 billion of Canadian assets had been acquired by non-Canadian business organizations.[20] While principal ownership resided with American based firms, German, Japanese, English, Dutch and other corporate nationalities were represented. This may mean, Levinson argues, that "the economic power of the union will be increasingly measured against the consolidated financial position of the world corporation rather than the national subsidiary with which it is doing the actual bargaining."[21]

One could speculate as to the occurrence of situations in which: industrial relations policies could be formulated and decisions made in locations far removed from the political jurisdictions within which the trade union functions; customers of goods formerly produced by strike-bound plants could continue to be supplied from operating plants in other countries; or perhaps production would be shifted from high labour cost countries to low labour cost countries, without diminishing the firm's servicing of its international markets.[22] A strike in a single plant or even an affiliated company therefore conceivably has reduced significance when taken in the context of the total conglomerate. The implications of this development for the balance of bargaining power between labour and management are quite clear.

In response to the challenge raised by the conglomerates, national and multinational alike, labour is seeking new alliances as well as re-casting its own structure along organizational lines more consonant with those of its corporate counterparts. Exemplifying these activities are the efforts to coordinate the collective bargaining of individual local unions and international unions and the amalgamation or merger of formerly independent unions in such industries as meatpacking, transportation and nonferrous metals.

Canadian unions, however, face an inescapable dilemma in selecting the appropriate modes of response to the rise of the multinational conglomerate. That is, the values and attitudes associated with an emerging nationalism seem to dictate reduced, not expanded, internationalism. Social and political forces are pushing Canadian locals away from their American international unions at a time when economic pressures are reinforcing existing structural and philosophical bonds.

GOVERNMENT STRUCTURE AND ADMINISTRATION. Though its emergence is recent, few would deny the importance of government in any of its roles (regulator, consumer or employer) to the present and future of industrial relations. Moreover, this importance is enhanced by an activism that formerly was absent from government. National and provincial goals such as full employment, price stability, balance of payments and equitable income distribution are imposed, priorities attached, and all efforts bent to secure them. Pursuit of goals by spending and taxation, manpower programmes, wage-price guidelines and the like have clearcut repercussions for industrial relations.

To the extent that an activist role is also taken regarding supervision and control of the hitherto autonomous relationship of labour and management, the governmental impact becomes equally substantial. Establishment of the labour court in Quebec and the arbitration tribunal in British Columbia and the increasing government expressions of concern for the efficiency of collective bargaining as a private decision-making mechanism both bear witness that the government is wresting initiative from the parties.[23]

The expansion of government's role as an employer is an additional aspect of social change having implications for the warp and woof of the Canadian Industrial Relations System. Public employment has expanded

---

[19] The significant growth of conglomerates during the 1960's as a new organizational force is illustrated by the manner of development of the following firms. Litton Industries started the past decade with revenue of $83 million (U.S.); by 1968 through the acquisition of sixty companies it had achieved gross revenues of $1.9 billion. Equally spectacular was Ling-Temco-Vought, which grew over the same period from $7 million sales to $2.8 billion, while gaining control of twenty-six other organizations. Gulf and Western collected eighty businesses, Textron collected sixty, and International Tel and Tel collected approximately fifty. A. M. Louis, "Ten Conglomerates and How They Grew," *Fortune,* May 15, 1969, p. 152. It is interesting to note, using 1967 statistics, that several of these multinational firms have revenues that exceed those of the Canadian Federal Government: General Motors ($20 billion U.S.), Standard Oil ($13 billion U.S.), Ford Motor Company ($10 billion U.S.), among others.

[20] For a summary of the study of foreign ownership prepared by Professor Melvill H. Watkins, see *Canadian Labour,* May 1968, p. 99.

[21] Charles Levinson, "Conglomerates," *Canadian Labour,* May 1969, p. 17.

[22] *Ibid.*

[23] See for example the statement of the Honourable John L. Nicholson, "New Role in a Changing Economy," *Labour Gazette,* January 1968, pp. 4-5.

by 50 per cent since 1946 and unionism among these workers at a considerably faster rate. As a consequence, two government employees' unions, the Canadian Union of Public Employees and the Public Service Alliance of Canada had become, by 1968, the fourth and fifth largest labour organizations in Canada.

It is in the public sector that the application of conventional industrial relations institutions and practices has been most seriously questioned. Although legislation has encouraged unionization and supported collective bargaining, the results have not met with wide-spread acclaim. Strikes have disrupted public services and disputes have recurred, seemingly with increasing frequency. Judge Rand, in commenting on bargaining by teachers, declared:

That school teachers should be remunerated suitably to their function is not questioned: but that any groups should be permitted, by such means, to compel the public to submit to arbitrary demands is repugnant to democratic government.[24]

His remedy was compulsory arbitration, a tool that, once adopted, could be applied to resolve private sector disputes, as British Columbia has attempted with the creation of its Mediation Commission.

A final consideration is the structure of governmental decision-making. In contrast to the increasing centralization of decision-making in labour and management structures, demands for greater autonomy and authority at the provincial and local level are pulling governmental decision centers away from Ottawa. Quebec, not alone, has sought to strengthen its provincial influence over such matters as education, taxation, medical care and related governmental activities. Thus, despite the growth of markets and the inter-provincial nature of much of the institutions of industrial relations, jurisdiction has continued to reside with eleven different political entities. One result is a lack of uniform treatment, contradictory results, and impediments to efficient collective bargaining. Another result of the re-emergence of provincialism is support for regional labour groups like the Quebec-based Confederation of National Trade Unions. With the spread of French Canadian nationalism, the CNTU has prospered in wealth and numbers, rivaling in size its CLC counterpart, the Quebec Federation of Labour.

Government, in all its facets, thus exerts its own set of pressures, akin to those generated by changes in enterprises, population, technology, and social beliefs.

---

[24] *Report of the Royal Commission Inquiry into Labour Disputes, p. 112.*

1

THE CANADIAN LABOUR MARKET

Sylvia Ostry

FACTORS IN LABOUR SUPPLY: GROWTH AND CHANGE

Canada is a large, rich, sparsely populated country which shares most of a continent with a larger, richer nation that contains ten times the population. These parameters — space, wealth of natural resources, proximity to the United States — plus the French fact underlie its economic, political and social development. The growth and changing patterns of use of Canadian manpower resources emerge from this matrix.

Since the native peoples of North America were and are pitifully few in number, the Canadian labour supply consists, in one sense, only of immigrants and the children of immigrants.[1] It is, however, more useful to distinguish between two sources of population growth — immigration and natural increase (including the children of immigrants) — which, together with trends in participation, have determined the growth and, to an important degree, the changing composition of Canada's manpower resources.

The first section of this article examines the main aspects of growth and change in Canada's labour supply and briefly considers its future. The following sections examine demand factors and emerging structural imbalances.

---

[1] It is interesting to note that our decennial census classification of the population does not provide an ethnic category titled "Canadian." Respondents who insist on replying to the question on ethnic origin in this fashion are usually classified N.E.S. — not elsewhere specified.

11

Growth

POPULATION.   A century ago, there were approximately 3.5 million
Canadians; today there are nearly 21 million. The decadal record in Table
1-1 depicts a persistent but by no means uniform rise during the hundred
years after Confederation. Intercensal increases range from a low of approximately 11 per cent over the depression decade, 1931-41, to the
surging advances of more than 30 per cent during the pre-World War I
and post-World War II periods. The difference between births and deaths
is natural increase — the "domestic" contribution to Canada's population. The difference between immigration and emigration is net immigration[2] — the "imported" contribution. This record of population growth
reflects the historical development and the interplay of domestic sources
— natural increase — and net immigration from abroad.

Table 1-1

POPULATION AND CHANGES IN POPULATION, 1861-1961

Year	Population	Numerical increase	Percentage increase
1861	3,229,633	793,336	—
1871	3,689,257	459,624	14.2
1881	4,324,810	635,553	17.2
1891	4,833,239	508,429	11.8
1901	5,371,315	538,076	11.1
1911	7,206,643	1,835,328	34.2
1921	8,787,949	1,581,306	21.9
1931	10,376,786	1,588,837	18.1
1941	11,506,655	1,129,869	10.9
1951a	13,648,013	2,141,358	18.6
1961a	17,780,394	4,132,381	30.3
1951b	14,009,429	—	—
1961b	18,238,247	4,228,818	30.2

a Excludes Newfoundland
b Includes Newfoundland
Source: 1951 and 1961 *Census of Canada.*

Underlying the contribution of natural increase to the growth of
the Canadian population are the *secular trends* in birth and death rates.
The steady long-run decline in the birth rate, familiar in all Western
countries, is observed with minor interruptions in every decade between
1861 and 1931. Late in the 1930's, the rate began to rise, most markedly
after World War II, and remained at a high level during most of the
1950's. The end of that decade marked a turning point and the rate
has been declining markedly since then.[3] Although the birth rate has been
the more important factor affecting fluctuations in the rate of natural

increase of Canada's population, the long-run, steadily declining mortality rate over the past century — from an estimated 22 per thousand in the 1861-71 decade to just over 7 per thousand today — has had a highly significant effect on the growth of the population. Both the birth rate and the mortality rate have important implications in the study of the labour force.

The domestic contribution has been a viable one, largely responsible for the fluctuations in the rate of increase from decade to decade. Although the flow of immigrants into Canada had been substantial, even by international standards, there has also been, in almost every decade, great numbers leaving Canada, primarily for the United States. Table 1-2 indicates that the contribution of net immigration to Canada's population over the 1861-1961 century as a whole has been far outweighed by natural increase. A reasonably reliable estimate would place the contribution of domestic supply at 85 to 90 per cent of the total increase in the Canadian population between 1861 and 1961.[4] Only in the decade preceding World War I, when the Canadian West was opened for settlement, and again in the most recent intercensal decade (1951-61) did net immigration have a substantial impact on decadal growth rates, contributing over two-fifths and one-quarter respectively to the growth in population.

The relative difficulty that Canada has encountered in attracting and holding both immigrant and native-born may partly be because "what is now Canadian territory has lain on the periphery of a vast settlement area, the shifting centres of which are and have been to the south and have

[2] The lack of accurate immigration data for Canada before 1921 makes any estimate of movements of persons into and out of the country open to question. A variety of estimates are available: *cf.* Frank T. Denton, *The Growth of Manpower in Canada,* one of a series of Labour Force Studies in the 1961 Census Monograph Programme, (Ottawa: Queen's Printer, 1969) for a review of the available data.

[3] The strength and timing of this decline came as a surprise to demographers and economists. Consider this quote from the final report of the so-called Gordon Commission, *The Royal Commission on Canada's Economic Prospects,* published in 1957. In discussing the assumptions on which the population projections were based, the Commission report states: "If the estimates of future fertility rates prove accurate, the birth rate will decline, but only moderately, moving down from where it stood in 1955 at 28.4 and varying between 24.2 and 25.6 over the period from 1960 to 1980." (p. 102.) Alas for the hazards of projection, by 1966 the crude birth rate had fallen to 19.4, the lowest Canadian rate on record.

[4] Based on data from *ibid. Cf.* also William C. Hood and Anthony Scott, *Output, Labour and Capital in the Canadian Economy,* (Ottawa: Queen's Printer, 1957). They estimate that net immigration amounted to about 6 to 7 per cent of the total population increase between 1851 and 1951 (p. 157). It should be noted that these estimates do not take account of the fact that natural increase during a decade may be affected by migration. Changes in size of the population and in age structure may affect both birth rate and death rates. *Cf.* Denton, *Growth.*

Table 1-2

POPULATION GROWTH AND ITS COMPONENTS, INTERCENSAL DECADES, 1861-1961

Decade	Population at beginning of decade	Population at end of decade	Total increase	Births	Deaths	Natural Increase	Immigration	Emigration	Net immigration
	'000	'000	'000	'000	'000	'000	'000	'000	'000
1861-1871	3,230	3,689	459	1,369	—760	609	260	—410	—150
1871-1881	3,689	4,325	636	1,477	—801	676	350	—390	— 40
1881-1891	4,325	4,833	508	1,538	—880	658	680	—830	—150
1891-1901	4,833	5,371	538	1,546	—878	668	250	—380	—130
1901-1911	5,371	7,207	1,836	1,931	—905	1,026	1,550	—740	810
1911-1921	7,207	8,788	1,581	2,338	—1,067	1,271	1,400	—1,090	310
1921-1931	8,788	10,377	1,589	2,612	—1,055	1,557	1,203	—1,171	32
1931-1941	10,377	11,507	1,130	2,403	—1,072	1,331	150	—351	—201
1941-1951a	11,507	13,648	2,141	3,245	—1,214	2,031	548	—438	110
1951-1961b	14,009	18,238	4,229	4,468	—1,320	3,148	1,543	—462	1,081

a Excludes Newfoundland
b Includes Newfoundland
Source: Frank T. Denton, *Growth of Manpower.*

inevitably attracted and, to a lesser extent, continue to attract peoples from the periphery."[5]

LABOUR FORCE. The historical data on the labour force are much more sparse than data on population; hence, the historical record is much more difficult to construct. Despite these data limitations, the main outlines of development are clear; not surprisingly, they are essentially similar to those described for total population. The contribution of net immigration to the labour force was far overshadowed by that of domestic sources except for the early part of the century and, more recently, during the first half of the 1950's. In fact, the years following World War II merit somewhat closer attention because of their greater relevance to present conditions and to policy discussion.[6]

As Table 1-3 indicates, labour force growth in Canada during the postwar period has been rather uneven. Following a sharp decline in the late 1940's, the rate began to pick up after 1950, mainly as a consequence of a large, sustained immigration that reached a peak of over 280,000 in 1957. The rate of increase in labour supply during the 1950's was a near record high for the century, although the source and pace of growth differed markedly between the first and second half. During the first half of the 1950's, roughly two-thirds of labour force growth derived from net immigration.[7] The rate of growth slowed perceptibly after 1957 and immigration declined steadily for the remainder of the decade. Between 1955 and 1960 the positions of the earlier quinquennium were reversed: one-third of the growth came from net immigration, two-thirds from domestic supply.[8] (A major component of domestic supply was female, as a consequence of the rapid increase in participation during this period.) Immigration in the 1950's played a key role in labour supply by offsetting the shortage of labour force entrants that arose from the low birth rates of the depression years. It is undoubtedly misleading to assess the impact of immigration during the 1950's or any part of the

---

[5] Dominion Bureau of Statistics, *Canada Year Book,* 1957-8, special article on immigration, pp. 154-76. For an alternative hypothesis, the displacement theory, which contended that those who left for the United States were "pushed" south, forced to leave because immigration created unemployment and depressed wages, cf. W. B. Hurd, "Demographic Trends in Canada," in *Annals of the American Academy of Political and Social Science,* September 1947, and "Some Implications of Prospective Population Trends," in *Canadian Journal of Economics and Political Science,* November 1939. Also cf. N. B. Ryder, "Components of Canadian Population Growth," *Population Index,* Volume XX, No. 2, (1954).

[6] Analysis of this period is greatly facilitated by the fact that current labour force data, in considerable detail, are available from the monthly Labour Force Survey initiated on a quarterly basis in November 1945 and on a monthly basis at the end of 1952.

[7] Frank T. Denton and Sylvia Ostry, "Labour Force: Growth and Change," *Canada, One Hundred,* (Ottawa: Queen's Printer, 1967), p. 272.

[8] *Ibid.*

Table 1-3

LABOUR FORCE, 1946-1967, ANNUAL AVERAGES

Year	Number of persons	Numerical increase	Percentage increase
	'000	'000	
1946	4,920	—	—
1947	5,035	115	2.3
1948	5,095	60	1.2
1949	5,136	41	0.8
1950	5,145	9	0.2
1951	5,200	55	1.1
1952	5,305	105	2.0
1953	5,397	92	1.7
1954	5,493	96	1.8
1955	5,610	117	2.1
1956	5,782	172	3.1
1957	6,008	226	3.9
1958	6,137	129	2.1
1959	6,242	105	1.7
1960	6,411	169	2.7
1961	6,521	110	1.7
1962	6,615	94	1.4
1963	6,748	133	2.0
1964	6,933	185	2.7
1965	7,141	208	3.0
1966	7,420	279	3.9
1967	7,694	274	

Source: Based on DBS *Labour Force Survey* data. Figures for 1946-1949 have been adjusted to include estimates for Newfoundland and for 1946-1952 to allow for the effects of differences in the frequency and timing of the Survey on the annual averages for this period.

postwar period solely in terms of numbers of persons without taking account of the "quality," or skill, and educational composition of the immigrant inflow. Canada experienced a very considerable net gain in the international movement of skilled and professional workers during this period.[9] This was not, however, an unmixed blessing. There can be little doubt that dependence on immigration during this period led to a neglect of training and education for high level manpower in Canada.

The decade of the 1960's achieved an even higher rate of labour force growth. Its opening years were not auspicious. In 1961 and 1962, under conditions of high unemployment and stagnation, immigration fell to its lowest point in ten years and its net contribution was close to zero. Although it climbed to "respectable" proportions toward the end of the decade, the main impact on labour supply in the 1960's stemmed from the "baby boom" children of the 1940's whose entry was delayed by more extended schooling and from the middle-aged and older married women who were entering the labour market in increasing numbers especially after the mid 1950's.

TRENDS IN PARTICIPATION. Changes in labour force participation have had little effect on the historical growth of labour supply in Canada. As Table 1-4 indicates, the overall rate has exhibited no long-run trend. Over the period for which data[10] are available, since the beginning of the twentieth century, the rate has been remarkably stable in view of the profound economic and social changes that have occurred during these years. Apart from the sharp rise between 1901 and 1911, a consequence of the massive immigration of those years,[11] the rate has varied by less than a percentage point from its highest to its lowest level.

As Table 1-4 reveals, however, the stability of the overall activity rate conceals marked, and markedly divergent, trends for men and women and for certain age groups within each sex. For this reason, while changes in participation rates have not affected the long-run growth of labour supply, they have had a decisive impact on its composition. A fuller understanding of many of the compositional changes to be discussed later requires some examination of these changing patterns of activity.

The total male participation rate has declined from close to 90 per cent at the beginning of the century to just over 80 per cent in 1961 and is currently about 77 per cent. Behind this substantial fall in the overall male rate lie the much steeper declines in activity for both teen-agers and older men (sixty-five and over): the first a consequence of prolonged schooling over the last half century, especially since the last war, the latter reflecting the trend toward earlier retirement. This delayed entry and hastened exit from the labour market should, in the absence of countervailing demographic developments, have had the effect of considerably shortening the average number of years in the male working life; however, improvements in life expectancy, due mainly to a decline in infant mortality, have more than counteracted these labour force trends so that the average number of years in the *working* life of males (at birth) rose from an estimated 39.6 in 1931 to 42.1 in 1961.[12]

---

[9] See Louis Parai, *Immigration and Emigration of Professional and Skilled Manpower during the Post-War Period,* Economic Council of Canada (Ottawa: Queen's Printer, 1965).

[10] The data in Table 1-4 have been adjusted to take into account changes in coverage and in concept in the differing censuses. See Denton and Ostry, *Historical Estimates,* for a description of the adjustment procedures.

[11] This was probably primarily a compositional (age) effect although perhaps strengthened by behavioural differences. The heavy weight of prime age males in the immigrant group would have raised the overall activity rate in the absence of native-born-immigrant differences in the propensity to participate.

[12] Frank T. Denton and Sylvia Ostry, *Working Life Tables for Canadian Males,* one of a series of Labour Force Studies in the 1961 Census Monograph Series, (Ottawa: Queen's Printer, 1969).

Table 1-4

LABOUR FORCE PARTICIPATION RATES, BY AGE AND SEX, 1901-1961

Year	Both sexes, 14 years of age and over	Men						Women					
		All ages 14 and over	14-19	20-24	25-34	35-64	65 and over	All Ages 14 and over	14-19	20-24	25-34	35-64	65 and over
	%	%	%	%	%	%	%	%	%	%	%	%	%
1901	53.0	87.8	—	—	—	—	—	16.1	—	—	—	—	—
1911	57.4	90.6	—	—	—	—	—	18.6	—	—	—	—	—
1921	56.2	89.8	68.4	94.3	98.0	96.9	59.6	19.9	29.6	39.8	19.5	12.0	6.6
1931	55.9	87.2	57.4	93.9	98.6	96.7	56.5	21.8	26.5	47.4	24.4	13.2	6.2
1941	55.2	85.6	54.6	92.6	98.7	96.1	47.9	22.9	26.8	46.9	27.9	15.2	5.8
1951[a]	54.5	84.4	53.7	94.2	98.2	95.0	39.5	24.4	33.7	48.8	25.4	19.8	4.5
1961[a]	55.3	81.1	40.6	94.4	98.4	95.3	30.6	29.3	31.7	50.7	29.2	29.9	6.1
1951[b]	54.3	84.1	53.5	94.0	98.1	94.8	39.1	24.2	33.4	48.5	25.1	19.6	4.4
1961[b]	55.1	80.8	40.5	94.2	98.0	95.0	30.4	29.1	31.7	50.4	28.9	29.5	6.0
1967[c]	55.5	77.5	39.4	86.0	97.0	94.1	24.7	33.8	31.6	56.6	34.4	35.9	5.9

[a] Excludes Newfoundland.
[b] Includes Newfoundland.
[c] Annual coverage based on twelve monthly observations from the *Labour Force Survey*. There are minor differences in coverage between these and the Census figures in the rest of the Table.

Source: Frank T. Denton and Sylvia Ostry, *Historical Estimates of the Canadian Labour Force*, One of a Series of Labour Force Studies in the 1961 Census Monograph Programme, (Ottawa: Queen's Printer, 1967).

The decline in male activity rates has been offset, in a most remarkable and perhaps not entirely coincidental way,[13] by increases in the participation of women. The proportion of women fourteen years of age and over in the labour market in Canada rose from about 16 per cent in 1901 to 29 per cent in 1961 and is currently well over 30 per cent. The increases have been especially dramatic since the 1950's. (See Table 1-4.) The rise in female participation has affected every age group except the very oldest (sixty-four and over) but it is much more marked for middle-aged and older women thirty-five to sixty-four, most of whom are married, than for teen-agers and younger women in the child-bearing and child-rearing years of life. This factor has, of course, greatly affected the structure of the female labour force. In 1901, the typical urban working woman(and there were not many) was young and single. Only the most unfortunate or most exceptional married woman ventured into the labour market. Today nearly 30 per cent of married women in Canada, many with children still living at home, participate in the labour force.

The essence of these significant labour force developments is the emergence of the so-called two-phased working life of women,[14] familiar in all Western industrialized countries. The two-phased participation profile for women developed in Canada during the 1950's, at least a full decade later than in the United States. (See Figure 1-1.) In the United States, moreover, female participation rates are very much higher than the Canadian rates at every age. As Table 1-5 indicates, Canadian rates are also relatively low by European standards. (See Table 1-5.) It is a reasonably safe assumption that Canadian rates have considerable room for growth if, as seems likely, international experience, particularly American experience, is a guide to future developments.

This transformation in the working life pattern of women, which

---

[13] *Cf.* Clarence Long, *The Labour Force under Changing Income and Employment,* (Princeton, 1958), Chapter 8. He suggests that older males have been "pushed out" of some sectors of industry by younger, better educated women. It has also been hypothesized that married women may work to keep their children [males only?] at school longer. The Canadian data on occupational and industrial trends do not support Long's thesis. The second hypothesis mentioned has not been tested because of lack of appropriate data.

[14] Detailed data from the 1961 Census allow us to trace the participation profile more clearly than is permitted by the more aggregated current (labour force sample) statistics. As of the 1961 Census the profile showed a sharp rise in participation from around 33 per cent, just after entry, to a peak of about 50 per cent for women aged twenty to twenty-four. After their mid-twenties, as most women married and began having children, a smaller and smaller proportion remained in the labour market. At the low point, around the age of thirty or slightly later, some 28 per cent of women were in the labour force. After this, the second phase of the working life cycle can be clearly seen with gradually rising participation to a second, though considerably lower, peak at ages forty-five to forty-nine. About one in three women of this age was in the labour force. Thereafter the rate declined, slowly at first, then after the age of fifty much more rapidly. See Sylvia Ostry, *The Female Worker in Canada,* one of a series of Labour Force Studies in 1961 Census Monograph Programme, (Ottawa: Queen's Printer, 1968).

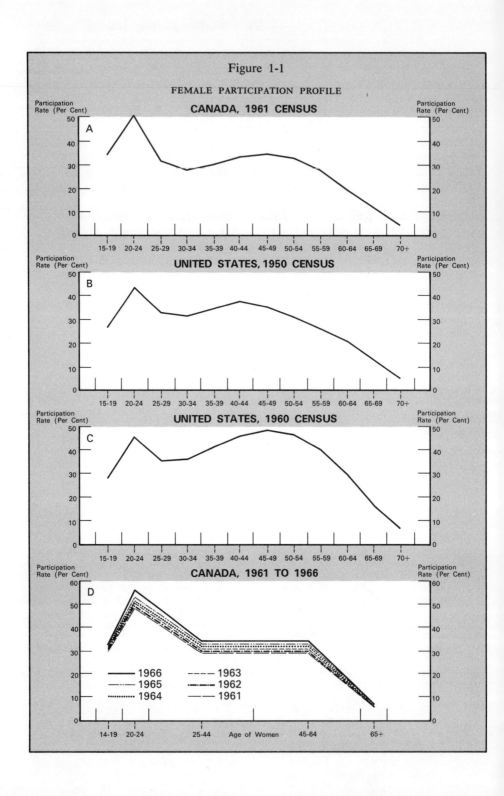

Figure 1-1

FEMALE PARTICIPATION PROFILE

Table 1-5

RATIO OF LABOUR FORCE TO TOTAL POPULATION IN
SELECTED COUNTRIES, 1962

Country	Both Sexes	Males	Females
Britain	47.7	64.9	31.4
France	42.3	57.9	27.4
Germany (F.R.)	47.8	64.2	33.1
Italy	41.3	61.0	22.5
Sweden	45.0	61.9	28.2
United States	40.0	54.5	25.9
Canada	36.3	52.7	19.5

Source: Illing, *Population*, Table 4-F, p. 86.

has the most fundamental and widespread economic and social implications, stems from and interacts with a number of equally fundamental and pervasive demographic and socio-economic developments in Canada. Some of these — the changing industrial and occupational patterns of the Canadian labour market, urbanization, rising levels of education — will be discussed in the section devoted to the changing composition of labour supply. Others — the reduction in working hours and the growth in part-time employment, improvements in household technology, the development of commercial substitutes for most household products, the values of an affluent society that places ever-greater emphasis on rising material standards of living, changes in employer attitudes and in community attitudes generally — can only be listed here, since their full exploration would extend this brief article into many volumes, requiring the efforts and skills of experts in a wide range of disciplines. Space limitations also justify only the mention of changes in marital and fertility patterns, although it is certain that they too have exerted a significant influence on these long-run trends.[15] The postwar generation of women in Canada married earlier, started their families earlier and were younger when their last child entered school.[16] Other demographic trends have also played

[15] For a discussion of these demographic variables see Jacques Henripin, *Tendances et Facteurs de la Fécondité au Canada,* 1961 Census Monograph Programme, (Ottawa: Queen's Printer, 1968).

[16] Further large reductions in the average age at marriage appear to be unlikely. Indeed the postwar decline has already abated because of extension of post-secondary schooling. See Wolfgang M. Illing, *Population, Family, Household and Labour Force Growth to 1980,* Economic Council of Canada, (Ottawa: Queen's Printer, 1967).

a role. In particular, the low birth rates of the 1930's and the consequent short supply of postwar new entrants created a very favourable economic environment for women entering the labour force. The proportionate decline of working age single women was especially conducive to the entry of married women.[17]

PROJECTIONS OF SUPPLY.[18]   The rate of growth of the Canadian labour force reached a record high during the 1960's, the most rapid since the early years of this century when the West was opened to the flood of European immigrants. The growth rate of the 60's, high not only by Canadian standards but exceedingly high by international standards, stemmed from sources very different from those of the earlier period. In the main, it was due to the arrival on the labour market of the plethora of post-war babies, now young adults whose level of education far surpassed that of the unskilled immigrants who settled the West or even that of the middle-aged and older workers who today form the mainstay of Canada's work force. The remarkable rise in female participation also contributed significantly to the burgeoning supply. Net immigration, however, was a factor of relatively limited importance.

While it is not anticipated that the present rate of growth will be maintained until 1980, the projected growth is none the less extremely high. (See Table 1-6.) The underlying sources are those of the 1960's:

Table 1-6

LABOUR FORCE GROWTH IN SELECTED COUNTRIES: 1965-1980

Country	Total Change in Force: 1965-80 Percent
Britain	4.4
France	13.5
Germany (F.R.)	5.5
Italy	1.7
Sweden	—0.3
United States	29.5
Canada	49.8

Source: Illing, *Population,* p. 77.

the baby boom, women and net immigration. Net immigration is expected to contribute about 17 per cent to labour force increases in the 1970's.

From 1967 to 1980, the labour force is projected to increase by almost 40 per cent, or by almost 3 million persons, to reach a level of over 10.5 million.[19] Women are expected to account for well over 40 per cent of the overall growth, reflecting the assumption that the total female participation rate should rise from its present level of about 34 per cent to 40 per cent by 1980. By 1980, women will probably comprise well over one-third of the Canadian labour force.

Table 1-7 presents the participation projections for 1980 and the actual labour force rates for 1967. It is evident that rates for teen-age and post-retirement males are expected to decline over the 1970's, but at a more moderate pace than in the previous two decades. Moderate decline is also probable in the twenty to twenty-four age group, because of extended post-secondary education. Little change is expected for prime age males, whose rates are both high and relatively stable. The trends for women are, of course, more striking. Only teen-age rates exhibit little change. For women over twenty, substantial increases in activity are expected. By 1980, the peak rate (women twenty to twenty-four) should be 62 per cent, a substantial gain over the present 57 per cent. By 1980, women twenty to twenty-four years of age should comprise 62 per cent of the labour force.

As Table 1-7 indicates, Canada probably will be making fuller utilization of her manpower resources by 1980. The overall participation rate is expected to rise by over three percentage points, from 55.5 per cent in 1967 to 58.7 per cent in 1980. (The ratio of labour force to total population will rise even more because of the slowdown in natural increase.) This rate will set a record high for at least a half century. It is mainly attributable to a greater proportion of persons being in the high participation groups and the increased participation of women.

These projected changes in participation will have an important effect on the composition of the labour force in 1980. Before we examine the projected changes in composition, however, we must consider the historical trends on which they were based.

---

[17] See John D. Allingham, *The Demographic Background to Change in the Number and Composition of Female Wage-Earners in Canada, 1951 to 1961,* Dominion Bureau of Statistics, Special Labour Force Studies, Series B, No. 1, (Ottawa: Queen's Printer, 1967). Cross-section econometric studies using 1961 Census data have sought to quantify the impact of a number of independent variables on female participation rates in Canada. See Ostry, *Female Worker,* Appendix, and John D. Allingham and Byran Spencer, *Women Who Work: Part 2,* Special Labour Force Studies, Series B. (Ottawa: Queen's Printer, December 1968).

The overriding importance of the stage of family formation is exhibited in all these analyses. The stronger impact of 'pull' variables (education or earnings of wife) than of "push" influences (education or earnings of husband) is also evident. The use of French Language and/or Catholic religion as a proxy for cultural influences shows up as a consistently negative and strongly significant influence on work activity.

[18] All projection data from Illing, *"Population, Family,"* Tables 4-B (p. 77), 4-D (p. 80), 4-E (p. 84), 4-G (p. 87), 4-I (p. 90).

[19] These figures are based on an assumption of average annual gross immigration of 100,000, the "medium" immigration assumption. See *ibid.,* p. 76.

Changes in Composition

AGE AND SEX. The major demographic and participation trends outlined in the previous discussion have left an imprint on the changing age-
sex structure of the population and the labour force. The effect of the
persistent decline in mortality rates is seen in the generally rising proportion of older people in the population while the long-run decline in
the birth rate until the late 1930's is reflected first, in the shrinking proportion of children under five years in all census records until 1941 and
second, in the rising median age of the population from just over twenty
years in 1881 to almost twenty-eight years in 1951. The increase in the
birth rate during and after World War II increased the population in the
younger age groups so that between 1951 and 1961 the median age declined by more than a full year.

Although it is sometimes difficult to disentangle the structural impact of immigration from the underlying birth and death rate trends,
the effects of heavy immigrant inflow are easily discerned in disproportionate increases in the young and middle-aged adult population and in the
sex ratio, because of its high male content. These effects are, of course,
much more marked for the working age population, fifteen to sixty-four,
than for the population as a whole. During the 1950's the large inflow of
immigrants aged twenty to forty helped to fill the gap created in working
age population by the low birth rates of the depression years.

Changes in the age-sex structure of the population will affect the
labour force through the "participation rate" and trends in participation
exert a powerful, independent influence on the structure of labour supply.
For example, while the male/female ratio of the working age population fell from 106.4 to 101.8 between 1901 and 1961, the female proportion of the labour force rose from 15 per cent to 26 per cent, a
consequence, of course, of the long-run decline in male participation and
the sharp rise in female rates. Similarly, the age distribution of the labour
force has been affected more by participation than by demographic
trends. For example, males under twenty accounted for about 28 per cent
of the working age population in 1921; this figure fell to about 24 per cent
in 1961 while the comparable labour force shares shrank by half, from
10 per cent to 5 per cent. For women, the changes were even more
marked. The steep rise in participation among middle-aged and older
married women (thirty-five to sixty-four years) is reflected in a tripling
of their labour force share, from about 4 per cent in 1921 to 12 per cent
in 1961, although the underlying changes in the population structure
were negligible in comparison. The median age of the female work force
rose by over five years between 1951 and 1961,[20] while the median age
of the base population increased by scarcely more than one year. The
1950's was the decade in which the return flow of women into the labour
force (the second phase of the working life cycle) first became evident
in Canada.

It is worth noting some of the structural changes projected for the
Canadian labour force by 1980. The proportion of women will likely
rise from just under 31 per cent in 1970 to almost 35 per cent in 1980.

Table 1-7

ACTUAL AND PROJECTED PARTICIPATION RATES BY AGE AND SEX:
ANNUAL AVERAGE, 1967-1980

Sex and Age	Actual 1967	Projected 1980*
Both sexes		
14-19 years	35.5	33.9
20-24 "	71.3	73.6
25-34 "	65.4	69.7
35-44 "	67.1	72.5
45-54 "	67.5	73.0
55-64 "	57.2	62.2
65 years and over	14.7	13.7
All ages — 14 years and over	55.5	58.7
Male		
14-19 years	39.4	36.7
20-24 "	86.0	85.0
25-34 "	97.0	97.3
35-44 "	97.6	97.7
45-54 "	96.0	96.0
55-64 "	85.8	85.5
65 years and over	24.7	21.7
All ages — 14 years and over	77.5	77.7
Female		
14-19 years	31.6	31.1
20-24 "	56.6	62.0
25-34 "	34.4	41.0
35-44 "	37.0	47.0
45-54 "	39.7	50.0
55-64 "	28.6	41.0
65 years and over	5.9	7.2
All ages — 14 years and over	33.8	40.1

* Medium immigration assumptions: 100,000 annual gross immigration.
Source: DBS *Labour Force Survey* and Illing, *Population,* Table 4-1, p. 92.

The proportion of women in the older age group, fifty-five to sixty-four, is expected to double. The most marked increases by age category for the labour force as a whole will be found in the young adult group aged

[20] See Sylvia Ostry, *The Occupational Composition of the Canadian Labour Force,* one of a series of Labour Force Studies in the 1961 Census Monograph Programme, (Ottawa: Queen's Printer, 1967), for an analysis of the changing age structure of the major occupational divisions of the labour force over the period 1931-61.

twenty to thirty-four. (See Table 1-8.) The distribution of the incremental supply is expected to be heavily weighted by workers under thirty-five who will account for over 60 per cent of the net addition to the total

Table 1-8

ACTUAL AND PROJECTED LABOUR FORCE BY AGE AND SEX:
ANNUAL AVERAGES, 1967-1980

Sex and Age	Actual 1967	Projected 1980	Percent Increase	Absolute Increase (distribution) No.	Percent
Both sexes					
14-19 years	816	911	11.6	95	3.2
20-24 "	1,090	1,657	52.0	567	18.9
25-34 "	1,599	2,813	75.9	1214	40.4
35-44 "	1,682	1,968	17.0	286	9.5
45-54 "	1,421	1,781	25.3	360	11.9
55-64 "	869	1,294	48.9	425	14.2
65 years and over	217	274	26.3	57	1.9
All ages — 14 years and over	7,694	10,698	39.0	3004	100.0
Male					
14-19 years	460	502	9.1	42	2.5
20-24 "	657	968	47.3	311	18.4
25-34 "	1,175	2,003	70.5	828	49.1
35-44 "	1,215	1,332	9.6	117	6.9
45-54 "	1,000	1,170	17.0	170	10.1
55-64 "	652	848	30.1	196	11.6
65 years and over	170	194	14.1	24	1.4
All ages — 14 years and over	5,329	7,017	31.7	1688	100.0
Female					
14-19 years	357	409	14.6	52	4.0
20-24 "	433	689	59.1	256	19.5
25-34 "	424	810	91.0	386	29.4
35-44 "	468	636	35.9	168	12.8
45-54 "	422	611	44.8	189	14.4
55-64 "	217	446	105.5	229	17.4
65 years and over	46	80	73.9	34	2.5
All ages — 14 years and over	2,365	3,681	55.6	1316	100.0

* Medium immigration assumptions: 100,000 annual gross immigration.
Source: DBS *Labour Force Survey* and Illing, *Population*, Table 4-B, p. 77.

labour force during the 1970's. There will, however, be a relative short fall in the thirty-five to forty-four age group, from which the recruits are drawn for executive and leadership positions in industry and government. These compositional changes suggest the possibility of more rapid promotion of young workers into positions of authority and emphasize the importance of better education and training and improved mobility as major goals of manpower policy.

GEOGRAPHIC DISTRIBUTION.   There have been marked regional shifts in the Canadian population and labour force in each decade of the twentieth century. During the period of rapid settlement in the West that marked the beginning of the great Wheat Phase of Canadian development, preceding World War I, the population in Saskatchewan and Alberta expanded by over 400 per cent, in British Columbia and Manitoba by 120 and 80 per cent respectively. Between 1901 and 1911 more than 60 per cent of the total increase in Canadian population was absorbed west of the Ontario border.

The western boom, however, was not sustained. Only British Columbia continued to experience rapid growth, tripling its share of population from under 3 per cent in 1901 to more than 9 per cent in 1961. The Prairies were severely hit by the Great Depression (population actually declined in Saskatchewan during the 1930's and 1940's) and they have achieved only moderate growth rates since World War II. Today they account for about 17 per cent of Canada's total population. The exception to the Prairie growth pattern is Alberta, which in recent decades has become Canada's fastest-growing province.

The most consistent patterns of growth over the century are found in the Central and Eastern regions of the country. Ontario and Quebec have enjoyed persistent and generally substantial increases. Today almost two-thirds of the labour force are located in Central Canada. (See Table 1-9.) At the other extreme, the Maritimes (and with the addition of Newfoundland, the Atlantic region) have suffered relative (and at times actual) decline throughout the twentieth century. In recent years this region has accounted for less than 10 per cent of Canada's working population.

These differential rates of regional growth in population and labour force were mainly the product of internal migration and the distribution of immigrants from abroad rather than differing rates of natural increase. The basic forces that have shaped the regional configuration of this country have been largely economic and technological, a response to broad underlying patterns of industrial change. Institutional and political factors have also played a role. The effort to achieve a more balanced growth for the country as a whole and to reduce if not to eliminate the distressingly high regional disparities in income and unemployment has long been an expressed object of federal and provincial government policy, a goal yet far from achievement. The problem of regional imbalance, as it is manifested in manpower terms, is treated in a later section of this essay.

Table 1-9

PERCENTAGE DISTRIBUTION OF THE POPULATION* AND LABOUR FORCE,
BY PROVINCE AND REGION: 1966

Province or Region	Population (June)	Labour Force (annual averages)
Canada	100.0	100.0
Atlantic Region	9.9	8.4
Newfoundland	2.5	1.9
Prince Edward Island	0.5	0.5
Nova Scotia	3.8	3.3
New Brunswick	3.1	2.7
Quebec	28.9	28.5
Ontario	34.9	36.6
Prairie Region	16.9	16.8
Manitoba	4.8	4.8
Saskatchewan	4.8	4.4
Alberta	7.3	7.6
British Columbia	9.4	9.6

* Excluding Yukon and the Northwest Territories.
Source: 1966 *Census of Canada* and 1967 *Labour Force Survey.*

URBANIZATION. Changes in the regional distribution of population in Canada have been accompanied by a steady and rapid pace of urbanization and an attendant shift from agricultural to non-agricultural activity. Urbanization and regionalization are the joint products of fundamental economic, technological and social forces. We can do little here except record the rise of urbanization and point out some of the consequences of this development for the growth and structure of labour supply in Canada.[21] (See Table 1-10.)

At Confederation, there were no large Canadian cities by contemporary standards and close to 85 per cent of the population lived on farms or in rural villages. A century later, a century during which the population had increased sixfold, the degree of urbanization reached 70 per cent. Moreover, 44 per cent of the population was living in large cities (100,000 and over) or larger metropolitan centres. By 1980 it is anticipated that the urban population will have grown to 80 per cent of the total population. Moreover the concentration in large cities is likely to be even more pronounced: some 60 per cent of Canadians will live in about twenty-nine major metropolitan areas.[22] Thirty years ago, 60 per cent of the rural population lived on farms, but by 1961 the proportion had fallen well below two-fifths and it is continuing to decline. Many persons living in rural non-farm areas commute to work in urban centres.

In labour force terms, the urbanization process in Canada is most clearly apparent in the marked shift from agriculture to industrial and occupational activity out of agriculture. (See below, for discussion of industrial and occupational changes.) The long-run relative decline of the farm labour force was transformed after World War II into a sharp absolute decrease in numbers. The movement of people off the farm (primarily young people, i.e. new labour force entrants) during the 1950's and early 1960's made a major contribution to manpower supplies during the postwar period. The farm-non farm shift, together with net immigration and rising female participation, provided an important offset to shortages of labour force entrants during the rapid economic expansion of the early and mid 1950's. The agricultural share of the industrial work force today has fallen to well under 10 per cent. Despite the projected increase in urbanization, the farm sector is not likely to be a significant source of labour supply in coming decades.

Table 1-10

DEGREE OF URBANIZATION: 1861-1966

Year	Total	Percentage of Population* Rural	Urban
	%	%	%
1851	100.0	86.9	13.1
1861	100.0	84.2	15.8
1871	100.0	81.7	18.3
1881	100.0	76.7	23.3
1891	100.0	70.2	29.8
1901	100.0	65.1	34.9
1911	100.0	58.2	41.8
1921	100.0	52.6	47.4
1931	100.0	47.5	52.5
1941	100.0	44.3	55.7
1951[a]	100.0	37.1	62.9
1961[a]	100.0	29.8	70.2
1951[b]	100.0	37.6	62.4
1961[b]	100.0	30.3	69.7
1966	100.0	26.4	73.6

* Excluding Yukon and the Northwest Territories.
a Excludes Newfoundland.
b Includes Newfoundland.
Source: Leroy O. Stone, *Urban Development in Canada,* 1961 Census Monograph Series and 1966 *Census of Canada.*

[21] For a full exploration of the subject see L. O. Stone, *Urban Development in Canada,* Dominion Bureau of Statistics, 1961 Census Monograph Series, (Ottawa: Queen's Printer, 1967).

[22] Economic Council of Canada, *Fourth Annual Review,* (Ottawa: Queen's Printer, 1967).

There is another important consequence of urbanization that is directly relevant to this discussion of labour supply, namely its influence on female participation rates. The labour force activity rates of women are much higher in urban than rural areas and appears also to vary directly, though not uniformly, with city size.[23] This variation can, in part, be attributed to differences in job opportunities — clerical jobs, other white-collar jobs and service jobs, etc. are more abundant in urban than in rural areas, in larger than in smaller cities. Other factors are also involved: family size, household technology, community attitudes, and customs for example. Whatever the complex of influences, the association between female participation rates and rural-urban residence is distinct and the gap in rates is substantial. Thus the shift of population from rural to urban areas, particularly the accelerated movement during the 1950's and early 1960's, was itself a factor contributing to the rise of female labour force participation in Canada. The continuing urban growth and the increasing concentration of population in large urban complexes, anticipated during the 1970's, may be expected to have a similar effect. Urbanization, (or the population "implosion") will have many other implications for manpower developments that deserve careful study. In particular, the location of jobs versus the location of living space and the manifold problems of travel-to-work patterns and costs will loom large in coming decades.

INDUSTRY AND OCCUPATION.   The transformation of Canada from a rural-agricultural society to a highly urbanized, industrialized society over the course of the twentieth century can be effectively traced in the changing occupational composition of the labour force. Changes in the kind of work people do (occupation) not only determine their livelihood and, therefore, their modes and standards of living but also affect their social status and their "world outlook." In more general terms, there is a strong relationship between the occupational deployment of a nation's labour force and its stage of economic development and pattern of social organization.

The changes that occur in the occupational structure of the working population are the result of changes in the industrial distribution of the labour force as well as modification of the occupational content of individual industries. The former reflects a wide complex of forces shaping the final demand for goods and services, and hence the derived demand for labour, as well as the technical relationships of production in and the productivity of individual industries. Within industries, occupational requirements respond to a great variety of pressures, the most pervasive and compelling of which is undoubtedly technological change. Furthermore, there is a continual interplay between changes in demand and changes in supply: in some periods independent developments on the supply side may play an important role in refashioning the pattern of labour force development by affecting relative prices and by means of inter- and intra-factor substitution. For example, the massive immigration of unskilled labour at the beginning of the century was reflected in structural changes of the work force. Over the long run, the most important element on the side of supply has been the extension of public education, to be discussed shortly.

From Table 1-11, it is apparent that the major changes in the industrial dimensions of the Canadian work force over the past three intercensal decades have been the drastic decline in agriculture, especially after 1941, and the impressive rise in service-producing industries — trade, finance, transportation, government, schools, hospitals and so on. The changes in the relative share of the goods-producing sector have been much more moderate. More current data, from the Labour Force Survey, but based on a different classification standard, show a continuation of these trends. (See Table 1-12.)

The much longer-run occupational trends depicted in Table 1-13 clearly indicate that the growth of the Canadian labour force in this century is characterized by two major occupational shifts obviously related to the industrial shifts described above[24] — a marked shift away from agricultural pursuits and a decisive movement toward white-collar jobs. The effect of long-run distributional changes on the relative share of blue-collar occupations has been virtually negligible in comparison.

Canada is not unique in this experience and these developments are well known in broad outline if not in precise detail and timing. What deserves noting, however, is that these changes have not evolved in a smooth and steady fashion over the course of the past six decades or more. This is apparent even in the case of the dramatic and persistent shift away from agriculture. The numbers engaged in farming continued to grow for the first three decades of this century, although at a pace outstripped from the beginning by those in the population with other occupational attachments. The much steeper fall of the agricultural share after 1941[25] reflects the combined effects of expanding off-farm job opportunities, and the increasing numbers of the rural population made unnecessary by the enhanced pace of mechanization and other improvements in farm production during those years. This produced both a relative and an absolute decline in farm occupations. During the 1960's, the agricultural share of occupations continued its steep descent, falling from just over 10 per cent to less than 8 per cent by 1967. (See Table 1-14.)

As with agricultural occupations, the growth path of the white-collar group has scarcely been smooth and steady. The pattern was marked by two phases of rapid expansion, one in the second decade of the century, which straddled World War I, and the more recent period, from 1941 to the present, which was initiated by World War II. The share of the white-collar ocupations has continued to rise during the 1960's, mainly because of a sustained growth in the professional and technical group.

---

[23] *Cf.* Allingham and Spencer, *Women Who Work,* p. 18, and Ostry, *The Female Worker,* Chart 3, p. 13.

[24] The extent and nature of the relationship has been analyzed in Meltz, *Changes in the Occupational Distribution of the Canadian Labour Force, 1931-1961* (Ottawa: Queen's Printer, 1965).

[25] During the 1930's, the wheat economy of the west was most seriously damaged, not only by the collapse of world wheat markets, but by severe drought, especially in Saskatchewan. However, the non-farm sector was in the throes of the Great Depression so that movement off the farm was discouraged and, indeed, some "backflow" probably occurred.

Table 1-11

LABOUR FORCE DISTRIBUTION BY MAJOR INDUSTRY GROUP: 1931-1961

Industry	1931 Number 000's	1931 Percent	1941 Number 000's	1941 Percent	1951 Number 000's	1951 Percent	1961 Number 000's	1961 Percent
Total Civilian Labour Force	3,917.6	100.0	4,196.0	100.0	5,214.9	100.0	6,342.3	100.0
Primary	1,293.3	33.0	1,320.6	31.5	1,111.7	21.3	903.3	14.2
Agriculture	1,124.0	28.7	1,082.3	25.8	827.2	15.9	640.4	10.1
Forestry and Fishing	97.5	2.5	145.0	3.5	180.6	3.5	143.6	2.3
Mining	71.8	1.8	93.3	2.2	103.9	2.0	119.3	1.9
Secondary	1,093.5	27.9	1,209.9	28.8	1,717.1	32.9	1,963.1	31.0
Manufacturing	800.0	20.4	983.9	23.4	1,364.7	26.2	1,494.7	23.6
Construction	293.5	7.5	226.0	5.4	352.4	6.7	468.4	7.4
Tertiary	1,530.4	39.1	1,657.4	39.5	2,328.8	44.7	3,344.1	52.7
Electricity, gas and water	28.1	0.7	25.9	0.6	62.0	1.2	70.5	1.1
Transportation and communication	317.0	8.1	292.3	7.0	433.5	8.3	500.2	7.9
Trade	395.6	10.1	468.4	11.2	711.3	13.6	931.8	14.7
Finance	93.1	2.4	90.4	2.2	144.2	2.8	229.7	3.6
Community and business service	251.4	6.4	277.7	6.6	431.2	8.3	764.4	12.1
Government service	100.8	2.6	117.2	2.8	203.5	3.9	363.3	5.7
Recreation service	18.8	0.5	17.7	0.4	28.7	0.6	39.8	0.6
Personal service	325.6	8.3	367.9	8.8	314.4	6.0	444.4	7.0
Industry not stated	0.5	0.0	8.0	0.2	57.2	1.1	132.0	2.1

Source: Noah M. Meltz, *Changes in the Occupational Distribution of the Canadian Labour Force, 1931-1961*, Table A-5, (Ottawa, Queen's Printer, 1965).

Table 1-12

PERCENTAGE DISTRIBUTION OF THE EXPERIENCED LABOUR FORCE BY INDUSTRY:

ANNUAL AVERAGES, 1961-1967

Industry	1961	1962	1963	Year 1964	1965	1966	1967
All industries	100.0	100.0	100.0	100.0	100.0	100.0	100.0
Primary	14.3	13.6	13.1	12.5	12.1	10.8	10.5
Agriculture	10.8	10.3	9.9	9.3	8.5	7.5	7.4
Forestry	1.9	1.6	1.6	1.5	1.3	1.2	1.2
Fishing and trapping	0.3	0.4	0.5	0.4	0.4	0.4	0.4
Mines, quarries, oil wells	1.3	1.4	1.2	1.3	1.9	1.7	1.5
Secondary	31.3	31.3	31.4	31.7	31.1	31.8	30.9
Manufacturing	24.0	24.1	24.3	24.9	23.8	24.4	23.9
Construction	7.3	7.2	7.1	6.8	7.3	7.4	7.0
Tertiary	54.4	55.1	55.5	55.8	56.8	57.4	58.6
Transportation, communication and other utilities	9.4	9.5	9.4	8.9	9.0	8.7	9.0
Trade	16.6	16.6	16.4	16.6	16.5	16.4	16.4
Finance, insurance and real estate	3.8	3.8	3.8	3.9	4.0	4.1	4.1
Community, business and personal service)	24.6	25.3	25.8	26.4	27.3	28.2	29.1
Public administration and defence)							

Source: Labour Force Survey.

Table 1-13

PERCENTAGE DISTRIBUTION OF THE LABOUR FORCE, 15 YEARS OF AGE AND OVER[a], BY OCCUPATION DIVISION, AS OF 1951, AND SEX, FOR CANADA[b]: 1901 TO 1961 CENSUSES

Occupation Division (as of 1951)	1901			1911			1921		
	T	M	F	T	M	F	T	M	F
All occupations	100.0	100.0	100.0	100.0	100.0	100.0	100.0	100.0	100.0
White-collar occupations	15.3	14.0	23.6	17.0	14.9	30.5	25.3	21.1	48.3
Proprietary and managerial	4.3	4.8	1.2	4.7	5.2	1.6	7.3	8.2	2.0
Professional	4.6	3.1	14.7	3.8	2.4	12.7	5.4	3.0	19.1
Clerical	3.2	2.9	5.3	3.8	3.0	9.4	6.9	4.7	18.7
Commercial	} 3.1	} 3.2	} 2.4	4.4	4.1	6.7	5.1	4.5	8.4
Financial				0.3	0.3	d	0.6	0.7	0.1
Blue-collar occupations	27.8	27.5	30.1	30.3	30.9	26.3	25.8	27.2	17.9
Manufacturing and mechanical	15.9	13.8	29.6	13.6	11.7	26.2	11.4	10.3	17.8
Construction	4.7	5.4	d	4.8	5.5	d	4.7	5.5	d
Labourerse	7.2	8.2	0.5	11.9	13.7	0.1	9.7	11.4	0.1
Primary occupations	44.3	50.5	3.8	39.5	44.8	4.5	36.2	42.1	3.7
Agricultural	40.3	45.9	3.8	34.4	39.0	4.4	32.6	37.9	3.7
Fishing, hunting and trapping	1.5	1.8	d	1.3	1.5	0.1	0.9	1.1	d
Logging	0.9	1.0	—	1.5	1.8	—	1.2	1.4	—
Mining and quarrying	1.6	1.8	—	2.3	2.6	d	1.5	1.7	d
Transportation and communication	4.4	5.0	0.5	5.6	6.3	1.5	5.5	5.9	3.0
Service	8.2	2.9	42.0	7.6	3.1	37.2	7.0	3.5	26.8
Personal	7.8	2.6	42.0	7.3	2.8	37.1	5.8	2.1	25.8
Not stated occupations	—	—	—	—	—	—	0.2	0.2	0.3

	1931			1941[c]			1951			1961		
	T	M	F	T	M	F	T	M	F	T	M	F
All occupations[a]	100.0	100.0	100.0	100.0	100.0	100.0	100.0	100.0	100.0	100.0	100.0	100.0
White collar occupations	24.5	20.2	45.4	25.3	20.5	44.7	32.0	25.4	55.4	37.9	30.6	57.3
Proprietary and managerial	5.6	6.4	1.6	5.4	6.2	2.0	7.4	8.7	3.0	7.8	9.6	2.9
Professional	6.1	3.7	17.8	6.7	4.5	15.6	7.3	5.3	14.4	9.8	7.7	15.5
Clerical	6.7	4.4	17.7	7.2	4.5	18.3	10.7	5.9	27.5	12.7	6.7	28.6
Commercial	5.4	4.8	8.3	5.4	4.5	8.7	6.0	4.7	10.4	6.8	5.6	10.0
Financial	0.7	0.9	0.1	0.6	0.7	0.1	0.6	0.7	0.1	0.8	1.0	0.2
Blue collar occupations	27.5	30.2	14.5	27.1	29.6	16.8	29.4	33.0	16.5	26.6	32.4	11.1
Manufacturing and mechanical	11.6	11.3	12.7	16.1	16.2	15.4	17.2	17.9	14.6	16.1	18.4	9.9
Construction	4.7	5.7	d	4.7	5.8	d	5.5	7.1	0.1	5.2	7.1	d
Labourers[e]	11.3	13.2	1.7	6.3	7.6	1.4	6.6	8.0	1.8	5.3	6.9	1.2
Primary occupations	32.4	38.2	3.7	30.5	37.5	2.3	19.8	24.6	2.8	12.8	16.1	4.3
Agricultural	28.6	33.7	3.6	25.7	31.5	2.3	15.7	19.3	2.8	10.0	12.2	4.3
Fishing, hunting and trapping	1.2	1.4	0.1	1.2	1.5	d	1.0	1.3	d	0.6	0.8	d
Logging	1.1	1.3	—	1.9	2.3	d	1.9	2.5	d	1.2	1.7	d
Mining and quarrying	1.5	1.8	—	1.7	2.1	d	1.2	1.6	d	1.0	1.4	d
Transportation and communication	6.3	7.1	2.4	6.4	7.5	1.7	7.8	9.2	2.9	7.7	9.7	2.2
Service	9.3	4.2	33.9	10.5	4.6	34.3	9.8	6.5	21.2	12.4	8.5	22.6
Personal	8.2	3.0	33.8	9.3	3.2	34.2	7.2	3.3	21.0	9.1	4.2	22.1
Not stated occupations	d	d	d	0.2	0.3	0.2	1.2	1.3	1.2	2.6	2.7	2.5

NOTE.—"Gainfully occupied" rather than "Labour Force" concept used prior to 1951. See 1961 *Census of Canada*, Bulletin 3.1-1, Tables 3, 3A and Introduction.

a 10 years and over in 1901.
b Excluding Yukon and Northwest Territories: including Newfoundland in 1951 and 1961.
c Excluding persons on active service, June 1941.
d Less than 0.05%.
e Labourers in all industries except those engaged in agriculture, fishing, logging or mining.
Source: Ostry, *Occupational Composition.*

Table 1-14

PERCENTAGE DISTRIBUTION OF THE EXPERIENCED LABOUR FORCE BY OCCUPATION: ANNUAL AVERAGES, 1961-1967.

Occupation	Year						
	1961	1962	1963	1964	1965	1966	1967
All Occupations	100.0	100.0	100.0	100.0	100.0	100.0	100.0
White collar	38.1	39.1	39.2	39.6	40.2	41.6	41.8
Managerial	8.8	8.9	8.9	8.9	9.0	9.1	9.1
Professional and technical	9.3	10.1	10.1	10.2	11.1	11.9	12.1
Clerical	12.8	12.9	13.1	13.1	13.2	13.9	13.9
Sales	7.2	7.1	7.1	7.3	6.9	6.6	6.7
Blue collar	30.8	30.7	30.8	30.5	30.9	31.6	31.2
Craftsmen, production process and related workers	24.8	25.1	25.3	25.0	25.5	26.3	26.5
Labourers and unskilled workers	6.0	5.6	5.6	5.6	5.4	5.3	4.7
Primary	13.4	12.7	12.3	11.6	10.9	9.8	9.6
Farmers and farm workers	10.8	10.3	10.0	9.3	8.5	7.6	7.5
Loggers and related workers)	1.8	1.6	1.6	1.5	1.3	1.3	1.3
Fishermen, trappers and hunters)							
Miners, quarrymen and related workers	0.8	0.8	0.7	0.8	1.1	0.9	0.8
Transportation and communication	7.0	6.7	6.6	6.6	6.4	5.7	5.6
Service and recreation	10.7	10.8	11.1	11.7	11.6	11.3	11.8

Source: Labour Force Survey, 1968.

The managerial and clerical occupations showed little change in relative numbers while the share of sales occupations actually declined in the latter years of the decade. (See Table 1-14.)

The rapid growth in white-collar occupations during the postwar period as a whole reflects the shift from industrial employment to the tertiary sector (which is heavily weighted with white-collar occupations), differential (below-average) productivity change in the service-producing industries and, especially in the case of clerical workers, changes in occupational composition within industry generally — the so-called "paper-work" revolution.[26] The slowdown in growth rates of clerical positions and especially sales occupations suggests that the strength and direction of these forces are undergoing change. These are precisely the areas, of course, which require intensive study if manpower projections are to be meaningful guides to policy and, alas, precisely the areas for which the dearth of information is most severe in Canada and elsewhere.

Within the blue-collar divisions, the manufacturing and mechanical occupations (skilled and semi-skilled) and the unskilled labourers have exhibited marked and often divergent variations in growth rates over the six-decade period. The rapid growth of the unskilled workers in the opening decade of this century (from just over 7 to almost 12 per cent) reflects the massive impact of Central and Eastern European immigration. It was not until 1941 that the Census recorded an absolute decline in the numbers of unskilled workers (for which the depression of the 1930's had paved the way.) This decline was halted temporarily by the wartime boom but it resumed once more during the 1950's and continued, at a reduced pace, throughout most of the 1960's. The share of the unskilled trade today is less than 5 per cent of the work force as a whole and about 6 per cent of the male work force. There is obviously not much scope for further decline.

A reverse growth pattern was exhibited by the largest component group in the blue-collar division, the skilled and semi-skilled manual workers. Their steady shrinkage in labour force share until 1931 was sharply reversed by the onset of World War II and, in the two decades following 1941, this group of occupations expanded at a slightly quicker pace than the total labour force. This modest growth was halted temporarily during the economic slowdown of the late 1950's and early 1960's. There was a very modest resurgence of these occupations, especially for males, since 1965. (See Table 1-14.) It is worth noting (in contradiction to the view that we are now a white-collar society) that this group of manual occupations still accounts for a very substantial share of the work force: about one-quarter of the working population as a whole and close to one-third of the male work force.

A majority of women, however, do work in a white-collar world today and for that reason alone some further comment on the service occupations is necessary. In 1901 more than two-fifths of women's jobs were in service

---

[26] *Cf.* Meltz, *Occupational Distribution,* Chapter 7 for a quantitative allocation of these factors.

occupations. Even today these occupations account for more than one-fifth of the female work force but well under 10 per cent of the male work force. The long-run trend for this group of occupations is by no means clear. Sharp declines in the female segment in the first two decades were reversed during the 1920's and 1930's but declines resumed during the war and early postwar period. Since the 1950's, the service share of women's jobs has remained fairly stable, at just above one-fifth of the total. The service share of male jobs, on the other hand, although still of minor proportions, has shown a steady increase in each decade since 1901. This slow but steady upward climb continued, with minor fluctuations, throughout the 1960's.

EDUCATIONAL CHANGES.   Changes in occupational structure are sometimes cited as evidence of the changing quality of the work force, but this is not necessarily true and this article will not assess them in those terms. A more direct, though by no means fully satisfactory, means of evaluating "quality" changes is by measuring the educational level of the working population, including formal, technical and vocational education and on-job training. Unfortunately, Canada has little data in this crucially important area. It should be remembered that there are ten different provincial systems of schooling to consider as well as the problems connected with the often radically differing experiences of the substantial immigrant population.

Little reliable historical data measuring even formal educational attainment on a consistent basis is available.[27] A reasonably effective alternative to piecing together the historical data is to use current statistics.[28] Table 1-15 shows the native-born[29] Canadian male population, in selected age categories, distributed according to its years of formal schooling. Each of the sex cohorts completed its education and entered the labour force at a different period in this century. Hence the differences in level of education between successively younger cohorts provide a reasonably good guide to the changing "quality" of labour supply over the past half century or so in Canada. As a rough measure of level of schooling we use the percentage difference in median years of schooling.

While there were consistent improvements in the quality of Canada's labour force population over the past six decades or more, the rate of progress in this respect was very slow in the earlier part of the century and, no doubt, even slower before then. A more marked improvement may be observed for those who completed their education during the Great Depression (the cohort born between 1911 and 1920) perhaps because massive unemployment and lack of jobs induced some, at least, to stay in school longer rather than venture into the working world. The greatest advance in educational levels was achieved by the men who finished their schooling in the 1940's, many of whom benefited from the Federal Government's assistance to returning war veterans. The experience of the 1940's was not repeated in the following decade of rapid economic growth and burgeoning job opportunities.

The progress in education over this century, while halting and uneven,

Table 1-15

IMPROVEMENT IN EDUCATIONAL LEVEL OF MALE POPULATION,[a] CANADA
PRE-1920 TO PRESENT

Age of Cohort in February, 1965	Period in which Cohort was born	Period in which most of Cohorts probably completed school	Percentage increase in Median Years of Schooling of Successive Cohorts
65 and over	1900 or before	Before 1920	
55-64	1901-1910	During 1920's	3.9
45-54	1911-1920	During 1930's	5.0
35-44	1921-1930	During 1940's	9.5
25-34	1931-1940	During 1950's	4.4
20-24	1941-1945	During 1960's	9.4

a Excluding immigrants who entered Canada since World War II.
Source: Denton and Ostry, *Canada One Hundred.*

has been substantial. Over 70 per cent of Canadians born before 1900 failed to reach high school level: over 40 per cent did not even finish primary school. Today, almost 80 per cent of the young Canadians who enter the labour force have had at least some high school education. Further progress in this direction is expected over the next decade. Rising enrolment and higher completion rates in secondary and post-secondary schooling are projected by the mid-1970's. By 1975, it is expected that 20 per cent of Canada's eighteen to twenty-four year olds will be attending university, compared with a dismally low 5 per cent in 1955-56.[30] This will help to narrow the currently substantial gap in both educational level and enrolment ratio between Canada and the United States.[31]

[27] For an examination of the Census data on the educational level of the major occupation groups from 1931 to 1961 see Ostry, *Occupational Composition.* For an historical analysis using a broader range of data sources, see also Gordon W. Bertram, *The Contribution of Education to Economic Growth,* Economic Council of Canada, (Ottawa: Queen's Printer, 1965).

[28] The data described here were derived from special questions added to the February, 1965 Labour Force Survey. For a fuller analysis see Frank J. Whittingham, *The Educational Attainment of the Canadian Population and Labour Force, 1960-65,* Dominion Bureau of Statistics, Special Labour Force Studies No. 1, (Ottawa: Queen's Printer, 1966).

[29] The native-born population living in Canada is, of course, depleted by the mortality and emigration of earlier decades and for this reason at least the use of current statistics as a substitute for historical data is not entirely satisfactory. Mortality is probably not highly selective by educational level but emigration certainly is. Difficulties of recall and other types of response error are probably more acute for the older respondents as well. (The sample of "native-born" included a few pre-World War II immigrants.)

[30] Economic Council of Canada, *Fourth Annual Review,* p. 69

[31] For a measure of the former, *cf.* Whittingham, *Educational Attainment,* and *ibid.*

A growing number of studies in various countries have suggested that education makes a highly significant contribution to growth rates and living standards. The seminal work in this area of analysis, Edward Denison's *The Sources of Economic Growth in the United States and the Alternatives Before Us,*[32] documented the proposition for the United States. Employing Denison's methodology and assumptions, a parallel Canadian study[33] concluded that roughly 25 per cent of the increase in real per capita income in the period 1911 to 1961 was attributable to the increased educational stock in the labour force. This compares somewhat unfavourably with the findings for the United States for which the relevant figure was more than 40 per cent. The Economic Council of Canada comments:

Thus, while education has made an important contribution to the growth of real income and productivity in Canada over the past half century, the even greater contribution of education to growth in the United States indicates that education has apparently been a factor tending to widen rather than narrow the differences in income and productivity between the two countries over this period.[34]

CHANGES IN DEMAND AND TECHNOLOGY

To trace the growth and changing structure of the labour force under the heading of labour supply is both arbitrary and artificial. Both the level and composition of the working population are jointly determined by the interaction of labour supply and demand. The manpower analyst, one confronted with the task of writing summary articles on manpower developments, must opt for brevity and simplicity of presentation and is, in the end, governed largely by the constraints of data availability. Demographic and labour force statistics in Canada, while by no means ideal, provide an *embarras de richesse* in comparison with the scanty and fragmented information on demand, productivity and technological change. It is the relative quantity and quality of data sources and not the relative significance of the subject matter that have determined the weight assigned to various topics in this article. The comments that follow, on demand and technological change, must be viewed against this preliminary note of explanation.

The Postwar Record of Growth

Viewed from a long-run perspective, growth rates in Canada during recent years have been unusually high. The average annual percentage change in real output, estimated at 3.5 per cent over the past century, reached more than 5 per cent during the long upward swing of the 1960's.[35] Over the postwar period as a whole, however, the growth process was highly uneven. The years immediately following World War II (1946-53) were characterized by consistently high employment and sustained increases in productivity and total output, a consequence of strong external and domestic demand forces and expansionary monetary and fiscal policies. By the middle and late 1950's many of these special and highly favourable expansionary forces had lost strength. A factor of great importance was the loss of momentum in the United States' economy. The period 1954-57 was transitional, marked by somewhat higher unemployment, slower gains in productivity and output and some deterioration in Canada's international position. It was followed by a period of serious stagnation, lasting from 1958 until the early 1960's. Along with large-scale unemployment averaging close to 7 per cent at the national level, other strains and weaknesses in the economy were exposed as productivity lagged and Canada's competitive position worsened. Public debates and concern focused on the source and nature of Canada's high unemployment and on the most effective policies to deal with it.

The early 1960's marked another turning point ushering in an era of long-term expansion and growth, the longest peacetime expansion in Canadian history. The "Great Expansion," as the Economic Council has dubbed it, was characterized by a strong thrust in the growth of aggregate supply, the manpower aspects of which have already been described. The enlargement of total demand was the corresponding side of the equation, without which the high growth rates in employment could not have been sustained. Major expansion of consumer incomes and expenditure in public sector spending on services and social capital, and in exports provided the necessary condition for high growth performance.

The powerful expansion of aggregate demand stimulated impressive gains in the level of total employment (over one million workers between 1961 and 1966). The composition of the increased demand affected the industrial and occupational distribution of the overall increment. (See Table 1-16.) For example, above-average rises in the demand for new machinery and equipment, for non-residential construction and for exports provided a stimulus to the lagging manufacturing and construction industries. This resulted in a modest improvement in their share of total employment despite substantial gains in productivity. The sharp advance in government expenditure for goods and services in the latter part of the period (from 1963) was reflected in the rapid growth of employment in community services (double the overall rate of growth) and in the expansion of the professional and technical groups (at better than 2.5 times the overall rate). As the expansion continued, cost and price advances accelerated. While there was no evidence of an overall shortage of labour

[32] Supplementary Paper No. 13, Committee for Economic Development, (New York, January 1962.)

[33] Bertram, *Contribution of Education*, p. 62.

[34] Economic Council of Canada, *Second Annual Review*, (Ottawa: Queen's Printer, 1965), p. 93. These differences have not, in fact, widened, pointing to the countervailing influence of other growth factors. *Cf.* Chapter 3.

[35] See *Annual Reviews* of the Economic Council of Canada for detailed analyses of growth over the post-war period.

Table 1-16

PERCENTAGE DISTRIBUTION OF EMPLOYMENT INCREASE: 1961-1966

Category	Distribution of Employed, 1961	Percentage of New Jobs
Industry		
Primary	14.2	—9.0
Secondary	30.2	37.8
Manufacturing	24.0	26.6
Construction	6.2	11.2
Tertiary	55.5	71.2
Transportation, communication and other utilities	9.3	5.2
Trade	16.9	14.1
Finance, insurance, real estate	3.9	5.7
Community, business and personal service	19.5	40.5
Public administration and defence	5.9	5.7
Occupation		
White Collar	39.8	56.8
Managerial	9.2	9.9
Professional and technical	9.9	25.4
Clerical	13.3	18.4
Sales	7.4	3.1
Blue Collar	29.2	40.4
Craftsmen, production process and related workers	24.2	36.5
Labourers and unskilled workers	5.0	3.9
Primary	13.5	—10.8
Transportation and Communication	6.8	—0.5
Service and Recreation	10.9	14.1

Source: Labour Force Survey.

(the unemployment rate averaged well over 4 per cent during the sixties), selective labour shortages in construction services and in some professional and technical occupations had begun to emerge by the end of the period. Public attention shifted from concern with the nature, source and incidence of unemployment to other issues: selective shortages, bottlenecks, rising prices, i.e. the problems of maintaining a buoyant economy without undue inflationary stress.

Technological Change

Some of the factors underlying the postwar growth in the productive capacity of the Canadian economy, which, in conjunction with changes in demand, have shaped the growth and composition of her manpower resources, have already been described in preceding sections. Increases in the quantity of resources (both human and physical) and in productivity have both played a role. Of significance, in respect to the latter, were important shifts in the deployment of resources (especially the farm-non farm transfer) and improvement in the quality of resources, in particular the rising educational level of the work force.

Among several other basic factors affecting productivity, technological change is of special interest to the manpower analyst. Whatever the overall contribution to growth and rising living standards, technological change will inevitably produce dislocations in the job market, because of its uneven impact on different occupations and communities. Because the market process operates so imperfectly, the adjustment to change can be slow, painful and costly to the workers and communities involved. A major concern of manpower policy, then, inevitably lies in the area of facilitating and anticipating adjustment to technological change.

There are, however, serious problems in planning effective policies in this area. The impact of technological change on employment levels and skill composition cannot be determined *a priori* nor can, if automation be considered in some sense a new form of technological change, its effect thus be made comprehensible by reference to the historical record. Theory and historical evidence can point the direction to the most fruitful lines of empirical investigation. Unfortunately, the measurement of technological change and its effects is fraught with conceptual and statistical difficulties so that a number of key issues — the pace of change, its determinants and diffusion; the nature; the source; the form; the interaction with other growth variables, and so on — remain essentially unsettled even in countries[36] where a large body of empirical research has been accumulated in recent years.[37] Thus, much of what follows by way of brief comment on Canadian developments must be viewed as extremely tentative.

Some of the effects of technological change on employment in Canada in recent decades are, however, visible to the naked eye. No sophisticated measures or analyses are required to relate the impact of mechanization in primary industries to the major reductions of employment in that sector. Rapid increases in productivity, associated with substantial capital investment and uncompensated by sufficient expansion of demand, have resulted in a substantial decline in numbers employed over the past two decades. (See Tables 1-11 and 1-12.) The process of adjustment, the rural-to-urban

---

[36] In Canada, the situation is particularly serious. Apart from ongoing research by the Department of Manpower and Immigration and by the Economic Council, only three published empirical studies in this area are available: Duncan R. Campbell and Edward B. Power, *Manpower Implications of Prospective Technological Change in the Eastern Canadian Pulpwood Logging Industry* (Ottawa: Queen's Printer, 1964), and Yehuda Kotowitz, "Technological Progress and Labour Displacement," *The Canadian Labour Market*, eds. Arthur Kruger and Noah M. Meltz, (Toronto, 1968).

[37] For a compendium of the results of recent studies see "Technology and the American Economy," Report of the National Commission on Technology, Automation and Economic Progress, *The Employment Impact of Technological Change, Appendix, Volume II*, (Washington: U.S. Government Printing Office, 1966).

shift of the labour force, has not been accomplished without heavy cost to individuals and communities, as witnessed by the still wide rural-urban gaps in income and manpower utilization in most advanced countries. The impact of changing production processes may be observed in the shrinking employment in such traditional occupations as locomotive firemen, pattern makers, metal polishers, boiler firemen, blacksmiths, weavers, coremakers, filers and grinders and stone cutters, and in the rapid growth of such new occupations as computer programmers, office appliance operators and a variety of inspection and quality control occupations in metal work and electronics, etc.

The case of the primary industries and the handful of specific occupations provide obvious examples of the impact of technological change in Canada in recent decades. But they provide little basis for generalizations about the consequences of technological change to employment and, therefore, are insufficient guides for policy makers. Much more evidence is required; for example, the statement "in general, an outstanding . . . consequence of technological change is to raise educational and skill requirements"[38] has not been documented. Evidence derived from studies in the United States point to no such firm conclusion. Case studies suggest either a *decline* in skill content or no significant change.[39] Regarding office automation, while some occupational upgrading is expected, "what is far from clear . . . is the nature, extent and tempo" of this effect.[40] Fundamental and far-reaching decisions about education and training policy must rest on firmer evidence.

What can be said of the pace of change during the postwar period and its effect on employment and unemployment? The most common measure of the pace of technological change is the rate of productivity increase, usually, although not ideally, output per manhour. The limited data available in Canada suggest that the rate of productivity improvement over the 1950's and 1960's was somewhat in excess of the long-run rate, implying an acceleration of technical change. Econometric analysis supports this view and suggests further that postwar technological change was, on balance, labour saving, in contrast with the neutral technological change of the prewar period.[41] During the late 1950's, the "structuralists" argued that the high levels of unemployment were due to an increase in structural unemployment arising from automation, i.e. accelerated, labour-saving technological change. This contention was proven incorrect by subsequent events. The unemployment rate receded with the expansion of aggregate demand during the 1960's. (See following discussion of structural unemployment.)

Finally, what of the underlying sources of technological change in Canada? A knowledge of the main determinants of technical change is essential in understanding its development and anticipating its future course.

Much of Canadian technology is borrowed from other countries and undoubtedly this will continue to be the case for many years. Of particular significance, in this respect, is the role of the United States' direct investment in Canada. It has been widely assumed that the spillover of technical innovation from the United States, via the subsidiary firm, is a major determinant of the rate of technological change in Canada;[42] recent investigation would not, however, support such a firm and unequivocal conclusion. Studies prepared for the *Report of the Task Force on Foreign Ownership and the Structure of Canadian Industry* (1968) suggest that "nationality of ownership is irrelevant to economic performance or that foreign ownership does not produce above-average benefits that can be perceived from data on productivity and size".[43] Rather, it would appear that "the nature of the Canadian environment within which firms operate is a more important determinant of their behaviour".[44] Increased competitiveness, tax changes and improvement in the training of entrepreneurs are recommended as growth-inducing policies.

Expenditures on research and development (R and D) is another important determinant of the pace of technological change. In 1963 Canadian expenditures on R and D were only 1.1 per cent of Gross National Product, compared with 2.3 per cent for the United Kingdom (1964-65) and 3.4 per cent for the United States (1963-64). Canada's ranking in terms of non-defence R and D, though better, is still low. Government expenditure comprised over one-half — about the same as in Britain and less than in the United States. Foreign-owned firms in Canada do more research relatively than resident-owned firms and given the size and technological leadership of the United States economy, this is clearly a net benefit to Canada.

Recent government policy measures designed to stimulate R and D — a programme of tax incentives was adopted in 1962 — and the proposals of the Economic Council to extend and improve these measures[45] should, if effective, help to close the research gap in Canadian industry. The effect of this development combined with another most important factor, the projected improvement in educational level of the work force (see p. 40), point to an improvement in the productivity advances in the future with all the consequences that it implies in terms of manpower adjustment problems.

[38] Economic Council of Canada, *First Annual Review,* p. 155.

[39] *The Employment Impact* — Appendix, Volume III, Part 3, p. 201.

[40] McDonald, *Impact and Implications,* p. 17.

[41] Kotowitz, *Technological Progress* and "Production Functions in Canadian Manufacturing 1926-39 and 1947-61," paper delivered at the Conference on Statistics, June, 1967.

[42] See, for example, North American Joint Conference on the Requirements of Automated Jobs and their Policy Implications, "Technological Change, Productivity and Employment in Canada", by J. P. Francis, O.E.C.D. (mimeographed) p. 6.

[43] Report of the *Task Force on Foreign Ownership and the Structure of Canadian Industry,* (1968), p. 80.

[44] *Ibid,* p. 82.

[45] *A General Incentive Programme to Encourage Research and Development in Canadian Industry,* December, 1965.

Table 1-17

SELECTED UNEMPLOYMENT RATES

Category	Year 1953	Year 1958	Year 1966
Total	3.0	7.0	3.6
Age and Sex:			
Males 14 years and over	3.4	8.1	4.0
14-19 years	7.2	16.6	9.7
20-24 years	4.9	12.7	5.3
25-34 years	3.2	7.7	3.1
35-44 years	2.5	6.1	2.7
45-54 years	2.8	6.7	3.3
55-64 years	2.9	6.7	4.3
65 and over	(3.1)	5.0	4.5
Females 14 years and over	1.6	3.6	2.6
14-19 years	(2.8)	7.4	6.4
20-24 years	(1.9)	4.0	2.5
25-34 years	(1.5)	3.1	(2.0)
35-44 years	(0.9)	(2.1)	(2.0)
45-54 years	(0.7)	(2.2)	(1.5)
55-64 years	0.0	(2.7)	(1.0)
65 and over	0.0	(3.0)	(2.2)

Category	Year 1953	Year 1958	Year 1966
Region:			
Atlantic	5.5	12.5	6.4
Quebec	3.8	8.8	4.7
Ontario	2.1	5.4	2.5
Prairie	1.9	4.1	2.1
British Columbia	4.0	8.6	4.5
Industry:[a]			
Agriculture	(0.6)	1.8	(1.3)
Forestry, fishing and trapping	11.4	29.2	15.7
Mining and quarrying	(4.2)	9.3	(4.0)
Manufacturing	3.1	7.2	3.2
Construction	9.4	19.0	9.3
Transportation, communication and public utilities	2.8	7.0	3.6
Trade	1.8	4.1	2.4
Service and finance[b]	1.6	3.4	2.0

[a] For 1953 and 1958, classification based on 1948 S.I.C., for 1966, classification is 1961 S.I.C. No occupational data are available before 1961.

Rates calculated from unemployed estimates of fewer than 10,000 are shown in brackets.

[b] In 1966, includes "Public administration and defence."

Source: Labour Force Survey.

PROBLEMS OF STRUCTURE AND ADJUSTMENT

Structural Imbalances

Tracing manpower trends in Canada, we have noted from time to time the emergence of structural imbalances and market maladjustment. During the postwar years, two major areas of concern have been the uneven incidence of manpower utilization, particularly as it is manifested in regional disparities in employment and income levels, and, more recently, the wage-price-employment adjustment mechanism, the so-called Phillips' curve discussion.

The uneven incidence of unemployment for different demographic socio-economic, geographic or labour market categories of the work force, whatever the overall level, was a phenomenon of interest mainly to statisticians in Canada until the late 1950's. (See Table 1-17.) For several years following 1957, during the serious stagnation of the North American economy, the economists' debate on the source and nature of the markedly higher unemployment focused attention sharply on the characteristics of the unemployed. Some economists and others outside the profession argued that the high unemployment (averaging close to 7 per cent in 1958 to 1962 compared with 3.5 per cent for the years 1946 to 1957) was caused by the demand shifts and by the accelerated technological changes of the 1950's. Cited as evidence was the concentration of unemployment in certain age-sex, educational, industrial, occupational or regional groups.[46] The remedy for this ailment, it was argued, was not an expansion of aggregate demand, which under the circumstances could serve only to stimulate increases in costs and prices, but selective measures designed to reduce unemployment of specific groups and to alleviate particular shortages and bottlenecks (evidence of which was not usually cited). Retraining and mobility was required to reshape the square pegs but, so the argument went, there was no shortage of round holes.

The debate about definitions and about the relevance or meaningfulness of some of the statistics and statistical tests and so on still continues[47] but, with the decline of unemployment during the 1960's, it has stimulated little public interest. The argument of the structuralists, i.e. that the high post-1957 unemployment was caused by an *increase* in the structural component, has been disproven by experience. The demand

---

[46] For a review of the debate see S. F. Kaliski, "Structural Unemployment — A New Stage in the Debate," *The Canadian Banker*, Autumn, 1967. Also P.-P. Proulx, "The Composition of Unemployment in Canada," in F. Bairstow (ed.) *Employment, Unemployment and Manpower*, Montreal, 1964 and F. T. Denton and Sylvia Ostry, *An Analysis of Post-War Unemployment*, Economic Council of Canada, (Ottawa: Queen's Printer, 1965). For a different approach to the problem, see Mahmood A. Zaidi, *The Labour Market and the Intra-factor Allocation Mechanism in Canada*, Economic Council of Canada, (Ottawa: Queen's Printer, 1967).

[47] *Cf.* J. L. Winter, "Structural Unemployment", in *The Canadian Labour Market*, ed. Arthur Kruger and Noah Meltz (Toronto, 1968).

shift has continued; there has been no cessation or reversal of technological change. Yet the level of unemployment continued to decline after 1961 and the decline was accomplished without more inflationary pressure than accompanied similar expansion during the 1950's. Unless the new manpower measures have been miraculously effective (an argument which no one would seriously defend), the decline in unemployment must have been largely the consequence of the Great Expansion of the 1960's.

While this particular structuralist debate about the nature and source of the increased post-1957 unemployment appears to be pretty well over, the problem of structural unemployment and related questions, low income, regional disparities, disadvantaged groups and so on, are matters of continuing concern. It is generally agreed that the *source* of unemployment cannot be identified by an examination of its *incidence,* yet identification of source is essential to the selection of the most effective policy mix (aggregative and selective) at any given time. Indeed, in line with this view, recent discussions have tended to reject the "mismatching" definition of structural unemployment, which dominated the earlier debate, and have focused attention on incidence, to policy-centred definitions such as those of Bergmann and Kaun[48] or Lipsey[49], which stress the trade-off between unemployment and price stability and cost-benefit criteria for selective policy measures. But what the more recent literature has chiefly revealed is that if the concept is complex, its measurement is more so. While it may be possible to detect a change in the structural component over time, a satisfactory absolute measure still eludes us.

Perhaps, for the time being, while the debate continues, the best answer to the question "how much of Canada's unemployment is structural?" is simply "too much." This provisional answer is most easily defended with respect to regional disparities in manpower utilization which have such important social and political as well as economic implications. Possibly for this reason, regional problems, more than any other aspect of structural imbalance in Canada, have been subjected to more intensive examination by a variety of governmental bodies (Royal Commissions, Federal-Provincial committees, task forces, agencies). It is noteworthy, in this regard, that immediately after the June 1968 election, Prime Minister Trudeau announced the creation of a new Department of Regional Development, charged with the responsibilty of providing "a more co-ordinated approach to the problems of areas that have not thus far shared fully in the economic growth of this country."[50]

Despite the intensive "official" scrutiny over many years and the various policy measures that it has engendered, a high and persistent degree of regional differentiation in every aspect of socio-economic development remains a striking feature of contemporary Canada. Although space limitations preclude any but the most cursory reference to this very large topic, there are several features of the manpower aspects of regionalism that are of particular relevance in this present discussion.

Regional Unemployment and Participation Differentials

The achievement of full employment in Canada (full employment is defined in terms of a minimal national rate of unemployment) will not of itself ensure a satisfactory balance of labour supply and demand in the five main regional markets. This is evident from observation of the raw data. (See Table 1-17.) A more sophisticated analysis permits an estimation of regional rates at given levels of the Canadian rate.[51] As Table 1-18 indicates, while regional unemployment rates rise and fall with the overall rate in Canada, (and evidence suggests that both the ranking and relative dispersion of these rates has changed little over the postwar period), a structural residue, especially in Eastern Canada, remains resistant to the forces of expansion in the national economy. When the national unemployment rate falls to 3 per cent one would expect to find unemployment in the Atlantic Region and Quebec well in excess of the full employment level, while shortages of labour are building up bottleneck pressures in the tight labour markets of Ontario and the Prairies.

Penetration below these highly aggregated data to smaller labour market areas reveals substantial intra-regional dispersion of rates and also shows that a disproportionate share of the persistent "surplus" or "depressed" areas are located in the Atlantic Region and Quebec.[52] Unfortunately, the scarcity of reliable data for small areas (only administrative data are available) has precluded the direct estimation and location of the structural components of regional unemployment in Canada.

[48] *Structural Unemployment in the United States,* Washington, 1966. The definition employed by the authors is: "Structural unemployment . . . is that amount of unemployment (less minimal frictional and seasonal) which cannot be removed by monetary and fiscal policy without creating substantial continuing inflation . . . deriving directly from shortages of labour" (p. 1). *Cf.* S. F. Kaliski, "Structural Unemployment in Canada: the Occupational Dimension," Paper presented to the Second Annual Meeting of the Canadian Economics Association, June 1968, (mimeographed) in which the Bergmann-Kaun approach is applied to Canadian data. The conclusion that, within the limitations imposed by data scarcity and quality, "expansions of the magnitude observed in the post-war period can take place without creating much additional demand for high skilled workers" (p. 30), is of considerable interest in view of the widely held public view of "serious" bottlenecks and scarcities of skilled and professional manpower.

[49] "Structural and Deficient Demand Unemployment Reconsidered," in A. Ross, ed., *Employment Policy and the Labour Market,* (Berkeley, 1965).

[50] Office of the Prime Minister, *Press Release,* July 12, 1968. The new Department will absorb a number of existing agencies which administer programmes dealing with aspects of regional development.

[51] Frank T. Denton, *An Analysis of Interregional Differences in Manpower Utilization and Earnings,* Economic Council of Canada, (Ottawa: Queen's Printer, 1966).

[52] *Cf.* S. Judek, "Canada's Persistent Unemployment Problem — Labour Surplus Market Areas", *Proceedings* of Senate Committee on Manpower and Employment, No. 7, (Ottawa: Queen's Printer, 1961).

Table 1-18

REGIONAL UNEMPLOYMENT RATES EXPECTED AT DIFFERENT
LEVELS OF THE CANADIAN UNEMPLOYMENT RATE*

Assumed unemployment rate in Canada	Expected Unemployment Rate in Region				
	Atlantic Region %	Quebec %	Ontario %	Prairie Region %	British Columbia %
2.5%	4.3	3.8	1.4	2.0	2.3
3.0%	5.1	4.4	1.8	2.3	3.0
3.5%	5.9	5.0	2.3	2.6	3.6
4.0%	6.8	5.6	2.7	2.8	4.2
5.0%	8.4	6.8	3.6	3.3	5.5
6.0%	10.0	8.0	4.4	3.8	6.8
7.0%	11.7	9.1	5.3	4.3	8.0

* Assuming average 1961-64 relationships.
Source: Frank T. Denton, *Interregional Differences.*

Persistent unemployment differentials reflect only one aspect of regional disparities in manpower utilization in Canada. They are reinforced by, and no doubt related to,[53] differences in total participation rates. A portion of these differences in overall activity rates is due to "compositional" effects, i.e. differences in the demographic structure of the regions, but, after accounting for these influences, a substantial gap remains in the "standardized" rates.[54] Thus in 1961 the Ontario rate, standardized for age, sex and marital status differences,[55] was a full 12 percentage points higher than the Newfoundland rate and about six points higher than the Nova Scotia, New Brunswick, and Quebec rates.[56] The differences, of course, were greater for females than males and greater for some age groups than for others, but the main point to be underlined here is that the combined effect of higher unemployment and lower overall participation in the Atlantic Region and, to a lesser extent, Quebec points to a serious problem of underutilization of manpower that cannot be solved by aggregative policies alone. While a full analysis would require examination of complex cyclical and seasonal influences and their interrelation,[57] a simple and admittedly rough measure of the total underutilization gap for 1966 — a year of close to full employment in Canada — clearly illustrates this contention. (See Table 1-19.)

Regional differences in manpower utilization have obvious implications for manpower policies, particularly mobility measures. But it is useful to place them in an even broader context. Thus differences in manpower utilization are a primary factor explaining the distressingly high interregional differences in per capita earned income in Canada[58] and

Table 1-19

REGIONAL GAPS IN MANPOWER UTILIZATION,* 1966

Region	Total	Underutilization Rate** Participation Component	Unemployment Component
Canada	10.4	9.0	1.4
Atlantic	21.6	17.5	4.1
Quebec	11.8	9.1	2.7
Ontario	6.8	6.7	0.1
Prairie	8.7	8.9	—0.2
British Columbia	11.2	9.2	2.0

* Manpower gap $= PE^1R^1 — PER$ where
     P = population, 14 years and over
     E = ratio of employment to labour force or unemployment rate
     R = labour force participation rate
     E^1 = average employment rate in Ontario, 1952-53
     R^1 = average participation rate in Ontario, 1952-53, for males.
       For females, R^1 was obtained by linear interpolation between average
       female participation rates for Ontario, 1952-53 and 1965-66 to take
       account of trend.
  Manpower Gap due to participation $= (PR^1 — PR)$
  Manpower Gap due to unemployment is derived by subtraction.
** Rates are ratios of manpower gap estimates to potential employment.
Source: Based on data from *Labour Force Survey.* Calculations are from D.B.S.
    Special Manpower Study, *Underutilisation of Manpower* by N. H. W. Davis
    and N. K. Tandan, Special Labour Force Studies, No. 8, (September, 1969).

[53] A regression analysis of age-sex specific participation rates against a number of independent variables, including unemployment, for 237 counties and census divisions in 1961, reveals a significant, negative association with unemployment rates for all groups including prime-age males.

[54] See Sylvia Ostry, *Provincial Differences in Labour Force Participation,* one of a series of Labour Force Studies in the 1961 Census Monograph Programme, (Ottawa: Queen's Printer, 1968).

[55] On the basis of the all-Canada structure. *Ibid,* p. 23.

[56] *Ibid.*

[57] On the cyclical sensitivity of participation rates in Canada, see S. F. Kaliski, "The Relation between Labour Force Participation and Unemployment in Canada", *C.P.S.A. Conference on Statistics,* June 1962 with comment by Frank T. Denton. For an analysis of this problem in British Columbia see J. T. Montague and J. Vandercamp, *A Study in Labour Market Adjustment,* (British Columbia: University of British Columbia, 1966). For seasonal aspects see Denton, *Interregional Differences.*

[58] For example, the difference in manpower utilization (unemployment and participation) accounts for roughly half the gap between the Atlantic Region and the Canadian average earned income per person. Denton, *Interregional Differences,* p. 8.

shaping the regional "profile of poverty" in Canada.[59] More generally, an examination of the relationship between income and unemployment or broken employment (including involuntary labour force withdrawal)[60] suggests a phenomenon of "poverty proneness", i.e. the simultaneous operation of a multiplicity of causes that together produce low income. Persons most liable to the risk of extended unemployment are also most likely to be poor earners when employed. The factors that increase the risk of extended unemployment of family heads appear also to impair the chances of other family members. It is apparent that there are strong regional aspects of "poverty proneness" in Canada of which we have stressed only one — the underutilization of manpower. But a particularly unfavourable set of interrelated economic circumstances in the Atlantic Region has created an area caught in a "vicious circle" of underdevelopment which can be broken only by a broad range of integrated policies — of which manpower policies must play an important role.

Finally, in this discussion of "structural imbalances" we have focused entirely on regional aspects for reasons already provided. There are, of course, other problems of disadvantaged groups which would merit close attention in a lengthier study. In 1963, a Special Committee of the Senate was appointed to "examine the problem involved in the promotion of the welfare of the aged and aging persons."[61] The proceedings of that Committee and the contributions to the Canadian Welfare Council's Conference on Aging[62] in 1966 revealed a number of adjustment problems confronting the older worker in Canada.[63] The exceptionally high male teen-age unemployment rates — more than double the overall male rate over the entire postwar period — point to underlying structural problems that have serious social as well as economic implications. It is of interest to note that teenagers and older males were among the very few groups in the population who appeared to have experienced some increase in structural unemployment during the late 1950's and early 1960's.[64]

The Adjustment Mechanism: Wages, Prices, Employment

It has been mentioned earlier, in the account of postwar developments, that as the high levels of unemployment receded during the upswing of the 1960's the emphasis of public debate and concern shifted away from problems of labour surplus and structural unemployment to questions of scarcities, bottlenecks, rising costs and prices and the fundamental problem of achieving compatibility of two basic goals: high employment and "reasonable" price stability. The most fruitful line of discussion centred on the "trade-off," the relationship between the unemployment rate and the rate of change of prices, since it focused attention on policy issues and also provided a new and helpful orientation to some other basic problems such as the issue of structural unemployment and of cost-push versus demand-pull inflation.

In this brief review of a very broad and complex topic, only a few areas of analysis can be explored. Although there are a number of estimates of both the Phillips' Curve (the wage-unemployment relationship) and the "trade-off" for Canada, only one set of price-unemployment relationships will be reviewed here. While the question of the "optimal trade-off" is essential to a full discussion of the policy issues, little empirical work exists in this area (not surprisingly, considering the formidable problems of estimation involved). All that will be attempted in this discussion is to place the role of manpower policy in the general context of the overall "trade-off" analysis, indicating some of the problems and issues involved.

The most extensive treatment of the "trade-off" is found in a Special Study, commissioned by the Economic Council,[65] which included a review of previous Canadian empirical work on the subject and of international experience and presented new estimates of both the wage-adjustment and price-level equations. Some of the main findings are briefly summarized here but the interested reader would do well to consult the source study which provides a full and detailed examination of the subject.

The best wage-change relationship estimated by the authors indicates that over 80 per cent of the variation in the rate of wage increase in Canada over the period 1953-65, was explained by variations in the unemployment rate; the level of unit profits in manufacturing (lagged half a year); the rate of change in United States average hourly earnings; the rate of change in consumer prices and Canadian average hourly earnings lagged one year. The "best" price-change equation (for the same period) reveals that the most important influences on the Consumer Price Index, the rate of change of Canadian prices were wages, import price changes and lagged price changes. These two relationships were reduced to a derived "trade-off" or, rather, a set of "trade-offs," corresponding to various assumptions about the independent variables, which the Economic Council called the "trade-off zone." The zone is a useful illustrative device to demonstrate the problem of conflict between policy goals of high employment and price "stability." The Council's Review depicts it in

[59] For a full discussion of the characteristics of low income families see J. R. Podoluk, *The Income of Canadians,* A 1961 Census Monograph, (Ottawa: Queen's Printer, 1969).

[60] See Sylvia Ostry, *Unemployment in Canada,* one of a series of Labour Force Studies in the 1961 Census Monograph Programme, (Ottawa: Queen's Printer, 1968), Chapter 5.

[61] See Senate of Canada, *Proceedings of the Special Committee on Aging,* (Ottawa: Queen's Printer, 1964).

[62] See *Proceedings,* The Canadian Conference on Aging, Canadian Welfare Council, (Ottawa: Queen's Printer, 1966).

[63] For an account of the employment and income picture of the older worker see Sylvia Ostry and Jenny Podoluk, *The Economic Status of the Aging,* prepared for the Conference on Aging, 1966.

[64] Denton and Ostry, *An Analysis of Post-War Unemployment,* pp. 13-14.

[65] Ronald G. Bodkin, Elizabeth Bond, Grant L. Reuber and T. Russel Robinson, *Price Stability and High Employment,* Economic Council of Canada, (Ottawa: Queen's Printer, 1966). A full bibliography of Canadian studies is included in Chapter 3. See also the Council's *Third Annual Review,* which deals with the general problem of the requirements for stable growth.

chart form but for our purposes it is simpler to select examples of particular trade-off relationships. Assuming that inflationary pressures from the outside are absent (the rate of change of import prices is set equal to zero); the rate of change of United States wages is equal to the Council of Economic Advisers' guidepost of 3.2 per cent and profits set equal to the mean of the 1953-65 period; the estimated "trade-off" indicates that the rate of unemployment "required" for price stability is 4.7 per cent or, alternatively, a 3 per cent unemployment rate entails an expected rate of inflation of 2.2 per cent. But the impact of changes in the external environments is appreciable. When international prices are assumed to rise at 2 per cent annually (and given appropriate values for the other variables) 3 per cent unemployment leads to a rise in the C.P.I. not of just over 2 per cent but of nearly 7 per cent per year. With an inflationary external environment some domestic deflation might "pay off": a rise in unemployment to 5 per cent would produce a decline in price change to 4.2 per cent. Beyond that the "trade-off" becomes excessive: 10 per cent unemployment is still associated with price rises of over 3 per cent and there is no value of the unemployment rate (over the period examined) that appears consistent with price stability.[66]

Further detail from these and other estimates, both for Canada and other countries, strongly confirm the existence of conflict between the goals of price stability and high employment: the problem of reconciliation is a "persistent and pervasive phenomenon and has nowhere lent itself to easy solution, even under widely differing economic conditions and developments".[67] The problem is greatly exacerbated in Canada by the openness of the economy which seriously reduces the "degrees of freedom" of Canadian policy-makers (even more so under conditions of a fixed exchange rate). Given external conditions and a limited ability to affect or offset them the problem of setting a policy objective that in some sense optimizes the "trade-off" in Canada is formidable indeed.

The circumstances of the postwar period, to which the "trade-off" estimates cited above relate, leave Canada with very little room to manoeuvre in pursuing an independent price-level policy. Historical evidence suggests that this was also true in the inter-war years. It appears therefore that the wage and price-change relationships have been remarkably stable despite the massive structural changes that have occurred in the economy. Some foreign studies suggest, however, the possibility of improving the "trade-off" by means of "new" policies, policies other than the traditional aggregative monetary and fiscal measures.[68] Among the "new" policies designed to shift the "trade-off" curve (in contradistinction to aggregative policies which have the effect of "moving along" the curve) are selective manpower measures.

The problem, of course, is more complex than this brief summary suggests. Are manpower measures to be implemented only when "unacceptable" rates of inflation are incurred, i.e. when aggregative policies have eliminated all demand-deficient unemployment? What is an "unacceptable" rate of inflation? If it depends on the public's preferences, how are these to be assessed? There is evidence that in Canada, during the postwar period, the monetary authority's penchant for price stability as opposed to higher employment was greater than could be explained on the basis of the relative costs of more inflation and more unemployment. Are manpower policies to be implemented on a cost-benefit basis in which the "benefit" is assessed in terms of the expected "shift" in the "trade-off"? Or is manpower policy an accepted policy instrument, such that cost-benefit analysis is reserved for the selection of particular measures within the range of available policies? Are minimum wage laws or union wage agreements — alleged to create or maintain structural unemployment and cost-push pressures — an appropriate target for manpower policy? If so, how are policies to be formulated in Canada where 90 per cent of the work force comes under provincial jurisdiction in matters of collective bargaining and labour standards legislation? The same question might well be applied to incomes policy.[69]

It is not difficult to extend this list of questions. It is, of course, extremely difficult to answer them or even to make a reasonable start in that direction. None-the-less, it is appropriate to the essay which follows to indicate the immense complexity of the problems facing policy-makers in this area.

[66] These estimates are derived from the "best" derived equation. Other equations, which the authors consider less realistic, suggest different results for the right-hand tail of the curve.

[67] Economic Council of Canada, *Third Annual Review*, p. 143.

[68] Bodkin *et al. Price Stability*, Chapter 8 and bibliography cited therein.

[69] See David C. Smith, *Incomes Policies*, Economic Council of Canada, (Ottawa: Queen's Printer, 1966), for a review of foreign experience and an assessment of the Canadian situation.

2

FEDERAL
MANPOWER POLICIES

Gerald G. Somers

THE DEVELOPMENT OF MANPOWER POLICIES

The preceding chapter stressed the serious challenge posed by dynamic changes and structural imbalances in the Canadian labour market. The response of federal manpower policies to these challenges in the 1960's has been impressive. Beginning at a modest level of activity at the start of the decade, the size, variety, and funding of manpower programmes grew to significant proportions at the end of the decade. These policy developments were characterized by a heartening spirit of innovation, not only in the components of the legislative package but also in their administration and implementation.

The list of programmes and their operating costs in Table 2-1 indicates certain trends during the decade. Federal payments for high school courses, adult training and apprenticeship programmes, relatively minor amounts in 1960, increased sharply by the end of the period. A somewhat similar growth in expenditures was experienced for the Winter Works Projects, the Vocational Rehabilitation Programme, and the research activities. Programmes such as Winter House Building, the Manpower Consultative Service and expenditures under the Manpower Mobility Programme, which were nonexistant at the beginning of the 1960's, achieved a respectable level of funding in the second half of the decade. Table 2-1 indicates, however, that the expenditures recorded for the first time in 1965-67 for the operation of the Manpower Division and the Research Branch of the Department of Manpower and Immigration represent a change in administrative functions rather than entirely new ventures in the manpower field.

What were the roots of this phenomenal growth, often cited as the "manpower revolution of the 1960's"? The foregoing discussion of changes in labour supply and labour demand, accompanied by structural imbalances and regional disparities, clearly provides a basis for increased federal intervention in the functioning of the labour market. Since the structural problems are of long standing, however, they cannot provide a sufficient explanation for the exceptional expansion of manpower policies in the past decade. The fact that the Canadian growth parallels the notable growth of similar policies in the United States, the United Kingdom and Sweden, countries that also had long standing structural imbalances within their labour markets, suggests that other causes were operative.

Manpower policies have long-term, secular objectives such as increased productive capacity as well as short-term, countercyclical purposes such as the reduction of unemployment and the dampening of inflationary pressures. The unprecedented growth of structural employment policies in recent years is related to these secular and countercyclical objectives. There has been a growing recognition of the contribution that investments in information and education can make to economic growth. There is some evidence that expenditures on occupational training for relatively disadvantaged workers may have an even greater impact on productivity and income than similar expenditures for general education. Long-term productivity is also encouraged by providing greater labour market information and by relocation subsidies to permit workers to move from depressed areas to areas of more buoyant employment opportunities. Even without rigorous documentation, many legislators have become convinced of the potential long-run benefits to be derived from manpower policies.

The countercyclical potential of structural policies was brought into focus by the unusually high level of unemployment that began in 1957 and persisted into the early 1960's. Governments appear to have been more convinced of the structural causes of this unemployment than were some economists. Subsequent events supported those who argued that a deficiency of aggregate demand was the root cause of the higher unemployment rate. At the time, however, the rapid advance of technological change in some sectors, coupled with complicating developments in labour supply, provided a basis for structuralist arguments and for manpower policies that had political appeal. Policies designed to attack what some considered to be cyclical unemployment were couched in terms of an attack on long-term structural problems.

The countercyclical role of manpower policies took a different form after 1965. As the level of unemployment declined under the impact of expansionary monetary-fiscal policy, resultant inflationary pressures began to demonstrate the limits of such aggregate policies. In Canada, as in a number of other Western countries in the period immediately following World War II, the Federal Government committed itself to achieve maximum levels of employment. In 1945, the White Paper on Employment and Income announced ". . . the Government has stated unequivocally its adoption of a high and stable level of employment and income . . . as a major aim of Government policy." In keeping with the current Keynesian tenor, it was assumed that these objectives would be attained primarily through aggregate monetary-fiscal measures. By the mid 1960's, however, there was a growing recognition of the trade-off between employment and price stability, of the persistence of pockets of unemployment even when

Table 2-1

OPERATING COSTS OF MANPOWER PROGRAMMES (IN THOUSANDS OF DOLLARS)

Programme	1960-61	1961-62	1962-63	1963-64	1964-65	1965-66	1966-67
Fed. Assistance to the Provinces for operating high school courses	N.A.	1,965	1,930	2,765	3,575	2,278	2,000
Fed. expend. on training programmes for adults	1,461	10,018	17,073	21,914	29,676	41,331	64,285
Fed. payments to the provinces for technical training and apprenticeship training	1,638	5,513	8,966	9,399	10,933	4,854	7,176
Fed. contribution toward payroll costs of approved municipal winter works projects	22,745	26,359	30,934	33,002	61,063	41,148	50,000
Fed. pay. under the Winter House Building Programme*	—	—	—	14,000	17,300	16,984	None for '67
Fed. pay. to the provinces for the vocational rehabilitation of disabled persons	144	196	333	517	652	844	750
Fed. expend. under Manpower Consultative Service	—	—	—	—	—	37	100
Expend. under Manpower Mobility Programme	—	—	—	—	—	49	1,200
Expend. for admin. of the National Employment Service	N.A.	N.A.	19,406	19,586	21,905	22,685	—
Expend. for operation of Manpower Division**	—	—	—	—	—	—	37,030
Expend. for the admin. of the Economics and Research Branch, including Research Grants	720	794	842	843	882	—	—
Expend. for admin. of Research Branch of Department of Manpower and Immigration	—	—	—	—	—	475	1,000

*Under Department of Labour.
**The Manpower Division is responsible for providing an employment service.
***The Research Branch of the Department of Manpower and Immigration has assumed responsibility for a number of studies initiated by the Economics and Research Branch of the Department of Labour.
Source: Prepared by the Program Development Service, Department of Manpower and Immigration, April 1967.

emerging inflationary pressures prevented the full development of monetary-fiscal policies. In this context, the countercyclical mission of active manpower policies became that of a handmaiden of aggregate policies in reducing unemployment without undue inflationary price increases. For some, manpower policies were "politically" more acceptable than aggregate monetary-fiscal policies.

Although these economic events and developments in technique provide the framework for the growth of manpower policies in the 1960's, the impetus given by institutional change should also be noted. The Economic Council of Canada was established in 1963 and commissioned to "advise and recommend to the Minister how Canada can achieve the highest possible levels of employment and efficient production . . ."[1] Fully accepting this statement of its responsibilities, the Economic Council became a principal spokesman for expanded manpower policies and thereby played a crucial role in bringing about both administrative changes and concrete programmes. In its *First Annual Review,* issued in December 1969, the Council strongly urged the adoption of an active manpower policy and called for the establishment of a special Division of Manpower within the Department of Labour. In its *Second Annual Review,* issued the following year, the ECC recommended the establishment of a separate manpower department. Even greater stress was placed on the need for improved education, training programmes, mobility subsidies, the collection of job vacancy data and other measures to reduce unemployment and to improve the efficiency of the labour market. In stressing the need for increased productivity and economic growth consistent with price stability, the Council's *Third Annual Review* and *Fourth Annual Review* in 1966 and 1967 again stressed the need for improved manpower and regional policies to reduce unemployment and to facilitate the adjustment to technological and other economic changes. Many of the manpower developments that occurred in this period were in response to the clear and persuasive recommendations of this influential body.

THE STRUCTURE AND ADMINISTRATION OF MANPOWER POLICIES[2]

The Economic Council of Canada, undoubtedly having the Swedish Labour Market Board in mind as a model, stated in its *Second Annual Review:*

[1] House of Commons of Canada, Bill C-72, "An Act to Provide for the Establishment of an Economic Council in Canada," 26th Parliament (1963), pp. 2-3.

[2] For a fuller discussion of the administrative developments described in this section, see Organization for Economic Cooperation and Development, *Manpower Policy and Programmes* (Paris, OECD, 1966); *Canada's Reply to Manpower and Social Affairs Committee, OECD,* prepared by the Programme Division Service, Department of Manpower and Immigration (Paris: OECD April 21, 1967); and Philomena Mullady, *Canada Manpower Policy and Programs,* Manpower Research Bulletin, U.S. Department of Labour, (November, 1968).

What is needed is a manpower agency which would be more than a place-ment service, important as this function is. It should be a key operational agency for implementing manpower policies and the sole coordinating agency of all policies and programmes related to the labour market.

In response to this recommendation, the Department of Manpower and Immigration was created by the Canadian Government on January 1, 1966. This reorganization brought together into a single ministry the various manpower services that were formerly a part of the Labour De-partment and the Immigration Services of the Department of Citizenship and Immigration. The functions of planning, coordinating and implement-ing manpower policies and programmes were thus consolidated in a single agency. The Department of Labour retained responsibility for labour standards, the administration of the Labour Code, labour relations under federal jurisdiction and Canada's relations with the International Labour Organization.

The new department, composed of six divisions and services, was headed by a cabinet Minister. The major operational units were the Man-power Division and the Immigration Division, each headed by an Assis-tant Deputy Minister. The Manpower Division has under its jurisdiction most of the former National Employment Service organization, in addition to the placement, settlement, and counselling services of the former De-partment of Citizenship and Immigration. The following functions from the Department of Labour were placed under the new department's juris-diction: training, rehabilitation, employment stabilization and the Man-power Consultative Services section. Five regional offices reported to the Director General of the Canada Manpower Division. There were 219 area offices, called Canada Manpower Centres, with responsibility for meeting community manpower goals, such as counselling, placement, training, mobility and data collection. Of special interest among the four support services of the Department is the Programme Development Service. Its branches include Research, Planning and Evaluation, Manpower In-formation and Analysis, Pilot Projects, and Advisory Council and Liaison. The Research Branch conducts long-range studies and provides informa-tion for action programmes.

One of the most far-reaching changes, in response to the Economic Council's recommendations, was the reorganization of the National Em-ployment Service. In contrast with its original role as basically a place-ment service, the new Manpower Division, working through its Area Manpower Centres, is described as a catalyst, a coordinator, and consultant to management and labour providing a professional consultant service to all parts of the world of work. The Division exists to help workers develop their maximum potential and to help them acquire jobs that match their skills, capabilities and personal needs. Employers are to be assisted in the recruitment function and are to receive advice on the supply of manpower and its effective utilization. The Division is given special responsibilities in preparing new manpower (through immigration or natural increase in the labour force) for effective entry and participation in the labour market. Special help is to be provided for the adaptation of labour and industry to economic and technological change. Finally, the Division is given a special charge to reduce seasonal and cyclical fluctuations in employment.

Although this administrative reorganization gives promise of productive results, it is important to recognize the limits on the federal structure and administration of manpower policies. Under the Canadian federal system, serious problems of jurisdiction over the development and administration of manpower policy arise between the central government and the ten provinces. Since education comes under provincial jurisdiction, the distinction between education and training must be finely drawn. Quebec has retained its right to establish a Provincial Employment Service in addition to the Canada Manpower Centres. The bilingual and bicultural division between Quebec and other sections of Canada creates especially serious problems in the administration and implementation of manpower policy. For example, the location and adaptation of immigrants and the operation of the labour mobility programme are inevitably affected by cultural and language differences as workers are moved across provincial boundaries. Execution of policy under the Canada Manpower Division understandably calls for careful consultation with provincial authorities.

THE CURRENT MANPOWER PROGRAMMES

Adult Training

As Table 2-1 shows, the Adult Training Programme receives a larger share of Federal Government expenditures on manpower policies than any of the other programmes. In 1967, the Adult Occupational Training Act, (OTA), replaced the Technical and Vocational Training Assistance Act of 1960. Whereas the earlier legislation had resulted in a significant advance in facilities for the technical training of students in vocational high schools, the OTA extends training services and training allowances to adults who can benefit from training. Under the 1960 legislation, the Federal Government had shared costs of training with the provinces and had assisted the provinces with the operating and capital costs of technical and vocational training at the secondary and post-secondary level, with much less emphasis on adult training and education. Under the OTA, the Federal Government provides 100 per cent of the cost of training allowances, paid directly to eligible adults. It also pays 100 per cent of the cost of operating employment-oriented adult training courses run by the provinces, and, in addition, the Federal Government makes loans to provincial governments to help with the purchase or construction of adult occupational training facilities. It may also make contributions to provincial research and development programmes related to adult training.

To be eligible for a training allowance under the OTA a person must have been working or seeking work for the last three years, except that a worker with dependents can qualify if he has been out of school for one year and if he is one year older than the provincial age for compulsory school attendance. Selection of trainees is made by the Canada Manpower Centres. The OTA changed the Unemployment Insurance Act so that the benefits of unemployed workers attending training courses would be protected while they were in their training courses. The minimum training allowance is $35 per week and the maximum $90, depending on family circumstances and living costs.

Because of provincial jurisdiction over education, the Department of Manpower and Immigration, through its five regional offices, must sign agreements with provincial governments to purchase adult occupational training authorized under the OTA from public institutions run by the provinces or municipalities. If there are no facilities in the area for giving a needed type of training, the worker may be sent elsewhere. If no other public training courses are available, the Manpower Centre may arrange to enrol eligible adults in private training schools. Arrangements may also be made for training adults in industry. To encourage training in industry, the Federal Government pays 100 per cent of the costs to an employer who sponsors or provides formal "classroom" training courses that develop skills that may be transferred to other employers or industries. Employers operating such courses are reimbursed for the wages they pay to employees while they attend training courses on company time; moreover, the Federal Government will pay an employer for operating on-the-job training courses, even when they result in skills that are specific only to that employer, provided that there is a threat of major technological change that would cause layoffs in the industry. Under the OTA, the Federal Government may also make thirty-year loans to provinces for the purchase or construction of occupational training facilities for adults. In some cases the Government will essentially pay for their construction by "renting" the facilities.

Of special interest for the discussion of evaluation below, is the provision in the OTA for research and development agreements with the provinces. The Federal Government pays 50 per cent of the cost to the province of research in connection with the adult training programmes and it pays 50 per cent of the costs to develop new courses and materials.

During the fiscal year 1966-67, 132,000 workers completed training. The number being trained is expected to increase during the next five years from .32 per cent of the labour force in 1966-67 to approximately 1.2 per cent of the labour force in 1972-73.[3]

Manpower Mobility

The Manpower Mobility Programme, begun in 1965, was liberalized and significantly changed in April 1967. The earlier programme had included both loans and grants to the worker, depending upon his period of unemployment in the home area; the new programme includes only grants. Any man who is unemployed or who has been notified of his permanent layoff is now entitled to a grant if there is little prospect of suitable employment in his home community and there is a definite job for him in a new area. Whereas the earlier grants were restricted almost entirely to the costs of moving, the 1967 amendments provide a grant of $500 to cover losses involved in the sale of a home in the old area and the purchase of a home in the new area; small grants are also available to enable unemployed people to look for work in the nearest area where there are better opportunities for employment. The grant not only covers the person's return travel expenses but includes a modest allowance to help support his dependents while he is away looking for work. Finally, the relocation provisions have recently been liberalized to permit payment to a worker who wishes to travel to an occupational training course outside of his home area; and under-employed workers are now also covered by the relocation grant system.

Although expenditures on the Manpower Mobility Programme have not been large to date, it is estimated that approximately $5 million may be spent in 1967-68 and a substantial expansion is anticipated in future years.

Training and mobility programmes are at the heart of manpower policies proper in Canada, as in other countries. However, brief mention should be made of other policies listed in Table 2-1 and some related structural policies.

Vocational Rehabilitation

The Vocational Rehabilitation Branch of the Canada Manpower Division has responsibility for administering the Vocational Rehabilitation of Disabled Persons Act, 1961. Special counselors in the Canada Manpower Centres refer handicapped workers to training programmes or to job opportunities. Under this legislation, the Federal Government has signed agreements with each of the provinces, covering a period of up to six years, by which it pays 50 per cent of the costs incurred by the provinces in a comprehensive programme for vocational rehabilitation of disabled persons. The federal-provincial Vocational Rehabilitation Programme had rehabilitated 12,918 handicapped persons by March 31, 1967. Veteran rehabilitation and workmen's compensation cases are covered under other legislation.[4]

Seasonal Unemployment

Under the Winter House Building Incentive Programme, 1963, the Federal Government provided a tax-free bonus of $500 to the original purchaser of a house during the winter. As noted in Table 2-1, payments were made in 1963-66, but the programme was discontinued in 1967 and was

---

[3] Mullady, *Canada Manpower* p. 57.
[4] *Ibid.,* p. 69.

changed to provide a flow of insured mortgage funds of $300 million to stimulate winter-built housing.

In 1963, the Federal government also expanded its programme of incentives to municipalities, encouraging them to launch public works during the winter. This programme, currently administered by the Department of Manpower and Immigration and Municipal Affairs, continues to flourish. (See Table 2-1.) A closely related programme is the Government Supplementary Construction Programme, designed to force the Federal Government to do some of its own construction during the winter. This programme is coordinated through the interdepartmental committee of government departments.

The Manpower Consultative Service

The Manpower Consultative Service was established in 1963 to assist in manpower adjustment problems resulting from technological or other changes. In 1966 it was transferred from the Department of Labour to the Canada Manpower Division of the Department of Manpower and Immigration. The programme encourages research and planning by unions and management at the plant or industry level to resolve problems resulting from technological change that might result in plant shutdown. The Federal government provides up to 50 per cent of the cost of the research needed to develop the recommended programme.

Immigration Policy

The Canada Immigration Division is responsible for recruiting immigrants and enforcing immigration standards. The Canada Manpower Centres provide the Immigration Division with information on job vacancies and other labour market data. These centres assist in the reception and relocation of immigrants and they provide counselling concerning social and economic adjustment. Arrangements are also made for educational programmes and job training.

Area Development

Under the Agricultural Rehabilitation Development Act of 1961, the Area Development Incentive Act of 1963, and the Fund for Rural Economic Development Act of 1966, funds are provided to improve employment opportunities and the status of workers in areas where annual unemployment rates have been unusually high over a number of years and where incomes are low. In addition to financial payments designed to encourage the development of employment opportunities, training programmes have been developed by the Canada Manpower Centres, and counsellors have been brought into rural areas to advise residents of the full scope of manpower programmes available to them.

Labour Market Information and Counselling

The provision of labour market information and the counselling of job applicants is a general function of the Canada Manpower Centres that support and enhance the more specific manpower policies discussed above. The expansion of information surveys and the development of a professional counselling staff constitute an important recent development in Canada's active manpower policy.

THE EVALUATION OF MANPOWER POLICIES

In spite of the impressive array of manpower policies described above and the growth of Federal expenditures on these programmes, they have not yet achieved their principal objectives. The process of evaluation has lagged seriously behind the process of implementation. Although extensive plans for evaluation are underway, only fragmentary data, falling far short of any full appraisal of effectiveness, are available to date.

A Planning and Evaluation Branch has been established within the Department of Manpower and Immigration with the following objectives: to review and evaluate the effectiveness of selected existing manpower programmes and to propose modifications where appropriate; to develop new methods and techniques for measuring the effectiveness of manpower and immigration programme activities; and to explore the use of systems analysis or operational research techniques as a basis for assessing the effectiveness of specific departmental programmes. The Research Branch of the department has also been assigned a role in providing a basis for evaluation, modification and development of manpower programmes. The Research Branch has a number of studies underway in the analysis of the labour market, two of which have special application to the evaluation of manpower policies: a benefit/cost analysis of the first six months of operations of the Manpower Mobility Programme has been completed and a follow-up survey of workers who have been relocated under the programme has also been conducted.

The Planning and Evaluation Branch is currently engaged in developing cost-benefit evaluation models for the newly amended Manpower Mobility Programme and for the new Occupational Training Act. With the aid of professional consultants, rather complex models have been developed, but only partial data estimates have been published as yet.

Adult Training

Although the OTA benefit/cost model is being used to produce preliminary estimates, the data made available on the functioning of the new programme of adult training are still sparce. They consist primarily of classifications by region and programme of gross costs and funds spent, of enrollment data, and a pilot mail follow-up survey. Although some detailed

Table 2-2

OTA PROGRAMME AGE OF TRAINEES BY TYPE OF AGREEMENT AND SEX, 1967-68
(PERCENTAGE)

Type of Agreement and Age Group	Male	Female	Total*
General Purchase			
19 years and under	4.1	7.2	4.7
20-24 years	29.6	35.0	30.6
25-29　"	20.3	16.0	19.2
30-34　"	13.4	9.8	12.5
35-44　"	17.3	16.8	17.1
45 and over	10.3	11.5	10.5
Age not reported	5.0	3.8	5.4
Total	100.0	100.0	100.0
Private Institutions			
19 years and under	3.3	6.3	4.8
20-24 years	30.5	33.5	31.7
25-29　"	21.4	13.9	17.5
30-34　"	16.2	9.5	12.7
35-44　"	17.5	17.7	17.5
45 and over	5.9	14.6	10.1
Age not reported	5.2	4.5	5.7
Total	100.0	100.0	100.0
Apprenticeship			
19 years and under	7.2	25.4	7.6
20-24 years	43.8	46.7	43.5
25-29　"	16.7	7.3	16.4
30-34　"	5.2	4.6	5.2
35-44　"	4.2	6.9	4.2
45 and over	1.3	5.7	1.3
Age not reported	21.6	3.4	21.8
Total	100.0	100.0	100.0

* Includes sex not reported.
Source: Department of Manpower and Immigration.

data on the characteristics of the trainees were available for the earlier programme, only tabulations by age have been made available for the new training act.[5] In 1967-68, approximately 10 per cent of the trainees in non-apprenticeship programs were over forty-five, with women tending to be older than men. (See Table 2-2.) A substantial proportion of the trainees were in the twenty to twenty-four age group under all types of OTA programmes, and young workers were especially prominent in the apprenticeship programme. There is little evidence here of an effort to compensate for the disadvantage of age in the labour market.

Table 2-3

EMPLOYMENT STATUS OF LABOUR FORCE PARTICIPANTS
BEFORE AND AFTER TRAINING

Employment Status	Week Before Course Started		Survey Week	
		%		%
Working for pay or profit	614	43.9	905	74.5
Unemployed and looking for work	769	54.9	309	25.4
Other	17	1.2	—	—
Total	1,400	100.0	1,214	100.0

The pilot follow-up survey provides the only currently available data on the post-training employment and earnings experience under the OTA programme. The study was based on a random sample of 4 per cent of the 70,649 full-time trainee authorizations in the fall of 1968. The response rate to the mail questionnaire was 74 per cent. Of the responding sample of 1,681 workers, 75 per cent had completed their training and 84 per cent passed their course. The pilot survey showed an emphasis on the "disadvantaged" from the standpoints of education and previous employment. Of the respondents, 41 per cent had eight grades of education or less and 55 per cent were unemployed in the week before their course started. Only 25 per cent were unemployed in the following survey week. (See Table 2-3.) Earnings also improved after training but not as markedly as employment. Mean weekly earnings increased from $81.50 to $97.40.

In comparing the benefits with a prediction yielded by the ORI benefit-cost model, the survey concludes that "The model as so far developed appears to be a reasonably reliable prediction mechanism." Unfortunately, the pilot survey utilizes no control group and makes no cost-benefit comparisons. Thus, it falls short of a fully reliable evaluation of even its restricted sample of trainees. In the absence of detailed benefit/cost evaluative data on the Canadian adult training programme, we can only fall back on such evaluations as have been made of similar adult training programmes in the United States. A few inferences are then drawn for possible application to the evaluation of the Canadian programme. Benefit/cost studies of adult training programmes in the United States demonstrate substantial gains. Four principal measures have been used in relating

[5] Department of Citizenship and Immigration, Research Branch, *Characteristics of Unplaced Applicants (NES) and Trainees in Programme 5, 1965-1966* (September, 1966). *Retraining of Adults in Canada,* (Paris: OECD, 1968); Department of Manpower and Immigration, *Report on Activities under the Occupational Training for Adults,* (Ottawa: The Queen's Printer, April 1969); F. D. Upex, *Pilot Follow-up Survey: Occupational Training for Adult's Program,* 1969; *Technical Summary of the Benefit/Cost Model of the Occupational Training for Adults Program,* developed by Operations Research Inc. (Ottawa: The Queen's Printer, January 1969).

benefits to the costs of training programmes for the unemployed and under-employed: *benefit/cost ratios* and other simple comparisons between the size of benefits and the size of costs; *pay-back period,* indicating the length of time needed to recoup the initial investment-cost outlay; *rate of return* on the initial investment-cost; and *present capital,* value of net benefits accruing from the training.

Methodological considerations cannot be discussed here; however, it should be noted that the findings summarized below are based on studies of varying research approaches. with varying degrees of departure from the "ideal" research methodology in benefit/cost evaluation.

BENEFIT/COST RATIOS.   As Cain[6] has noted, the determination of a bene-fit/cost ratio is itself based on simple arithmetic and the substance of the evaluation lies in the calculation of the benefits and costs. For the deter-mination of benefit/cost ratios, as well as the other measures discussed below, private benefits are usually determined as the present value of a lifetime stream of increased earnings that can be attributed to the training programme (i.e., in comparison with the earnings of a control group of nontrainees). To calculate the social benefit, the increased earnings are construed to be a marginal addition to national project (sometimes ex-panded on the basis of a "multiplier") and, frequently, increased tax payments and reduced transfer payments are included in social benefits. The computation of present values presupposes selection of an appropriate discount rate (customarily varying between 4 and 10 per cent), and a decision whether the increased earnings of trainees are assumed to be constant through a lifetime or some period ending before an expected work life. The determination of costs customarily includes the prorated capital costs of buildings and equipment, administrative costs, instructional costs, subsistence costs and the opportunity costs of the trainees' foregone income during the training period.

In his study of training programmes for unemployed workers in Connecticut, M. E. Borus[7] found that under the most restrictive assump-tions, the benefit/cost ratio was 3.2 for an average worker. Assuming a service life of ten years, a discount rate of 5 per cent and a multiplier of 2.0, the benefit/cost ratio for society ranged from 73.3 to 157.0, depend-ing on the assumptions made concerning the trainees' use of their new skills.

D. A. Page,[8] in his evaluation of the effects of retraining programmes in Massachusetts, found a benefit/cost ratio of about 6.0. The benefits were measured in terms of increases in earnings after training and reduc-tions in transfer payments and they were adjusted for cyclical changes in the economy. The improvement in per capita annual earnings was estimated at $976, attributable primarily to increased employment during the year rather than increased pay per job. The increased family earnings of $9.60 per week found by E. Main[9] in his nationwide follow-up survey of MDTA trainees was also attributed primarily to the increased employ-ment of trainees rather than to higher wages while the breadwinner was employed.

At a somewhat lower level of methodological sophistication, the Department of Health, Education, and Welfare (1965) concluded that

Table 2-4

REPORTED WEEKLY EARNINGS FROM MAIN OCCUPATION
BEFORE TRAINING AND AFTER TRAINING

Weekly Wage	Before Per Cent of Clients	After Per Cent of Clients
$1 — 19	2.2	0.6
$20 — 39	6.5	2.9
$40 — 59	19.8	10.2
$60 — 79	24.8	24.3
$80 — 99	18.2	21.7
$100—124	15.2	19.4
$125—149	5.4	9.1
$150—199	5.2	8.1
$200 and over	2.7	3.7
SUB-TOTAL	100.0	100.0
Not employed		36.5
Not reported	19.4	15.0
Mean Wage Before Training*	$81.5	
Mean Wage After Training**	$97.5	

* Calculated from ungrouped data
** Calculated from ungrouped data

an investment of $13.3 million in training resulted in gross earnings of $148 million in five years — a return of $2.24 on the dollar.

Based on different conservative and realistic assumptions about the appropriate measures of the costs and benefits, G. Cain[10] found cost-benefit ratios for Job Corps trainees ranging from 1.02 to 1.70. His conclusion that these ratios, being higher than those on many other government investments, called for increased expenditures on the Job Corps

[6] Glen G. Cain, *Benefit/Cost Estimates for Job Corps,* Institute for Research on Poverty, University of Wisconsin (September 1967), Mimeo.

[7] M. E. Borus, "A Benefit-Cost Analysis of the Economic Effectiveness of Retraining the Unemployed," *Yale Economic Essays,* Vol. 4, No. 2 (Connecticut: Fall, 1964) pp. 371-430.

[8] D. A. Page, "Retraining Under the Manpower Development Act: A Cost-Benefit Analysis," *Public Policy,* Vol. 13 (Massachusetts: 1964) pp. 257-267, (Brookings Reprint No. 86); G. G. Somers and E. W. Stromsdorfer, "A Benefit Cost Analysis of Manpower Retraining," *Industrial Relations Research Association Proceedings* (West Virginia: December 1964) pp. 172-185.

[9] Earl Main, "A Nationwide Evaluation of M.D.T.A. Institutional Job Training," *The Journal of Human Resources* (Winter, 1968). See also, the favourable rates of return of M.D.T.A. trainees relative to other technical school students in *The Role of Technical Schools in Improving the Skills and Earnings Capacity of Rural Manpower,* O.M.P.E.R. United States Department of Labour (September, 1966), Mimeo.

[10] Cain, *Benefit Cost Estimates.*

could be even more forcefully applied to the foregoing studies of MDTA and ARA retraining programmes.

PAY BACK PERIOD. Cain, Stromsdorfer and Somers[11] have indicated in their study of trainees in West Virginia that the investment costs of these retraining programmes for unemployed workers (from the standpoint of society) can be paid back in as little as eleven months for male trainees and thirteen months for male and female trainees together. Given the relatively smaller costs of these programmes from the standpoint of society as well as from the standpoint of training, the increase in their earnings as a result of training provides a relatively rapid period of payoff, even if we ignore any tax benefits and the implications of other government payments to the trainees and control groups.

Page[12] has found that the savings in unemployment compensation alone were large enough to pay off the initial investment in the retraining course in about five years, without taking into account increases in additional taxes paid by the trainees after their course.

The study by the Department of Health, Education, and Welfare cited above concludes that in federal income taxes alone, trainees repaid the costs of training in five years.

RATES OF RETURN. The general formula for rates of return is:

$$f(r) = \sum_{t=1}^{n} \frac{C_t - B_t}{(1 + r)^t} = 0$$

where C_t and B_t are the costs and benefits per time period t, and r is the rate of return that equalizes the present values of the costs and benefits.

Cain and Stromsdorfer[13] indicated that the rate of return for all trainees in the West Virginia sample was 92 per cent; for male trainees, 109 per cent; for female trainees, 29 per cent. These were the rates of return to society, which were much lower than the private rates of return.

EXPECTED CAPITAL VALUES. Net expected capital values exceed the returns. The formula used to estimate the capital value is:

$$V = \sum_{t=a}^{66} \frac{E_t}{(1 + r)^{(t + 1 - a)}}$$

where V is the capital value of the returns to a given group of trainees; a, the average age of the group of trainees; E, the net earnings differential of the trainees over the nontrainees (this will be negative during the training period and will generally be a positive but declining amount for all periods in the post-training period). The rate of decline is the same as that used in the calculation of rates of return — r represents the selected rate of discount.

Cain and Stromsdorfer[14] found that the capital value of the net earnings benefits per male trainee is $3,985, given a 5 per cent discount factor and the private concept of measurement. Under societal concepts, the corresponding figure is $14,200 per male. The capital value per female trainee of the programme is $80 or $1,239 for private and social measures respectively, at a 5 per cent discount rate. The use of a 10 per cent discount rate reduces the largest benefits to about 40 per cent of what they are at 5 per cent.

Studies that focus on the employment gains of individual trainees following their training also show substantial improvement. However, there is little about the impact of the training on national levels of unemployment or on the price level. We can infer that adult training has contributed to income and probably to productivity; but we cannot draw meaningful conclusions about its countercyclical effects.

The training costs under the Canadian OTA have been estimated to be $5.58 per training day, plus $10.29 per day for allowances; a total of $15.86 per day.[15] There is an estimated average of seventy-five days of training per trainee, giving a total cost per trainee of under $1200. Since the average cost of institutional training under the Manpower and Development and Training Act in the United States is frequently cited as approximately $1300 (U.S.), average costs are slightly higher in the United States. Unfortunately, benefit data are not available for Canada and comparable benefit/cost measures cannot be devised.

Although these studies imply that the training programmes have redistributed employment opportunities and income to trainees, much more research is needed in evaluating the effects of the United States and Canadian programmes on cyclical patterns. Their broader economic implications are in question.

IMPLICATIONS FOR AGGREGATE ECONOMIC POLICY[16]
THE EFFECTS ON AGGREGATE UNEMPLOYMENT RATES

As heartening as the results may be for the favourable impact of adult training courses on the economic welfare of the trainee, they do not necessarily demonstrate the achievement of the economic objectives of society as a whole. Those who have arrived at much higher benefit/cost relationships for society as a whole than for the individual trainees obviously have an opposite view, or have at least worked on the hypothesis that

---

[11] These students are included in Somers (ed.), *Retraining the Unemployed* (University of Wisconsin Press, 1968). Stromsdorfer's article, "Determinants of Economic Success in Retraining the Unemployed: The West Virginia Experience," appears in *The Journal of Human Resources* (Winter, 1968).

[12] Page, *Retraining*.

[13] Somers, *A Benefit Cost Analysis*.

[14] *Ibid.*

[15] Mullady, *Canada Manpower*, p. 57.

[16] This section is adapted from the author's *Economic Implications of Large-Scale Training Programmes*, prepared for presentation to the Manpower Division of OECD (October, 1968).

the indirect effects, which they have considered, have not been outweighed by invisible negative effects. There are at least two schools of thought concerning the aggregate employment effects of manpower training and retraining programmes. The controversy remains primarily in the realm of theory since existing empirical studies provide only partial answers, largely on the fringes of the central question. Although the discussion below centers on retraining, much of it is also applicable to other structural manpower policies.

On the one hand, some contend that it is very unlikely that manpower training programmes have contributed significantly to the reduction in the unemployment rate that occurred between 1961 and 1967. Some of these critics contend further that even a substantially larger training and retraining program, taken by itself, would not result in significant reductions in the aggregate unemployment rate. Their arguments center on the following four points.

First, because employers hire workers in order to produce goods and services that people buy, only an increase of income and demand on the part of the purchasers of goods and services will create an increased demand for workers. Since retraining, by itself, does not bring about increased income or demand on the part of purchasers, it will not by itself generate more jobs and employment. The crux of this argument is that increased demand for labour, that is, increased jobs and employment, comes about only through increased aggregate demand. Only expansionary monetary-fiscal policy brings about such an increase in aggregate demand. Even if large scale government expenditures on training programmes could be construed as a major increase in aggregate demand, it is argued that the government funds spent on training programmes thereby reduce roughly equivalent government expenditures that might have occurred in some other sector and for some other purpose.

Second, although training programmes cannot create new jobs, it may be argued that they can reduce unemployment if the unemployment problem is substantially a structural one. If many job vacancies exist in the face of pools of unskilled, unemployed labour, then training and retraining programmes to bring the unemployed workers up to the level of skill required to fill the vacancies would serve to reduce the rate of unemployment in the economy as a whole. Implicit in the views of many who argue against the likelihood of this effect is a belief either that the unemployment problem is not a substantially structural one or that the unemployed are so unskilled, uneducated and disadvantaged that they cannot be brought up to the level of skill required to fill the relatively high-skilled job vacancies.

Third, even if it could be established theoretically that government training programmes could create jobs and/or reduce unemployment, it is argued that the scale of the federal training and retraining programmes in Canada and the United States in the 1960's has not been sufficiently large to bring about any significant results. Since the inception of the training programme, enrollments have averaged approximately 5 per cent of the unemployed; the number of OTA or MDTA trainees available to contribute to a reduction of unemployment in any particular year is relatively small. If we take a broader concept of unemployment and underemployment as well as a broader concept of manpower training policies, the potential impact of these programmes is no more significant. A committee in the United States has concluded that "The most gross estimate indicates that less than 10 per cent of persons needing the job training programmes can be enrolled in them." The committee's report goes on to indicate that in individual states, cities and neighbourhoods the numbers reached are frequently much less than 10 per cent.[17] The Economic Council of Canada has recently expressed similar views concerning the limited impact of current policies in reducing the numbers of the "working" poor.[18] If a broad concept of "underutilized manpower" were adopted in Canada, as in a recent labour force study, the gap between actual and potential enrollment in training and retraining programmes would be even greater.[19]

Fourth, for these reasons, the impressive showing of benefits derived from training to the trainees must not be construed as similar benefits in employment in the economy as a whole. It is possible that the trainees' improved employment status was achieved at the expense of a decline in the status of other unemployed workers competing for available jobs. The kinds of jobs taken by most of the trainees are probably at such a skill level that they could be fairly readily filled by nontrainees who were given the proper information and advice.

On the other hand there is a group of economists who adopt a more optimistic attitude toward the aggregate employment effects of government manpower training programmes. They feel that the training programmes to date have been sufficiently large to bring about some reduction in national unemployment and that if the training programmes were greatly expanded they could have a very significant impact on aggregate unemployment. Their arguments include the following tenets.

First, unemployment is reduced because the training programmes take unemployed workers off the unemployment rolls during their period of training quite apart from any employment effects following the completion of training. Utilizing enrollment in four United States manpower programmes (Neighborhood Youth Corps, MDTA On-The-Job Training, Community Action (paid professionals) and college Work Study) Malcom Cohen estimates that, for the period 1965-67, enrollment in these programmes constituted a reduction of .15 of a percentage point in the overall unemployment rate in 1965, .3 of a percentage point in 1966, and .4 of a percentage point in 1967 (from 4.2 per cent to 3.8 per cent).[20] While enrollment in these programmes satisfies the statistical definition of

[17] *Opening the Doors: Job Training Programs,* A Report to the Committee on Administration of Training Programs, Part 2, (February, 1968), Greeleigh Associates, pp. 62-63.

[18] Economic Council of Canada, *Perspective 1975,* Sixth Annual Review, (September, 1969), pp. 121-122.

[19] N. K. Tandan, *Underutilization of Manpower in Canada.* Dominion Bureau of Statistics. Special Labour Force Studies No. 8 (September 1969).

[20] Malcolm S. Cohen, "The Direct Effects of Federal Manpower Programs in Reducing Unemployment," *Journal of Human Resources* (Fall, 1969), pp. 491-507.

employment used in United States household surveys, some would claim that the critical question is how successful such persons are in obtaining employment after they leave the programme.

In somewhat similar vein, Gosta Rehn[21] discusses the extent to which training programmes can be utilized to regulate the labour supply in the short-run as a countercyclical device. He notes that this procedure is utilized in Sweden. In periods of national unemployment, more trainees are enrolled in training programmes and they are retained in training programmes for a longer period of time as a contribution to the reduction of aggregate unemployment. In periods of tight labour markets and inflationary wage-price pressures, enrollment and duration of training programmes are reduced.

If government funds are used to establish training programmes that relate training to a work situation in such a way as to be classed as "employment," the government can go far toward taking workers off the unemployment rolls and in reducing aggregate "unemployment." In Cohen's model, utilizing a broad definition of employment, the unemployed workers are given "jobs" and "employment" by enrolling in a government-sponsored training-work programme. In Rehn's model the unemployment rate is reduced by taking workers out of the labour force, that is, reducing the labour supply by placing workers in a training programme. If the training-work programmes in Cohen's scheme were based on government public works or public employment of some kind, it is conceivable that the programmes could be expanded sufficiently to make a very substantial contribution to the reduction of aggregate unemployment, especially among the poor and disadvantaged. If the government were forced to rely on training-work programmes in private industry, the limits would be established by the size of the incentive subsidies and by employers' willingness to take on additional work-trainees in response to subsidy incentives. Cohen's estimates for the four programmes in 1965-67 could be used to porject the reduction in national unemployment that might occur with a 10, 25 or 50 per cent increase in programme enrollment.

Second, quite aside from the direct employment effects of enrollment in training programmes, these programmes create jobs if the government expenditures on training facilities, instruction and allowances augment aggregate and regional demand and do not merely replace other expenditures that would have been made in the absence of training. In depressed areas, especially where unemployment rates are high, large-scale government expenditures on manpower training programmes would have a significant impact on total expenditures and would not be offset by a decline in other expenditures in that area. The multiplier effect of such training programmes might serve to increase aggregate demand and employment significantly.

Third, studies have indicated that lack of skilled workers in a depressed area acts as a deterent to the establishment of new plants, and that the improvement of local skills can be an important inducement to industrialization. Retraining programmes in depressed areas would create new jobs if the availability of newly retrained workers induced employers to establish new plants, which would not have been established elsewhere, in these areas.

Fourth, training programmes can create jobs if any decrease in expenditures made elsewhere, as a result of the training expenditures, is in a sector that is capital-intensive. Such a decrease in spending would not decrease employment as much as the hiring of the retrained workers would increase employment. Since retraining reduces the real costs of labour, employers may be induced to hire more of the cheaper factor relative to capital. Furthermore, the lower cost of labour that results from training programmes might induce some shift from savings to consumption for jobs that will be created by retraining programmes, if employers become more willing to hire trainees because of their new skills even though the employers had no job vacancies before the trainees presented themselves.

Fifth, unemployment will be reduced by training programmes if structural causes are considered important. This argument is based on the structural hypothesis and assumes a substantial number of job vacancies which could be filled by upgrading the skills of the unemployed. Unemployed workers with new skills can fill the jobs that are vacant because qualified workers had been unavailable. If filling one vacant job removes a bottleneck and permits the hiring of additional workers, the training programme could have a multiplier effect in reducing unemployment. Some deny this premise. Further studies are needed to provide a factual basis for the optimism of the proponents of training on this score.

In summary, there are cogent arguments for the belief that training programmes can reduce aggregate unemployment levels through direct enrollment effects as well as through post-training experience. The contribution of training can be greatest if accompanied by a vigorous expansionary monetary-fiscal policy. As Rehn has noted, in some situations it is possible to pursue these expansionary policies thanks only to training programmes preventing inflationary pressures, namely by improving the mutual matching of labour supply and demand. However, the particular Canadian and American situation in the 1960's gave rise to independent pursuance of both structural and aggregate policies to reduce unemployment. It would be empirically difficult to disentangle the employment contributions of the training programmes from those of the monetary-fiscal policy; however, it is possible to construct a theoretical model that gives a significant independent role to retraining programmes in the reduction of aggregate unemployment. Up to a point, the larger the scale of the training programmes, the larger the reduction in unemployment. However, where diminishing returns would begin is difficult to determine theoretically or to estimate empirically.

[21] Gosta Rehn, "A Note on the Importance of Manpower Programmes — Exemplified by Adult Training for the Short-term Variability of Labour Supply" OECD, (Paris, 1967), pp. 6-12, mimeo.

Reduction in Inflationary Pressures[22]

There are some who feel that government subsidized retraining programmes can be fully justified only in a period of tight labour markets and inflationary pressures. They reason that government retraining programmes in a period of general labour surplus may merely change the composition of the unemployed. In time of labour shortages, however, public retraining can become an important anti-inflationary force. Retraining can thus play a major role in policies designed to bring about full employment by reducing the inflationary pressures created by expansionist monetary-fiscal policy as the economy approaches full employment.

Although this position has merit, there are caveats that must be observed. First, in a period of tight labour markets, the remaining unemployed are likely to be heavily concentrated among the hard-core disadvantaged. These are the very workers who are least likely to be trained for the critically short occupations. These occupations usually require a higher level of general education than is customarily found among the most disadvantaged. (Of course, general educational levels can be raised before training commences). Second, private employers can be expected to increase their own training efforts in a period of labour shortage. Since the evaluation of the economic impact of federal retraining should be based on the determination of what would have happened in the absence of this public activity, a period of full employment may be one in which the social net "benefits" of subsidized retraining are less than one would suppose. Third, even if the benefits of retraining increase in a period of full employment, the costs of retraining may also increase in such a period. The costs of instructors and facilities will be higher and the opportunity costs of the training will rise.

Although there are *a priori* grounds for believing that retraining programmes can help move the economy to higher levels of aggregate employment at lower levels of inflationary pressure, the contribution of retraining to this effect depends upon the structural hypothesis once more. If there is a serious imbalance and mismatching between the composition of the unemployed and the composition of the additional demand for labour induced by expansionist monetary-fiscal policy, the increased expenditures will result in rising prices rather than increased output in employment.

Studies are not yet available to show the extent to which retraining has helped reduce any imbalance that might exist between the increase of job vacancies and the remaining unemployed, in a period of expansionist monetary-fiscal policy. Lacking detailed information on job vacancies as well as detailed characteristics of the unemployed, we cannot take the first step in appraising the extent of the structural imbalance, let alone appraise the contribution of retraining in resolving that imbalance. Whereas the government retraining programmes have probably made some dent in the hard-core occupational shortages that have become almost a tradition in the labour market, there is no evidence that the impact has yet been a sizable one. In spite of the many courses offered in such occupations as draftsmen, welders, auto mechanics, secretaries and nurses' aides, these occupations continue to suffer national shortages.

Recent discussion of inflation in Canada and the United States has focused attention on the relationship between inflation and unemployment. The structure of labour and product markets yields a Phillips curve relationship between the rate of inflation and the rate of unemployment. These seem to indicate that thus far it has been possible to have a lower rate of unemployment only at the cost of a higher rate of inflation. Fiscal and monetary policies alone have been incapable of attaining full employment and price stability simultaneously. Policy measures designed to influence the structure of the market, such as manpower policy, are designed to alter this relationship.

A large-scale occupational training programme is an element of both manpower policy and fiscal policy. Expenditures on training or financial incentives for training affect not only market structure but also aggregate demand. To the extent that there is a relationship between inflation and unemployment, it is not immediately clear, therefore, whether a large-scale training programme will cause a shift of the curve or a movement along it, or both.

One might attribute a shift in the Phillips curve since 1962 to the expanded manpower training programme in Canada and United States. This would be difficult to verify, although the Cohen estimates above are suggestive. It is difficult not only to distinguish occupational training from other causes but also to separate that part of the training programme that affected aggregate demand from that part that affected market structure. The analysis used in the Phillips curve does not lend itself to this separation.

It is often hypothesized that wage inflation occurs under full employment because of a shortage of skilled workers. The implication of the skilled worker hypothesis, if a training programme is to resist inflationary forces, is that attention should be focused on the problem of skill shortages rather than on the problem of employability of the disadvantaged. Unfortunately, training of the hard-core unemployed does little to inhibit an increase in the level of money wages; in fact, it may even promote wage inflation to the degree that it creates an excess demand for skilled labour in on-the-job training. Moreover, attention is concentrated on the provision of general training that can be transferred from one firm to another, rather than on training that is specific to a firm. This raises a problem for on-the-job programmes, in which the firm is motivated to provide specific training. Proposals to provide "insurance" to compensate firms for labour turnover or subsidies for OJT, however, could provide a solution to this problem.

Much of the analysis of wage inflation is preliminary to an analysis of price inflation. From a simple Phillips curve relating change in money wages and the unemployment rate we can derive a relationship between the change in price level and the rate of unemployment, if we assume that a change in price level equals change in wage level minus change in productivity. An analysis of the impact of occupational training is complicated by the fact that productivity appears both in the wage equation,

[22] I am grateful to Duncan MacRae for his contribution to this section.

perhaps through its proxy profits, and in the price equation. Training that increases productivity moderates price inflation in the price equation but adds to it in the wage equation through the enhancing effect on wage inflation.

The findings of the research performed thus far have barely begun to describe the relationship between occupational training and the relationship between inflation and unemployment. The Phillips curve approach to inflation is at too high a level of aggregation to be of direct use. Among other theories so far propounded, the skilled worker hypothesis of money wage determination has direct implications for a manpower training programme. If this hypothesis is correct, then to combat inflation, occupational training should either concentrate on developing skilled workers or achieve an adequate supply of skilled workers by the training of unskilled or semiskilled workers who, having entered at the usual recruitment levels, will rise to higher levels. If large scale on-the-job training programmes in the future disproportionately employ skilled workers as trainees they will contribute to inflation. Thus, in Canada as elsewhere, hypotheses concerning the impact of training on inflation remain untested.

Economic Growth

The proponents of large scale retraining programmes argue from a stronger position when they leave the area of possible short-term countercyclical effects and concentrate on the long-term effects of retraining on productivity. Because the basic purpose of the training programme is to increase skills and productivity, their ultimate failure to contribute to an increase in real Gross National Product would constitute a major indictment against training programmes. A number of recent studies have shown the important contribution of education, training and other investments in human capital to economic growth. They are too familiar to require elaboration here.

The work of Ribich, Weisbrod, and Hansen shows that the effect of occupational training, especially among the disadvantaged, may be more important than the effect of general education in contributing to employment and incomes. Lester Thurow has estimated that under certain circumstances, a 10 per cent increase in current expenditure in education and on-the-job training would cause the potential rate of growth of output to rise by 0.08 percentage points. The same increase might be achieved with a smaller investment in OJT alone.[23]

EFFECTS ON INCOME DISTRIBUTION, POVERTY

Many of the points raised in the discussion on the aggregate employment effects of manpower training programmes also apply to the aggregate income effects. However, by concentrating on the lowest-income, disadvantaged groups, the retraining programmes could have an important effect in reducing poverty, regardless of its impact on the aggregate level of income in the economy. MDTA data in the U.S. show that 81 per cent of institutional trainees and 50 per cent of on-the-job trainees who were family heads and who were in training in 1966 had earnings of less than $3,000 or had no earnings for the last full year before entering training.[24] Since a number of the training-related programmes of the war on poverty, such as the Job Corps and the Neighborhood Youth Corps, are directed to more disadvantaged groups than are found among MDTA trainees, it is likely that the total national training effort has had a significant effect in raising the incomes of those in the lowest income category. Most of the detailed follow-up analyses have shown a significant increase in income after training as compared to the period before training. The partial Canadian follow-up data currently available provide similar implications. Mangum, who has made the most detailed study of this question, concludes:

Although its contribution to the over-all reduction of poverty is small, MDTA has made a significant contribution to the income of its poor enrollees. To have helped between 175,000 and 225,000 low income persons in a period of more than four years, half of whom were probably heads of families, to raise their incomes from just below the poverty line to a little above it is gratifying, particularly when compared with experiences of other programs. However, the dent made in the problem of the 9,000,000 poor families is hardly noticeable.[25]

Obviously, a substantial expansion of training programmes geared to the needs of the disadvantaged would serve to further the escape of additional families from poverty.

It is in this realm that the external benefits of retraining programmes become most obvious. If the reduction in poverty, as a result of new skills, new jobs and higher income, is accompanied by a reduction in crime and delinquency, society gains additional benefits. A number of studies have indicated the existence of such a relationship. Along this line, a number of experiments have shown that training programmes within correctional institutions serve not only to increase employment and income after release from the correctional institution, but also serve to reduce recidivism.

Tax Revenue and Transfer Payments

The possible effects of retraining programmes on increased government tax revenue and on the reduction of welfare and unemployment payments depend upon the success of these programmes in reducing unemployment

---

[23] Thomas Ribich, *Education and Poverty* Brookings Institute, (1968); Burton A. Weisbrod, "Preventing High School Dropouts," in Robert Dorfman (ed.), *Measuring Benefits of Government Investments* (Brookings Institute, 1965); W. Lee Hansen, Burton A. Weisbrod and William Scanlon, "Determinants of Income: Does Schooling Really Count?" University of Wisconsin, (December 1967), Mimeo; Lester Thurow, in *Toward a Manpower Policy,* R. A. Gordon, (ed.) (New York: John Wiley, 1967).

[24] Garth Mangum, *MDTA, Foundation of Federal Manpower Policy,* (John Hopkins University Press, 1968), Chapter 4.

[25] *Ibid.*

and raising income. A few of the studies designed to evaluate the economic effects of retraining programmes, such as those by Hardin and Borus and Gibbard and Somers, have indicated that the successful employment and income effects of retraining programmes have indeed resulted in increased tax payments by the trainees and, especially in the case of the West Virginia studies, in a substantial reduction in post-training welfare payments as compared with a control group of nontrainees. But these are only benefits for the government. Society as a whole has gained nothing since changes in government expenditure and income affected only the distribution, not the size, of total national income.

Mobility Programme

A refined benefit/cost analysis of the current mobility programme is underway. A sophisticated model has been developed,[26] but no data have been published. A. N. Polianski has conducted the only available benefit/cost analysis to date;[27] unfortunately, his analysis refers to the earlier version of the programme rather than the amended measure of 1967. He found that, on the average, relocatees increased their income from $2,577 per annum to $4,646 as a result of their move. The average estimated outlays for all types of assistance were $475. The present value of benefits for individual relocatees was estimated to be $5,482, giving a benefit/cost ratio of 12/1. For the government, the benefit/cost ratio was estimated to be 8/1, and for society as a whole, 34/1. Methodological problems confronting studies of this nature are dealt with later in this essay.

Whether these favourable findings would be duplicated in other studies of the old programme cannot be determined, and no such results are yet available for the new programme. However, some data are available on characteristics of the 6,000 workers who received relocation grants in 1967-68, on the direction of their movement and on the factors associated with successful mobility. The mobile workers are relatively young. The majority are under thirty-four years of age, but one-fourth have four or more dependents. Over three-fourths moved within the boundaries of their own province, but in one-fifth of the relocations the move was out of a designated "development area" to a non-designated area.[28] An analysis of 1,143 workers from October to December 1967 indicates that Ontario experienced both the largest out-flow of mobile workers (39.6 per cent) and the largest influx (50.3 per cent). Quebec was second among the provincial areas as both a point of departure and a point of destination.[29]

Another study by the Programme Development Service indicates that the best "risk" for a successful relocation is found among those with higher level skills, relatively high levels of education and vocational training, little previous unemployment and those married, with one to three children. These findings are not surprising, but they raise a note of caution in interpreting the results of the promised cost/benefit analysis: since the "successful" relocatees were also approximately the most successful workers before their move, the true net effect of the mobility programme must be guaged with care.

A follow-up survey of the mobility programme was conducted in 1968 by a consulting firm under contract with the Department of Manpower and Immigration. It covered workers receiving relocation grants in the period between April 1 and June 30, 1967. Although the survey suffered from major problems in contacting a reliable sample of relocations and falls short of a full-fledged evaluation, it provides some useful and interesting insights.[30] The non-response rate was such as to permit only a range of quantitative conclusions. The year after their move, between 33 per cent and 50 per cent of the relocatees were still employed in the job to which they had moved. An additional 20 to 23 per cent were still in the new community working at another job. However, between 20 and 26 per cent of those who had been unemployed before their move were still unemployed at the time of the survey. Movers had a median real income gain of $800 to $1,100, or 21 to 27 per cent compared with their income before the move.

These favourable findings must be tempered by the fact that 75 per cent of the movers stated that they would have moved even if the government had not had a mobility programme. This points to the serious methodological deficiency of a study that attempts to evaluate the "net" effects or "value added" of the government's role in encouraging mobility.

If the magnitude of earnings increase under the new mobility programme is found to approach that of Polianski's earlier study, given the average $600 moving cost and $60 exploratory-visit cost of the present programme, the programme is likely to be given a favourable evaluation in economic terms. As in all mobility projects, however, the social-psychological costs of migration cannot be readily measured. The effectiveness of counsellors in mitigating these costs can only be surmised from existing reports.

METHODOLOGICAL PROBLEMS IN MOBILITY EVALUATIONS[31]

Policy-makers have a special interest in knowing the gains and costs and the returns to personal and social investment in manpower relocation; as the following papers suggest, however, a precise evaluation of costs

[26] Robert A. Jenness, "Manpower Mobility Programs", G. G. Somers and D. W. Wood, (eds.) in *Cost-Benefit Analysis of Manpower Programs,* Queen's University and University of Wisconsin, 1969.

[27] Manpower Mobility Program — A Pilot Project in the Method of Evaluation of Government Programs," 25th Interstate Conference on Labour Statistics (June 15, 1967), Mimeo.

[28] Paper delivered by W. R. Dymond at the Round Table on Manpower Mobility, Economic Council of Canada, Ottawa, (September 5, 1968).

[29] *Ibid.*

[30] *Manpower Mobility Program Follow-up Survey.* Department of Manpower and Immigration, Mimeo, no date.

[31] See Somers, (ed.) "The Returns to Geographic Mobility: A Symposium," *Journal of Human Resources* (Fall, 1967); and "Conceptual and Data Problems in Evaluating Relocation Projects," Symposium of the International Manpower Institute, U.S. Department of Labor, April, 1969.

and gains is impeded by theoretical and methodological difficulties. First, returns to the investment in mobility are crucially influenced by other investments in human beings. The interactions are complex and not easily disentangled. Investments in training, education and labour-market information are likely to further geographic mobility and to enhance the economic benefits derived from mobility. Although the gains resulting from each of these related investments can be theoretically and statistically identified, the allocation of their costs is a formidable task. How much of these private and public expenditures, valued for their own sake, should be charged as a "cost" of the mobility they enhance?

Second, there is a lack of symmetry between gains and costs. Whereas the gains of mobility are found to be primarily economic, namely improved employment and income, the significant costs are non-economic. Numerous studies have disclosed that mobile workers consider the actual monetary costs of their move to be of secondary importance to their loss of friends, relatives, and familiar surroundings. Non-economic factors always present a problem for the analysis of returns to human investments. The problem is usually disposed of, rather than solved, through an explicit recognition of its existence and explanation of its intractability, and an apologetic decision to omit non-economic costs and benefits from the formal analysis. Because socio-psychological variables are concentrated on one side of the equation, however, their omission can introduce a substantial bias in the evaluation of mobility programmes. When sizeable economic benefits are set against the minor monetary costs of moving, while considerable, socio-psychological costs are excluded, an explosive rate of economic return may be recorded. And yet, the reluctance of many workers to leave economically depressed areas in spite of such potentially high rates of return raises serious questions concerning this type of measure. Current efforts to integrate quantitative measures of noneconomic costs and benefits into the formal investment analysis will hopefully remove some of the obstacles to assessment.

A third conceptual problem facing analysts in this field is the appropriate area designation for the calculation of social benefits. In a sense, this is merely a sub-type of the general problem of external factors, common to the determination of benefits of education and other investments in human beings. But in evaluating the benefits of geographic mobility, these considerations take on an important physical aspect, as well as a conceptual one. It may be found that the only positive benefits of mobility are external to the area from which the movement originates, and yet relocation subsidies are frequently included as part of regional development programmes.

The area from which workers migrate is likely to suffer losses in potential production, consumption and infrastructure. Although local welfare costs and unemployment may be reduced because of outmigration, even these results are not assured, given the selective composition of the migrants and the impact of their departure on area income and consumption. On the other hand, receiving areas may benefit greatly from geographic mobility by increased production and in the demand for goods, service and facilities. Although some costs are also transferred from depressed areas along with the migrants, there are indications that an area's benefits from immigration greatly outweigh its costs.

There is a complex relationship between costs and benefits of geographic mobility, as they pertain to the individual, to area redevelopment policy and to national economic welfare. While most analyses measure returns to the individual, the effects on the productive efficiency of particular regions and on the nation's Gross National Product are equally important (but less readily measurable) results.

Fourth, and finally, the designation of appropriate control groups presents a problem to an accurate evaluation of costs and benefits. This too, is a general problem in the study of human resources, but it presents special complications in the analysis of the returns to mobility. As in other evaluations of human investment, it is necessary to know what difference mobility makes, what results can be specifically attributed to it and what results would have occurred even in its absence.

Should the experience of mobile workers be compared with their own premobility status or with the status of nonmobile workers? If the former, how can the analyst ensure that general economic conditions have remained the same while the worker moved from one area to another? If the latter type of control group is deemed more appropriate, should the comparison be made with nonmobile workers in the old community or in the new community? And how can the analyst ensure similarity in the characteristics of the mobile and nonmobile workers? The choice of a comparison group can vitally affect the findings. Since the motivation to move geographically is closely linked to the worker's current economic status, the employment and income of most mobile workers differs significantly from that of nonmobile workers even before the move. Without careful controls, a *post facto* mobile-nonmobile comparison may simply reflect the *status quo ante* rather than measure the impact of mobility.

These methodological problems plague evaluations of subsidized mobility in Canada, in the United States and in other countries. Until they are resolved, the ratio of costs and returns of the mobility programme remain open to question.

Evaluation of other Programmes

Given the paucity of concrete data for evaluation of the two key programmes in an active manpower policy — training and mobility — quantitative precision in the evaluation of other policies is unlikely. Indeed, discussions of such aspects as the consultation service, the labour market information system,[32] and the employment service functions are usually in terms of rather general qualitative appraisals and recommendations rather than specific measurable results. This is unfortunate because there are some reasons to believe that increased labour market information may

---

[32] See Noah M. Meltz, *Study of Labour Market Information Systems,* Department of Manpower and Immigration (June, 1968).

constitute the principal contribution of government in the manpower field. Other policies, such as the measures to stabilize employment and to encourage regional growth, are appraised in terms of dollars spent rather than labour-market success.

The current lack of detailed evaluation of Canadian manpower policies is typical of the experience in a number of countries where such policies have a much longer tradition. There is a tendency to accept the value of manpower policies on faith, to simply state the fact that training and mobility programmes have reached only a small fraction of eligible workers who might benefit from them, to recount some gains without a controlled comparison and therefore, to urge the expansion of manpower policy. As long as legislators are willing to act on these same assumptions, the cry for evaluation and the conduct of evaluation may largely remain an academic exercise.

There is some evidence, however, that in Canada as well as the United States and even Sweden (the model of an active manpower policy) legislators are no longer willing to accept unsupported assertions or the benefits derived from government expenditures in this field. Careful evaluation may thus become essential for an expansion in manpower policies in the 1970's comparable to that of the dreading decade. A recognition of these facts of life is now noticeable in the statements of those in the Department of Manpower and Transportation and in the Economic Council of Canada.[33] Such views bode well for evaluation research in the future.

[33] William R. Dymond, "The Role of Benefit-Cost Analysis in Formulating Manpower Policy," in *Cost-Benefit Analysis of Manpower Policies*, pp. 42-55; and Economic Council of Canada *Sixth Annual Review* pp. 164-166.

3

THE
DIRECTION of UNIONISM
in CANADA

Arthur M. Kruger

INTRODUCTION

Consideration of the direction of unionism in Canada will be related in this essay to the issues that are raised in the other articles in this volume.

Frequently we speak of "organized labour" or "the labour movement" as if there were a cohesive institution with a clear-cut identity that was designated by these terms. Even a cursory look at our unions indicates that this concept is not true. Canadian labour is not a unified movement with a structured hierarchy and clearly defined goals. Rather, Canadian unions are decentralized and have diverse views of their objectives and methods. This is not to deny that unions have much in common, or to imply that no generalizations about unions are possible; however, the effort of any analysis usually focuses on common characterstics. In Canada the decentralization of labour demands that attention be given to the numerous exceptions to any generalization.

As this article will emphasize, the development of labour organization in Canada did not occur in a vacuum. A study of labour must embrace the context within which the unions developed. This context primarily includes the legal, market and institutional environment. In Canada, the study must embrace many special features of the environment, including the impact of the United States on Canada, the constitutional divisions of responsibilities between the federal and provincial governments, and the French-English division in Canadian society.

The next section briefly reviews the nature of the environment, focusing on the elements that have conditioned the development of unionism

Table 3-1

PERCENTAGE DISTRIBUTION IN CANADA OF VALUE ADDED OR NATIONAL INCOME ORIGINATING*, BY INDUSTRY, SELECTED YEARS 1870-1955.

Year	Primary Industries					Secondary Industries				Tertiary Industries			Total Industry	Adjustment**	Grand Total***
	Agriculture	Fishing and Trapping	Mining	Forest Operations	Total Primary	Manufacturing	Construction	Total Secondary	Public Utilities	Government	Other Service Industries	Total Tertiary			
1870	33.3	1.1	0.9	9.6	44.9	19.0	3.0	22.0	—	—	—	20.9	87.8	12.2	100.0
1880	32.0	1.9	1.0	8.6	43.5	18.9	3.8	22.7	—	—	—	22.4	88.6	11.4	100.0
1890	27.0	1.6	1.4	6.6	36.6	23.5	4.6	28.1	—	—	—	26.7	91.4	8.6	100.0
1900	26.7	1.6	3.3	4.9	36.5	20.8	4.2	25.0	—	—	—	29.4	90.9	9.1	100.0
1910	22.8	0.9	2.6	3.9	30.2	22.7	5.1	27.8	—	—	—	33.6	91.6	8.4	100.0
1920	19.4	0.9	2.5	3.8	26.6	24.2	5.5	29.7	—	—	—	35.3	91.6	8.4	100.0
1929	12.1	0.6	3.9	1.7	18.3	24.5	6.1	30.6	12.8	8.0	35.8	56.6	105.5	—5.5	100.0
1930	11.3	0.4	3.5	1.4	16.6	22.6	5.6	28.2	12.7	9.6	39.6	61.9	106.7	—6.7	100.0
1933	7.6	0.3	4.7	1.3	13.9	22.8	2.8	25.6	14.1	15.1	40.5	69.7	109.2	—9.2	100.0
1939	11.7	0.3	6.8	1.6	20.4	26.6	3.4	30.0	11.6	10.5	33.1	55.2	105.6	—5.6	100.0
1945	11.8	0.6	2.8	1.6	16.8	27.5	3.5	31.0	11.0	18.0	24.9	53.9	101.7	—1.7	100.0
1950	11.7	0.5	3.9	1.8	17.9	30.7	5.6	36.3	10.2	8.1	30.1	48.4	102.6	—2.6	100.0
1951	13.4	0.5	4.0	2.2	20.1	30.1	5.0	35.1	10.2	8.2	28.4	46.8	102.0	—2.0	100.0
1952	11.4	0.4	3.6	2.0	17.4	29.4	5.6	35.0	10.7	9.0	29.4	49.1	101.5	—1.5	100.0
1953	9.9	0.3	3.2	1.7	15.1	29.7	6.4	36.1	10.8	9.5	29.8	50.1	101.3	—1.3	100.0
1954	7.3	0.3	3.4	1.9	12.9	28.8	6.6	35.4	10.9	10.7	31.5	53.1	101.4	—1.4	100.0
1955	7.8	0.3	3.8	1.9	13.8	28.7	7.0	35.7	10.7	10.6	30.7	52.0	101.5	—1.5	100.0

* For 1870 to 1920 inclusive, the figures represent value added by each industry. For 1929 to 1953, the data pertain to income originating in industry as given in the National Accounts.
** Adjustment item comprises rent, indirect taxes, less subsidies, plus net income for 1870 to 1920 inclusive, and national income of nonresidents for 1929 to 1953.
*** Covers gross national product for 1870 to 1920 inclusive, and net national income at factor cost for 1929 to 1953.

Source: O. J. Firestone, *Canada's Economic Development, 1867-1953, with Special Reference to Changes in the Country's National Product and National Wealth* (London: 1958), Table 68; DBS, *National Accounts, Income and Expenditure, 1950-1955*, Table 20. Reproduced by permission from Caves and Holton, *The Canadian Economy*, Harvard Economic Studies, Harvard University Press, p. 604.

in this country. The third section, entitled "The Development of the Canadian Labour Movement," will describe the evolution of labour organization in Canada; in the fourth section, entitled "Canadian Labour Today," the focus will shift to an examination of Canadian unions today. The final section, "The Problems and Prospects of the Labour Movement," will treat the principal problems currently confronting organized labour and will forecast the problems and development of Canadian unionism in the near future.

THE ENVIRONMENT

The factors in the environment that influence trade unions are developments in markets (both labour and product markets), the nature of legislation bearing on unions and collective bargaining, and the relative status of labour, management and government in the society. These subjects are treated at length elsewhere in this volume and in specialized works.[1] Here, we will merely indicate the highlights of these features of the environment.

The Growth of Canadian Industry[2]

A trade union movement is more likely to develop in urban societies where output and employment are concentrated in manufacturing, construction and transportation than in rural societies where agriculture, fishing and trapping predominate. Once a union movement does develop, its character is strongly influenced by the relative importance of the various sectors of the economy and by the nature of the predominant technology. Table 3-1 indicates how the relative importance of various sectors of the economy as measured by the value of output originating in these sectors has changed. Note the secular decline in the primary sectors and the growth in the position of the secondary and tertiary industries. You also will observe the significant rise in the relative position of the tertiary sectors in recent years.

These shifts have been accompanied by other changes in the nature of Canadian business that also have influenced the characteristics of the labour movement. The size of business firms in many sectors has increased enormously over the years, partly in response to technological change. There is some controversy concerning the degree to which selling markets

---

[1] For a further discussion of this approach, see S. M. A. Hameed's article in this volume. Also see J. Dunlop, *Industrial Relations Systems* (New York: H. Holt & Co., 1958).

[2] For further information see R. Caves and R. Holton, *The Canadian Economy* (Cambridge: Harvard University Press, 1961); G. W. Wilson et al, ed., *Canada: An Appraisal of Its Needs and Resources* (Toronto: University of Toronto Press, 1965); and W. T. Easterbrook and H. G. J. Aitken, *Canadian Economic History* (Toronto: Macmillan Co., 1956).

have become more or less competitive. Numerous examples of both increased and reduced competition are readily available to support either contention. The development of our extractive and manufacturing sectors
has been achieved through a vast influx of foreign capital, primarily from
the United States, accompanied by foreign ownership and control over a
very significant portion of these sectors.[3]

Shifts in the relative importance of the various sectors have changed
the location of Canadian industry. Areas dependent on agriculture, fishing
and forestry have become relatively less important as sources of output
and employment than areas where manufacturing and services are concentrated. This will become more evident in the discussion of population
and labour force changes.

Canadian Population and Labour Force Trends[4]

Industrial change and population change go hand in hand. The Canadian
population has grown rapidly as a result of both natural increase and
immigration. Within Canada, population has shifted geographically as
industry and employment opportunities moved to certain regions.

Elsewhere in this volume, labour force trends are discussed at length.
Here, we will merely point out the following important facts:[5]

a. the significant urbanization of the Canadian population and the growing
concentration in certain parts of the country;
b. the rapid growth in the proportion of workers engaged in the service
sectors in recent years and the long-term relative decline in employment in the primary sectors;
c. the growing proportion of workers employed in white-collar occupations. White-collar work has increased in importance in many sectors
including some (e.g. manufacturing) that have traditionally been
thought of as overwhelmingly blue-collar.
d. the rapid rise in female participation in the labour force and the concomitant growth in the female proportion of the labour force.

Canadian Labour Legislation[6]

The provincial governments, rather than the Federal Government, set
the legal framework for labour organization and collective bargaining for
most of the labour force. Although legislation differs among jurisdictions
in a number of important matters, there is enough uniformity in the
approach of the eleven governments to permit us to speak of a Canadian
system. The Canadian system follows the American practice of letting
workers in an "appropriate bargaining unit" decide which union, if any,
will bargain for them. This is usually decided by majority vote of those in
the unit. Once a union is designated as bargaining agent, no other
union can act for those in the unit and the chosen union must represent
everyone in the unit, members and non-members alike. Following a union's
certification as exclusive bargaining agent for a given group of employees,
both the union and management must negotiate "in good faith" with a

view to drawing up the terms of a collective agreement. The law prohibits work stoppages during the term of a collective agreement.

Certain categories of employees are singled out for special treatment. Some are not permitted to belong to larger bargaining units (e.g. supervisory staff, foremen etc.); others are restricted to specified organizations (e.g. Ontario civil servants cannot choose any union other than the Civil Service Association of Ontario); and some employees are prohibited from striking (e.g. policemen).

The Status of the "Actors"

The final environmental determinant of union growth is the relative position of the "actors" (union leaders, employers and government officials) who participate in collective bargaining. Determination of status involves judgments which are difficult to document.

There is little doubt that the status of union leaders has improved greatly over the years. In the nineteenth and early twentieth centuries, these men were viewed as outlaws or at least dangerous radicals whose activities had to be controlled by legislation and the courts. On the other hand, property rights and the corresponding rights of management always have had strong support in our society. Managers tend to possess certain characteristics (wealth, income, education, family background and so on) that make them highly esteemed. A marked change in attitude began to take place during the 1930's when business leaders lost prestige in the face of economic collapse. World War II hastened the change. Legislation was enacted favouring union organization and collective bargaining. Union leaders were soon invited to participate as representatives of labour on numerous public bodies.

Nonetheless, suspicion of union leaders persists and the labour elite have not as yet arrived at a status comparable to that of either management or government leaders. This contention is supported by Canada's leading authority on Canadian elites, Professor John Porter, who concludes that the labour elite does not enjoy the prestige of other elites (business, government, religion, academic etc.) in this country.[7] Porter sums up his findings in the following comments:

[3] See Canada, Privy Council Office, *Foreign Ownership and the Structure of Canadian Industry* (Ottawa: Queen's Printer, January 1968) for a well documented treatment of this subject.

[4] For further information, see H. D. Woods and S. Ostry, *Labour Policy and Labour Economics in Canada* (Toronto: Macmillan Co., 1962), Chapter X, XI and XII; and Caves and Holton, *The Canadian Economy.*

[5] See S. Ostry's article in this volume.

[6] See also S. M. A. Hameed's article in this volume, and H. D. Woods and S. Ostry, *Labour Policy and Labour Economics in Canada* Part I (Toronto: Macmillan & Co., 1962), and E. Lorentsen "Fifty Years of Labour Legislation in Canada," *Labour Gazette,* September 1950.

[7] See John Porter, *The Vertical Mosaic: An Analysis of Social Class and Power in Canada* (Toronto: University of Toronto Press, 1965), Chapters XI and XVIII.

Labour leaders rarely share in the informal aspects of the confraternity of power. They do not, as we have seen, have the range of honorific roles that the corporate elite does. Nor does the power of labour leaders extend beyond their institutional roles. They do not have the power, for example, to exploit non-economic areas of social life and harness them to the commercial principle as the corporate elite has with the world of sport.[8]

Labour leaders are, therefore, on the periphery of the over-all structure of power, called in by others when the 'others' consider it necessary, or when the labour leaders demand a hearing from the political elite.[9]

The American Influence[10]

In addition to these forces, the United States has influenced Canadian trade unions. American unions followed the example of American corporations and extended their operations north of the border; in many cases, the firms involved were not American-owned. However, there is little doubt that the speed and extent of the penetration of international unions was influenced by the degree of American ownership of Canadian industry. In Canada, the American corporations and unions found an environment similar in many ways to that below the border and thus adapted readily to Canadian conditions. In turn, American ownership of industry and the presence of American based unions reinforced the Canadian tendency to follow American practices.

Even without these institutional links to the United States, the fact that Canada shares most of this continent wih a large English-speaking neighbour would have exposed us to American patterns in any case. The communications media have, of course, had a much stronger impact on the English-speaking than on the French-speaking parts of Canada. Quebec's tendency to follow a somewhat different course of union organization and legislation than the other provinces, has had its impact on the course of labour relations in that province.[11]

THE DEVELOPMENT OF THE CANADIAN LABOUR MOVEMENT

All of the environmental forces discussed above have operated to influence the development of unionism in this country. This section of the paper highlights the historical changes in the growth and the structure of Canadian unionism.

The Evolution of Canadian Unionism[12]

Labour organization in Canada began long before Confederation. The earliest recorded strike occurred among the voyageurs at Lac la Pluie in 1794.[13] Unions were important enough in Nova Scotia to provoke legislation to curb labour organization as early as 1816.[14] By the 1830's, there were a considerable number of union locals in Canada including the York Typographical Society, founded in 1832, which has had a continuous existence to this day. By the middle of the nineteenth century, British and American unions had entered Canada and established local branches of their unions. Foreign influence was also felt when British immigrants, with experience in unions in their native land, became active in labour organization in Canada.

However, most of these early unions were weak and very few of them survived for long. They were isolated from each other with little cooperation among locals in a given city or in a particular trade.

Some union leaders recognized the need to coordinate union activity to achieve labour's economic and political goals. As early as 1834, unions in Montreal combined to set up the Trades Union to coordinate their activities. This, and similar early efforts, failed. By the 1870's, some cities had established permanent and effective central bodies. Thereafter, municipal labour councils were established in many urban centres and today virtually every industrialized town or city in Canada has such a body.

By the 1870's, a growing number of Canadian locals had been organized by, or were affiliated with, American-based international unions. Although a few British affiliates carried on into the twentieth century, direct British influence was never significant. The role of the British immigrant leaders mentioned earlier persisted as a major influence in Canada and immigrant leadership is an important factor in some Canadian unions today.

National unions also have a long history in Canada. Among the unions that developed spontaneously in this country were the Provincial Workman's Association, the Quebec-based Catholic unions and the Canadian Brotherhood of Railway, Transport and General Workers Union. Other unions, such as the One Big Union (OBU) were offshoots of, or breakaway groups from, American unions. In 1873, the Canadian Labour Union was established to bring together organized workers from every craft in every part of the nation. It seems to have disappeared about 1878. In 1879, workers in Nova Scotia established the Provincial Workman's Association which included in its membership a variety of unions in that province. In 1886, the Canadian Trades and Labour Congress

---

[8] *Ibid.*, p. 539.

[9] *Ibid.*, p. 540.

[10] See J. Crispo, *International Unionism* (Toronto: McGraw-Hill, 1967).

[11] See the article by A. F. Isbester in this volume.

[12] For a more complete treatment of the history of Canadian unions, see H. A. Logan, *Trade Unions in Canada* (Toronto: Macmillan Co. of Canada Ltd., 1948); S. Jameson, *Industrial Relations in Canada* (Ithaca: Cornell University Press, 1957); J. T. Montague, "The Growth of Labour Organization in Canada 1900-1950," in *Labour Gazette*, September 1950.

[13] See H. A. Innis, *The Fur Trade in Canada* (New Haven: Yale University Press, 1930), p. 245.

[14] C. Lipton, *The Trade Union Movement of Canada 1827-1959* (Montreal: Canadian Social Publications Ltd., 1968), p. 7.

(TLC) was established, uniting workers in a variety of unions across Canada. The TLC, unlike its counterpart in the United States, the American Federation of Labour or AFL, embraced international craft unions; branches of the Knights of Labour, an American reformist union founded in 1869; affiliates of British unions; and purely Canadian unions. The TLC membership was concentrated at the outset in Ontario and Quebec and was quite small. As late as 1901, all Congress affiliates combined had a total membership of 8,381.[15]

Originally, the Knights had been in the majority in the TLC, but after 1894 the Knights declined in membership and the internationals soon dominated the TLC. Their parent unions in the United States had always been unhappy about the presence of the Knights and other unions in the TLC and pressed for a purge of "dual unions."[16] In 1902, the TLC finally succumbed to this pressure and expelled the Knights along with other unions. The purge was not complete and pressure from the AFL persisted. In 1913, the TLC expelled its last British-based affiliate, the Amalgamated Society of Carpenters, and in 1921, the Canadian Brotherhood of Railway Employees (CBRE) was forced out of the TLC on the charge of dual unionism.

The TLC began as an all-embracing house of labour; however, it soon faced the conflict between the exclusive jurisdiction principle that its international affiliates considered almost sacrosanct and the desire to accommodate national unions. This problem was exacerbated by the fact that the internationals were organized largely on craft lines and excluded the unskilled from membership, while the Knights and many national unions were based on the industrial union principle of organizing all workers, skilled and unskilled, irrespective of craft, in a given industry. Organized labour on this continent had long been divided on the issue of the appropriate form for union organization. Many bitter debates have been held on the subject. Furthermore, in practice, industrial unions frequently found themselves in conflict with one or more craft unions in their efforts to organize firms where skilled workers were employed. The purge of 1902 was only the first round in a long and continuing battle between proponents of these two forms of organization.

The TLC remained strong in spite of the members lost through these purges. Unions outside the TLC made several attempts to form rival central bodies which, in most instances, were composed of national unions hostile to international unions. In 1902, the expelled unions set up the National Trades and Labour Congress which was reorganized as the Canadian Federation of Labour (CFL) in 1908. By 1914, however, the CFL had very few affiliates. The next attempt to establish a rival congress occurred in 1919 when dissident locals of a number of internationals mostly in Western Canada, severed their ties with the internationals and established the One Big Union (OBU). The OBU emphasized both the need to break the ties with the American unions and the need to organize workers on a broader basis than by craft. The OBU remained a very small organization but continued to operate until the 1950's when most of its affiliates were absorbed by Internationals.

Of greater significance was the creation of the Federation of Catholic

Workers of Canada in 1921. This body, confined to workers in Quebec, emphasized national unionism and multiple forms of organization, both craft and industrial, from the outset. Later, this group changed its name to the Canadian and Catholic Confederation of Labour (CCCL), and in 1960 it was reorganized under its present name — the Confederation of National Trade Unions.

Outside Quebec, attempts to establish a national body that would rival and replace the TLC continued. In 1927, the remnant of the old CFL combined with the Canadian Brotherhood of Railway Employees to form the All Canadian Congress of Labour (ACCL), a body that stressed the desirability of national unions. Left wing unions in the 1920's and 1930's grouped themselves in the Trade Union Unity League, later renamed the Workers Unity League. In the mid-1930's, new industrial unions were established in the United States to organize mass production industries such as automobiles, steel, rubber and so on. These unions soon set up branches in Canada as well. Before long, they found themselves in conflict with the craft unions. In 1937, the AFL expelled these new unions; the TLC, succumbing to pressure, followed suit in 1939. These new unions combined with the ACCL to form the Canadian Congress of Labour (CCL). National and international unions managed to coexist in the CCL largely because the new industrial-based internationals generally had granted greater autonomy to their Canadian districts than had been the case with the AFL affiliates and because all of the CCL unions accepted industrial unionism. The CCL grew rapidly and, while never as big as the older TLC, it was the only national labour centre ever to pose a serious challenge to the TLC. In 1956, the TLC and CCL merged to form the Canadian Labour Congress (CLC).

Today the CLC and the CNTU are the only union centres of any significance in Canada.[17]

The Changes in the Composition of the Canadian Union Movement

The earliest unions were organized on a craft basis with the unskilled worker largely outside the union fold. Skilled workers were more readily organized for a number of reasons. Some of them were immigrants with union experience in their native lands. They were better educated and because they possessed scarce skills, they were more secure than the unskilled in conflicts with employers who opposed the unions. Skilled workers

[15] E. Forsey, "History of the Labour Movement in Canada," *The Canada Year Book 1957-58,* (Ottawa: Queen's Printer, 1958).

[16] A dual union is defined as one that attempts to organize workers considered to be in the jurisdiction of some other union. On this continent, unions have long argued for exclusive jurisdiction over a given occupation or industry by a single union and have labelled dual unionism as undesirable. In other countries, dual unions are often accepted as part of the normal state of affairs.

[17] Apart from the CLC and the CNTU, there are two very small organizations claiming to be national union centres — the National Council of Canadian Labour and the recently formed Council of Canadian Unions. Both oppose international unions. Neither is large enough to warrant further discussion here.

Table 3-2

UNION MEMBERSHIP 1911-1968, WITH ESTIMATES OF TOTAL PAID WORKERS
IN NON-AGRICULTURAL INDUSTRIES IN CANADA, 1921-1968

Year	Union Membership* (Thousands)	Total Non-Agricultural Paid Workers (Thousands)	Union Membership as a Per Cent of Total Non-Agricultural Paid Workers*	Year	Union Membership (Thousands)	Total Non-Agricultural Paid Workers (Thousands)	Union Membership as a Per Cent of Total Non-Agricultural Paid Workers
1911	133	—	—	1940	362	2,197	16.5
1912	160	—	—	1941	462	2,566	18.0
1913	176	—	—	1942	578	2,801	20.6
1914	166	—	—	1943	665	2,934	22.7
1915	143	—	—	1944	724	2,976	24.3
1916	160	—	—	1945	711	2,937	24.2
1917	205	—	—	1946	832	2,986	27.9
1918	249	—	—	1947	912	3,139	29.1
1919	378	—	—	1948	978	3,225	30.3
1920	374	—	—·	1949	1,006(a)	3,326	30.2
1921	313	1,956	16.0	1950	—(b)	—	
1922	277	2,038	13.6	1951	1,029	3,625(a)	28.4
1923	278	2,110	13.2	1952	1,146	3,795(c)	30.2
1924	261	2,138	12.2	1953	1,220	3,694	33.0
1925	271	2,203	12.3	1954	1,268	3,754	33.8
1926	275	2,299	12.0	1955	1,268	3,767	33.7
1927	290	2,406	12.1	1956	1,352	4,058	33.3
1928	301	2,491	12.1	1957	1,386	4,282	32.4
1929	319	2,541	12.6	1958	1,454	4,250	34.2
1930	322	2,451	13.1	1959	1,459	4,375	33.3
1931	311	2,028	15.3	1960	1,459	4,522	32.3
1932	283	1,848	15.3	1961	1,447	4,578	31.6
1933	286	1,717	16.7	1962	1,423	4,705	30.2
1934	281	1,931	14.6	1963	1,449	4,867	29.8
1935	281	1,941	14.5	1964	1,493	5,074	29.4
1936	323	1,994	16.2	1965	1,589	5,343	29.7
1937	383	2,108	18.2	1966	1,736	5,658	30.7
1938	382	2,075	18.4	1967	1,921	5,953	32.3
1939	359	2,079	17.3	1968	2,010	6,068	33.1

* Does not include members of professional associations, even where they engage in collective bargaining.
** Calculated from columns (2) and (3).
(a) Includes Newfoundland for the first time.
(b) Data on union membership for all years up to and including 1949 are as of December 31. In 1950, the reference date was moved ahead by one day to January 1, 1951. Thus, while no figure is shown for 1950, the annual series is, in effect, continued without interruption. The data on union membership for subsequent years are also as of January.
(c) Figures for all years up to and including 1952 are as of the first week in June. Data for subsequent years are as of January.

Source: Labour Organizations in Canada (Ottawa: The Queens Printer, 1911).

in such industries as construction, printing, and transportation, being among the first workers to be organized, are today among the most highly organized groups in Canada.

Once industrial unionism took hold, union organization followed more closely the growth and the pattern of distribution of the labour force discussed above. There are, however, some important exceptions:

a. Unions have been stronger in the urban centres than in small communities.
b. Blue-collar occupations have been more likely to organize than white-collar workers.
c. Unions have been much weaker in the service industries than in the goods-producing sectors.
d. Very small firms are less likely to be organized than larger ones.
e. A much smaller proportion of female workers than of male workers belong to unions.

Table 3-2 shows the change in the size of the labour movement over most of this century and compares this with changes in non-agricultural paid employment in the same period. The figures on non-agricultural paid employment provide the best available approximation of the potentially organizable. Many in this group, however, are not likely to join unions, e.g. management officials, doctors, or lawyers. The data in Table 3-2 illustrate the close relationship between union membership and growth in the non-agricultural labour force.

Union growth was also affected by periods of buoyant labour demand and favourable public policy during World War I and in the immediate postwar years. Employer hostility in the 1920's and the failure of the unions to reach the growing mass production industries, where industrial rather than craft organization was required, explains much of the union's decline in the decade. In the latter case, existing unions were mostly wedded to the craft base and legislation did not provide the support necessary for organizing the unskilled.

The onset of the depression in 1929 created heavy unemployment which, while it reduced the absolute number in the organized work force, did not affect the unionized share of the employed non-agricultural labour force. This was, in part, attributable to the advent of the new CIO industrial unions in the mid-1930's. By securing a measure of public support, these new unions began to penetrate the steel, automobile and other mass production industries. This campaign continued during and after World War II.

Union membership surged during World War II as labour demand rose rapidly and public policy shifted markedly in support of organization. Now that legislation and market forces favoured organization, the new CCL unions with their stress on industrial unionism were well suited to capture the large unorganized plants. During these years union membership doubled and the percentage of the paid labour force in unions rose sharply to over 25 per cent by the end of the war. In the years since World War II, the labour movement has continued to grow, but at a much slower pace than in the period 1936-46. Indeed, its growth has not been quite as rapid as that of the labour force, with the result that the percentage of organized workers in the labour force has slipped from above one-third to somewhat below one-third of the potentially organizable.

Although prosperity and favourable public policy served to promote union growth in the postwar period, other forces were working in the opposite direction. First, the most easily organized workers, the skilled craftsmen and those in large plants, were almost all organized by 1946. Unions then had to address themselves to workers who were more difficult to organize, including employees of small firms in small communities, professional workers and female labour. Furthermore, in the postwar years, the hard-to-organize white-collar, female and service sectors grew at the expense of the blue-collar, goods-producing sectors, which have been the traditional basis of support for unions. Consequently, growth of Canadian unions in the last two decades has been sluggish as compared with the dramatic gains in the late 1930's and the 1940's.

The above discussion indicates that the rate of growth of labour organization has largely followed the growth of the Canadian population and labour force. The composition of our union movement has reflected to a considerable degree the distribution of employment, which itself is largely determined by the composition of our Gross National Product. The relative facility with which different segments of the labour force are organized is itself the result both of market shifts in demand for commodities and services and of technological change.[18] The shift in public attitudes in favour of unions during both World Wars and in the depression was a major factor in union success in these years. Only with public support were unions able to secure favourable legislation and obtain the support of the various agencies implementing and adjudicating the relevant legislation. Labour legislation since World War II has promoted both craft and industrial unions, especially the latter. Legislation does not permit the British pattern of multitude of unions in a single bargaining unit. Our unions tend to concentrate on more limited jurisdictions than many in Britain and elsewhere but within its jurisdiction each union seeks total control.

CANADIAN LABOUR TODAY

This section describes the contemporary Canadian Labour movement, focusing on its size, distribution, structure and government.

Union Membership — Industrial and Geographic Distribution[19]

Table 3-2 indicates that Canadian unions today have a total membership of just over 2 million and account for very close to one-third of all non-agricultural paid workers and over one-quarter of the labour force. There are approximately 165 unions of which 110 are international and 55 national. Most of the more than 9,200 local unions in Canada are affiliated to a national or international union.

Table 3-3

UNION MEMBERSHIP BY CONGRESS AFFILIATION, 1968

Congress Affiliation	Number of Locals	Membership	
		Number	Per Cent
Canadian Labour Congress	7,312	1,571,514	78.2
AFL-CIO/CLC	4,569	1,222,249	60.8
CLC only	2,743	349,265	17.4
Confederation of National Trade Unions	1,030	201,292	10.0
American Federation of Labour and Congress of Industrial Organizations Only	10	678	*
Unaffiliated International Unions	347	107,833	5.4
Unaffiliated National Unions	451	77,489	3.9
Independent Local Organizations	123	50,927	2.5
Total	9,273	2,009,733	100.0

* Less than 0.1 per cent.
Source: Economics and Research Branch, Canada Department of Labour, *Labour Organizations in Canada, 1968* (57th ed.) p. xiii.

Tables 3-3, 3-4, and 3-5 provide further data on the composition of the contemporary labour movement. From Table 3-3, we can see that about three-quarters of those organized are in unions affiliated with the CLC and the overwhelming majority of these are internationals, also affiliated with the AFL-CIO in the United States.[20] The CNTU accounts for approximately 10 per cent of all Canadian union members. The balance consists of international, national and local unions unaffiliated with either congress. Table 3-4 highlights the key role of international unions, which account for about two-thirds of the entire unionized sector of the labour force and about two-thirds of the unions in Canada. Table 3-5 demonstrates the wide range in the size of our unions (both international and national) as measured by membership. Approximately 20 per cent of our international unions and 13 per cent of our national unions are

[18] See N. M. Meltz, *Changes in the Occupational Composition of the Canadian Labour Force 1931-1961* (Ottawa: Queen's Printer, 1965).

[19] The best source for statistics on Canadian unions is Canada, Department of Labour, Economics and Research Branch, *Labour Organization in Canada*, published annually by the Queen's Printer in Ottawa.

[20] Since these figures were published, the large and important United Automobile, Aerospace and Agricultural Implement Workers of America (U.A.W.) with about 91,000 Canadian members has left the AFL-CIO but continues to be affiliated with the CLC.

Table 3-4

Type and Affiliation	Number of Unions	Number of Locals	Membership	
			Number	Per Cent
International Unions	108	4,967	1,345,331	66.9
AFL-CIO/CLC	91	4,569	1,222,249	60.8
CLC Only	3	41	14,571	.7
AFL-CIO Only	5	10	678	*
Unaffiliated Railway Brotherhoods	2	109	8,114	.4
Other Unaffiliated Unions	7	238	99,719	5.0
National Unions	54	3,990	690,260	29.4
CLC	21	2,529	319,062	15.9
CNTU	12	980	193,709	9.6
Unaffiliated Unions	21	451	77,487	3.9
Directly Chartered Local Unions	193	193	23,215	1.2
CLC	143	143	15,632	.8
CNTU	50	50	7,583	.4
Independent Local Organizations	123	123	50,927	2.5
Total	478	9,273	2,009,733	100.0

* Less than 0.9 per cent.
Source: Canada Department of Labour, *Labour Organizations in Canada, 1968,* p. xiii.

very small with under 500 members. About one-half of our unions (including both national and international unions) have under 5,000 Canadian members. About one-seventh of our unions (including both national and international unions) are quite large with 20,000 or more members.

This disparity in size shows up even more markedly if we look at the extremes. The five largest Canadian unions as of January 1, 1968 were the following:[21]

1. United Steelworkers of America
    (AFL-CIO/CLC)   145,000 members
2. International Union, United Automobile,
    Aerospace and Agriculture Implement Workers
    of America
    (AFL-CIO/CLC)[22]   127,000 members
3. Canadian Union of Public Employees
    (CLC)   116,000 members
4. Public Service Alliance of Canada
    (CLC)   97,800 members
5. United Brotherhood of Carpenters and
    Joiners of America
    (AFL-CIO/CLC)   77,900 members

Table 3-5

INTERNATIONAL AND NATIONAL UNIONS BY SIZE, 1968

Member-ship Range	International Unions		National Unions		Total	
	Number of Unions	*Member-ship*	*Number of Unions*	*Member-ship*	*Number of Unions*	*Member-ship*
Under 500	23	3,555	7	1,508	30	5,063
500— 999	3	2,348	4	2,887	7	5,235
1,000— 2,499	12	19,359	10	16,965	22	36,324
2,500— 4,999	14	47,735	10	35,608	24	83,343
5,000— 9,999	17	122,671	11	87,440	28	210,111
10,000—14,999	11	130,195	3	33,830	14	164,025
15,000—19,999	8	137,575	1	16,104	9	153,679
20,000—29,999	11	253,886	3	73,928	14	327,814
30,000 and over	9	628,007	5	321,990	14	949,785
Total	108	1,345,331	54	590,260	162	1,935,591

Source: Canada Department of Labour, *Labour Organizations in Canada, 1968,* p. xiii.

Canada's smallest national and international unions in the same year included at least sixteen with under 100 members. The five smallest known unions in Canada (all internationals) were:
1.   The International Association of Siderographers
(AFL-CIO/CLC)   6 members
2.   Cigar Makers International Union of America
(AFL-CIO/CLC)   8 members
3.   International Mailers Union (ind.)   18 members
4.   Switchmen's Union of North America
(AFL-CIO/CLC)   27 members
5.   International Alliance of Bill Posters,
Billers and Distributors of the United
States and Canada
(AFL-CIO)   25 members
Many foreign observers remarked on both the large number of unions operating in Canada and the small size of many of them. Although Canada's labour force is only about one-tenth that of the United States, most American unions, along with the Canadian-based unions, are active in this country. Comparison with most European countries further demonstrates the relatively fragmented structure of the Canadian labour movement.

[21] See Canada, Department of Labour, *Labour Organization in Canada,* 1967.
[22] See fn 20 above.

Table 3-6

UNION MEMBERSHIP BY INDUSTRY, 1967

Industry	Locals	Membership
Agriculture	15	865
Forestry*	41	43,907
Fishing and Trapping	7	3,285
Mines	190	57,929
Manufacturing	2,747	758,802
Construction	528	209,558
Transportation and Utilities	2,198	361,605
Trade	247	78,416
Finance	11	890
Service Industries	696	169,382
Public Administration	1,456	206,788
Industry not Reported	11	3,617
Adjustment Entry**	—	25,661
No Return	532	—
Totals	8,678	1,920,647

* Includes some sawmilling.
** This entry represents the difference between total membership as reported in the survey of union headquarters and the total obtained in the survey of local unions.
Source: Based on DBS Standard Industrial Classification (1960) DBS Cat. No. 12-501.

Tables 3-6, 3-7 and 3-8 provide information on the industrial and geographic distribution of union membership in Canada in 1967, the most recent year for which such data are available.[23] From Table 3-6, we see that well over one-half of all union members and of all union locals are in the manufacturing, transportation, utilities and construction sectors. This is not surprising. Organization in manufacturing, forestry, construction and mining has increased slowly in recent years so that union membership in these sectors in 1967 accounts for about the same proportion of total membership as it did in 1962. The relative importance of the transportation-utilities sectors has increased in this same period from 18.8 per cent of the total membership to 23.3 per cent of all organized workers. More interesting is the large and growing number of union members in the service sectors, particularly in public administration. This sector now accounts for over 10 per cent of all union members, a much higher proportion than in the past. Similarly, the proportion of union members who are employed in trade has risen from 3 per cent in 1962 to 4.1 per cent in 1967. Workers in the service sector now account for 8.8 per cent of all union members compared with 7.1 per cent in 1962. This reflects the rapid growth in employment in these sectors and as we noted earlier, unionization has not kept pace with this growth.[24]

Table 3-7

THE INDUSTRIAL DISTRIBUTION OF UNION MEMBERSHIP AND OF EMPLOYMENT,
CANADA 1967

Industry	No. of Union Members	No. of Paid Workers 12 Month Average 1967*	Per Cent of Employees Organized**
Agriculture	865	99,000	.9
Other Primary	105,121	183,000	57.4
Manufacturing	758,802	1,716,000	44.2
Construction	209,558	396,000	52.9
Transportation & Utilities	361,605	625,000	57.9
Trade	78,416	1,010,000	7.8
Finance, Insurance and related	890	293,000	.3
Community, Personal and Other Services	169,382	1,532,000	11.1
Public Administration	206,788	443,000	46.7

* Figures rounded to nearest thousand
** Calculated
Source: Canada, DBS, *The Labour Force Special Tables,* Table 3(C), Special
   Surveys Division D.B.S.
   Canada, Department of Labour, *Labour Gazette,* Feb. 1968, p. 92, Table 1.

Table 3-7 compares the industrial distribution of union membership
with the industrial distribution of the labour force. The uneven penetration
of union organization is quite evident — organization ranges from the
highly unionized transportation and utilities sectors to the virtually
unorganized finance and agricultural sectors. What is also apparent is
that unions have reached near capacity penetration in their traditionally
strong sectors and future growth hinges on their ability to expand their
base in the trade, finance, service and public administration industries
where employment is growing rapidly and where most workers remain
outside the union movement.

Table 3-8 shows the geographic distribution of union membership
and compares this with the geographic distribution of the labour force.
British Columbia is the most highly organized province and the Atlantic
provinces are the least organized. Most differences can be explained

---

[23] These data are obtained from local unions. They are not as reliable as the
information in Tables 3-3, 3-4 and 3-5, which is obtained from the national
offices of the unions.

[24] See Canada, Department of Labour, "Industrial and Geographic Distribution
of Union Membership in Canada in 1967," *Labour Gazette* Vol. LXVIII, No.
2, (February 1968), page 91.

Figure 3-1

THE STRUCTURE OF THE CLC-AFFILIATED SEGMENT
OF THE CANADIAN LABOUR MOVEMENT[25]

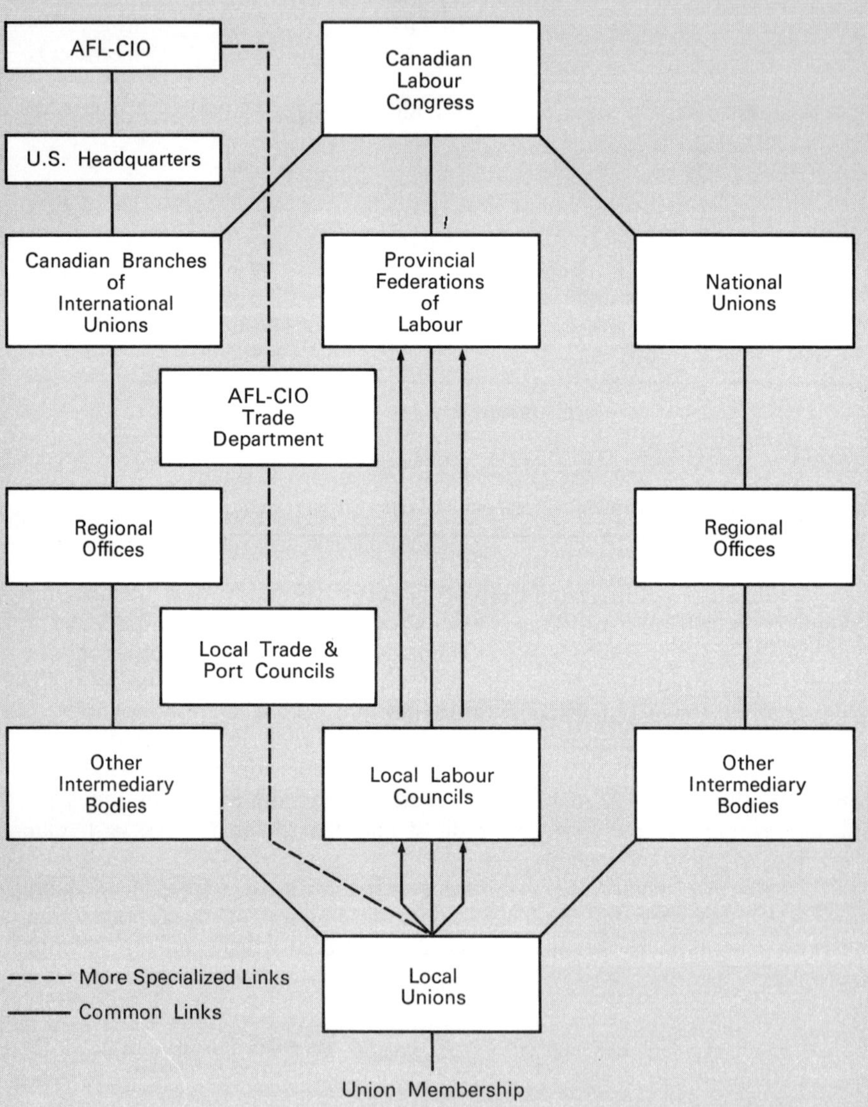

Table 3-8

GEOGRAPHIC DISTRIBUTION OF UNION MEMBERSHIP AND
OF NON-AGRICULRURAL EMPLOYMENT, CANADA 1967

Provinces	No. of Union Members	Employed Non-Agricultural Labour Force Week ended Nov. 11, 1967**	Employees Organized** Per Cent of Non-Agricultural
Atlantic	120,707	584,000	20.7
Quebec	569,430	1,967,000	28.9
Ontario	721,581	2,605,000	27.7
Prairies	198,151	1,002,000	19.8
British Columbia	240,228	716,000	33.6
Canada	1,920,647	6,874,000	27.9

* Figures rounded to nearest thousand
** Calculated
Source: Canada, Department of Labour, *Labour Gazette*, (Feb. 1968), page 94,
Table 3 and page 117, Table A-1.

by the differences in industrial employment among provinces and the uneven industrial penetration by unions that we noted earlier. Other factors include the degree of urbanization, the size of plants and the other cultural differences among regions that influence worker attitudes toward unions.

The Structure of the Contemporary Labour Movement

This section examines the way in which the Canadian labour movement is structured, focusing on the organization of the Canadian Labour Congress. Of the many organized workers remaining outside the CLC, most are in the CNTU.[26]

In many organizations, power is centralized and the greatest influence resides at the top of the organization chart. As Figure 3-1 demonstrates, this is not true of the CLC. The CLC is a loose confederation of largely autonomous international and national unions. The CLC's major functions

[25] I am indebted to Professor John Crispo for this organizational chart. See J. Crispo, *International Unionism: A Study in Canadian-American Relations* (Toronto: McGraw-Hill, 1967) p. 167.

[26] For further information on the CNTU, see the article by A. F. Isbester in this volume.

include lobbying with the federal government, representation on international bodies,[27] and on national bodies,[28] and mediating disputes among affiliates. None of these functions is central to the purpose of Canadian unionism — the negotiation and administration of collective agreements. The CLC does have a small research staff which is available to advise affiliates in this activity. In those few cases in which workers belong to locals directly affiliated to the CLC, Congress officials bargain for those workers.

The provincial federations and local councils that appear in the centre of the chart have functions similar to that of the CLC at the provincial and municipal levels. The important power centres are shown on the right and left hand sides of the chart in the slots designating the national and international unions. In most internationals, the U.S. headquarters holds considerable power governing inter-union relations, and often bargaining and strike policy as well. There are some cases, notably the United Steelworkers of America, where the Canadian district is virtually an autonomous unit within the international.

The regional offices administrate at the local level, with regional autonomy varying greatly among unions. Trade departments and local councils, on the other hand, are arrangements for coordinating the action of unions in similar or closely related jurisdictions. The degree of coordination also varies greatly among councils but seldom involves the surrender of autonomy by any union.

At the bottom of the pyramid are the local unions to which the membership has its most immediate tie. The locals are often quite powerful and in many cases formulate their own bargaining and strike policies with little interference from above. In other cases, local leaders have little power because policy is determined at the national or international level, and even contract administration is handled by representatives from central offices. In addition, the central office often holds a veto over the locals and can place dissident locals in trusteeship. The degree to which the locals are self-governing in practice varies greatly among unions and depends on the issue.

While there is considerable diversity among the individual unions in the degree of decentralization of power, this is not true of the multi-union congresses and federations. Clearly, it is the affiliated international and national unions that are the principal centres of power. These affiliates can leave the congresses at will and seldom have suffered as a result of severing this relationship.

THE PROBLEMS AND PROSPECTS OF THE LABOUR MOVEMENT

In this section, we will examine the problems and shortcomings of the contemporary labour movement and its prospects for the future. Several matters should first be clarified. Our focus on deficiencies does not in the least imply union failure or an inability to recognize the numerous achievements of organized labour. The previous two sections described the historical development of the labour movement and its present size, distribution and organization. Even in this brief survey, the significant achievement of union organization, particularly over the past thirty years, should be apparent. Union growth has been rapid; labour unions are now accepted by employers and by society as a permanent and even a positive force in our industrial community. Among many important gains, collective bargaining for workers has resulted most notably in replacing the absolute and often arbitrary authority of management with contractual provisions as well as creating a bilateral procedure for adjudicating grievances.

Any comment on union success and failure, must employ some standard. Over the years, there has been considerable conflict, both within the union movement and outside its ranks, concerning the appropriate role of unions.[29] Some have urged unions to concentrate on leading the working class to a revolution designed to overthrow capitalism and replace it with some variant of a worker controlled system. Others have suggested that unions focus on political action geared to the reform of the existing social system. For most union leaders and union members on this continent, collective bargaining designed to improve the lot of their membership at the work place, is the major goal of organized labour. Worker organization, higher wages and fringe benefits, and improved working conditions are what most unionists expect from unions. Although some also hope for effective political action, this is secondary, for the majority, to the union's function as an instrument of change at the work place. In appraising unions, the standard this discussion will employ is the standard set by most Canadian unionists themselves, namely success in organization and effectiveness in representing workers through collective bargaining.

Organizing the Unorganized

It was noted earlier that only about one-third of the non-agricultural labour force has been organized in trade unions. It is precisely in the most rapidly growing sectors (white-collar occupations, service industries, and female employees) that unions have had the least success in organizing.

---

[27] CLC delegates sit on the International Labour Organization (ILO) and on the International Confederation of Free Trade Unions (ICFTU).

[28] Often the CLC is asked to designate labour representatives to public agencies. Examples are the Economic Council of Canada and the Canada Labour Relations Board.

[29] For various views on the purposes of trade unions see S. Perlman, *A Theory of the Labour Movement* (New York: Macmillan Co. 1928); R. F. Hoxie, *Trade Unionism in the United States* (New York: Appleton Century-Crofts, 1923); S. Webb and B. Webb, *Industrial Democracy* (London: Longmans, Green and Co. 1897); F. Tannenbaum, *A Philosophy of Labour* (New York: Alfred A. Knopf, 1951); K. Marx, *Selected Works* (New York: International Publishers, 1936); and C. Kerr and A. Siegel "The Structuring of the Labour Force in Industrial Society" *Industrial and Labour Relations Review,* January 1955 p. 155 ff.

This has led some observers to predict a long term decline in the power and influence of the labour movement as its traditional areas of support become less significant. This would seem to imply that collective bargaining will also become less important as a device for setting terms and conditions of employment.

Others point to factors which indicate that this decline is not inevitable and that unions may well expand their organization and influence. In some countries, notably Sweden, a very high percentage of white-collar and professional workers belong to unions. Even in this country large numbers of white-collar workers in public service, transportation and manufacturing establishments are union members. Teachers have used their professional associations for bargaining for many years and have been highly effective. Some nurses, doctors and engineers are now following this same pattern and becoming more militant in the process. The traditional barriers to white-collar organization are disappearing. Women increasingly view paid employment as a more or less permanent feature in their lives. This should lead them to seek greater control over their work environment and re-muneration than was the case when paid work was viewed by women as a temporary phenomenon. The militancy of some nursing associations and teacher groups dominated by women in recent years is a reflection of this new attitude.

Among professional employees, there is a distinct trend away from self-employment to salaried employment. This is true even among the traditionally independent practitioners of medicine, law and pharmacy. It is even more apparent among engineers, architects and accountants. Professionals are gradually adapting to the new situation and seeking effective means of influencing their working conditions. In many cases, where employment units are small and the practitioner feels he has con-siderable bargaining power, he is content to negotiate his own terms of employment. When the employment unit grows, management is often com-pelled to formalize salary schedules and working conditions. Individual bargaining is confined to narrow limits and professionals must then act collectively to share in the determination of the formal rules governing them. This is already apparent in hospitals where salaried doctors and nurses have moved toward collective bargaining as the requirements of the provincial government regulations increasingly limit the discretion of local hospital administrators.[30]

This loss of face-to-face contact between employers and employees, applies with even greater force to the mass of non-professional white-collar workers employed in organizations of ever-increasing size. These workers (apart from those in public service) are still largely unorganized. Like the professionals, they resist joining unions, because they consider them organizations appropriate for lower status, blue-collar workers and beneath the dignity of the white-collar employee.[31] Unlike the professionals, they do not have professional organizations which can be and have been adapted for purposes of bargaining. It seems unlikely that many Canadian white-collar workers will join existing unions. More likely is the develop-ment of associations of white-collar workers at the level of the firm which then may spread to industrial, regional and national groupings similar to what is already common among blue-collar workers.

If this appraisal is accurate, within a decade we may well see new national associations and a new confederation of associations called something other than unions, with no formal ties to existing unions. This is the pattern in Sweden where there are three national groupings of employees covering professional and non-professional white-collar workers, and blue-collar workers respectively. Our traditional unions will decline in importance, although not necessarily in absolute size; however, the collective bargaining process will be spread by these new forms of organization to groups which now are largely unorganized. The first prediction, then, is that unions will decline but that collective bargaining will be extended through new organizations to a majority of the employed labour force. For many of these workers, particularly those in public service and the professions, the strike probably will not be an acceptable procedure in the bargaining process. The parties will have to evolve some mode of arbitration that will be acceptable to all concerned.

The Structure and Government of Canadian Unions

Some of the peculiarities of the Canadian Labour movement — the crucial role of the internationals, the split in Quebec between the CNTU and the CLC and the multiplicity of unions in this country — were discussed above. In addition, there are some newly emerging internal union problems, revolving around the issue of the rights of union members *vis à vis* both their unions and the collective agreements made on their behalf.

The first problem is the matter of union structure. The presence of international unions accounts for most of the peculiarities of the Canadian labour movement. Our numerous small unions can operate only because they are affiliated to the American-based internationals. If they had to operate independently, there is no doubt that most of them would not have been organized along existing lines. Rather there would be fewer, larger Canadian unions with a multi-craft, multi-industry base of organization. The fragmentation of our unions acts, in turn, to perpetuate American control over the smaller Canadian organizations.[32] In many cases, the Canadian membership is too small and too scattered to permit important staff functions such as research, education, publicity, organization and even contract administration to be conducted from Canadian headquarters.

---

[30] See D. Bell "Capitalism of the Proletariat," *Encounter*, February 1958. Reprinted in D. Bell, *The End of Ideology* (Glencoe Ill.: Free Press, 1960).

[31] This view of relative status reflects the nature of the work environment and tradition rather than differences in skill and income. Indeed, many union members earn far more than most white-collar workers and have greater skills than office employees. One union leader recently referred to the white-collar clerks as "a mass of unskilled labour."

[32] A different point of view is expressed by C. Brian Williams in his article in this volume.

The members of most of our international unions are dependent on the American headquarters for this assistance.[33]

This sometimes means that Canadian members receive little service from their internationals or that the assistance received is inappropriate. For example, many internationals publish newspapers entirely in the English language. This is suitable for most of their members, but of no value to French Canadian unionists, who are annoyed by the failure to recognize the French fact. Similarly, international representatives sent to Canada by American unions often are unfamiliar with Canadian legislation or Canadian conditions. Attempts to transfer American practice to Canada do not always work.

The existence of the CNTU as a separate trade union centre is largely a reflection of French Canadian separatist tendencies in many facets of our social life. However, the relations between the CNTU and the CLC are probably more strained than they would otherwise be because most of the CLC unions are internationals. The CNTU would be more willing to cooperate if not to merge with a purely Canadian union movement. CLC unions would have greater freedom to work out arrangements for such cooperation if they were not tied by rules set by the internationals.

Union fragmentation combined with the difficulties of organizing the unorganized, have produced bitter inter-union battles for the allegiance of workers. Unions find it increasingly easier to raid rival unions than to extend organization to those outside the union fold. The result is a union game of musical chairs with workers shifting among unions but little in the way of net additions to the union movement as a whole. This absorbs the time and energies of union leaders and much of the union's treasury. It also often results in adverse publicity. With fewer unions, there would be less raiding and perhaps more success in extending labour organization.

Although much of this discussion has been critical of the role of international unions in Canada, there is a great deal to be said in favour of the link to American unions. Organization of workers in Canada would have been retarded in the absence of assistance from the United States, and Canadian workers continue to benefit from the advice and resources available to them in international unions. Canadian unions can disaffiliate, albeit at some sacrifice, yet few have chosen to do so. Through the leverage gained in international bargaining with United States based corporations, Canadian workers in the tin can, automobile and other industries have won unprecedented wage increases, which they could not have achieved otherwise. Professor Crispo in his study of the impact of international unions concludes "from the point of view of international unionism itself, the relationship is clearly positive".[34]

Yet the link with American unions has produced a peculiar kind of structure in our unions. Both Canadian nationalism and French Canadian separatism are on the ascendancy in Canada. The resolution of these conflicting trends is difficult to foresee. What is already clear is that unions in which French Canadians are unable to play a leading role are unlikely to survive in Quebec. In effect, this means that few internationals will survive in that province. Furthermore, it would seem that even in other parts of the country, Canadian workers will seek greater independence, even at some sacrifice of bargaining power. Those internationals that are large enough in Canada and are possessed of foresight may make concessions sufficient for their survival in Canada. However, most internationals will be unwilling or unable to do so. This may result in a rupture of the relationship through rebellion of Canadian workers perhaps assisted by Canadian legislation. Our prediction then is that over the next decade, the ties of Canadian workers to American-based unions will be loosened or dissolved. This will be accompanied by the merger of many existing unions to form fewer, larger and stronger Canadian unions. It would be foolhardy to predict the future relationship between workers in Quebec and those elsewhere in Canada, or the precise way in which the union movement may be restructured.

The other key matter involving internal union affairs is the relationship of union members to their unions. Perhaps the greatest achievement of unions has been the curb placed on the arbitrary exercise of managerial authority and the opportunity provided for the impartial adjudication of worker grievances. In the course of attaining these objectives, workers find that new threats to their freedom have emerged. In a few unions, the rank and file has lost control to autocratic leaders who in some instances have abused their power to enhance their own wealth and influence. Democratic procedures are not followed. Corruption and favouritism prevail. Leaders sign "sweetheart" contracts to the disadvantage of the members and union funds are misappropriated. It should be emphasized that such practices are rare. Most unions are run reasonably democratically and honestly. This is not easy in organizations geared to constant combat where dissent and treason are readily confused. Yet the disclosure of union abuses both in the United States and Canada is cause for concern.[35]

The CLC and the majority of honest unions are unable to check the abuses in these few cases. Too often the members are equally helpless in securing reforms. The disclosure of abuses within some unions, however, damages the public image of all unions. There seems little doubt that over the next few years, governments will intervene to ensure that minimum standards of democratic procedures and financial practices are adhered to. Governments will regulate union operated, hiring halls and other institutions to protect workers from discriminatory or arbitrary practices. Unions will

---

[33] By far, the best study of international unions is J. Crispo, *International Unionism: A Study in Canadian-American Relations* (Toronto: McGraw-Hill, 1967). On page 169, Professor Crispo shows that research, public relations and education staff are found in some of the larger Canadian unions but are totally absent in unions with less than 10,000 Canadian members.

[34] See J. Crispo, *International Unionism*, p. 321.

[35] See *Hearings and Final Report of the Select Committee on Improper Activities in the Labour or Management Field*, U.S. Senate, Eighty-sixth Congress (Washington: Government Printing Office, 1960) and *Report of the Industrial Inquiry Commission on The Disruption of Shipping* (Ottawa: Queen's Printer, 1963).

resist further public controls but are unlikely to prevent the passage of new legislation.[36]

Even in the unions that are run honestly and reasonably democratically, workers often find themselves at odds with their union leaders. Union leaders are concerned with the survival of their unions and with their own relationships to the corporate and government officials with whom they deal. In the course of their day-to-day activities, the union officers may find it expedient to concede some matters for the sake of good will and with the expectation that in the long run management will repay these favours. To the workers, such actions are often viewed as a "sell out." Furthermore, the collective agreement itself is becoming burdensome. This is paradoxical because such agreements were intended to liberate workers from arbitrary rule by spelling out the respective rights of the parties. These contracts have become so increasingly lengthy, detailed and complex that workers often are unable to understand their rights. Employment conditions have come to be rigidly defined with less opportunity to accommodate special cases. For example, in many agreements time allowed for the use of washroom facilities is defined to include specified periods of the day (e.g. ten minutes in mid-morning and ten minutes in mid-afternoon).

Contemporary trend in our society is to go against the number of restrictive rules under which we live. In the area of public law, legislation regulating personal morality is under attack. In our schools, students have successfully undermined rules governing dress, deportment, smoking and even attendance requirements. This trend will inevitably spread to the work place and leaders of unions and managers of corporations will have to adapt to these new demands. As in the schools, habit and tradition will stand in the way of successful adaptation. On the other hand, the success of collective bargaining and the amiable relationships built up between management and union officials in many situations will open up the opportunity for successful adaptation where the parties have the foresight to initiate change.

Our prediction is that there will be growing pressure from workers for less rigidly defined contractual terms of employment and more emphasis on mutual trust between managers and the managed. Where this is not forthcoming, there will be violent strikes, often with ill-defined objectives and frequently led by rank and file workers in opposition to the official union leadership.

Bargaining in the Public Service: The Canadian Experience

The growing interest in collective bargaining within the public sector in both Canada and the United States is obvious. This is apparent both in the figures on unionization of public service employees at all levels of government and in the increasing discussion in labour relations literature of the problems of collective bargaining in the public sector. Most of the discussion focuses on the problems of adapting private sector bargaining practices to the particular situation of government employment relations.

Although it is acknowledged that there are many similarities in the employer-employee relationship in public and in private employment, the focus has been on the differences.

Many arguments propose that the employer-employee relationship in the public sector demands a special bargaining process. The foremost of these arguments involves the sovereignty of the state. The role of "participant" in the collective bargaining process, it is argued, constitutes a threat to the sovereignty of the state. Furthermore, the state cannot be seen to yield to the dictates of a group of its employers under the pressure of a strike, or even to the decrees of an arbitrator or arbitration tribunal without some loss of its sovereignty. Yet, most proponents generally agree that the issue is not serious. The state engages in negotiations with all sorts of private firms for the purchase of various goods that it requires. Contracts are signed and, during the negotiations, the state often faces the threat of a refusal to enter into contract by the private firm. No one has ever alleged that a loss of sovereignty is involved. As for arbitration, the state often submits to suits against it in the courts of the land and abides by the decision of these courts. Again no one would argue that there was any challenge to the sovereignty of state involved.

In the following quotation Jacob Finkelman has succinctly commented on this issue:

Ideological concepts such as sovereignty are often no more than political myths functioning to preserve the existing social structure. Even looking at the matter from a theoretical or philosophical point of view, there is no greater surrender of sovereignty in a legislature delegating to an arbitration tribunal authority to make a decision in the area here under discussion than there is in the enactment of a statute which provides that the courts shall have power to adjudicate certain types of disputes between the state and a private citizen and award damages to the latter which the state is required to pay. The concept that the sovereign can do no wrong, that actions in tort cannot be brought against the state, and that actions in contract can only be instituted against the state if express consent to their institution is granted by the sovereign to the citizen, say by petition of right, is now generally recognized as being outmoded, and it has been abandoned in many jurisdictions without any great outcry that the legislature in so doing has surrendered its sovereignty. There would appear to be no reason in theory, then, why the sovereignty concept should be perpetuated in the field of labor relations.[37]

There is no single model which can be described as the Canadian model in collective bargaining for public servants. The practices vary

---

[36] A possible model for new Canadian legislation is provided in the American Labour Management Reporting and Disclosure Act, 73 Stat., 519, Public Law 83-267, especially Titles I-IV.

[37] J. Finkelman "When Bargaining Fails" in K. O. Warner (ed.) *Collective Bargaining in the Public Service: Theory and Practice,* (Chicago: Public Personnel Association, 1967) p. 120.

greatly among different levels of government — federal, provincial and municipal. Municipal employees have long operated largely under legislation very similar to that applicable in the private sector, with the exception of policemen and firemen who are forbidden to strike under various acts.

Provincial bargaining arrangements vary throughout Canada. In Ontario, the civil service employees, with the exception of workers in liquor stores, provincial police and a few other groups, are organized in a single large association. The Civil Service Association of Ontario bargains on behalf of about 43,000 employees. Because strikes are illegal in public employment, the parties have agreed to submit unresolved interest disputes to a tripartite arbitration tribunal. The arbitration tribunal's awards are final and binding insofar as the provincial government has always agreed to implement them. There is no reason to expect that the province will deviate from past practice unless it felt that there was a real threat to the public interest in the arbitration award.

Saskatchewan, Quebec and New Brunswick go even further in providing for the right of employees in the provincial civil service to engage in strikes. The legislation providing the right to strike for public employees was first enacted in Saskatchewan in 1944. Quebec followed in 1964 with provision for strikes among provincial civil servants, hospital employees, and teachers. More recently the province of New Brunswick enacted legislation that provides public service employees with the right to strike. In all cases arbitration is an alternative to strike but only if both sides agreed to submit to binding arbitration. In all cases, there is provision for preventing strikes among employees engaged in essential services. In Quebec, there is provision for delaying a work stoppage in the case of strikes endangering "public health or safety" or "interfering with education" for a period of eighty days by act of the provincial government while an inquiry proceeds. In Saskatchewan, in 1966, an Essential Emergency Act was passed under which the provincial cabinet could forestall or end a strike in a named list of public services deemed to be essential.[38] In these cases compulsory arbitration applies. In New Brunswick the withdrawal of the services of certain employees is designated to be a threat to the "health, safety or security of the public." These employees cannot engage in strikes even though other members of the same bargaining unit may be permitted to strike. New Brunswick legislation also contains an interesting provision that outlaws picketing but also outlaws the employment of the strike-breakers by the provincial government.

The Canadian Federal Government's approach to collective bargaining is probably the most interesting experiment in Canada. It covers the largest number of employees but, more important, it includes most of the innovations found in the provincial legislation as well as some unique features of its own.[39] Most federal employees come under the Public Service Staff Relations Act (PSSRA). The exceptions are members of the armed forces, the Royal Canadian Mounted Police and those federal employees in agencies that fall under the Industrial Relations Disputes Investigation Act.[40] Confidential and managerial employees are excluded from this legislation; however, the definition of confidential and managerial in the federal legislation is quite narrow. Indeed many supervisory employees who, under legislation covering the private sector, might be considered managerial are in fact permitted to organize and engage in collective bargaining. They are permitted to belong to the same union as those whom they direct and in some cases, they can be included in the same bargaining unit as those they manage. Only about 3 per cent of federal civil servants have been excluded from bargaining because of their managerial or confidential capacity. The Public Service Staff Relations Act covers over 200,000 employees, most of whom are civil servants under the jurisdiction of the Treasury Board acting as the employer. It also includes eight separate employers covering workers in the following agencies: The Atomic Energy Control Board, The Centennial Commission, The Defense Research Board, The Economic Council of Canada, the Fisheries Research Board, The National Film Board, The National Research Council and the Northern Canada Power Commission. Workers covered by the PSSRA are scattered among seventy-five departments and agencies across Canada; some of them even serve overseas. They cover a wide range of occupations from unskilled labour to highly skilled research scientists, lawyers, physicians and so on. The bargaining units are unusual, including as they do a very large group of professionals (doctors, lawyers, dentists, engineers).

Almost all eligible federal employees have elected to engage in collective bargaining and have joined together in certified bargaining units. The legislation is administered by the Public Service Staff Relations Board, which has been established specifically to deal with the collective bargaining arrangements in the federal civil service. The Board is tripartite in nature and has many of the functions found in labour relations boards covering employees in the private sector. The Board decides on the appropriate bargaining unit, conducts certification proceedings, certifies the bargaining unit, hears questions of alleged unfair labour practices, and so forth. (The Board has other functions which are not normally carried on by labour relations boards that cover private employees.) The Chairman of the Board is a permanent appointee of the government who is acceptable to all concerned. In addition to the Chairman, there is a panel of employee nominees from the various major unions engaged in bargaining with the government and there is a panel of employer nominees. All cases that go before the Board are heard by a tripartite panel where employer-employee representatives appear in equal numbers.

[38] The Saskatchewan essential services emergency act of 1966 covers water, heat, electricity, gas, hospitals. The cabinet in these cases can impose arbitration. The chairman of the arbitration board must be a judge and if the parties cannot agree on the chairman, the cabinet appoints him. This tends to load the boards in favour of the government. Illegal strikes can result in the certification by cabinet order.

[39] The New Brunswick legislation is modelled very closely on the federal act.

[40] The IRDI Act is the one which covers employees in the private sector under federal jurisdiction. It includes workers in the crown corporation such as the Canadian National Railroad, The Canadian Broadcasting Corp. etc.

There is also a tripartite arbitration tribunal established to hear interest disputes. The tribunal has a permanent Chairman who is acceptable to all parties. In addition it has a panel of employer nominees and a panel of employee nominees. Each arbitration case is heard by a three man panel, consisting of the Chairman plus a nominee from each of the panels. The decisions of the tribunal, however, are the decisions of the Chairman.

The final piece of machinery established by the government to fulfill its purposes is the appointment of an adjudicator to handle grievance disputes under the collective agreements. There is a chief adjudicator who is acceptable to all parties and his efforts are supplemented by other adjudicators who assist him. The grievance machinery is open not only to those who are eligible to engage in collective bargaining and choose to do so but to other employees who either choose not to bargain or are ineligible for collective bargaining.

The legislation significantly differs from the private sector in its definition of the scope of collective bargaining. Certain matters that are specifically precluded from collective bargaining include the following.
1. Anything that requires action by Parliament, except for the granting of money to carry out the collective agreements is precluded from bargaining.
2. Matters covered by the following legislation, the Government Employees Compensation Act, the Government Vessel Discipline Act, the Public Service Employment Act, and the Public Service Superannuation Act are precluded from bargaining.

The latter pieces of legislation are designed primarily to protect the merit principle of appointment, transfer, and promotion which are excluded from collective bargaining. They also cover matters such as superannuation, death benefits and accident compensation which are also outside the scope of bargaining. All of these issues are open to discussion by the parties through the National Joint Council composed of most of the major associations engaged in bargaining with the government and the representatives of the government. The discussions, however, are advisory to the government only. The government also exercises unilateral control over the classification system and job assignments.

Under the federal legislation, the bargaining agent is given the option of choosing between two possible routes for resolving any dispute that cannot be resolved through negotiation. The bargaining agent may choose to submit the dispute to a conciliation board. Should the board fail to resolve the dispute the bargaining agent is then free to engage in a strike. The alternative is to submit the dispute to arbitration with conciliation by a conciliation officer as a possibility prior to arbitration. The government is bound under the legislation to accept the decision of the bargaining agent as to the route chosen. This provides the bargaining agent with a very powerful weapon in collective bargaining. Groups that are unwilling or unable to engage in effective strike action can compel the government to submit disputes to compulsory arbitration. Other groups that may find the strike an effective weapon can in fact engage in work stoppages. The bargaining agent is free to alter its choice of route from one set of contract negotiations to the other. It must, however, designate the route to be followed prior to beginning of collective bargaining on a given contract.

At the end of 1969, of the 110 instances in which a bargaining agent has designated the route to be chosen, ninety-eight bargaining agents bargaining for 158,900 employees had chosen arbitration while only twelve bargaining units with 37,700 employees had selected the conciliation board strike route in the event that negotiations fail.

In order to handle the problem of emergency services, which are defined under the federal legislation as services which if not performed threaten the "safety and security of the public," there is provision for designating employees who are not permitted to engage in strikes. The bargaining agent is entitled to some information on the likely number of designated employees prior to its selection of the appropriate bargaining route. It can ask the employer to submit a list of employees who the employer wishes to designate should a strike occur. The employer is required to submit such a list very soon after request is received. The bargaining agent may choose to accept some or all of the employer's notion of designated employees. Should it decide to challenge a portion of the list of designated employees, the case is decided by the Public Service Staff Relations Board. Once the number of designated employees is known, the bargaining agent then proceeds to select the appropriate route. Thus far, in all those cases where the bargaining agent has requested a list of designated employees, about 13.6 per cent of employees in these bargaining units have been designated. Of course, the proportions designated will vary greatly among bargaining units.

The disputes that are submitted to arbitration are subject to a variety of stipulations. The most important would appear to be the following.

1. No matter may be brought before the arbitration tribunal that has not been raised earlier in collective bargaining. All matters that are excluded by law from bargaining are of course not subject to arbitration.

2. In addition, there are certain issues that are bargainable but not subject to arbitration. Arbitration is limited under Section 70 to "rates of pay, hours of work, leave entitlement, standards of discipline and other terms and conditions of employment directly related thereto." Under Section 56, Arbitration Tribunals cannot deal with matters that require action by Parliament, except for the expenditure of the funds. Arbitration under Section 70 specifically cannot deal with the merit principle of appointment assignment, lay-off or release nor can it deal with matters involving workers not in the bargaining unit who are disputed before the arbitration tribunal. For example, while the parties are free under Section 70, to deal with a matter such as union security through negotiations, the Arbitration Board cannot deal with such a matter should the parties fail to resolve it during the process of bargaining.

The most significant problems experienced under the federal legislation appear to be the following.

1. *Fragmentation of the bargaining units.* The certification procedures followed under the Act have resulted in a very large number of bargaining

units in the federal public service. Some fragmentation was necessary and desirable, given the enormous size and diversity of employment in the public service; however, the degree of fragmentation has probably been excessive. It leaves many of the bargaining units too weak to find the strike option a really effective one. Strikes could occur in many of these bargaining units for considerable periods of time with little pressure on the employer for any kind of settlement. Fragmentation also opens the question of whip sawing by the bargaining agents as they use either the strike or arbitration process to secure a gain for one group of employees, which they then attempt to spread to other groups of employees. Finally, too many issues are constantly being negotiated. The employer is constantly bargaining simultaneously with various bargaining agents. Some of the larger associations bargain for a sizeable number of bargaining units and they too are constantly engaged in collective bargaining with the same employer. In each of these bargaining sessions the same issues come up again and again, particularly in the fringe benefit and working conditions area. The parties too often are bargaining with an eye to what precedents may be set in other groups. This creates all sorts of problems in collective bargaining and also for the arbitration process because the arbitrators must be conscious of the implications of their decision in a given case on other groups of employees. If arbitrators take this consideration too seriously then they may refuse to innovate in the area of fringe benefits and working conditions for fear of opening up the possibility of whip saw.

2. *Limitations on the scope of arbitration.* Since the subjects that can be dealt with under arbitration are much narrower than those that can be dealt with through the collective bargaining process, the bargaining agents often find that the employer can use the threat of forcing arbitration in order to compel the bargaining agents to agree. Thus the employer may indicate his willingness to make concessions on certain matters not subject to arbitration only if the bargaining agent foregoes arbitration. Otherwise the employer may refuse to concede these matters and, in effect, impose arbitration.

Public Concern Over the Substantive Issues in Collective Bargaining

North American legislation has focused on promoting collective bargaining procedures by facilitating union organization, requiring "good faith" bargaining and providing facilities for mediation of disputes. The premise behind our legislation is that the interest of the state ends once the parties are brought to the bargaining table. The actual terms of agreement that result from the bargaining process are assumed to be of interest only to the parties directly involved. This attitude has undergone some change over the years. Minimum wage laws as well as legislation restricting working hours and regulating vacations, safety conditions and so on have placed a floor on conditions which may be negotiated in agreements. This kind of regulation has a long tradition in laws governing child and female labour, some of which predate collective bargaining. In recent years, however, statutory regulation of labour standards has increased. We may expect state regulation to expand further in the future.

Related to the state's interest in minimum standards at the work place is a growing government involvement in minimum incomes and services for all citizens, whether in or out of the labour force. Public pensions, health insurance and other similar programmes are constantly expanding in scope. As they expand, they make fringe benefits negotiated through collective bargaining less significant. A wide variety of welfare benefit programmes has been initiated through collective bargaining. However, these benefits are unequally distributed and large sectors of society are excluded from coverage. Public pressure has intervened to force the creation of universal programmes which tend to displace negotiated fringe benefits, and as some fringe benefits are removed from the bargaining table, unions demand and secure new programmes. With time many of these will also be taken over by the state.

A final consideration is the most controversial area of public policy as it relates to collective bargaining. In the years since World War II we have increasingly delegated to the state, the responsibility for achieving our national economic goals. The goals most frequently stated as generally accepted in our society include full employment, stable prices, rapid economic growth, stability in our foreign exchange rate and greater equity in income distribution.[41] It would appear that the simultaneous achievement of these objectives is impossible in an economy where prices and wages are determined by market forces and where markets are subject to "imperfections" that cause them to operate quite differently from what is predicted by the economist's model of perfect competition. Among these market imperfections, we include unions and collective bargaining. Experience in a number of countries suggests that, as we move closer to our objective of achieving full employment, we face stronger inflationary pressures. This, in turn, puts pressure on our foreign exchange and also adversely affects income distribution. Conversely, when inflationary pressures subside, unemployment becomes more serious. This, in turn, inhibits economic growth and also adversely influences income distribution.[42] Governments face strong pressures to achieve all of these goals simultaneously. The obvious solution would appear to lie in public control over market decisions on prices and wages. The degree of control that is advocated ranges from outright nationalization of industry to wage and price controls or to mere requests that those wielding economic power exercise self-restraint.

This is not the place to evaluate the various solutions proposed to resolve the policy dilemma we now face. Clearly, both labour and

---

[41] See Economic Council of Canada, *Fourth Annual Review, The Canadian Economy from the 1960's to the 1970's* (Ottawa: Queen's Printer, 1967).
[42] See Bodkin et al, *Price Stability and High Employment: The Options for Canadian Economic Policy: An Econometric Study* (Ottawa: Queen's Printer, 1967).

management will face increasing pressures to justify publicly the decisions they have taken. Where the public finds these decisions unacceptable, it seems likely that the state will be forced to alter these private decisions. Governments may intervene directly to control these decisions by setting ceilings on wages and prices or indirectly by curbing the market power of unions and management.

The latter course is expected to be the route preferred in our economy. This would imply action to strengthen the anti-combines legislation and to find comparable machinery for limiting the bargaining power of unions. Achieving such controls is not easy; identifying and measuring market power is also difficult. Curbing market power often leads to undesirable effects in other areas.[43] If these difficulties are not resolved, governments will probably turn to more direct forms of regulation which, over a period of time, may make unions obsolete or at least force a drastic revision in what we now view as the role of unions.

---

[43] For example, large firms may be necessary for efficiency. Large powerful unions may be the only effective devices for processing worker grievances and protecting workers rights.

4

THE PHILOSOPHY
OF THE CANADIAN
LABOUR MOVEMENT

Aranka E. Kovacs

INTRODUCTION[1]

This essay examines the basic objectives and attitudes that have motivated the Canadian labour movement. Within the framework of the essay, the origins, emergence and growth pattern of Canadian unionism are examined and the philosophy that has been and is the moving force behind the organization will be discerned. At the outset, the concepts of "philosophy" and "movement," as they apply in this discussion, must be defined. An organization emerges when a group of people who share a common situation accept a common objective that may be realized for the collective group. Hoxie explained the origins of unions in this way:

It goes back in its genesis ultimately to the common needs and problems of the wage-workers; it arises immediately out of the consciousness of the common or group character of those needs and problems; it exists for common action looking to the betterment of the living conditions; it appears primarily as a group interpretation of the social situation in which the workers find themselves.[2]

[1] The study under examination has received financial support on a number of occasions from the Canada Council and the Department of Labour — University Research Committee. I gratefully acknowledge their support for the research. A preliminary paper on the subject matter has been published. See A. E. Kovacs, "A Tentative Framework for the Philosophy of the Canadian Labour Movement," *Relations Industrielles Revue Trimestrielle, (Industrial Relations Quarterly Review)*, Laval University, Vol. 20, No. 1, (January 1965).

[2] R. F. Hoxie, *Trade Unionism in the United States*, (New York: D. Appleton & Co., 1920), p. 59-60. By permission Hawthorne Books Inc.

The goals and attitudes that are conditioned by the environment or common situation constitute the philosophy for any organization and the philosophy to which the group adheres gives it the motivating drive that allows the organization to develop. A basic assumption of this study is that the Canadian labour movement is motivated by a philosophy that has given the movement its purpose and identity. Such a philosophy may embrace both short-term objectives and a long-term ideology and aims.

Any definition of the Canadian labour movement must recognize that the movement is composed of many diverse and autonomous labour unions. The existence of separate unions, however, does not constitute a "movement"; it is when these individual labour organizations voluntarily unite under a formal structure and when they endorse and adopt a common philosophy that they can be called a "movement." A labour movement, then, is held together and sustained by a broadly defined purpose and a common direction. As an institution it represents many complex relationships contingent not only upon economic forces, but also on psychological, political and social motivations and drives. Since the labour movement is a dynamic force in society, it is subject to change in a progressive economy. Trade union organizations also change with the alterations occurring in a progressive nation; conversely, by changing and adopting, the labour movement also acts on and influences the direction and evolution of the social structure in which it exists and functions. That is, while the development of the trade union movement is affected by the social, political and economic structure in which it is allowed to grow, as a social force it too is influential in shaping that environment, directly or indirectly, through its collective activities and policies.

The labour movement, then, is defined in this study as a dynamic organizational instrument created by workers and emerging as an institutional force independent of the state and the employers. It embraces a philosophy which provides the movement with the institutional drive necessary for its survival and development. Since the movement is an evolutionary force, its philosophy is also subject to alteration with the times. Composed of a wide variety of union organizations, the labour movement is thus continuously facing pressures in its internal relationships and from its external environment. The movement in any period or age may, therefore, be motivated and impelled by a philosophy that is not the same as the one held in the previous period; furthermore, that philosophy will not necessarily be adopted in the future. Consequently, because the Canadian labour movement, as a dynamic institution, has passed through various stages of growth and development, the philosophy behind the movement cannot be examined without referring to its historical evolution. For the purpose of this study, the philosophy of the labour movement will be related to three distinct stages of union growth.

The nature of the subject matter demands generalizations about the labour movement as a whole, because union philosophy is not clearly and precisely articulated. Because the philosophy of the labour movement is not given to us as an academic formula or as an intellectually conceived plan of society, it is necessary to interpret the words of labour leaders as they reflect the "grass roots" philosophy of the rank and file union member. Throughout the history of the movement, the leadership has been an extremely important influence on union development. The recent Woods Report maintained that,

One of the advantages of a pluralistic society is the multiplicity of organizations competing to serve different interests. In this sense, the labour movement has often mirrored the wider society. It is made up of myriad individual units which frequently differ in structure or philosophy or both . . . Philosophically, the spread covers everything from a small number of unions purportedly dedicated to the radical transformation of society to a large number of craft unions interested in the preservation of the existing system. Between lies the bulk of the labour movement, with a membership primarily interested in bread and butter gains, and a leadership determined to provide those gains while working toward the gradual reform of society.[3]

In the past, the Canadian leaders have been enthusiastic, practical and outspoken men who have rebelled against certain injustices in the work situation, and not intellectuals looking at labour in the abstract and rebelling against what they consider to be injustices in society. Union leaders in the past have come up from the ranks and, in most instances, what they lacked in formal education was made up by a keen awareness of practical issues. For this reason it often appears that labour organizations pursued their work-conscious policies pragmatically, being content to have their idealism articulated through the broader base of the central Congresses. If we attach great importance to leadership in the movement and if the leadership is more formally educated in the future, it is possible that the philosophy, the common goals and the direction of the movement will be significantly altered.

A labour economist has stated:

In considering the intellectual basis for broad social movements, the strictures of precise scientific method must obviously be strained. Such resources as interpretive analysis and even insight, with the test of reasonableness, must necessarily be involved.[4]

Because the labour movement does not lend itself readily to the precision and rigour of theoretical economic analyses, the division of union growth into three stages of development is an attempt to provide a framework for the analysis. First, in the *formative* stage of union growth, the unions emerged. There was a display of fraternal dedication and loyalty to a cause which gave unionism a sense of mission and idealism. Second, in the *establishment* stage, the trade unions that comprised the labour movement were legally allowed to function and grow. It was in this stage that

---

[3] The Report of the Task Force on Labour Relations, *Canadian Industrial Relations*, (The Woods Report), Ottawa, 1965, p. 105.
[4] L. Reed Tripp, *Labour Problems and Processes*, (New York: Harper and Brothers, 1961), p. 57.

collective bargaining became widespread, and a pragmatic philosophy permeated the movement. Third, in the *power* stage of development, labour organizations took on features of large scale enterprise, expanding their scope and power and exerting a relatively greater degree of influence on public policy and on society.

A basic assumption of this analysis is that Canadian unionism originated in response to industrialism. In other words, unionism is a worker movement emerging to meet certain conditions that arose from industrial capitalism. Although the philosophy of the movement has changed, with the changing nature of capitalism, pragmatism and idealism are considered in this article as a philosophy. Viewing the labour movement as a response to industrial capitalism is a traditional approach that follows the theories of the labour movement as developed by the Webbs, Marx, Perlman, and Tannenbaum. Yet the analysis is unique in that the three-part approach is developmental and evolutionary.

THE FORMATIVE YEARS

In the formative stage of labour organization in Canada, the union was a vehicle for protest against the grievances arising from the job situation and against the inequalities experienced by workers in the broader economic and political environment. The craft labour unions protested against the loss of status as the early skilled tradesmen met the impact of technological progress. By joining together into trade unions the craftsmen believed that they could more effectively protect their waning status in the changing stream of industrialization.[5] Protection and security on the job were the chief concerns of these early craft workers. As industrialization progressed and the composition of the labour force changed, the new industrial workers protested against low wages and poor working conditions in the factories. Both the craftsmen and the industrial workers were concerned with their status, the former in preserving it and the latter in defining it. In 1898, D. A. Carey, the outgoing President of the Trades and Labour Congress pointedly summed up the function of unionism when he stated that trade unions:

represent the aggregate expression of the discontent of labour with existing economic, social and political misrule.

He further maintained:

the trade union is the best form of organization for the toilers to protect their present interests and work out their future welfare.[6]

With the spread of industrialism and the growth of the factory system, the labourers were soon tied to the machines in the production process and thereby to the new organizational structure. Those who were directly affected by the rate of change in the working environment shared a culture, distinct from that of other segments of society. Tannenbaum's analysis provides a functional explanation for the original emergence of organization among workers in western industrial states:

What the workers had in common was their employer, the industry they worked in, the hours they labored, the bench or the machine they worked at, the wage rate they received, the foremen who ruled over them, the materials they worked with, the whistle that called them from their labors. In addition, they had each other in common. They worked together at the same bench, inside the same mill or mine, struggled with the same refactory materials, and were dependent upon one another's co-operation. Here was a new social factor. The same process that had gathered these laborers together had forged a "society" in which a sense of identity became inevitable. Their mutual association and experience, their similar skills, their relationship at the work bench, the tools they used, and the materials with which they worked gave them a common language. They acquired the language of the craft, the job, the shop, and the industry.[7]

Neither the working environment described by Tannenbaum nor the grievances arising in the workplace were alien to the development of industrialism in Canada. Poor working conditions, low wages, long hours of work and a sense of alienation and insecurity characterized the situation. Although the labour organizations that emerged were concerned with raising the labourer's wages and reducing the hours of work, the new unions were also very much concerned with the "dignity" of labour and with the "humanization" of industry. This concern was emphasized by the leaders in such statements as the following:

Labor is the only line of greatness that has survived the swift and devastating changes of time. You are laborers and ought to be proud of it . . . Yield not an inch of your just dues and true dignity to any hostile forces. Measure your dues by your merits, and let your dignity be commensurate with your honour and self-esteem.[8]

Thus, early unions were voluntary organizations in which labourers were brought together by common discontent and a search for status and security. Daniel J. O'Donoghue remarked,

The trade-unions are the legitimate out-growths of modern society and industrial conditions. They are not the creation of any man's brain. They

---

[5] A. E. Kovacs, "The Knights of St. Crispin in Canada," *Canadian Labour,* Ottawa, Vol. 11, No. 4, (April, 1966). The shoemakers represent only one example of the early formation of trade union organization for the protection of the status of the craft workers, who were affected by technological progress that was transforming the industry.

[6] D. A. Carey, *14th Annual Convention Proceedings,* Trades and Labour Congress, (1898).

[7] F. Tannenbaum, *A Philosophy of Labour,* (New York: Alfred A. Knopf, 1951), p. 59.

[8] *The Labour Union,* Knights of Labour newspaper, Hamilton, Ontario, February 10, 1883.

are organizations of necessity. They were born of the necessity of the workers to protect and defend themselves from encroachment, injustice and wrong. They are the organizations of the working class, for the working class, by the working class;[9]

While the trade union became a vehicle for grievance protests against the immediate job conditions, unionism also became a crusade for humanitarian working conditions. Labour and the workers were idealized; their dignity and honour were stressed. Spokesmen urged that

It should be the pride and pleasure of every workingman in the city to join heartily in this movement for the elevation of his class.[10]

and

Men must be roused to a full consciousness of their dignity as men, their power as citizens and their rights as toilers to equal opportunities and an equal share of natural resources.[11]

More radical organizations, such as the One Big Union which embraced a left-wing political philosophy, stressed not only class conflict but the worth and dignity of labour:

In assimilating the platform of the One Big Union [the worker] is doing something for himself and his family and for his class at the same time. His happiness lies in the hope inspired by the better understanding of his position and the position of his class.[12]

Unionism emphasized that the union member, through his union organization, gained a sense of self-respect and security that mechanization tended to obliterate or suppress. The search for identity and security was an important element in the emergence of early trade unionism. As the movement became imbued with an idealism and missionary zeal that looked towards a vision of a better life in the future, labour leaders reiterated:

Underlying all trade union purposes is a great yearning to remove the causes of human injustice and to enable all to have a chance to develop and find satisfaction in living.[13]

The idealism pervading the movement gave it a vitality and vigour that carried it forward even when the struggle for recognition and acceptance became acute. The new organizing drives were led by men who believed they were crusaders for a cause; the environment, therefore, was often charged with emotional and moral currents. Spreading their convictions and beliefs to the unorganized was the chief duty of the leadership in their attempts to unionize the workshop. Leaders and workers belonged to the same labouring group and they identified their common grievances with injustices beyond the immediate job situation. Demands for shorter hours, better working conditions and higher wages were naturally blended with social goals such as justice, equality and welfare.

To join the union took considerable courage, but once in the labour movement a man was caught up in the struggle to lift the burden of ignorance, poverty, and injustice that pressed on every hand. The need of the times drew out a sense of dedication in Canada's labour leaders, and a concern for social good, that could hardly be matched in any other group. Labour was urging manhood suffrage, free schools, safety precautions on railways, factory inspection, and a separate court for juvenile offenders. What were other sections of the community saying on these matters?[14]

Characteristic also of the formative years of unionism in Canada was an awareness of a "working class" and a consciousness of union members that they belonged to a class. In Canada, this structure was loosely regarded and the theoretical labour-capital division was not rigidly emphasized except by unions that adhered to a leftist ideology. Even when the emerging unions met bitter resistance from employers, the "labour-capital" conflict was used as propaganda to fight individual managements rather than being a rigidly held ideology as a basis to change the existing social structure. Yet the awareness of a working class remained, as labour protest was channelled into discontent and resentment of local employers, even though the struggle for recognition was not transferred to a struggle for working class domination of industry. The fight for recognition gave the working class a militant spirit, and it was this militancy that carried it forward.

With the struggle for recognition and the accompanying militancy, cleavages developed between the radical and conservative elements within the unions. Division and factionalism within created diverging ideologies. The more conservative elements emphasized the role of unions to be that of reform instruments pressing for changes in labour legislation, the wage system, and factory conditions. They regarded the unions as avenues of gradual social reform. The position of the conservative "working classes" was expressed by the President of the Trades and Labour Congress at the turn of the century when he stated:

The processes of reform are gradual, but our enterprising should be constant; we never want to weaken our forces by concluding that because our needs are not met quickly we ought to despair. We have no right to expect that our aims and objects should be brought about by revolution, for even revolutions have to be matured by an evolutionary process. Thus,

---

[9] D. J. O'Donoghue, "Canadian Labour Interests and Movements," *Encyclopedia of Canada*, 1900, p. 258. (A photostat copy of O'Donoghue's article was made by the T.L.C. and this is now deposited in the library of the Canadian Labour Congress, Ottawa).

[10] *The Labour Union*, February 3, 1883.

[11] Ibid, March 3, 1883.

[12] *One Big Union Bulletin*, January 17, 1920, p. 5. (The O.B.U. Bulletin is available on microfilm in the Department of Labour Library, Ottawa).

[13] Charles Dickie, Secretary-Treasurer of Division 4, Railway Employees, A.F.L., "Aims and Ideals of the Trade Union Movement," *Canadian Congress Journal*, (official journal of the T.L.C.), Vol. XI, No. 12, (December, 1932).

[14] Doris French, *Faith, Sweat and Politics, The Early Trade Union Years in Canada* (Toronto: McClelland and Stewart Limited, 1962), p. 87.

I think the spirit of constant, and especially reasonable methods should be the desire of this National Congress.[15]

More radical elements within the union movement saw the unions as instruments for social revolution though class conflict. Unions such as the One Big Union and the Industrial Workers of the World adopted revolutionary policies. The One Big Union took the following position:

Being firmly built upon the class struggle, the O.B.U. seeks not only to organize the workers for the immediate struggle for wages and conditions, but it labours objectively to the end that the workers shall take over the industries of the country and administer them for the benefit of all who work.[16]

Left-wing militancy became more pronounced and took stronger hold in some parts of Canada, especially in Western Canada. Impatience with evolutionary reform through the existing social system was displayed as such unions adopted and advocated an ideology based on the class struggle for the overthrow of the existing structure.

In Canada, however, it generally was the more conservative elements that gave the labour movement its direction. With a few exceptions, the Canadian labour movement became preoccupied with attempts to modify what appeared to be injustices and inequities within the system, rather than concentrating their efforts towards the replacement of the structure. Adopting a broad social reform base, the labour movement sought the advancement and improvement of the position of the working classes within the framework of the existing wage system. Strong emphasis was placed on economic means rather than on political ideology to achieve demands that included not only economic welfare but educational benefits and greater social and cultural involvement. It has been observed,

. . . the trade unions did demonstrate a broad social philosophy outside their normal activities: in education, in finance, and economic development, in welfare measures, in the franchise. . . . The broader social responsibility and concern were more apparent in Canadian unions than in American unions, and even though the American influence has since weighed largely on Canadian developments this difference was never completely lost.[17]

Imbued not with a Marxian class consciousness based on class warfare, but with a reforming class consciousness based on gradual improvement, the Canadian labour movement was not based on the view that unions were the instruments of social revolution in which the workers were unconsciously caught up in the class conflict of a capitalist system. Rather, the formative stage of Canadian unionism was based on a working class awareness in which labour organizations were regarded as avenues for gradual reform through which the economic status of the workers could be improved. It became a strong belief that only through union organization could workers participate in the decision-making areas of industry that had an impact on their working lives. It was this attitude regarding trade unions that became the dominating principle and that influenced the direction that the developing labour movement was to take.

Yet it should be emphasized that there were exceptions to this general observation. The labour movement experienced many complex divisions, splits and re-alignments in its historical growth pattern. Not only has the main path of unionism diverged into radicalism occasionally, but the movement has also experienced ties with the social doctrines of the Roman Catholic Church in the province of Quebec. However, since the divergences from this pattern constitute a separate study on their own merits, for the purposes of this study, attention will be centered on the main pattern of union growth.

The central question, then, that arises is why the development of the labour movement in Canada took the more conservative direction. The rejection of a leftist ideology did not signify a lack of interest in political parties. The records show that discussions on political matters were not absent from conventions of organized members in the youthful stage of union growth. Nor were attempts to form a labour party or to place labour candidates in provincial and federal elections absent at such meetings. Although the same close political ties that characterize many European labour movements did not develop, the labour movement in Canada cannot be said to have been or to be without political orientation. In its early history, even before the widespread organization of industrial workers, the labour movement urged the support of labour candidates in provincial and federal elections, and intermittently recommended the formation of an independent labour party. Whenever dissatisfaction was voiced with the progress of legislation on behalf of labour, recommendations for the organization of a labour party followed. The view was expressed in the 1880's at the annual conventions of the Trades and Labour Congress that a third party on a labour platform be formed to represent the working classes in Parliament. But in a realistic fashion reminiscent of the Gomper's stand, the Convention also urged:

where no labour candidates are nominated all labour organizations be advised to act unitedly in support of the candidate who pledges himself to vote for most planks of the platform of the Congress.[18]

Unlike the American Federation of Labor policy regarding political parties, the Trades and Labour Congress convention in 1917 urged the formation of an independent labour party of Canada, and called for a conference to organize provincial labour parties. Although a small number of labour candidates were successful in getting seats in legislatures during these years of active interest in politics, a labour party of any significance was

---

[15] R. Smith, President, Trades and Labour Congress, *Proceedings of the 17th Annual Convention*, 1901.

[16] *One Big Union Bulletin*, October 26, 1926, p. 4.

[17] Doris French, *Early Trade Union Years*, p. 153.

[18] Canadian Trades and Labour Congress, *Second Convention Proceedings*, (1886).

not formed.[19] However, at its 1923 Convention the Trades and Labour Congress reconsidered its stand on political action. While advocating the need for labour representation in Parliament in order to secure the passage of favourable legislation on behalf of labour, the Convention passed the resolution that the Congress "continue to act as the legislative mouthpiece for organized labour in Canada independent of any political organization . . ." [20] Thus, the Trades and Labour Congress reverted to its role as a legislative pressure group, a role that it held until the merger with the Canadian Congress of Labour in 1956.

It cannot be substantiated, however, that worker protest in Canada was principally political in nature. Demands for economic reforms on the job situation did not become subordinate to the demands for political reform. The view has been expressed that, in Britain:

much of the intensified worker protest that has been associated with early industrialization was principally political in origin and reflected desires to widen political participation and was not so closely related to economic development as it once appeared to be.[21]

However, this was not the case in Canada. It is certainly true that the influence of British trade unionism was felt in Canada. The reforming class consciousness apparent in the formative stages of union development was to a large extent a heritage of the British connection. British artisans emigrating to Canada were conscious of their craft status while at the same time they were "a settled generation that eschewed the radicalism of their fathers, and accepted the industrial society in which they had been raised."[22] In the 1880's the new model unions of England, such as the Amalgamated Society of Engineers and the Amalgamated Society of Carpenters and Joiners, established locals in Canada. Even earlier, the first indigenous locals or labour circles in the 1830's and 1840's were under the leadership and influence of British trade unionists who had come to settle in Canada. Daniel J. O'Donoghue, referring to the labour movement in Canada in the late nineteenth century made the acute observation that:

The predominant idea of British trade unionism governs but modified so as to embody the chief principles governing the American Federation of Labour. Nevertheless there is a smattering of moderate socialism interwoven in the Canadian labour movement, . . . which asserts itself occasionally, as opportunity offers.[23]

The attitudes and policies of the early Canadian unions on such matters as the movement for shorter hours to provide a better life through more leisure, social, health and medical insurance, equality and human rights were coloured by the British outlook. "The Canadian trade union movement while closely linked to the U.S. movement has been greatly influenced by the British movement from whence the early membership originated."[24] Although the extension of American unions into Canada soon had its strong impact on the Canadian labour movement, there is no doubt that the early influence of British unionism left its mark.[25]

The first international unions in Canada were British.[26] Under the British influence the early Canadian trade unions emphasized improvements in labour legislation through the parliamentary procedure and stressed the support of labour candidates. Gradually the impact of American unionism was more strongly felt in Canada, but the working class consciousness in the British tradition was never completely erased. In the Canadian labour movement it was the radicalism of class conflict that was rejected and not the consciousness of a working class. Perlman's thesis,[27] with reference to the United States, is that individualism and private property, as foundations of the American system, have tended to erase the class emphasis one might expect in the trade union movement. These fundamental values apply to the Canadian nation too, but in the formative years of union growth job consciousness went hand in hand with class consciousness. This basic difference from the American labour movement becomes apparent when examining the philosophy of Canadian unionism. American "international" unionism had an impact on the general philosophy of the Canadian labour movement and this philosophy reflects the accepted values of capitalism in both countries, but it is also true that the philosophy of Canadian unionism shows a more marked

[19] The first union member to be elected to a provincial legislature was Daniel J. O'Donoghue in 1874, representing Ottawa. Other labour candidates were elected in the 1880's and the 1890's, and in these two decades labour candidates in various industrial centres were put in the running although not always successful in elections, by the Toronto District Trades and Labour Council, by the Montreal Trades and Labour Council, the Knights of Labour, the Provincial Workmen's Association of Nova Scotia, and the British Columbia and Winnipeg labour unions. In 1900 the first labour candidate from Winnipeg was elected to the Federal House of Commons. A. W. Puttie of the Winnipeg Typographical Union was the first labour candidate in the Federal House. See *The Trades and Labour Congress of Canada: An Historical Review, 1873-1955,* (Ottawa, Trades and Labour Congress, 1955). This publication is now in the library of the Canadian Labour Congress, Ottawa.

[20] *Ibid,* p. 19.

[21] Clark Kerr, J. T. Dunlop, F. Harbison, Charles A. Myers, *Industrialism and Industrial Man,* (Massachusetts: Harvard University Press, 1964), p. 8. By permission Harvard University Press and Heinemann Educational Books Limited.

[22] H. C. Pentland, "The Development of a Capitalistic Labour Market in Canada," *Canadian Journal of Economics and Political Science,* Vol XXV, No. 4, (November, 1959); and reprinted in A. E. Kovacs, ed., *Readings in Canadian Labour Economics,* (Toronto: McGraw-Hill of Canada Ltd., 1961), p. 14.

[23] O'Donoghue, "Canadian Labour Interests and Movements."

[24] D. J. Saposs, *Ideological Conflicts in the International Labour Movement,* Monograph No. 1, (Honolulu: Industrial Relations Centre, University of Hawaii, 1964).

[25] H. A. Logan, *Trade Unions in Canada,* (Toronto: The Macmillan Co. of Canada Ltd., 1948), Chapter 1.

[26] Claude Jodoin, "The Influence of International Unions on the Canadian Labour Movement," *Business Quarterly,* University of Western Ontario, Fall, 1959.

[27] Selig Perlman, *A Theory of the Labour Movement.* Perlman's theory was first published in 1928. Reprinted by Augustus M. Kelley, Publishers, New York, 1949.

emphasis on political involvement, advocacy of public and co-operative ownership, and economic planning.

Thus in the early stages of labour organization unions were voluntary protective organizations formed for the purpose of protesting against grievances and injustices found in the employment situation. In addition to the strong economic base of unionism, these early organizations were also motivated by an ideology which offered a broader vision than was discernible on the immediate employment scene. Furthermore, the economic and political motivations underlying the early trade union movement in Canada were supported by a psychological force which provided the work force with a feeling of dignity and of belonging. It has been pointed out that,

Thus the trade union movement being the vehicle of expression of the ideals of the worker must play an ever-increasing part in all that tends to regulate his conditions of life. The aims and aspirations of our labour movement are not useless verbiage and declarations, but the real ideal and highest conception of what human life should be. Labour's philosophy is the philosophy of democracy.[28]

While political interest was not absent in the pioneering days of Canadian unionism, the practical problems attached to the employment situation became the real issues for many rank and file members. Even in the midst of an era of lively political interest the President of the Trades and Labour Congress stated in 1896 that "practical reform is far superior to theoretic," and he called on the convention delegates to "avoid as much as possible those questions whose object is purely speculative or experimental." [29] The practical reformist nature of the movement was also apparent in a statement from the next Trades and Labour Congress President (who was also an M.P.P. in the British Columbia legislature), three years later, when he remarked:

It is easy for us to be prophets of future Utopias, and whilst high ideals are of great value, impossible and extravagant ones are of doubtful utility; our strength increases proportionately to the abandonment of impossible things . . .[30]

Thus, direct political alliance was not taken until the 1940's. Even as late as 1935 the executive board of the All-Canadian Congress of Labour, which merged with the Canadian CIO Committee to form the Canadian Congress of Labour in 1940, stressed that the prime objective of unionism was to improve the living standards of labour in a developing country, and in order to achieve that goal there was "no need of adherence to any fine-spun theory of government or social organization." Furthermore, "Unions which are but the instruments of political doctrines are incapable of serving the workers in the industrial struggle."[31]

While the pioneering stage of union growth displayed a keen political interest and emphasis, the economic function became the overriding issue as the movement continued to grow. The fading missionary cause and the decline of political involvement were replaced by the pressures of collective bargaining. Though the political reform element was not completely erased, the time-and-effort-consuming business of collective bargaining brought the pragmatism of the labour movement to the attention of the public. Idealism faded as the economic nature of unionism captured the participation and interest of both membership and leadership alike.

THE ESTABLISHMENT YEARS

In the establishment stage the chief union function became the business of collective bargaining. The legal framework permitting trade unions to operate within the existing social structure had a tremendously important bearing on the establishment stage of union growth. The attitude of government and the support of public opinion are elements contributing to the spread of collective bargaining.

Although the right to form trade union organizations in Canada was given to workers under the Trade Union Act of 1872 and the amended Combines Act of 1892, a positive policy of recognition and acceptance was not granted until the enactment in 1944 of the Wartime Labour Relations Regulations, P.C. 1003. These Regulations provided for a formal certification process for compulsory collective bargaining and for the continuation of the principle of compulsory conciliation. This principle has dominated dispute settlement legislation since the beginning of the twentieth century, with the Industrial Disputes Investigation Act of 1907, which first contained the provision of compulsory conciliation that is embodied in present legislation.

Although the legal position of unions was protected in this second stage, the unions still faced resistance and hostility from employers; often, their resort was a long and bitter strike. Although collective bargaining and conciliation were used as approaches to settle differing interests, the period was characterized by instability in industrial relations. Attempts were made to settle conflicts through compromise, negotiations and conciliation, but the fear and distrust on both sides did not readily lead to co-operation.

While legally the areas of conflict were narrowed by being removed from the realm of collective bargaining,[32] strikes and lockouts were fre-

---

[28] Charles Dickie, "Aims and Ideals."

[29] D. A. Carey, President, Trades and Labour Congress, *12th Convention Proceedings*, (1898).

[30] Ralph Smith, President, Trades and Labour Congress, *15th Convention Proceedings*, (1899).

[31] Executive Board Report, *Convention Proceedings*, All-Canadian Congress of Labour, (1935), p. 17.

[32] H. D. Woods, "Canadian Collective Bargaining and Dispute Settlement Policy: An Appraisal," *Canadian Journal of Economics and Political Science*, Vol. XXI, No. 4, (November, 1955), and reprinted in A. E. Kovacs, ed., *Readings in Canadian Labour Economics*.

quently the resort of the disputing parties. Under Canadian federal law recognition disputes were removed from the area of conflict through the provision for legal certification in the labour relations statute. Furthermore, potential and actual discontent arising in the workplace was now formally channelled through the grievance procedure, which is an integral part of the collective agreement. Under federal legislation in Canada, the present Industrial Relations and Disputes Investigation Act makes it mandatory that every contract contain provisions for the settlement of differences concerning the interpretation and violation of the agreement. Such a provision is similarly required by some of the provincial statutes in Canada. Thus, the grievance process, with the arbitration clause as the final step, provides for the settlement of conflicts in the day to day labour management relations without a work stoppage during the term of the collective bargaining agreement.

Although legal provisions narrowed the areas of conflict and thereby reduced some of the tension between the parties, the period of establishment is characterized still by unrest on the industrial relations scene. Strikes and lockouts were legally resorted to when the negotiating parties did not resolve their differences over the terms and conditions of the collective bargaining agreement. The time period, which was legally established and through which the parties had to pass in the compulsory conciliation process, put a restraint on the work stoppage, but did not legally prohibit strikes or lockouts. Interest disputes tended to dominate labour-management relations in this stage of union growth as the representatives of both parties worked out their operational relationship.

Legal recognition does not always signify actual recognition by employers, but once certification was obtained, the open resistance met by unions had to face the daily problems encountered in the job situation. Unionism became involved with collective bargaining and this became the chief function occupying the labour movement.

Because collective bargaining is a continuous and a dynamic process and because it consumes both time and effort, unionism became highly involved in "bread and butter" issues and the labour movement became motivated by goals related to the immediate economic improvement of the group. The business of collective bargaining was demanding and success was felt when immediate objectives were met and achieved. With the emphasis on collective bargaining the labour movement took on the features of what has been called "business unionism" in the United States.[33] The philosophy of the labour movement in Canada became one of pragmatism. Motivated by forces from within, this pragmatic philosophy permeated the labour movement. The "bread and butter" demands extended into extremely imaginative fringe benefits. The main concern of the workers was security and "fringes" were extended to make provisions for seniority, unemployment benefits, guaranteed incomes, pensions and health and accident benefits. The emphasis of unionism was on the improvement of the economic welfare of the membership. It was in this sense that labour organizations took on the dominant function of business unionism which was analyzed by Hoxie.[34] Any long-term ideology that would embrace social reconstruction was rejected in favour of goals to obtain more and more of the current "fruits" of economic progress. Thus, the concern of the labour movement in the establishment stage centred on short-term pragmatic goals that brought improvements in the economic and industrial sphere to the membership.

The effectiveness of collective bargaining in winning immediate demands emphasized bargaining power as the union's means of survival. The objective became the attainment of a maximum number of benefits in the form of increased wages, improved workshop conditions and greater welfare fringes. The progressive economic development of Canada gave to the working population an improved standard of living which union members attributed to the impact of labour organization. The material affluence accompanying economic growth in Canada benefited the total population but union members in particular maintained that the improved standard of living that they had achieved had been won by direct collective bargaining through their unions. Although prominent economists and labour spokesman pointed out[35] that economic forces, rather than union pressures had been responsible for increasing the real income of the wage earning group, unionized labour insisted that the improvements were the result of an increase in union bargaining power.

As unions thus became more and more engrossed in the process of collective bargaining to secure increasing economic reforms, the philosophical foundations of the labour movement became more narrow. Unions interested in protesting against the evils of industrialism give way to unions interested in surviving as institutions through a shifting of bargaining power. Although, as Chamberlain points out,[36] the reform element that was so strongly present in the formative years of union growth was never wholly absent in the labour movement, this distinctive pioneering feature of trade unionism began to fade in the establishment stage. The affluence of society was reflected in union philosophy as the idealism of the formative years waned and was held in check by a "conservatism" that adhered to the existing modified "free enterprise" system to a much greater degree than in the emerging years of unionism. In Canada, in the establishment stage, the labour movement's interest in political parties appeared in its endorsement of the C.C.F. as "the political arm of labour" by the Canadian Congress of Labour and this policy was adhered to "through thick and thin, mainly thin" in the years from 1943 to 1956.[37]

The prosperous years of Canadian economic development provided

---

[33] R. F. Hoxie, *Trade Unionism.*

[34] *Ibid.*

[35] See Milton Friedman's article, "Some Comments on the Significance of Labour Unions for Economic Policy," in *The Impact of the Labour Union,* David McCord Wright, ed., (New York: Kelley and Millman, Inc., 1956), Ch. X, p. 204. A similar view was also expressed by Dr. Eugene Forsey, Canadian Labour Congress, as reported in the *Globe and Mail,* April 22, 1962.

[36] Neil W. Chamberlain, *Labour,* (New York: McGraw-Hill Book Co., 1958), p. 40.

[37] E. Forsey, "The Movement Towards Labour Unity in Canada: History and Implications," *Canadian Journal of Economics and Politcal Science,* Vol. XXIV, No. 1, (Feb. 1958), and reprinted in A. E. Kovacs, ed., *Readings.*

the opportunity for unions to develop an aggressive demanding quality and this militancy became formalized through the collective bargaining process, with work stoppages as the final step if settlement over the terms and conditions of the contract was not reached. In this stage of union development there was little scrutiny about the direction of the labour movement and there was little soul-searching with regard to the ultimate role of the labour movement in the modified competitive system. No effort was made to articulate the nature and extent of the goals of the labour movement as the leaders and membership were caught in the rapidly changing social and economic environment in which they functioned.

In the establishment stage of union growth, the union worker became less class conscious than he was in the formative years. Higher wages, greater leisure, more comforts, better housing and greater opportunities for travel and cultural activities allowed the worker to identify himself with middle class aspirations. Although in his present occupational status the worker might remain immobile due to lack of education, inadequate training, and due to seniority provisions and pension benefits on the job, he nevertheless strives for social mobility for his children. A sense of social flexibility was experienced as workers in the socio-economic environment associated with the success of a job-oriented union philosophy with their own aspirations. Perlman made the observation that,

. . . in a labour movement which has already gone beyond the emotional stage and acquired a definite rationale of its own, an appeal for common class action, be it through a sympathetic strike or through joint political action, will only be likely to evoke the response which is desired if the objective of the proposed common undertaking be kept so close to the core substance of union aspiration that Tom, Dick and Harry could not fail to identify it as such.[38]

Thus the objectives and demands of the labour movement centred on internal goals associated with the micro-economic environment. This is not necessarily a static approach because unionism became caught up in the changing conditions with more and more involvement in "progress," which brings improvements in working conditions. Perlman maintained that an unsophisticated idealism still motivates the labour movement in the "business unionism" stage of its development. He asserted

even "business unionism", shows idealism both in aim and in method; only it does so in the thoroughly unsophisticated way of "Tom, Dick, and Harry idealism". All unions sooner or later stress "shop rights", which, to the workingman at the bench, are identical with "liberty" itself, . . . And, after all, is not this sort of liberty the only sort which reaches the workman directly and with certainty and that can never get lost en route, . . .[39]

While this point is relevant, it is also true that the aims and objectives of unionism reflected a pragmatic philosophy that dominated the labour movement in the establishment stage and that idealism as a strong original motivator of union organization faded as collective bargaining became a "business" of growing importance for the unions' survival. This stage of unionism centred around the organizing campaigns preparing for certification, around the process of negotiations and, more dramatically, around the strike or lockout, when interest disputes are not settled after attempts at conciliation and mediation fail. The reforming zeal was submerged in this stage of union growth and the expanding and demanding business of the collective bargaining process dominates the industrial scene. This point was emphasized at an early Canadian Congress of Labour Convention:

We are all aware that the labour movement is primarily concerned with the economic interests of the workers; it deals with questions of wages and working conditions, the negotiations of agreements with employers through the process of collective bargaining and matters of this nature.[40]

As unionism passed from the formative years of development to an era in which organization became established in the fabric of Canadian society, the evangelical atmosphere is replaced by dedication to unions that function as "service organizations."[41] Ross maintains that unions that began as voluntary organizations and were motivated by a working-class ideology are now changing into organizations which serve their membership as "public utilities." While this view may be valid to explain the establishment stage of union development in Canada it is also noticeable that the Canadian labour movement, in the power stage of union growth, extends its scope beyond the micro needs of its membership. But in the establishment stage of union growth it is evident that

Unions may be looked upon as power centres concerned with advancing the welfare of their members. The basic objective of unions in industry is improved working conditions of those they represent.[42]

As the collective bargaining environment faced altered conditions, new problems arose that necessitated differing approaches to achieve objectives. Therefore, the following observation made in the Woods Report becomes meaningful:

"As collective bargaining changes, so must trade unionism. Business unionism may have to be replaced by institutions whose philosophies reflect the new tasks of collective bargaining."[43]

In the next stage of union development it is evident that union organizations have become an additional power bloc in society, wielding economic force and containing the potential for greater political participation as a labour bloc.

[38] Perlman, *A Theory*, p. 277.
[39] *Ibid*, p. 274-5.
[40] A. R. Mosher, *Address* to Third Convention of the Canadian Congress of Labour, 1942.
[41] A. M. Ross, "Labor Organization and the Labor Movement in Advanced Industrial Society," *Virginia Law Review*, Vol. 50:1359, (1964), and Reprint No. 252, Institute of Industrial Relations, University of California, (Berkeley, 1965).
[42] *Report of Task Force on Labour Relations in Canada*, p. 36.
[43] *Ibid*, p. 38.

IV. THE POWER YEARS

With the spread of collective bargaining as a chief function of unionism and with a pragmatic philosophy dominating the labour movement in the stage of establishment, the question of whether the expanded power of unions reflects a change in philosophy in the future stages of union development poses itself. Does the Canadian labour movement take on a more direct role in "social transformation" through greater participation in the political arena in the future?

Political involvement, directly or indirectly, has not been absent in the Canadian labour movement as we know from viewing the history of trade unionism in Canada.[44] Ideological differences have contributed to numerous factions and divisions within the labour movement, but historically organized workers in general have rejected any attempts to radically transform society by adhering to left-wing ideology. Organized labour has accepted the basic societal form in Canada with the goal of gradual reform and it is in this sense that "trade unionism is an instrument of social transformation as well as an agent of collective bargaining . . ." [45] It has been predicted that the philosophy of the Canadian labour movement will not change in the next decade.[46] While its approach and tactics must adapt to the changing conditions, its basic motivating force will be generated by aims that are based on fundamental human needs for security and freedom. It is claimed that the pragmatic philosophy of the labour movement embraces an idealistic concept of social justice, as well as a materialistic approach for improved economic conditions. For example:

Unions do indeed spend the majority of their time and effort on bread and butter issues. But that is only part of the story. Running through the labour movement from its earliest days has been a highly idealistic conception of its role in the fight for social justice. The labour movement has always regarded itself as a missionary for a better world, . . .[47]

Thus, it is conceded and agreed that "a trade union movement without something larger than a wages philosophy tends to become sterile."[48] Where does the Canadian labour movement get its dynamism for future growth and expansion of power? An examination of the figures for union membership and their application as an index of union growth and power indicates a long-term increase in membership.[49] But looking at growth merely in terms of numbers does not fully explain this trend. In addition to external factors contributing to the growth patterns of unions, i.e., wars, favourable legislation, growing labour force, there are internal forces at work that contribute to this development.

The labour movement in Canada, appears to be moving towards the adoption of a philosophy that embraces both social and economic action as well as, to a more limited extent, political action. The "bread and butter" demands are solidly engrained in unionism as we noted in examining the establishment stage of development, but along with such pragmatic concerns for its union membership, a concern for social justice also has an impact on both the organized and unorganized labour force. The collective bargaining process has been very successful in attaining unionists' demands for "immediate" economic improvements in the working environment. But the scope of unionism has extended beyond the local employer-employee relationship to include matters dealing with international labour organizations and with social legislation and public policy on manpower training, automation, economic growth, education and human rights. The pragmatic philosophy was not replaced; due to an extension of union power, however, the objectives and goals of the labour movement were expanded to wider areas of social concern, with more effectiveness than in the formative years of growth. As early as 1900, a labour leader observed that:

. . . the trade union movement will be judged, not by its results in improving the position of any particular section of workmen at any particular time, but by its effect on the permanent efficiency of the nation.[50]

The labour movement in its economic function, has been successful through the process of collective bargaining and has had some influence in the social sphere as a pressure group. Yet, is it necessary for the labour movement to play a significant role in the political field in Canada? Historically, the labour movement has always shown interest and participation in politics, although its degree of involvement depended on the prevalent situation. As early as the 1880's the first central congress endorsed political action by encouraging labour representation in the legislatures. The Trades and Labour Congress followed this policy and its 1917 convention recommended the formation of an independent labour party for Canada. But in the subsequent years the Executive Council of the Trades and Labour Congress warned of the danger of political domination which might submerge and destroy the existing trade union movement. As a result, the 1923 convention of the Trades and Labour Congress

[44] For histories of the Canadian labour movement see: H. A. Logan, *Trade Unions in Canada: Their Development and Functioning,* (Toronto: Macmillan Co. of Canada, 1948); Stuart Jamieson, *Industrial Relations in Canada,* (Ithaca, N.Y., Cornell University Press, 1957); A. E. Kovacs, ed., *Readings.* Charles Lipton, *The Trade Union Movement of Canada,* 1827-1959, (Montreal: Canadian Social Publications Limited, 1966); John Crispo, *International Unionism,* (Toronto: McGraw-Hill of Canada, 1967); Gad Horowitz, *Canadian Labour in Politics,* (Toronto: University of Toronto Press, 1968).

[45] Report of the Task Force on Labour Relations, p. 39.

[46] John L. Fryer, "Labour's Changing Role," *Canadian Labour,* Vol. 13, No. 6, (June, 1968).

[47] *Ibid,* p. 15.

[48] N. J. Ware, *Labor in Modern Industrial Society,* (Boston: D. C. Heath and Co., 1935), p. 379.

[49] M. C. Urquhart, editor, and K. A. Buckley, assistant editor, *Historical Statistics of Canada,* (Toronto: Macmillan Co. of Canada, 1965); *Labour Organization in Canada,* (Ottawa: Canada Department of Labour, Economics and Research Branch, Annual).

[50] R. Smith, President, Trades and Labour Congress, at the 16th Annual Convention, (1900).

endorsed the policy that the Congress remain independent of any political party but that it continue to press for legislative reforms on behalf of organized labour. Its Political Action Committee was simply to provide information to members about political candidates and legislatures but the Congress would not directly affiliate with or endorse any political party. This policy was continued and the 1942 convention of the Trades and Labour Congress passed the following resolution:

. . . be it resolved that labour political autonomy be left in the hands of the established labour parties . . . and . . . that this Congress continue to act as the legislative mouthpiece of organized labour in Canada independent of any political organization engaged in the effort to send representatives of the people to Parliament, the Provincial legislatures or other collective bodies of this country.[51]

Until the merger of the Trades and Labour Congress and the Canadian Congress of Labour in 1956, the Trades and Labour Congress continued to endorse this policy. The delegates to the Trades and Labour Congress conventions were often enthusiastic about active support of and participation in politics, but the executive of the Congress, more strongly influenced by the American Federation of Labour policy and under closer pressures from that body, continued to resist open and direct political action.

It was the newly established Canadian Congress of Labour formed in the 1940's which went beyond such indirect participation. At its 1943 Convention, the Canadian Congress of Labour endorsed "the C.C.F. as the political arm of labour in Canada," and recommended its affiliated and chartered unions to affiliate with the party. Following this policy some controversy developed over the matter in subsequent conventions, and the outcome was the formation of a C.C.L. Political Action Committee which outlined its own programme supporting such policies as full employment, social security and public ownership of insurance, war plants, coal mines and transportation. The Canadian Congress of Labour programme was then submitted to the various political parties, and it was the C.C.F. party that gave assurance that such a programme would be adopted in its own platform. As Professor Logan points out:

Having found it difficult to get the membership to agree on politics and parties, it seemed better to lay down the conditions and have the parties choose the Congress.[52]

The Canadian Congress of Labour continued to support the C.C.F. as the political arm of labour and internal opposition was not strong enough to force an alteration of this policy. In the late 1940's and early 1950's a number of Communist-led affiliates were expelled from the Congress and thus opposition to the endorsement of the C.C.F. was largely quieted. The Canadian Congress of Labour maintained its support of the C.C.F. until the merger with the Trades and Labour Congress in 1956. After the merger, the newly established Canadian Labour Congress played an important role in the formation of the New Democratic Party in 1961, the successor to the C.C.F., and since then political affiliation of union membership has been encouraged. The Canadian Labour Congress however, as the central Congress, is not affiliated to the New Democratic Party because it maintains its traditional stand that the labour movement must not be politically dominated by a single party and must be free to criticize or support any political platform. The Congress position, however, is that the N.D.P. is the party in Canada that has a programme in line with the objectives and aims of the labour movement, and therefore the Congress urges that organized workers give strong support to N.D.P. candidates. This stand is in contrast with the policy of the Confederation of National Trade Unions in Quebec which does not openly give support to any particular political party in Canada. At the same time the Confederation of National Trade Unions does not lack a "reformist" attitude, and it has been noted that the

C.N.T.U. declarations on the capitalist system are more biting and critical than those of the C.L.C. and have in them the ring of the ideological socialist.[53]

What indications are there that organized workers are interested in a labour movement oriented towards party politics? It appears that labour leaders are keenly encouraging political orientation and they emphasize that,

A labour movement that is without interest in political matters is a labour movement that is evading one of the most fundamental responsibilities.[54]

Many labour leaders, while pointing to the economic function of unionism as its primary aim and holding the view that "It is the economic function which keeps the union alive,"[55] at the same time also emphasize political involvement. In its changing economic function the labour movement must become more politically conscious in its new role:

. . . the attitude of the Labour movement towards governments and towards political action must be reconsidered, with a view to determining whether or not the time has come for the adoption of political policies and closer association with political parties . . . It would appear that, in its own interests, the labour movement can no longer stand aloof from political action, and that, unless it has a voice and influence in the political field, it will be unable to make its full and proper contribution to the public welfare.[56]

---

[51] Resolution passed at 58th Convention of the Trades and Labour Congress, held in Winnipeg, 1942.

[52] H. A. Logan, *Trade Unions*, p. 560.

[53] Quoted by J. Crispo, *International Unionism*, p. 240.

[54] C. Jodoin, "The C.L.C. and Politics," *Canadian Labour*, Vol. 6, No. 9, (September, 1961), p. 5.

[55] Andy Andras, *Labour Unions in Canada, How They Work and What They Seek*, (Ottawa: Woodsworth House Publishers, 1948).

[56] A. R. Mosher, address to the Canadian Congress of Labour Convention in 1943, *Convention Proceedings*, p. 13.

Union leadership is voicing increasing concern over issues and problems that cannot be solved through collective bargaining. Political sentiment and involvement is a British tradition impregnated in the Canadian labour movement, and it is not alien to workers to look towards government for the remedies to a great many problems affecting the labour force. It has been pointed out that:

The Canadian union movement has never limited itself to a collective-bargaining role in society . . . In seeking both the "bread-and-butter" objectives of good contracts and broader social goals, unions must be concerned with the kind of legislation that is enacted in their municipality, province and country.[57]

In Canada, organized labour has given more emphasis to political participation than their counterpart organizations in the United States.[58] This difference is important in examining the philosophy of the Canadian labour movement because the "job-conscious" mentality that Perlman believed applicable to the American labour movement is not wholly applicable to Canadian unionism. Granted the significant influence of international unionism, the Canadian labour movement has also acted independently and has adopted a philosophy that is broader in outlook. The "job conscious" concept has taken on an added meaning in the Canadian labour movement and the impact of international unionism has not completely erased the early idealistic concept of its role in society. After passing through the establishment phase when a pragmatic philosophy sustained unionism and its adoption allowed the movement to grow and gain power, the next stage of development displays a return to a more widening outlook and attitude. It is argued that this broader scope of the labour movement will not mean that its commitment to collective bargaining is sacrificed, rather that it is strengthened.

The formative and pioneering days of unionism, however, are past and the same missionary zeal, idealism, emotionalism and humanitarianism, is not likely again to inspire the more educated leaders and the more sophisticated membership of present and future unions. The new role that the labour movement is assuming in the power stage of development, while admittedly embracing idealism, is not the same as the role it had in the formative years. Its status and image of the movement have changed; the historical economic, social and political conditions in which it moves have changed; the composition and nature of the labour force about which the movement is concerned have changed; and the working environment has changed, both technologically and psychologically. The "traditional" role of the labour movement is changing. Some claim that the movement has outlived its original purpose, although they do not think it will disappear from society. Galbraith argues that the labour movement's effectiveness is greatly reduced by the spread of industrialism. He states:

In fact the industrial system has now largely encompassed the labour movement. It has dissolved some of its most important functions; it has greatly narrowed its area of action; and it has bent its residual operations very largely to its own needs. Since World War II, the acceptance of the union by the industrial form and the emergence thereafter of an era of comparatively peaceful industrial relations have been hailed as the final triumph of trade unionism. On closer examination it is seen to reveal many of the features of Jonah's triumph over the whale.[59]

Galbraith maintains that the rise of industrialism has considerably weakened the union as a social force. Unionism will lose its position of power when the era of industrial development passes in which it rose to that status. On the contrary, the thesis of this article emphasizes that a stage is reached by the labour movement in the new technological system in which labour unions will not lose their position of power in society but will strengthen it. They derive their power from three sources:

As an institution, it derives its formal social recognition through certification; as a voluntary association it is vested with authority by its members in the agreed constitution and by-laws and by the extent of member's loyalty; and finally, in its bargaining it increases its power through contractual obligations imposed on management which guarantee it as an independent institution.[60]

A labour elite has emerged in the power stage of union growth and through their power in decision-making they exert a strong impact not only in the industrial area but also on the social scene. The importance of the labour elite in the power structure has been noted:

Along with the corporate elite there is in the economic system another elite group whose decision-making has important consequences for the society. This second group is made up of trade union leaders. Their power in economic decision-making stems from the control which in varying measure they have over the supply of labour. The power of these two elites in the economy is by no means equal because the corporate elite has that consolidated power which comes from the traditions of property institutions, whereas the labour elite has emerged after struggles aimed at reducing such power.[61]

Unionism grows in size and power and is nurtured by a deeply engrained pragmatism carried over from the establishment stage. This power derives not only from its role as an economic institution but also as a social institution. Its extension of scope, interest and power is given recognition by society as more and more labour representatives are invited to represent workers' interests on government boards and commissions. The encouragement and support of provincial governments in the

---

[57] Editorial, *Canadian Labour,* Vol. 13, No. 6, (June 1968), p. 5.

[58] J. Crispo, *International Unionism,* op. cit., Ch. 7.

[59] J. K. Galbraith, *The New Industrial State* (New York: Signet Books, 1967), p. 290.

[60] H. D. Woods, "Men and Industry," in *Proceedings of the 5th Annual Industrial Relations Conference,* McGill University, 1953.

[61] John Porter, *The Vertical Mosaic, An Analysis of Social Class and Power in Canada,* (Toronto: University of Toronto Press, 1965), p. 309.

establishment of joint labour-management councils is another indication of the public recognition of the power of unionism in its impact on the public interest and welfare of the country.[62]

But the labour movement as an important power bloc in society faces internal problems which take over as the union structure becomes larger and more bureacratic. Leadership begins to assume more administrative positions as central control expands. There is a tendency towards greater centralization as bargaining strength increases. This requires larger staffs of experts and specialists to interpret and solve the various problems arising in the collective bargaining process. With more centralization and specialization the internal relationship between membership and leadership changes. With greater central control over policy affecting the rank and file, the problem of the rights of the individual within the group becomes serious and takes on a new importance:

Where social justice once meant economic and political opportunity for the group, it has come to mean democracy and civil rights for the individual within the movement.[63]

The spirit of unionism has changed, but the goal of social and economic justice has not disappeared. It is expressed in more structured channels such as the grievance procedure, or participation on joint boards of one kind or another. Furthermore, the psychology of labour as "consumer" is replacing the conception of labour as "producer" and the "working class" image is fading as the labour movement extends its influence in the socio-economic area. Its success has been proven in the economic sphere and, as the present technological system provides more leisure opportunities, unionism is also becoming conscious of cultural activities as an area of participation.[64] Although a "working class" interpretation of the labour movement is considered outmoded even by labour, yet the union member has been associated with a certain image and social status "which, though it may be glossed over on the surface by the material well-being and conspicuous spending of the workers, is nevertheless made prominent by noticeable differences in cultural interests and social habits and customs." [65] It is that barrier that the Canadian Labour Congress wishes to "crack through."

Unionism as a social and economic force will continue to exert a strong influence on society, but as a political "labour" bloc its future is less certain. Although the leadership strongly urges political involvement, the general rank and file membership in the labour movement has not committed itself to the support of a socialist party. It has been speculated that only a "take-off" in the N.D.P. would draw labour support, but at the same time, "Union support is necessary for the take-off; but the take-off is a prerequisite for support from these unions."[66] In the political arena it becomes more difficult to speculate about the role of the labour movement in the future. Although the leadership may be committed to direct political participation, union membership has not demonstrated its active support at the polls.[67] It appears that the labour movement in Canada, although not rejecting political involvement directly, is moving in a direct-tion that will give strength to the collective bargaining process through more direct participation on the industrial and social scenes.[68] But there is an acute awareness that achievement in those areas can only be reached in a political climate conducive to their attainment. Thus, it is unlikely that the Canadian labour movement, in the future course of its development, will reject political action as a potential approach to reach its goals.

In the power stage of union growth, the Canadian labour movement must consider its political orientation, must re-examine its structure and government[69] and must review its approach to organizing, to bargaining and to the social and economic problems created in the transformation of society through the impact of automation. If the reappearance of a reforming consciousness is to be effective, the labour movement, with its gained power, must work not only for short-term pragmatic goals but for the betterment of the human condition on the macro level. The image and status of "business unionism" acquired in the establishment stage of union development must be broadened to include humanitarian values in a society urgently and anxiously searching for a meaningful existence.

V. CONCLUSION

In this examination of the philosophy of the Canadian labour movement, the approach centers on stages of union development. In the emerging and formative years of labour organization, unionism displayed a loyal dedication to a cause. A sense of common purpose inspired labour unions and the discontent experienced with the job environment was associated with an idealism that praised the dignity and worth of labouring. The desire

---

[62] See A. E. Kovacs, "A Study of Joint Labour-Management Committees at the Provincial Level in the Provinces of Canada," a study prepared for the Task Force on Labour Relations, Research Project No. 56.

[63] Mark Perlman, "Labour Movement Theories: Past Present and Future," *Industrial and Labour Relations Review,* Vol. 13, No. 2, (April 1960).

[64] See the article in the *Globe and Mail,* May 26, 1969, regarding the proposed policy of the Canadian Labour Congress to "crack through the cultural black-tie barrier" by participation on arts councils presenting cultural programmes.

[65] A. E. Kovacs, "A Tentative Framework for the Philosophy of the Canadian Labour Movement," p. 46.

[66] G. Horowitz, *Canadian Labour,* p. 262.

[67] See A. E. Kovacs, "Tentative Framework," p. 43, for a discussion of possible reasons why active political involvement appears uncertain.

[68] A contrary view regarding the direction that the Canadian labour movement is taking has been expressed by Anthony Carew, "Canadian Labour — The Need for Social Renewal," *Relations Industrielles Revue Trimestrielle,* (Industrial Relations Quarterly Review), Vol. 23, No. 4, (October, 1968).

[69] For a discussion on the recommendations of the C.L.C. committee which studies its Constitution and structure see the articles: L. Sefton, "The C.L.C. Commission on Constitution and Structure", and S. T. Payne, "Opinions syndicales sur les structures syndicales," in *Relations Industrielles Revue Trimestrielle, (Industrial Relations Quarterly Review),* Vol. 23, No. 4, (October, 1968).

for reform was to be achieved through a working-class spirit and a militancy that adhered to a philosophy advocating gradual change through the parliamentary system in Canada. In time this missionary zeal did succumb to change and labour organizations became engrossed in the business of collective bargaining, as the legal framework allowed them to exist and to function. In the second stage of the growth pattern, the labour movement was motivated by the acceptance of a flexible standard of living and the demands of "more and more" were based on the optimistic assumption that the economy is one of continuous progress and improvement. Unionism existing as an established institution became involved in a highly complex industrial relations system. Its pragmatic philosophy was motivated by the success which was realized in the microeconomic sphere. There was no effort to transform society through political involvement, but only through demands for welfare fringes. Such pragmatic short-term programmes also have long-term implications and effects on the organized as well as on the unorganized segments of the labour force.

As the labour movement acquired power in its dynamic process of development, the establishment stage gave way to a philosophy that adhered to a broader purpose and direction. In the public stage of growth, the Canadian labour movement gained public recognition of that power. The motivating force comes from the existence and identity of unionism as a powerful institution in society, as well as from an idealism that has become structured. The idealism of the formative years represented a desire for reform, a faith or belief in improvements for the working class. The road to achievement experienced many difficult struggles and battles and gradually the idealism of the pioneering days was translated into gains and improvements on the employment scene. The idealism of the power stage still provides a motivating purpose for the labour movement, but now there is a greater economic affluence, and a macro approach which was lost sight of in the establishment stage is no longer an "impractical" and "extravagant" orientation. Thus, in the power stage of the labour movement in Canada unionism adheres to a philosophy that does not reject an ideology moving towards social action and to a more limited extent political action on the national scene. This direction does not reject political orientation because there is an awareness of the increasing role of the state in the socio-economic environment as the labour movement works within the existing political structure. The trend towards an emphasis on social action is one that the labour movement can now afford. After an era of impressive economic achievements and reaching the stage of power that it has, the labour movement can become more effective in realizing its ideals than it was able to in the formative years of union growth. But only the future will show how and to what extent the Canadian labour movement develops in that direction.

5

TRADE UNION

STRUCTURE

AND PHILOSOPHY:

Need for a Reappraisal

C. Brian Williams

INTRODUCTION

This paper examines the present state of the Canadian organized labour movement and attempts to assess its future role in Canadian society. The preceding paper by Aranka Kovacs states the issue quite clearly: "Where does the Canadian labour movement get its dynamism for future growth and expansion of power?" Alternatively, as she quoted from Norman Ware, ". . . a trade union movement without making something larger than a wages philosophy tends to become sterile."

Whereas the previous paper looks at the future with optimism, this paper offers little but despair. Yet, they both agree that the answer to the question of labour's future role, function, and effectiveness depends upon its ability to develop a structure and philosophy that will permit it to meet and deal effectively with the challenges of the future. The thesis advanced here is that its present structure and philosophy is obsolete and it is unlikely that a recasting of its structure and philosophy will be forthcoming.

As Kovacs has pointed out, any attempt to assess the contributions of organized labour must come to grips with the problem of measuring it. Just how does one measure the contributions of the Canadian trade union movement to Canadian society? Is it sufficient to quote membership figures? In January 1967, the Canadian trade union movement claimed 1,920,647 members in 8,679 locals of 110 international, 55 national, and 333 independent organizations. Is it sufficient to say that the 1,920,647 members are covered by over 10,000 collective agreements with Canadian employers? Is it sufficient to quote changes in membership? From January 1966 to January 1967, union membership climbed by 185,000 which represents a gain of 10.6 per cent and the highest percentage increase for any year since 1952. Union membership totaled 32.3 per cent of all non-agricultural paid workers, or 26.1 per cent of the total Canadian labour force.

The Canadian Labour Congress, the larger of Canada's two national centres, has affiliated unions representing 1,450,619 members, or 76 per cent of the total union membership. This represents an increase of 168,000 members or 13.1 per cent over the previous year. In January 1967, the Confederation of National Trade Unions had a membership of 198,000 with a reported increase of 10,000 members or 5 per cent over the previous year.

International unions, with 1,272,884 members in Canada, accounted for just over 66 per cent of total union membership. National and regional unions accounted for 30 per cent of Canada's trade union membership. Directly chartered local unions constituted 1.5 per cent of the total, and independent local organizations comprised less than 3 per cent of the total.[1] Are membership and collective agreement figures sufficient, or must other criteria be used in an attempt to measure the contributions of the Canadian trade union movement? While the labour movement is pleased with recent organizing successes, it is by no means complacent. A recent article which commented enthusiastically on its organizing success closed on a less enthusiastic theme.

With all this stirring in the world of trade union organization and labour-management relations, a number of issues remain unresolved. They can not remain unresolved indefinitely. Management, labour and the public are looking to new solutions to both old and new problems, and time won't stand still while these are being worked out.

What will happen in the court injunction issue? What will happen about implementing the Freedman report on automation and management's rights? What will happen about implementing the Macpherson report on railway problems affecting a major industry? What will happen in the field of compulsory arbitration, already invoked in the past in Ontario Hydro, in the railway system, now a part of the negotiating procedures in Ontario hospitals and in the federal civil service and still hanging over the ILA settlement? What will happen in the field of manpower studies, training and retraining?[2]

In drawing up a balance sheet of labour's contribution, is it sufficient to limit attention to work done in the name of the Canadian working class? Should one measure its contributions to the Canadian economy, or even to Canadian society at large? Should one look closely at the structure and philosophy of the movement to assess its compatability with the social and economic climate in which it must operate. If this were done, would labour's net valuation be an asset or a liability?

In terms of membership and collective agreements, the Canadian trade union movement has come a long way from its origins in the 1840's. However, when left to its own devices, and before the statutory dictum of compulsory collective bargaining, with its aid to membership growth and formulation of agreements, its growth and development in terms of membership, agreements, structure and philosophy was troubled, cumbersome, irregular and painfully slow. Before its tenth birthday, the pains of a distorted structural growth and a divided philosophy foreshadowed recurring weaknesses that still plague it in the present day. From within the ranks of labour, rose the question of political representation *versus* collective bargaining and of international trade unionism *versus* national trade unionism. For the next thirty-six years, these two issues drained the strength of the infant structure-seeking movement.

A century ago, when the Canadian economy was largely agricultural and concentrations of population and industry were few, labour organization extended little beyond local units, despite the fact that a few labour unions were in existence in Canada as early as the 1820's. Today, union locals number more than 8,600 and most of their central organizations are affiliated with one of the two national centres of Canada — the Canadian Labour Congress, the larger of the two, or the Confederation of National Trade Unions, which operates almost exclusively in Quebec.

Union membership is nearing 2 million and is widely dispersed industrially, occupationally and geographically. About one in every four members of the labour force and about one in every three non-agricultural paid workers belong to the union movement.

A unique feature of the Canadian labour movement is its international character. The growth of the union movement in this country has been greatly influenced by events and developments in the United States. Although there have been several attempts in the past one hundred years to "nationalize" the labour movement in Canada, only the portion within the CNTU, a few national unions in the CLC, and a few independent unions have no international connection.

THE DEVELOPMENT OF THE STRUCTURE AND PHILOSOPHY OF INTERNATIONAL UNIONISM[3]

International trade unionism in this country began in the decade preceding Confederation, when unions operating in the United States began to form locals in Upper Canada. Not until 1873, after Confederation, was an attempt made to form a national federation of unions. In that year, thirty local unions in Ontario formed the Canadian Labour Union.

[1] *Labour Gazette,* Vol. 66, No. 12, (December 1966), p. 730, and *Labour Organizations in Canada,* 1967. (Ottawa: Queen's Printer, 1967) p. vii-xiii.

[2] "Union Growth in Canada," *Canadian Labour,* Vol. 11, No. 10, (October 1966). p. 20.

[3] "100 Years of Labor Organization," *Labour Gazette,* Vol. 67, No. 7, (July 1967). p. 444-45.

The CLU held conventions for several successive years but the organization failed to thrive; however, a Canadian Assembly organized in 1881 by the Knights of Labour, which had been established in the United States in 1869, was able to claim a membership of 16,000 by the end of the 1880's. The Knights organized workers regardless of trade or occupation.

In 1886, still searching for structure and philosophy, the Canadian movement established its legislative watchdog, the Dominion Trades and Labour Congress of Canada. In 1893, it became the Trades and Labour Congress of Canada, a body that existed under that name for the next sixty-three years. The Trades and Labour Congress of Canada, created in the image and shadow of the American Federation of Labor and born at the height of the controversy over international trade unionism, precipitated the inevitable question of dual jurisdiction. The debate continued. Finally, overwhelmed by AFL sentiment, the TLC convention of 1903 acceded to the Berlin Declaration.

[The TLC] shall form organizations in localities where none at present exist into local unions, but in no case shall any body of workingmen belonging to any trade or calling at present having an international or national union be granted a charter. In the event of the formation of an international or national union of the trade or calling of the unions so chartered being formed, it shall be the duty of the proper officer of the Congress to see that the said union becomes a member of said international or national union. Provided that no national union be recognized, where an international union exists.[4]

Out went the dualist and with their ouster came the parade of Canadian nationalists — the National Trades and Labour Congress, the Canadian Federation of Labour, and the All Canadian Congress of Labour — until finally in the late 1930's the nationalist battle cry of "Canada for the Canadians" was lost in the ever popular appeal of "industrial unionism" and its servant, the Canadian Congress of Labour.

Another separation from the mainstream of international trade unionism occurred in 1919 when a group objecting to the emphasis on craft unionism in the TLC, and advocating more direct political action in preference to legislative submissions, formed the One Big Union. This union group sought to organize by industry rather than by trade. It gained prominence after the Winnipeg General Strike of 1919, at which time it claimed a membership of 41,500. But it soon began to decline and, at the time of its entry into the Canadian Labour Congress in 1956, it had only 6,000 members. In 1927, dissidents from the Canadian Federation of Labour joined with the Canadian Brotherhood of Railway Employees and the remnants of the One Big Union to form the All-Canadian Congress of Labour. The ACCL objective was complete independence for the Canadian labour movement. The Depression arrived soon after the birth of the ACCL, however, and its membership went into a decline (as did that of the TLC). Union membership did not pick up again until after 1935.

In 1935, the Wagner Act was passed in the United States. This Act protected labour's right to join unions and to bargain collectively with employers. Six leading industrial unions in the AFL formed the Committee for Industrial Organization and began to organize workers in mass production industries. In Canada, agitation grew for legislation similar to the Wagner Act. Unions belonging to the Committee for Industrial Organization lent assistance to similar Canadian organizing efforts. In 1936, the AFL suspended the unions that had formed the Committee on the grounds that they were fostering dual unionism. In 1937, these unions were expelled; they then set up a new central organization, the Congress of Industrial Organizations. The TLC avoided a similar split in its ranks until 1939 when its executive concluded that it could no longer ignore the dual unionism advocated by the CIO unions and expelled the Canadian branches of the CIO unions.

Its strength weakened by the general decline in union membership during the Depression and by the defection in 1936 of a group of unions that left to form a new Canadian Federation of Labour, the All-Canadian Congress of Labour saw new hope for its policy of industrial unionism. In 1940, it joined with the expelled CIO unions to form the Canadian Congress of Labour.

The years from 1886 to the 1940's were good years. Canadian labour was alive, vibrant and dynamic. It had something to say and a voice with which to say it. Debate on structure and philosophy was ever present and occupied the central stage of labour's deliberations. Labour was concerned about its problems and it actively sought answers to them. It was a thinking and inward looking labour movement. It had committed leadership and was determined to establish its rightful role in Canadian economic and social life. It stood on its own two feet. What a contrast to compare the exciting dialogue of this period to the humdrum dialogue of today.

The Canadian trade union movement has had a rich, full and exciting history. Surely, in any assessment of labour's contribution, this history must be recognized as a positive contribution. Yet is it sufficient to cite numbers and history, or must successful social organizations have demonstrated their ability to adapt and change in response to the environment in which they find themselves? Must they stand the test of time? What of labour today?

THE STATE OF LABOUR MANAGEMENT RELATIONS TODAY

To most observers, 1966 was a year of noticeable increase in labour unrest in Canada, and the year set records for the number of strikes and man-days lost due to work stoppages. The generally accepted measure of labour peace, the man-days lost due to work stoppages, nearly doubled over the 1965 level. The 629 stoppages resulted in a loss of over five million

---

[4] As quoted in C. Brian Williams, "Development of Relations Between Canadian and American National Centers, 1886-1925," *Industrial Relations* (Laval): Vol. 20, No. 2, (April 1965). p. 349.

man-days.[5] Not only did strike activity increase in 1966, but there was also a pronounced quickening of interest in labour affairs in Canadian press, radio and television. As a result, the Canadian public at large has become increasingly aware of labour developments in Canada.

Except for the share increase in man-day's lost due to work stoppages over 1965, it could be argued that the labour unrest of 1966 was no greater a problem than the problems of earlier years, such as those encountered during the period of readjustment in 1946-48. Viewed in perspective, the man-days lost represented only .33 per cent of total man-days worked by the non-agricultural labour force and this loss was greatly exceeded by man-days lost due to sickness and absenteeism. Of consequence is the fact that labour's activities, particularly labour-management affairs, received much more public attention and were much more a part of the fabric of Canadian news reporting and public discussion.

During 1966, there were five work stoppages that received minute examination — airline employees, meatpackers, railway employees, Ontario truckers, and Vancouver longshoremen — and four settlements that received equal attention — longshoremen, 80¢ over two years; seaway workers, 30 per cent over two years; British Columbia loggers, 40¢ over two years; railroaders, a minimum of 24 per cent over three years. Out of this experience there has arisen increasing concern over work stoppage, which is not in the public or national interest, and the settlement, which is not in the public interest, especially in the face of inflationary pressures.

Whether these stoppages and settlements were or were not in the best interest of Canadians is very difficult to prove, and to date no one seems particularly interested in finding out. In the field of political and public affairs, however, proof is not a prerequisite of acceptance. The reporting media has suggested damage and the public at large is all too willing to accept this suggestion as proof. Possibly a truer representation of the state of affairs will come out of the two commissions appointed as a result of the 1966 experiences — the inquiry into the use of the labour injunction headed by former supreme court judge, the late Ivan Rand, and the Federal Task Force on Industrial Relations headed by Dean H. D. Woods of McGill University. The Task Force has explored all aspects of labour-management relations in Canada and its relation to public policy in this area. Other issues that have received considerable attention include the suggestion of Canadian-American wage parity in the automobile and steel industries, trade union militancy as evidenced by inflated requests and an increase in membership's refusal to accept recommended settlements, a lack of optimism over the recently introduced system of collective bargaining in the provincial and federal Civil Services, and labour's desire to see the principles of the Freedman report adopted as public policy. In addition, there are negotiations underway in 1970 which, if not peacefully concluded, will result in severe criticism of the collective bargaining process — the automobile industry, Air Canada and the Canadian Airlines Employees Association, locomotive engineers and firemen, hospital employees and several other agreements in the public service.

As this quickening of public interest in labour affairs continues, it appears that the labour movement of Canada is rapidly losing public support and sympathy and, more importantly, the support and sympathy of the provincial and federal governments. Increasingly, the programmes, activities and image of the Canadian trade union movement are failing to stand up before the scrutiny of the Canadian reporting media and the Canadian public. Traditionally, the Canadian trade union movement has had the support and comfort of many non-participating individuals in Canadian society and, to some extent, the success of Canadian labour is a result of this support. For many years, both provincial and federal governments, have been friends of labour. Public sentiment, always divided and although not positively assisting, has, through its neutrality, not frustrated labour's efforts. The Canadian intellectual community, although it was never granted a legitimate role in labour's efforts, has traditionally been in sympathy with trade union efforts.

The 1960's brought considerable change in the list of friends of the Canadian labour movement. The labour movement seemed to stand in relative isolation. The long standing support from government crumbled before the economic and social realities of the sixties. No longer gripped by labour's championing the cause of the underdog, public sentiment saw the labour movement as the enemy of economic and social progress, blocking the Canadian economy's every effort to advance. Disenchanted by labour's lethargy and its complete refusal to take measures to retain its legitimate place in Canada's economic and social life, the Canadian intellectual community is no longer one of its supporters. One student of labour, writing in 1965, expressed his feelings this way:

> *Traditionally, Labour Day speakers eulogize the past achievement of the trade union movement and hold out even more promise for the future. While I intend to follow the same general pattern, I will spend relatively little time extolling the accomplishments of times gone by and devote most of my remarks to the challenges which lie ahead.*

> *I stress the word challenges because of my conviction that organized labour cannot count on an illustrious future unless it is prepared to adapt to the needs of the times. The periodic transformations which have marked the history of the labour movement in North America bear witness to this view . . .*

> *While I do not consider myself an alarmist on the subject I do feel that the labour movement faces a crisis. A crisis, not in the sense that its very existence is threatened, but in the sense that it cannot continue to play the full part in our society that it has a right and obligation to play unless it puts its own house in order.*[6]

---

[5] "Time Lost in Strikes Doubles," *Financial Times,* March 23, 1967.

[6] John H. G. Crispo, "Looking Back and Looking Forward: Can Organized Labor Stand the Test of Time," *Industrial Relations* (Laval), Vol. 20, No. 4, (October 1965), p. 700.

The importance of the developments of 1966 do more than merely point out the apparent need for not only better methods of accommodating labour-management differences and conflicts, but also better methods of reporting on them. More importantly, they have questioned the ability of the Canadian trade union movement to accommodate effectively the Canada of the 1960's. If 1966 is any indication of the ability of the Canadian trade union movement to advance its cause and manage its affairs in contemporary Canada, it is certain that future years shall witness its diminishing role as a determinant of labour conditions in Canada.

Although it is not possible to charge this loss of support to any one cause, it does appear that labour is no longer able to define for itself an accommodative role in contemporary economic and social affairs. It is as though it were living in the past, completely unaware of changes that have taken place around it. Its structure and philosophy is obsolete and its image is riddled with criticism. In answer to public and government commitment to higher productivity, it offers the fifty year old dictum of business unionism. To concern over the problem of interunion rivalry and jurisdiction disputes, it cites the aged Scranton Declaration and adopts weak constitutional proscriptions.[7] Its solution to the complex problems associated with the introduction to automation and technological change is the Freedman Report.[8] Its reply to criticisms over work stoppages affecting "national and public interest" is its revered right to strike.[9] Its solution to problems of higher prices is higher wages. The record is clear: these answers are not good enough for the problems of Canada in the 1970's.

Concomitant with declining support in many quarters has been a flurry of commentaries which not only diagnose labour ills but also prescribe a cure. Some call for rationalizing labour's structure, arguing that there are too many unions and that a rationalized structure would consolidate numbers and reduce the number of overlapping jurisdictions. Some urge unions to abandon their pragmatic member-satisfying collective bargaining philosophy, with stress on immediate returns, favour of greater emphasis on labour's role in the economic and social realities of today. There are those more inclined towards the numbers game, who note that trade union membership is lagging behind the growth of the non-agricultural labour force and urge it to organize the as yet largely unorganized occupations in the service sector. There are those who note that much of the growth in trade union membership and collective agreements is in areas where the traditional labour movement appears to have no interest, control or influence — the so called professional occupations such as school teaching, nursing, dietetics, and the civil service. There are those who charge that labour's call for support by the working class is steeped in memories of the hardships, unemployment and low wages of the Great Depression and, as such, has little appeal to the comparatively affluent young members in the Canadian labour force. These people are better educated, hard to convince and are not satisfied with the emotional "underdog" appeal. Some claim that labour is more interested in relying on collective bargaining rights set out under statute law rather than working to make the system more effective. There are those who claim that labour is irresponsible in its exercise of the right to strike and urge caution in its use, lest an impatient public and government take the right away.

There is no shortage of diagnoses and proposed cures; in reviewing the list of current commentaries, however, one wonders how many of these observations are really little more than symptoms of the ills facing Canadian unionism. It appears, in fact, that labour is suffering from structural inadequacies and an obsolete philosophy. Consequently, it finds its image deteriorating and stands condemned for emphasizing collective bargaining gains over the need for a social awareness and a participation in Canadian national affairs. In terms of structure and philosophy, Canadian labour was ill-equipped to face the challenges and realities of the 1960's and to set the course for change through the 1970's.

Because of a structural deficiency, Canadian labour a. is condemned for its position on inflation, b. is labeled irresponsible for calling stoppages contrary to the national interest. Because of an obsolete philosophy, it a. is labeled irresponsible for calling stoppages over jurisdictional issues within the union, b. appears unable or uninterested in extending its organization and influence, c. appears unable to win the support of the younger members of the labour force, and d. is condemned for its position on the introduction of technological change to Canadian industry.

SOME VIEWS ON DEFICIENCIES IN STRUCTURE

The structure of the Canadian trade union movement is predominately international. Of the 160 unions operating in Canada as of January 1, 1969, 101 were international and 59 were national in character. Of the 8,378 affiliated local unions, 4,470 were affiliated with international unions and 3,908 were affiliated with national unions. In terms of membership, over 65 per cent of Canadian trade unionists were in locals that had international affiliation. Only 8 national unions had a membership of over 20,000 persons.[10] According to one expert, a union with a membership of less than 20,000 persons has little chance of success. From the point of view of practical day-to-day trade unionism, the small membership of national unions at present raises a number of problems in the ability of the union to service its members effectively. William Mahoney, Canadian

[7] "Notice of Non-Compliance in Dispute Procedure," *Canadian Labour,* Vol. 11, No. 2, (February 1966), p. 22, and "Executive Council Report," *Canadian Labour,* Vol. 11, No. 5, (May 1966), p. 12.

[8] "Automation — A National Program," in *Canadian Labour,* Vol. 11, No. 5, (May 1966), p. 33.

[9] "CLC Statement on the Right to Strike," *Canadian Labour,* Vol. 9, No. 11, (November 1964), p. 17.

[10] *Labour Organization in Canada, 1969.* (Ottawa: Queen's Printer, 1969), p. xii-xiv.

Director of the United Steel Workers of America, had this to say on the subject:

> *There is a very real connection between the fact that most successful unions are those which have passed the 20,000-mark in Canadian membership. This seems to be the figure which permits: Canada-wide organizational activity, including Canadian specialists operating from a Canadian headquarters; and a Canada-wide membership service structure.*
>
> *We must keep two points in mind. Firstly, it costs more to provide routine staff service to any union membership in Canada than it does in the United States, or in some geographically smaller nation with a larger population concentration. Secondly, in addition to routine service, modern unionism requires a great deal of specialized service to counterbalance the increasing specialization of management. To be most effective in Canada, these specialists must be thoroughly grounded in Canadian legislation and procedures.*
>
> · · ·
>
> *Our population is very small in comparison with the size of our country and, except for a concentrated central core in southern Ontario and the Montreal area, it is very thinly spread across the land. We must, therefore, provide more service staff per member than they do in other countries and our travel and communication costs are very high in ratio to dues-payers. We have found that, if a union has less than 20,000 Canadian members, it must either provide less than adequate service to all locals and do less organization or it must concentrate exclusively on the central core while ignoring the rest of the country.*
>
> · · ·
>
> *Another reason for added expense is bilingualism. We have always taken the position that, where French is the predominantly used language, union information and union service must be available in the French language if the union is to be most effective. The same position has been taken by other successful unions. This, of course, costs more than unilingual services in a country such as the U.S. or most other countries in the western world.*
>
> *Thirdly, Canadian workers are cribbed and confined by a lot of unnecessary, unfair and expensive regulations and laws. Collective bargaining in Canada is more regulated by more laws than in most countries of the free world; far more, for that matter, than other countries in the North Atlantic community. Most employees come under provincial jurisdiction and this means, not only differing sets of labour relations laws, but different sets of workmen's compensation, safety laws, etc. The legal costs per member in Canada, if a union is at all active and agressive, are higher than in most other free countries; the more laws, the more lawyers.*
>
> *Lastly, Canadian strikes are more costly to central treasuries. In certain Canadian industries, particularly those located in remote areas,*

employers tend to ignore the general patterns of bargaining and tend to resist unionism very rigorously. In parts of the mining industry, for example, we must still simply assume that the employer would force employees to choose between abject bargaining surrender or strike action very early in any local union's history. Since the local union has had no chance to build up its own resources, since local unionists have not been able to accumulate personal reserves because of low pay, high costs and lack of social security laws, and since there has been no alternative work available as is frequently the case in highly populated areas, strikes in this industry have been long and costly.

Over the first twenty years of our union's operations in Canada, the cost of maintaining service, expanding organization and financing strikes have required, in addition to Canadian dues dollars, a subsidy of many millions of dollars from our U.S. fellow-members. We are now in the positon where Canadians can pay their own way under normal circumstances, but it is still very close to the line. A long, expensive strike will make the difference between operating in the black or in the red.[11]

In view of the close relationship between labour's means and ends, international trade unionism is a logical structural form and it has worked well throughout most of the history of Canadian labour.[12] Recent developments, however, give prominance to the question of whether it can continue to work well in the face of the new challenges. The labour movement itself is looking for an answer to this question. The sixth biennial conference of the CLC, held in Winnipeg in September 1966, established a Commission on Constitution and Structure ". . . to examine the entire question of structure mergers, affiliation, and unity and to submit recommendations to the 1968 Canadian Labour Congress convention on these subjects." [13] Speaking on the proposal, CLC President, Claude Jodoin, noted that with the tenth anniversary of the founding of the CLC ". . . the time seems appropriate to take a further look at our structure."[14] Subsequently, Donald McDonald, Secretary-Treasurer of the CLC, was appointed Chairman of the Commission. The six member commission had equal representation from national and international unions and invited two types of briefs from CLC affiliates: on the constitution and structure of the CLC and on the labour movement in general, particularly mergers. In subsequent hearings called by the commission, the Canadian Union of Public Employees reportedly urged that the more than one hundred unions

---

[11] "Large Unions More Efficient," *Canadian Labour*, Vol. 10, No. 11, November 1965), p. 26-27.
[12] The reader interested in exploring the development of international unions in Canada should consult C. Brian Williams, "The Development of Canadian-American Trade Union Relations: Some Conclusions," *Industrial Relations* (Laval), Vol. 21, No. 3. p. 332-353.
[13] "CLC Structure Commission Begins Hearings," *Canadian Labour*, Vol. 11, No. 11, (November 1966), p. 45.
[14] "Structure Commission," *Canadian Labour*, Vol. 11, No. 5, (May 1966) p. 17.

in Canada amalgamate into ten national industrial unions. In its brief, it was reported that it argued ". . . that fragmentation into many unions was a basic fault of the Canadian labour movement, and that some international unions limited their Canadian members' autonomy in matters that were purely Canadian." It also urged a complete reorganization of the CLC's structure in order ". . . to eliminate the system of too many chiefs and too few indians."[15]

In December, 1966, the official publication of the Canadian Labour Congress commented on the work of the commission:

An intensive study that may have a marked influence on the structure and operations of the Canadian labour movement in the years to come was launched when the CLC's Commission on Structure and other matters held its first sessions in Vancouver early in November.

. . .

Hearings will continue at various centres across the country until early February; but the initial stages of the enquiry have been adequate to demonstrate the serious and constructive approaches being made by many sections of the movement.

Behind the entire project is a strong feeling that a labour movement must be prepared to keep abreast of the times and to equip itself to meet new and changing conditions if it is to fulfil its responsibility to the membership.

The first ten years of the merged Congress comprised what might be considered to be a period of consolidation. It was natural, for example, that in framing a constitution for the new Congress, which came into being in 1956, many concessions had to be made by various groups in order to reach an agreement.

There is a strong feeling that the time has now been reached when this situation can be reviewed and a somewhat different approach is possible if it is required.

The basic task of the Commission will be to determine just what is required, within the Congress and between affiliated unions, in order to meet the challenging times that lie ahead. The work of the Commission should provide a most valuable basis on which to build for the future.[16]

Canadian labour has traditionally used collective bargaining as its method of achieving its ends of "more, more, more." In its enthusiasm to establish the collective bargaining principle, it not only embraced international trade unionism but also eagerly greeted government's offer to legislate the practice, and at every opportunity it has encouraged its adoption. In the vast majority of cases, collective bargaining in Canada takes place at the lower levels of economic activity, usually at the plant or multi-plant level.

Ever since it was first introduced in Canada in the 1840's, international trade unionism has received criticism from without and from within the Canadian labour movement. Some objected to imposing the international constitution on Canadian members and to the old AFL imposing its constitution on the equally old Dominion Trades and Labour Congress. Some objected to the export of membership fees and dues to the United States. More recently, some have objected to the international's rejection of settlement terms agreed to by its Canadian local membership and the imposition of the AFL/CIO's wishes on Canadian jurisdictional disputes in the Canadian Labour Congress. There are those who fear that the internationals operating in Canada will conduct their affairs not in the interest of its Canadian membership but in the interest of its American membership. Some regard any participation of United States organization in Canada with suspicion.

All of the above fears and suspicions arise from the fundamental fact that, in a North American trade union committed to collective bargaining, the structure is designed to maximize bargaining power. In its attempt to maximize power, local autonomy must inevitably be surrendered to the central authority. This is certainly the case with an international union; and a national union pursuing the same objectives through collective bargaining would be structured in a similar way. Consequently, even with a national union structure, the same criticisms noted above appear to hold true.

Although studies of Canadian labour structure are few, there is simply no evidence that the international structure has any interest other than the well being of its Canadian membership; the same is true for its leadership, both Canadian and American. There is, however, one aspect of the international structure which not only has received insufficient attention, but also may be used to question seriously the ability of the Canadian labour movement, under its present international structure, to confront the challenges it faces in the next decade. On the one hand, under the international structure, the Canadian portion of the movement is not sufficiently free nor sufficiently encouraged to undertake the much needed examination of its collective bargaining policies and the acceptance of these policies by Canadian society. On the other hand, it is the collective bargaining policies of the Canadian sections of international unions that are the centre of criticism, as the events of 1966 have so aptly demonstrated. To be sure, the international conventions of the international unions spend a great deal of their time discussing and formulating collective bargaining policies, but the policies are national (i.e. United States) and it is the application of these policies in Canada that is being questioned. For the large part, there is no similar collective bargaining policy determining forums in Canada. One of the two propositions advanced in this essay is that the international trade union structure is not one that makes it likely that the international Canadian labour movement will be able to maintain its role

[15] *Labour Gazette,* Vol. 67, No. 8, (August 1967), p. 477, and *Labour Gazette,* Vol. 66, No. 9, (September 1966), p. 499.
[16] "CLC Structure Commission," *Canadian Labour,* Vol. 11, No. 12, (December 1966), p. 4.

and influence in Canadian society, because its structure does not permit sufficient attention to be given to the question of Canadian collective bargaining policies.

Note the words of William Dodge, Executive Vice-President of the Canadian Labour Congress, when he wrote recently on the influence of international unions in Canada.

During the past few years both labour and management in Canada have been engaged in a vigorous discussion of economic planning and their roles in it. As a result of these discussions, exciting new agencies have come into being — the Economic Council of Canada and numerous regional planning bodies.

Labour and management are both being obliged to think out their roles in economic planning in a very profound way. They are beginning to realize that their demands upon the economy must take into account the national interest. They are moving inexorably toward exploration of such concepts as incomes policy, industrial rationalization and more government intervention in economic affairs.

It is in such areas that the independence of Canadian management and labour becomes important, because it is by no means clear that the economic interests of Canada can be served adequately by adopting policies similar to those followed in the United States or acceptable to government, business and labour in the United States.[17]

Under the international structure, the basic collective bargaining policies of Canadian branches are greatly influenced by the policies set down in the constitutions and conventions of the international organizations, organizations in which the large majority of members and contracts are located in the United States. As a result, the collective bargaining policies of Canadian branches of international unions have been arrived at in the light of the economic and social realities of the United States. It is these policies that the international membership is duty bound to uphold and follow.

It may be argued that several international unions do call together their Canadian membership for the purpose of setting policies to govern Canadian activities. The policy conference of the steel workers is an example. Similar sessions are held by the meat packers, auto workers, oil-chemical workers, operating engineers, and the Canadian Railway Labour Executive Association; however, only a few of the 111 international unions in Canada hold such meetings. In addition, and this is the main point, the reported proceedings of unions that do hold Canadian policy conferences reflects the sentiment and philosophy of the collective bargaining policies set down by the international unions. Very little time, if any, is spent discussing basic collective bargaining policies. Most of the time is spent formulating the specific requests for the upcoming negotiations. There can be little doubt that the decisions reached in these meetings are greatly influenced by the basic philosophy and policies arrived at in the American proceedings. In other words, the American proceedings set out the basic general terms of reference and provide a back-stop against which the specific Canadian decisions are made.

It is not suggested here that international unions intentionally restrict ". . . the freedom of Canadian branches to make decisions based on national needs, aspirations and conditions . . . ."[18] Nor is it suggested that the international is forcing Canadian branches to adopt international collective bargaining policies. In both situations, the ability of the international to influence Canadian branches is no different than its ability to influence United States branches. This ability varies considerably from one union to another. As pointed out in several recent studies, both contentions cannot be supported by the facts. What is suggested is that the international structure ". . . national needs, aspirations and conditions . . . ." *are not sufficiently* stressed in the formulation of the collective bargaining policies to be followed by the branches of international unions operating in Canada.

Except for those international unions that provide some type of forum within which to develop the policies to be followed in its Canadian section, it is difficult to see how these issues can receive the amount of attention they must have under the present structure. It is unrealistic to look to the Canadian Labour Congress for leadership. First, the Canadian Labour Congress, being a creation of its affiliates, is able to concern itself only with matters of which its affiliates approve. It is unlikely that affiliates would accept CLC leadership on matters within the collective bargaining arena. The discussions at CLC conventions are largely void of any meaningful examination of the collective bargaining policies to be followed by its affiliates. The CLC's inability to introduce and successfully operate procedures for the settlement of inter-union jurisdiction disputes is a good example of its affiliates' attitude toward CLC attempts to regulate or influence the labour management field. In addition, in a recent editorial, the CLC's publication *Canadian Labour* emphasized that the CLC undertook three functions on behalf of its affiliates — legislative, coordinating, and service.[19]

In an article entitled "The Influence of International Unions," William Dodge, Executive Vice-President of the CLC, undertook to show that the CLC and its affiliates are not under United States control. He attempted to do this by identifying a number of areas where the CLC and its affiliates' position was contrary to the AFL/CIO and its affiliates' position. These areas were: a. political action, b. international affairs, c. world trade union affairs, d. economic planning. It is interesting that the first three of these areas do not relate directly to the labour management field. The fourth area — economic planning — does. Here are some of the words used by Mr. Dodge on this subject:

[17] "The Influence of International Unions," *Canadian Labour,* Vol. 10, No. 11, (November 1965), p. 22. Emphasis added.

[18] Bryan M. Downie, "The Influence of International Unions on Collective Bargaining in Canada," (Queen's University: School of Commerce, September 1965), p. 1, Mimeo.

[19] Editorial, *Canadian Labour,* Vol. 9, Nov. 11, (November 1964), p. 3.

The Canadian labour movement has declared itself for economic planning but labour in the United States is still hesitant and suspicious. Canadian labour may eventually be obliged to make choices and perhaps commitments which will meet with stern disapproval among labour leaders in the United States.

This may very well require independent action on structure and policy which will present many complex problems. It will be difficult to effect mergers or revise jurisdiction and structures to suit Canadian policy requirements if such decisions are not simultaneously being made in the United States. I say difficult but not impossible, I think it has been established that we are capable of making our own decisions in Canada and determined to act in the interests of our own country and our own people.[20]

Although the events of 1966 were not unique in the history of Canadian labour management relations, they have brought forth unprecedented comment from all quarters of Canadian life. As Mr. Dodge pointed out, this situation is largely a result of increased concern over the health of the Canadian economy and increased attention with the concept of economic planning. The labour management disputes and the terms of settlement which were so widely heralded in 1966 run counter to this increasing commitment to a smooth functioning and well planned economic system. In the areas of management of the economy and progress towards economic planning, there is an ever increasing gulf between Canadian and American thinking and practice. The economic underpinnings of Canada are not the same as those of the United States. The structure of our industry and the role of industries in our economy are quite different. As a result, Canadian collective bargaining policies, which assume a transferability from the United States to Canada, are having and will continue to have difficulty finding acceptance in Canada's contemporary economic and social scene.

The economic and social scene in contemporary Canada dictates that the economic and social realities of Canada be reflected in the collective bargaining policies of all trade unions operating in Canada. Because these collective bargaining policies are hammered out in international conventions and by executive decision, the Canadian unionist does not have a forum, such as a convention, where these issues could be examined in the light of the realities of the Canadian scene. A most cursory examination of the proceedings of Canada's national labour centre, the Canadian Labour Congress, clearly illustrates that this is not a forum for working out collective bargaining policies in Canada. Unlike proceedings of the national American centre, the AFL/CIO, very few collective bargaining policies are ever debated at CLC conventions. When debate does occur, it simply reflects the decisions reached in international proceedings. The CLC, to quote labour itself ". . . is the creature of its affiliated organizations."[21]

David McDonald, International President of the United Steelworkers, in a taperecorded message to the 1964 steelworkers policy conference, implied that most international unions do not allow the Canadian Labour Congress and branches of internationals in Canada exclusive jurisdiction over labour policies in Canada.

We accept and respect the authority of our AFL/CIO in U.S. matters. We accept and respect the authority of the Canadian Labour Congress in Canadian matters.

We respectfully suggest to all other international unions that they should study the successful results of such a policy, results which show clearly in the size and growth of the Canadian section of the United Steelworkers.[22]

The 1960's has demonstrated repeatedly that collective bargaining today, even though carried out at a local level, receives national attention in the Canadian press, radio, and television. Faced by this reality, Canadian labour stubbornly clings to its traditional structure. Not only does it not have a forum in which to formulate its policies on agreements that are now of national concern, but also it does not have a vehicle for expressing itself at the national level. The greatest tragedy of the international structure is that it prevents Canadian labour from meaningfully confronting the issues faced by Canadian unionists. The Canadian movement is largely devoid of a meaningful research effort. Educational efforts in Canada are carried out at the discretion of American decision-makers. The agenda on collective bargaining and other trade union policies is held in the hands of American unionists. Debate takes place on American soil and in an American context where Canadian realities and Canadian labour issues receive little consideration and have little effect on the outcome of the discussion. The result — and it is a great tragedy — is that Canadian unionists have no effective forum in which they can formulate Canadian policies and programmes for Canadian labour issues. Unlike the earlier days of the international trade union structure, the rapid divergence of Canadian and American industrial interests demand the separation of the collective bargaining policies used by trade unions in the two countries.

SOME VIEWS ON DEFICIENCIES IN PHILOSOPHY

It is difficult to separate Canadian trade union structure from Canadian trade union philosophy. The structure of the movement is the organizational manifestation of its philosophy; consequently, a change in one affects the other. International trade unionism not only has molded the structure of the Canadian movement, but also has shaped its philosophy; an international trade union structure means an international trade union philosophy.

This paper has suggested that the international trade union structure contributes to some of the issues facing the Canadian trade union movement today. It was also argued that continued adherence to this structure

[20] "The Influence of International Unions," *Canadian Labour,* Vol. 10, No. 11, (November 1965), p. 22.

[21] Editorial, *Canadian Labour,* Vol. 9, No. 4, (April 1967), p. 5.

[22] "Steel Workers Policy Conference," *Labour Gazette,* Vol. 64, No. 6, (June 1964), p. 476.

will make it increasingly difficult for Canadian labour to find its much needed accommodative role in contemporary Canadian society. Other issues faced by the Canadian movement today are likewise the result of the accompanying international trade union philosophy. Continued adherence to this philosophy will also make it difficult for Canadian labour to meet challenges as they arise.

Previous sections of the article portrayed the history of the trade union movement in structural terms; it is important to realize, however, that it was not simply the structure that was the subject of such heated controversy and debates, but also the philosophy that was attached to or part of each of the structural forms advocated. In terms of philosophy, this same structural history of the Canadian movement reflects two primary schools of trade union philosophy — class collaboration and class consciousness.

The philosophy of class collaboration is the philosophy of international trade unionism. It was this philosophy that was manifested in the Dominion Trades and Labour Congress of 1886 and in the international trade unions, and it is the current philosophy of the Canadian Labour Congress. The philosophy of class conscious trade unionism was the philosophy of organizations that were set up in opposition to the philosophy of international trade unionism. Organizations such as the National Trades and Labour Congress, the All Canadian Congress of Labour, the Canadian Federation of Labour, the One Big Union and, to some extent, the Canadian Congress of Labour are the best examples.

The essential elements of these two opposing schools of trade union philosophy are not difficult to identify and are well documented in the platforms, proceedings and records of each organization. In broad terms, differences focus on: a. the role of trade unionism in society, b. the means or methods whereby the trade union movement is to advance the cause of the working class and, as a corollary, c. the structure to be adopted in order to effectively advance this role and method.

The philosophy of international trade unionism was the philosophy of class collaboration. It was this philosophy that emerged after great debate in the platform of the American Federation of Labour in 1886, and by the turn of the century was the predominant philosophy of the American labour movement. It was the philosophy of "pure and simple business unionism" and of "Gomperism." It was a philosophy that was arrived at after an examination of alternative positions.

The philosophy of class collaboration accepted not only the existing system, but also the form of government that went along with it. The role of the trade union movement was one of wringing improvements in wages, hours and working conditions from reluctant American employers. A pragmatic philosophy, it cast government's role in secondary terms. Its method was collective bargaining and its weapon was the work stoppage. Its structure in turn was shaped to maximize its chosen method — organization within exclusive jurisdictions by crafts, surrender of local autonomy to the central body of the craft, the international trade union, internal government by constitution and bylaws and the development of a "defense" or strike fund. It sought to organize workers wherever non-union labour or products met the competition of union labour or products. Emphasizing solidarity of the craft or trade, the central organization of the craft or trade was given complete autonomy in matters of collective bargaining and the strike. To the national federation, The American Federation of Labour, fell the responsibilities for acting as the spokesman for all of organized labour and for advancing labour's legislative cause within the established political framework. It adopted an independent political stance. The cornerstone of this philosophy was self-centred — self help and sole reliance on the resources within the "House of Labour."

The philosophy of class consciousness was diametrically opposed to the philosophy of class collaboration. The following words, drawn from a recently published class conscious interpretation of Canadian labour history, illustrate:

> *In the period under review, trade union progress demanded a fighting wage policy, organization of the unorganized, unity, industrial and Canadian unionism, political action. Yet the dominant trade union officialdom in Canada, and its ally, U.S. international headquarters resisted. Why? One reason was class collaboration. Not the word or ideological trend, although it was a word and ideological trend. Not collective bargaining or legislative representations to governments. But something distinct: Subordinating the movement's interest to reconciliation with the employers, settling for less than it was possible realistically to get.*[23]

The philosophy of class conscious trade unionism rejected the existing economic and political systems. As replacements, it advocated various degrees of reform, ranging from direct worker control of the means of production to direct worker representation in the existing economic and political system. In answer to the dictum of organization by crafts, with a central union having exclusive jurisdiction, the philosophy called for a loose organization of all workers in an industry, whether skilled or unskilled, into one organization. This philosophy placed great emphasis on the unity and solidarity of labour regardless of one's trade or calling. It de-emphasized collective bargaining and the strike as the method of protest against an employer, in favour of political action and the demonstration of labour solidarity through the general or industrial strike.

The philosophy of class collaboration trade unionism was introduced in Canada with the establishment of the Dominion Trades and Labour Congress of Canada in 1886. Through the years, with the rise of the CIO in the United States and the CCL here in Canada, its organization by craft theory was broadened to include organization by industry, semi-skilled and unskilled workers, although still within the context of the notion

---

[23] Charles Lipton, *The Trade Union Movement of Canada, 1827-1959,* (Montreal: Canadian Social Publications Limited, 1966), p. 237.

of exclusive jurisdiction. Today, the class collaboration philosophy represents the philosophy of all but a very small section of the Canadian trade union movement. It is a philosophy that is subscribed to by national unions as well as international unions.

Although there have been several attempts to introduce various degrees of class consciousness into the Canadian trade union movement, these attempts have been repeatedly rebuffed by Canadian trade unionists. On this point, it is sufficient to say that the philosophy of class collaboration has worked well in the past, yet one wonders whether it can continue to do so when confronted by the requirements of the next decade. As a meaningful trade union philosophy, it may be obsolete. The role assigned to national and international unions is too narrow and the emphasis placed on self-centered-self help is too great. In short, and this is the second of the two main propositions advanced in this essay, the two major philosophical cornerstones of business unionism — the limited role of national and international unions and the emphasis on self-centered-self help through the employer-employee collective bargaining relationship — will make it difficult for the Canadian trade union movement to find the accommodative role it urgently needs in contemporary Canada.

There are those who will say that some of the above charges represent failings on the part of collective bargaining and not Canadian trade unionism. They will say that it is collective bargaining that is ill-equipped to handle the issues arising in contemporary labour-management relations. It is not collective bargaining that is obsolete, however, but the philosophical setting within which it is asked to work by Canadian labour — a setting that in turn makes it difficult for collective bargaining to continue to do the job that we have asked of it.

There is nothing inherently wrong with the class collaboration philosophy itself, but recognizing the present transformations in our social and economic system, it is a philosophy that runs counter to the values held in contemporary Canadian society. It is a philosophy that unduly restricts the role of national and international trade unions, and places far too much reliance on a narrowly conceived self-centred-self help collective bargaining method.

THE ROLE OF NATIONAL AND INTERNATIONAL TRADE UNIONS
IN THE CLASS COLLABORATION PHILOSOPHY

Within the philosophy of business unionism, national and international unions are encouraged to play a relatively limited role in extending trade union organization and influence throughout all levels of the economic system. The philosophy supports the exclusive character of a union's area of influence, with the result that it is deeply committed to jealously protected and well defined occupational or industrial jurisdictions. This area of interest and of influence extends only to the craft or industry, not to the economic system as a whole. Because of this acceptance of and emphasis on protecting and working within established occupational or industrial jurisdictions, the labour movement ostensibly has little interest in either extending its jurisdiction to new occupational classes or industries or in changing established occupational classes and industries, even though occupational and industrial definitions are rapidly changing. It shows little concern with national issues and seems indifferent to the impact of decisions in their craft or industry on the national scene. In terms of what the national and international unions *should* be concerned about and who they should be concerned about, this philosophy grants an extremely limited role to these organizations.

Many of the new occupations such as school teachers, nurses, and public servants, which have extended the labour management area, are represented by organizations that are not part of the traditional trade union movement. That is, they are not within the jurisdiction of established trade union organizations. In most cases these occupations are most reluctant not only to affiliate but even to be associated with the traditional trade union organizations. They find the image of the traditional trade unions quite repulsive.

If the trade union movement of Canada is to re-establish its role in Canada social and economic affairs, it must adopt a philosophy that not only encourages extending organization beyond established occupational and industrial jurisdiction, but also quickens the interest and concern of national and international trade unions on the impact of developments within the craft or industry on the national scene. It must replace rigidity with flexibility and self-centred interest with national interest. It must actively work to extend its concern to the labour force as a whole, and to organize and assist all persons seeking improvement in their position within Canadian society, through collective bargaining or otherwise. In order to do this, it must adopt a philosophy that grants national and international trade unions a much more active and participative role. Specifically, it must confront and solve problems of jurisdictional disputes, raiding, extension of trade union organization to new occupations and industries, and the impact of trade union activities within a craft or industry on the national economy.

Like the matter of structure, some members of the Canadian trade union movement are equally concerned over the restrictive character of international trade union philosophy. In January 1964, an editorial in *Canadian Labour* spoke on the role of the Canadian trade union movement.

The whole labour movement is today critically appraising its role in society. Inevitably, as society changes and develops, the labour movement will adapt to meet those changes and developments. The Canadian Labour Congress, as the focus of the labour movement on the national scene, will undoubtedly be called upon to reflect sharply those changes in the service of its members across Canada.[24]

[24] Editorial, *Canadian Labour*, Vol. 9, No. 1, (January 1964), p. 3.

Earlier in 1962, Wilfred List, labour reporter for the Toronto *Globe and Mail* and a friend of labour wrote:

Organized labour in Canada is groping toward an uncertain future, clouded by the rapid changes taking place in the composition of the work force and the emergence of a universal middle class no longer attracted by traditional union slogans.

. . .

Imaginative new approaches are needed if labor is to continue as an influential force and bargaining instrument in the future. The challenge is only now being given serious recognition, but the response is still one of groping for a solution.

. . .

The warning signs are plain enough, but organized labor is still basically tradition-rooted and difficult to arouse to the challenge of the changing times. Here and there, as gadflies on the body politic of organized labour, some union leaders are raising their voices in a warning of the crisis ahead.

. . .

Pure and simple business unionism divorced from any philosophy or ultimate goals still dominates much of the union movement, particularly in the building trades. Unions will have to demonstrate that their vision goes beyond the immediate wage goal.

. . .

The solution to many of the labor movement's difficulties may lie in the area of greater central direction of union affairs, as is the case in Sweden. But jealously guarded jurisdictions and rivalries, as well as the fact that some of the larger unions are outside the Canadian Labour Congress makes any approach toward a more central form of authority difficult indeed.[25]

Attempts within the House of Labour to establish effective self administered machinery for resolving jurisdictional disputes and eliminating raiding have met with only limited success. In 1960, the Executive Council of the Canadian Labour Congress adopted a code of organizing practices which was designed to eliminate raiding by replacing it with orderly organizing methods. In 1964, the CLC convention adopted an Internal Disputes Procedure, designed to resolve conflicting jurisdictional claims. However, when faced by the commitment of national and international unions to the traditional jealously guarded jurisdictions, the CLC simply has no way in which it can make the outcome of the machinery stick. The Canadian Labour Congress is the creature of its affiliated organizations.

William Dodge, Executive Vice-President of the Canadian Labour Congress has stated the problem this way:

I think, however, there is a great deal of misunderstanding about our role in the settlement of jurisdictional disputes and raids. It must be remembered that, when the TLC and the CCL merged in 1956, we created the greatest hodge-podge of jurisdictional overlaps imaginable, and this was done in the firm belief that unions had to learn to live together in peace and harmony, or perish.

The Conventions of the CLC have adopted a Constitution which gives limited authority to deal with jurisdictional disputes. We can use our powers of persuasion, and have done so successfully on a great many occasions, but we have no disciplinary po⸱ ers. This is understandable, because the jurisdictional lines between unions are so blurred as to make the exercise of such powers almost impossible.

In the case of raids, however, we do have disciplinary power. We have the power to suspend or expel from the Congress a union which violates the constitutional provisions on raiding. This latter power is not vested in the officers, nor in the Executive Council. It is vested in the Convention, and is carried out by the vote of the delegates from all affiliated unions.

· · ·

This power was not granted with a "tongue-in-cheek" attitude, as I recall it. We all felt that we were ushering in a great new era of friendly relations — friendly rivalry, if you like — between unions within one family. More important, we felt that, unless we could achieve a rule of law in our relations with one another within the CLC, we might as well say goodbye to our hopes for organizing the vast army of unorganized workers who remained and still remain outside of the Labour movement.[26]

To be sure, the Congress has been successful in resolving hundreds of jurisdictional disputes and raids, and it is fair to say that most national and international unions accept CLC involvement and are prepared to comply. In other cases, however, the CLC's "persuasion" and constitution have not proven sufficient, and it is these disputes that have been brought so forcefully to public attention. It is these few disputes that are proving to be so damaging to the image of the Canadian trade union movement. In April of 1960, the CLC convention expelled the International Brotherhood of Teamsters for deliberate, premeditated, and repeated raiding of other affiliates of the CLC. Most people found the conduct and attitude of the Teamsters quite obnoxious. In February 1966, the National Plate Printers, Die Stampers, and Engravers Union of North America and the United Steelworkers failed to comply with the decision of the International Dispute Procedures and, consequently, the executive was forced to issue a notice of non-compliance. At the 1966 convention of the CLC, the Executive Council report commented on the effectiveness of the procedures.

The internal disputes settlement procedure adopted as amendments to Article III of the Congress Constitution at the last Convention has proven to be quite successful. Experience to date would indicate that, while it is a great improvement on the previous procedure, it still has a number of weaknesses, and it is hoped that further experience will serve to demonstrate what steps should be taken to make it even more effective.[27]

---

[25] Wilfred List, "The Future of Labor," *The Commerceman*: Vol. XVII, 1962. p. 41-43.

[26] "The Congress and Jurisdictional Disputes," *Canadian Labour*, Vol. 5, No. 12, (December 1960), p. 11.

[27] "Executive Council Report," *Canadian Labour*, Vol. 11, No. 5, (May 1966), p. 12.

The existence of "blurred jurisdictional lines between unions" not only permits disputes over jurisdiction and encourages raids, but also has the effect of concentrating organizational efforts in those traditional occupations and industries. However, the Canadian labour force and Canadian industry is undergoing rapid structural change and, as this occurs, new occupations and industries are not receiving the much needed attention of the Canadian trade union movement. As William Dodge has congently stated:

> *These unorganized workers are for the most part white-collar workers, workers with some scientific training, and workers in the service industries, all notoriously difficult to organize. If we cannot show conclusively that we have within the CLC a united Labour movement, determined to outlaw unethical practices, and to organize the unorganized, instead of disorganizing the already organized, we are going to get nowhere in our efforts to bring these new people into our movement.*[28]

In order to find an accommodative role in contemporary society, the Canadian trade union movement must once and for all, through mergers and consolidations, define for itself a much broader jurisdiction for national and international unions within the class collaboration philosophy. The philosophical element of rigid occupational and industrial jurisdiction, an element of philosophy that dates back to the Berlin Declaration of 1903, is obsolete because it unnecessarily confines the role of trade unionism in contemporary society. It provides the basis for possible jurisdictional disputes and raids which are detrimental to the union image and does not permit the movement to respond easily to the ever increasing occupational and industrial changes in Canada. It is an aspect of philosophy that reinforces much of what the public dislikes in the Canadian labour scene.

THE CONCEPT OF SELF-CENTRED — SELF HELP IN THE CLASS COLLABORATION PHILOSOPHY

Because of the emphasis on self-centred-self help, the major concern of national and international unions is directed to the employer-employee level and the identification of results are limited to gains set out in the collective agreement. Broader labour welfare issues such as housing, education, human rights, immigration, international affairs, manpower policy and economic policy — issues that go beyond the local employer-employee relationship and the collective agreement — are left to the national center, the Canadian Labour Congress. The impact of the terms of settlement on the national economy, and the resultant issue of wage restraint are likewise left to be dealt with by the CLC. In matters of collective bargaining, the unions affiliated to the CLC retain absolute autonomy; recent experiences indicate, however, that activity at the employer-employee level and the results of these activities extend far beyond this level and are viewed as matters of national concern.

Unfortunately, the concept of self-centred-self help implies that the role of Canadian trade unionism is limited to activities and efforts at an employer-employee level in a given craft or industry. It suggests that the consequences of these activities and efforts, at levels other than the employer-employee level, are of no concern to the trade union movement. It suggests that activities and efforts at the employer-employee level can be thought of as isolated events set apart from, and not related to, other levels of Canadian economic and social affairs. While this may have been an acceptable proposition in the early days of the class collaboration philosophy, it is not acceptable in the contemporary scene. Whether there is, in fact, a relationship or not (and to date no one has satisfactorily defined the relationship of decentralized collective bargaining decisions on the national economy) the press, radio, television, and a good many observers of the labour scene present the results of these "isolated" events in terms of their impact on the larger scene. It is as if local employer-employee decisions are made from within a fish bowl with all of Canada on the outside looking in and rightly or wrongly interpreting the impact of these decisions on the country as a whole without giving too much thought to whether there is an impact or not. Given the ever increasing awareness and concern of the Canadian public on Canadian economic affairs, its commitment to a smooth well functioning economy and its commitment to economic planning, the concept of self-centred-self help is completely untenable. To continue to hold to this element of philosophy is to drive the labour movement further and further away from what could be a most sympathetic and understanding public and government response.

Because of its deep commitment to self-centred-self help, the movement is often labeled irresponsible; that is, in reaching decisions at the employer-employee level, it fails to take into account the impact of these decisions at other levels in Canada.

To succeed in contemporary Canada, the national and international unions must begin to redefine their role from one of self-centred-self help (on the employer-employee level) to one of social awareness and concern (on the national level). In short, the national and international unions must become intimately involved in topics that as yet have been mostly the concern of the Canadian Labour Congress, for example, the subjects of manpower development and utilization, adjustment to technological change, and wage restraint. In these three cases, the subjects are primarily and, in the first instance, employer-employee "action areas" and consequently must be the concern of national and international unions. The attitudes of the national and international unions have so far suggested that they do not think these are their problems. They are quite happy to leave them in the hands of the Canadian Labour Congress. This is a very poor attitude.

The issue of manpower development and utilization is assumed by the trade union movement to be a national issue and hence the concern of the CLC despite the fact that the decisions affecting manpower are made

---

[28] "The Congress and Jurisdictional Disputes," p. 11.

at the employer-employee level. By placing such great emphasis on the role of the Federal Government in this issue, the trade union movement seems to look to the Federal Government for initiative in this area. Note the emphasis on Federal Government involvement in the following excerpt from the recently issued CLC statement of manpower policy.

We propose that the government take steps immediately to co-ordinate manpower programs under a single agency within the Department of Labour . . . The NES should be given the necessary increases and improvements in funds, facilities and professional staff so that it can become the core of a new manpower agency, which might be called the National Manpower Service. This would be the key operational agency for implementing manpower policies and the sole co-ordinating agency of all manpower programs . . . .

We also urge the government to close the major gaps in manpower policy — particularly in the fields of research, training of the unemployed, and the geographic mobility of labour . . . We feel that the federal government should assume the full cost of living allowances to unemployed trainees and then raise the level of these allowances to a least three-quarters of an average industrial wage in each region. In regard to geographic mobility, the government should pay transportation costs, removal allowances, "settling-in" allowances (including cash benefits to sustain the worker until his first pay cheque in the new region) and, in the case of workers attending a training school away from home, a second residence allowance.[29]

Recalling the failure of the national manpower legislation of 1960, it should be clear to all that it is imprudent to look to the Federal Government for effective leadership and initiative. As it is not in a position to make the decisions affecting manpower, it is hardly in a position to initiate leadership. If anything, its role is one of facilitating and coordinating. It is equally clear, both here in Canada and in the United States, that the successful manpower programmes are those that have received firm leadership and initiative at the employer-employee level. If the parties at the employer-employee level do not recognize their responsibility, it is extremely difficult to see how the initiative needed to deal with Canadian manpower problems can be developed. Repeated suggestions that initiative in this area must come from the Federal Government makes it extremely easy for the participants at the employer-employee level to continue to avoid their true responsibilities. This they are quite prepared to do, as the manpower field has many knotty and complex problems. Finding solutions will not be an easy or an inexpensive task.

In the area of adjustment to technological change, the Canadian labour movement seems to follow the same basic approach. Again, it becomes a problem for the Federal Government and great emphasis is placed on seeking legislation that incorporates the principles set out in the eagerly received Freedman report, which places responsibility for adjusting to technical change at the employer-employee level. Here is what appears to be labour's solution to this complex problem:

It is too much, said Commissioner Freedman, to expect that trade unions will stand idly by while employers arbitrarily make changes which deprive workers of their jobs or drastically alter working conditions. He clearly pointed out that the doctrine of the exclusive right of management is pernicious not only in its effect on the labour-management relationship, but also on the employees concerned and on the communities which may be affected. He consequently made a number of recommendations to correct this situation. The recommendation which is of the greatest consequence in terms of labour-management relations is one which calls for a modification of the managerial prerogative as exercised hitherto. Commissioner Freedman argues convincingly that there is an obligation on the part of management to defer any technological changes until the trade union with which it has relations has been notified and been given an opportunity to treat it as a negotiable item. Commissioner Freedman suggests that an appropriate way of forcing them to do so would be through an amendment to the Industrial Relations and Disputes Investigation Act...

The Canadian Labour Congress urgently demands that the federal government at once implement the Freedman recommendations. Furthermore, we call upon all provincial governments to amend their relevant statutes in a similar fashion. Such actions would ensure that throughout Canada organized labour would have the right to bargain collectively over the introduction of automation and technological change.[30]

Although there is nothing inherently wrong with legislating a requirement to take the introduction of technical change to the bargaining table, one wonders if this approach would lead to the cooperation and understanding that experience tells us is so important in making the necessary adjustments. As in matters of manpower management, the successful programmes have relied on the exercise of initiative at the employer-employee level. Again, the decisions affecting and relating to the introduction of technological change are made at the employer-employee level. It is the employer-employee level that is the action level. Solutions to both manpower management and technical adjustment problems are hard to come by and most of the successful ones have been developed through experimentation. Governments and National Centres are not in a position to experiment. Experiments take place at the employer-employee level and, as such, the support, cooperation and good faith of the parties is the first requirement for success.

While the existing trade union structure and philosophy have served the Canadian labour movement well, as measured by membership, growth in membership, members of the labour force covered by collective agreement and its history, there are signs that its usefulness will be sharply challenged in the succeeding decade. Earlier, Kovacs concluded that ". . . unionism as a social force will continue to exert a strong influence on society . . ." This article does not agree with that statement. Unless

[29] "CLC Manpower Policy," *Canadian Labour,* Vol. 11, No. 1. p. 7.
[30] "Automation — A National Program," *Canadian Labour,* Vol. 11, No. 5. p. 32.

the Canadian trade union movement is prepared to reshape its structure and philosophy drastically, it will continue to have great difficulty in carving for itself an accommodative role in Canadian economic and social affairs.

First, an increased public awareness of the Canadian labour management scene has resulted in demands for increased accountability in the labour-management relationship. This demand for greater accountability, in turn, has as its roots a strengthening of Canadian commitment, both public and private, to a smooth functioning and well directed Canadian economic system. The labour movement for its part, still clinging to aged concepts of structure and philosophy, increasingly finds itself committed to courses of action that run counter to this demand for a smooth functioning Canadian economy.

With respect to structure, its international character chokes off the dialogue among Canadian trade unionists over Canadian trade union issues and challenges. Because of this structure, the movement is without a voice, is intellectually deprived and lacks institutions that could speak with authority on the challenges thrown before it. With respect to philosophy, the role and function assigned to the national and international trade unions is to narrow and the emphasis placed on self-centred-self-help is too great. As a result, the movement seems incapable of reconciling its continued future development with the challenges thrown before it in the contemporary scene. These challenges include: a. its rigid position on the introduction of automation and technological change; b. its apparent inability to resolve internal jurisdictional disputes; c. its apparent disinterest in extending its influence to new occupational groups and to the younger members of the labour force; d. its commitment to immediate collective bargaining ends over a commitment to greater social awareness and participation in Canadian economic and social affairs.

6

CANADIAN COLLECTIVE

BARGAINING:

Analysis and Prospects

Syed M. A. Hameed

Literature on Canadian collective bargaining seems to fall into two broad categories. There are a large number of descriptive essays and comments on the provisions of collective agreements relating to a variety of topics, such as technological change, seniority, work rules, pension plans, vacations, hours of work and wage increases. These are primarily produced without any reference to a theoretical framework and belong to the phase that ended with the establishment of the Woods Task Force in 1967. Those studies that were commissioned by the Task Force were required to follow a certain theoretical framework,[1] resulting in a relatively greater analytical rigour and the occasional possibility of predicting the future perspectives of collective bargaining. What is disconcerting in the latter category of studies is an indiscreet use of the Craig model, a modified and useful version of the Dunlop and Easton approaches,[2] which essentially is an industrial relations model and not a framework for the analysis of collective bargaining. Yet no one has made a conceptual or definitive distinction between collective bargaining, which is only a conversion mechanism in Craig's model, and the industrial relations system, which is a much broader concept.

---

[1] The framework adopted by the Task Force was developed by Alton W. J. Craig, *Canadian Industrial Relations* (The Report of the Task Force on Labour Relations), Privy Council Office, December 1968, p. 9.

[2] John T. Dunlop, *Industrial Relations System* (New York: Henry Holt and Company, 1958); David Easton, *The Systems Analysis of Political Life,* (New York: John Wiley and Sons, 1965).

A THEORETICAL FRAMEWORK FOR THE ANALYSIS OF
COLLECTIVE BARGAINING

Any theory of collective bargaining should explain, in operational terms:
a. the logic of collectivity as expressed through the formation of unions;
b. management resistance to unions;
c. the structure of bargaining relationship, i.e. local, regional, national or industry wide set-up;
d. the type of collective bargaining relationship in the continuum of perfect harmony to hostility, defining the degree of conflict;
e. the process of collective bargaining as defined by the mechanism of third party intervention, work stoppage and emergency settlement;
f. the outcome of negotiation or the content of an agreement.

This collective bargaining theory must be based squarely upon an integrated system of theories[3] such as Common's theory of the labour movement, marginalist-behaviouralist theories of the firm or the Stevens-Somers negotiation model.

In this section a cause and effect relationship will be established between the dependent and independent variables outlined in Table 6-1. An expected change in the exploratory variables will define the degree of unionism, the nature of management resistence, the structure and process of collective bargaining and the likely contents of collective agreements.

The problems involved in making the above concepts operational and the possibilities of their quantification have not been explored sufficiently, although there are indications that the use of quantitative techniques may yield useful results.[4] The following analysis, however, will be in terms of qualitative and casual relationship with the possibility of subsequent quantification.

Expansion of Markets

Three significant landmarks in the history of unionism have been selected to highlight the analytical and casual importance of expanding markets.[5] They are:
a. the establishment of British international unions, their lack of substantial growth and their subsequent disappearance;
b. American international unions and their continued relevance;
c. the growth of Canadian locals, trade councils and national trade union centers.

Canadian unionism, from its origin, in 1816, without legislative foundation, in the province of Nova Scotia to its present day entrenchment in the social, political and economic life of the country, may be explained in terms of expanding markets. Between 1827 and 1844, printers, shoemakers, carpenters and stone cutters were organized in the developing eastern cities of Montreal, Hamilton and York. Consciousness of separate industrial classes was born as journeymen recognized that their interests were separate from merchant-master and thus realized a need for protective organizations. However, menaces of the market, namely 'scabs'

Table 6-1

DEPENDENT AND INDEPENDENT VARIABLES

Theoretical Antecedents	*Independent Variables*	*Dependent Variables*
Common's theory of the labour movement	Expansion of markets	Degree of unionism, structure of unions, and collective bargaining
Marginalist-behaviour-alist theories of the firm	Management maxi-mization, satisfying function	Management resistance to unions
Stevens-Somers model	Power as a negotiational base	Type of collective bargaining relationship and the contents of collective agreements
Common's legal framework of capitalism	Legal foundations of conflict resolution	Process of conflict resolution

and interstate producers against whom the early craftsmen sought shelter in unions, had an upper hand in the battle since craftsmen were scattered and lacked solidarity and experience in the formation of stable collective units. The journeymen's organizational success came later with the Toronto Typographical Union which claims a continuous existence since 1844.

Continuity and relative stability became a feature of the Canadian trade union movement in the middle of the nineteenth century. The purely indigenous character of the labour movement, without extraneous influences, was a short lived phenomenon lasting for only thirty-four years, (1816-50). A significant point in the history of the trade union movement in Canada, not often emphasized, is that labour, product and money markets within Canada were relatively less connected with each other than they were with the markets in England and the United States.[6] This

[3] S. M. A. Hameed, "A Theory of Collective Bargaining," *Relations Industrielles,* Vol. 25, No. 3, (August, 1970).

[4] For various approaches to quantification, see S. M. A. Hameed, "Theory and Research in the Field of Industrial Relations," *British Journal of Industrial Relations,* (July 1967).

[5] Robert Ozanne, "The Labor History and Labor Theory of John R. Commons: An Evaluation in the Light of Recent Trends and Criticism," in G. G. Somers (ed.) *Labor, Management and Public Policy* (Maidson: The University of Wisconsin Press, 1963).

[6] C. Brian Williams explains international unionism in terms of international trade, labor migration and American investment in Canada. These three factors are comparable with John R. Commons product, labour and money market expansion. C. Brian Williams, "The Development of Canadian-American Trade Union Relations," *Industrial Relations,* Vol. 21, No. 3, (July, 1966).

explains not only the international character of Canadian unionism but also the fact that, given the nature of market expansion at the time, it could not have been any other way.

In terms of labour market expansion, Canada was and still is a net recipient of labour from England. Because this one-directional flow could not be a threat to job territory in England, there was no incentive for the British labour movement to organize workers in Canada. British unions that organized locals in Canada, because of the outflow of ideas and cultural or political affinity, were the Amalgamated Society of Engineers, ASE, (1850) and the Amalgamated Society of Carpenters and Joiners, ASCJ (1860). There was, however, no economic logic to sustain such unions for any length of time: "The ASE was absorbed into the International Association of Machinists in 1920 and the ASCJ, into the United Brotherhood of Carpenters and Joiners in 1914, though some branches seceded in 1922 and resumed their status as locals of the British organizations until 1925, when the latter formally withdrew."[7] These international unions of British origin had greater stability and relatively higher survival qualities than the early Canadian unions. Since internal Canadian market linkage was less effective, in terms of economic transactions, than the linkage with the British markets, this linkage with England could have become viable and lasting if the flow of labour had been from Canada to Britain.

Expanding markets and the enlightened self-interest of the American unions, on the other hand, made American international unions economically feasible and tenacious. Within the short span of a decade (1861-70), important American unions like the Iron Moulders (1861), the Locomotive Engineers (1864), the National Typographical Society (1865), the Cigar Makers (1865), the Knights of St. Crispin (shoemakers, 1867) and the Railway Conductors (1868) made their inroads in Canada. Purely Canadian locals, primarily in the domestic trades such as baking, tailoring, bricklaying, stone-cutting, book binding and longshoring, which were also emerging during this period, were not directly helped by this Canadian-American market linkage. They had to wait for internal market expansion which came gradually — first, in the form of trade councils in the notable Eastern cities and, second, in the form of national central organizations which were, to begin with, scarcely national in character.

In Toronto, five craft unions formed the Toronto Trade Assembly (1871) and in Ottawa and Hamilton, Trade Councils were formed (1873 and 1857 respectively), while attempts to form a national organization were made by the Toronto Trades Assembly in 1873. A convention in 1873, attended by thirty-one locals of fourteen unions from Ontario, established the Canadian Labour Union which met for four consecutive years without a Western representation. In the depression of the 1870's, both trade councils and the Canadian Labour Union disappeared because with the lack of railroads linking East and West markets, the formation of national unions at this time was premature. In the decade following the start of railroad construction (1881) and protective tariffs (1879), however, union membership grew and a number of significant developments took place. Trade councils were revived or freshly started in Toronto, London, Montreal, Ottawa, Brantford, Vancouver and Victoria. A national centre, the Canadian Labour Congress, was set up in 1883 and three years later, in 1886, it became the Canadian Trades and Labour Congress. During the two subsequent conventions, delegates were all from Ontario, but from "1889 on, there was always a substantial delegation from Quebec; in 1890 British Columbia sent two and Manitoba one. New Brunswick sent its first delegate in 1897, Prince Edward Island in 1908 and Nova Scotia in 1903, but in 1905 and 1906 there were no Maritime delegates at all. Provincial Executives for British Columbia and Manitoba were elected in 1895, for New Brunswick in 1896, and for Nova Scotia and Prince Edward Island in 1901. Saskatchewan and Alberta were represented from the beginning of their existence."[8]

Railroad expansion, a significant phase in the economic growth of this country, represented a new emphasis on factory production and a different assortment of threats to labour market security, namely child labour, long hours, immigrants and foreign products, all of which required stronger unions as protective organizations. For the first time, closer ties were established between the Trades and Labour Congress and the American Federation of Labour over the question of labour market expansion. In 1896, the Congress felt concerned about the American Alien Contract Labour Law which was being applied to the Canadian workers and complained to the Federation, which laid the basis for continued exchange of delegates at their conventions.

Historical development of the trade union movement during the nineteenth century coincides with the history of collective bargaining. For this reason, our analysis beyond this point is not relevant to our subsequent discussion of collective bargaining and its other determinants. It may be said in conclusion that the Canadian trade union movement, its continued relations with its American counterpart and the sequence of events, such as the expulsion of the CIO unions from Canada in 1939 and the subsequent merger and establishment of the Canadian Labour Congress in 1956, give a testimony to John R. Commons' theory of the labour movement.

STRUCTURE OF UNIONISM.   A critical factor in the growth and pattern of unionism is the market organization in which a union operates. Some industries locate in localized geographic areas in order to take advantage of manpower, fuel or accessibility to consumer markets, yet others are not as restricted. Market characteristics of industry may thus help in identifying the following basic models of unionism in Canada:

The craft unions. There is a large variety of craft unions in Canada — the carpenters, the bricklayers and the sheet metal workers. The United

---

[7] Eugene Forsey, "History of the Labour Movement in Canada," *The Canada Year Book*, 1957-58, p. 795.
[8] Eugene Forsey, "History."

Brotherhood of Carpenters and Joiners of America, affiliated with AFL-CIO/CLC, for example, was the fourth largest union in Canada with a membership of 77,300 in 1967. There are other craft unions which are somewhat difficult to categorize because they are organized in mass production industries. A well known example is the International Brotherhood of Electrical Workers, affiliated with AFL-CIO/CLC. It was the eighth largest union with a membership of 48,500 in 1967.

The industrial unions. The industrial unions are organized in the mass production industries such as automobile, aircraft, steel and agricultural implements. Examples of these unions in Canada are the United Steelworkers of America, the largest union with a membership of 130,000 and United Automobile, Aerospace and Agricultural Implements Workers of America, the second largest union with a membership of 98,880.

The service industries. Unionism in service industries is relatively weaker that the above two categories. Hotel, restaurant and retail clerks are unionized in adequate number but are not very effective in raising their wages. Federal Department of Labour studies, prior to the passage of the Standard Labour Code in 1967, revealed that a large number of employees receiving less than the minimum wage of $1.25 were in these trades. A notable exception to this are teamsters who are notorious for their militancy. In Canada, 54,700 workers belong to the International Brotherhood of Teamsters, Chaffeurs, Warehousemen and Helpers of America and maintain an independent existence.

The Civil Service and public utilities. This is a very promising and growing section of Canadian unionism. The Canadian Union of Public Employees with 106,100 members and Public Service Alliance of Canada with 92,800 members constitute almost two-thirds of the total CLC membership from national unions. In 1967, with the exception of the United Steelworkers of America, they both reported the largest number of membership increases among all the unions surveyed. Their recent growth is explained directly in terms of legislative support granting collective bargaining rights to public employees and indirectly through the impending market role of the government which is becoming the largest single employer in the economy.

The railroad unions. Historically, these unions, both in Canada and the United States have been treated separately in law and public policy. The Canadian Brotherhood of Railway, Transport and General Workers is the tenth largest union in Canada, accounting for 34,900 members and the third largest national union affiliated with the CLC. There are also unaffiliated railway brotherhoods which do not constitute an impressive membership (only 8,264 or .4 per cent of the total union membership in Canada).

The white-collar and professional unions. A contemporary and somewhat universal phenomenon of technological change has introduced structural changes in the composition of the labour force and has brought about an unprecedented growth in white-collar and professional employees. Unionization of these new categories of workers was regarded with considerable skepticism in the late 1950's, however, teachers, nurses, engineers, clerks, and motion picture and television employees are the new breed of trade union mmbers.

Maritime unions. Longshoring and stevedoring unions and various craft and semi-industrial unions such as building trades may be placed in this category.

Management Maximization — Satisficing Function

The development of unions, their structure and their industrial and geographic distribution, as outlined in earlier chapters and briefly synthesized in the preceeding section of this paper, reveal the extent to which unions have been successful in their attempt to obtain management and social recognition. Historical evidence suggests that management does not take very kindly to union growth. Professor Tripp has recorded the incidence of early conspiracy cases to show the typical management attitude in the beginning of the nineteenth century:

The famous Philadelphia cordwainers case of 1806 illustrates a not atypical employer reaction to . . . union groups and the ultimate resort to law to oppose their activities. Employers sometimes would offer to negotiate. More often than not, they would refuse, try to advertise for non-union men, and endeavour to break up the union organization. One can find advertisements in the early papers of these eastern cities for "sober young men from the country" to take the jobs when labor troubles arose. The masters in the Philadelphia cordwainers society accused the union of forming a combination and conspiracy to raise wages to benefit themselves and to injure those not joining the cordwainers society or union."[9]

The conspiracy doctrine that developed in British common law was applied to unions in the United States. "Of some six conspiracy cases between 1806 and 1815, four verdicts were adverse to the workingmen."[10] The prevailing economic doctrine favoured atomistic competition and condemned all forms of combination, meaning that corporations were as much in contravention of economic thinking as were trade unions. Nevertheless during the 1930's and 1940's, incorporation laws were enacted without parallel recognition of the unions in public policy. The first judicial recognition came to the unions in 1842 with the criminal conspiracy charges being set aside in the *Commonwealth vs. Hunt* case, but continued use of injunctions until the early 1930's greatly helped management ignore the growing demands of the labour movement and thus keep costs of production low.

The basic entrepreneurial need for keeping costs down is a continuing phenomenon and it received legislative and judicial backing when it clashed with union demands. Consequently, unions would never have

[9] L. Reed Tripp, *Labor Problems and Processes,* (New York: Harper and Brothers, 1961), p. 6.
[10] *Ibid,* p. 6.

grown strong enough to negotiate higher wages and better terms of employment except for three important developments after 1930, which did not alter management cost-consciousness but rather brought about changes in economic thinking and public policy measures. First, the depression of the 1930's evoked enthusiastic support for the underconsumptionist doctrine. Both the Hobsonian and Keynesian approaches felt the need for creating additional purchasing power since lower income groups, because of their higher marginal propensity to consume, could create effective demand for the volume of products which otherwise would glut the markets. Acceptance of these ideas was the first blow to the management maximization function and the entrepreneurial prerogative in maintaining an "optimizing" behaviour. Employer prestige diminished while employer resistance to unions and collective bargaining was considerably reduced. Second, therefore, was a projection of these ideas into a public policy that extended legal support to union organizations and collective bargaining. The development of this legal framework will be discussed in the next section. Third, was the increased demand for production during World War II which has by no means come to an end in the postwar period because the continued prosperity and opportunity for higher profits still exists.

The current management attitude consists of the over-all management attitude in the economy and the management attitudes and decisions pertaining to unions and collective bargaining in unionized plants. Distinguishing these two parts allows a possible prediction about the growth of unionism and the extension of collective bargaining. For example, the overall management attitude in recent years is characterized by a "satisfying," rather than "maximizing" or "optimizing," behaviour, and directly derives from the fact that a larger section of Canadian business has now grown to a size that requires theories of bureaucracy in order to explain the decision-making function. The management of these businesses does not essentially maximize its profits; it can and does indulge in other luxuries. The size of the business has additional economic ramifications. Oligopolistic business, for instance, by virtue of its control of the consumer market, can fix target rates of return and thus can afford to accommodate inflated union wage demands. To this extent a generalized softening of management attitude toward unions can be expected, unless the government intervenes through anti-combines legislation or policies of moral suasion to reduce business autonomy. However, another economic factor has a significant counter effect. The value of Canadian international trade, as a percentage of G.N.P., is one of the highest in the world, thus imposing a strict standard of international competition. Canadian business, therefore, has to remain constantly cost-conscious and to adopt a generally hard-line attitude toward union demands.

The Organizational Behaviour Research Unit at the University of Alberta has recently conducted one of the few[11] surveys of Canadian attitudes.[12] The sample comprised 650 middle and upper management personnel, drawn from across the country. Mean age of the group was 36; 89.5 per cent of them did not belong to any union; 56.9 per cent had high school or higher education; 66.4 per cent were Protestants; 78.4

per cent held a staff position or supervised a department. Their answers with regard to the existence and usefulness of unions seem to crystalize current management attitudes. There was a substantial resignation to the idea of union existence and, although only 21 per cent agreed that Canada would be better off without them, 68.5 per cent agreed that "the way they are run now, labour unions do this country more harm than good."

Appraising the attitude of Canadian management toward unions in an historical perspective, The Task Force viewed labour-management relations along a continuum of hostility-acceptance:

The history of industrial relations in this country reveals that the posture of management is a critical determining factor in the nature of the union-management relationship. Employers can, as in the United States, choose from a range of strategies in charting their industrial relations course. At one end of the spectrum is active hostility to unions which can at best lead only to strained relations. Further along the spectrum is the possibility of deliberately trying to compete with unions for the loyalty of employees, almost to the point of failing to recognize the prevalence of dual loyalties in this area. Here again the result is likely to be continuous conflict. Still another alternative is that which characterizes most large corporations to-day. They usually accept unions as part of the system and visualize collective bargaining as a straight power struggle."[13]

Resistance to unions is inherent in management maximization or satisficing function. It is revealed overtly in the non-unionized sector of the economy, but remains latent in the unionized plants and comes to the surface during periods of economic stringency and government non-intervention. During the 1960's, for instance, concern about the balance of payments and inflationary wage settlements, accompanied with the Liberal government's non-intervention policy, crystalized into a hard-line management attitude in the areas of wages and working rules. A number of bitter disputes in this period may be attributed to this situation, especially the dispute of 1966 when the number of man-days lost as a percentage of estimated working time was the highest (0.34) since the postwar year, 1946.

In the previous sections, attention was given to three of the four factors that have made the capitalist market arrangement viable: the development of the trade union movement in Canada, the degrees of its acceptance or non-acceptance by management, and the incidence of a government intervention policy. The fourth factor, the federal and provincial enactment and administration of labour laws, can be examined

---

[11] J. J. Wettlaufer, G. Forsyth, and A. Mikalachki, *Management's Views of Union-Management Relations at the Local Level*, Task Force Study.

[12] I wish to thank Charles McMillan for making these results available to me. I am also indebted to Rodney Schneck who agreed to release these figures prior to publishing his own study on Canadian attitudes.

[13] *Canadian Industrial Relations*, The Report of the Task Force on Labour Relations, Privy Council Office, December 1968.

against the background. It is advisable to make a distinction at this point and categorize existing labour laws in Canada into the following categories: laws governing labour standards such as minimum wages, maximum hours, annual vacations, general holidays, etc; laws governing industrial safety and workmen's compensation, which define compensation, the nature of disability benefits, medical aid, etc; laws governing industrial training and apprenticeship which cover the problems of certification, term of apprenticeship and minimum wage payment; laws governing labour-management relations, covering such aspects as certification of bargaining agent, duty to bargain, conciliation procedure, mediation, arbitration and inquiry, and other matters relating to the setting up of Labour Relations Board, picketing and boycotting etc. It is the last category which is most pertinent to our discussion.

Historical Development

Prior to the passage of the Trade Union and Criminal Amendments Acts of 1872, unions in Canada had no legal existence, and were tried under the criminal conspiracy and anti-combines laws which originated in eighteenth and mid-nineteenth century England.[14] Table 6-2 summarizes the development in Federal Legislation. Phase I, characterized by repressive measures against unions and the absence of a manifest legal attempt to resolve labour-management conflict, formally ended in Canada with the passage of the Trade Union and Criminal Amendments Acts of 1872. Phase II, which started at this time with an explicit recognition of unions as legal entities, did nothing beyond tolerating the existence of unions, in legal, social or managerial context. This phase virtually continued till the introduction of P.C. 1003, in 1944, which recognized the workers' rights to organize and also made collective bargaining compulsory. Phase III, although it is a distinct phase in the development of the Canadian labour-relations laws, is not specifically a period of encouragement comparable with the post-Wagner Act period (up to 1947) in the United States.

The passage of the Wagner Act in 1935 gave active legal encouragement to American unions when labour-management relations in that country became established within a framework of compulsory collective bargaining and a right to strike. No government intervention was envisaged for the settlement of industrial disputes until the postwar enactment of the Taft-Hartley Act. Thus, it is possible to identify four distinct phases in the development of the American labour relations law: phases of repression (until 1842), tolerance (1842-1935), encouragement (1935-1947), and intervention (1947 onward). The last two phases are not identifiable in the Canadian labour relations law.

Although intervention, in the form of conciliation, has been an outstanding feature of the Canadian dispute settlement policy, the Federal Government was a relatively late entrant in this field with the Conciliation Act of 1900, while the provinces had already assumed an intervention policy: Ontario in 1873, British Columbia in 1883, Nova Scotia in 1888 and Quebec in 1901.[15] The Federal Conciliation Act was patterned after the United Kingdom Conciliation Act of 1896 and was prompted by serious mining unrest in British Columbia. Conciliation, as introduced at this time, was on a purely voluntary basis, authorizing the Minister of Labour to provide such services when requested by either party to the dispute. The element of voluntarism outlived its utility, at least in a particular segment of the economy, within the short period of three years, and the Canadian parliament was prompted to pass the Railway Disputes Act in 1903 as a result of a prolonged strike by trackmen on the Canadian Pacific Railway. Two significant factors in the passage of the Conciliation Act and the Railway Disputes Act were that the enactments took place following a mining strike and a Canadian Pacific Railway strike with the specific intention of resolving industrial conflict and that the first piece of legislation was patterned after a British law but the second one borrowed the dispute settlement technique from the American use of arbitration boards in the Massachusetts railroad strike of 1877. The second factor represents the beginning of the American legal influence and an end to further borrowing from the British labour-relations law. The Conciliation and Labour Act of 1906, a subsequent piece of legislation patterned after the British law, proved inadequate and was replaced, although technically it is considered in existence even now.[16] Subsequent evolutionary stages in the enactment of legal techniques of conflict resolution were reached with the passage of the Industrial Dispute Investigation Act (IDI) of 1907, P.C. 1003 of 1943, and the Industrial Relations and Dispute Investigation (IRDI) Act of 1948. The IDI Act, like the Conciliation Act and Railway Disputes Act, was passed following an emergency situation due to a strike in a Western Canadian coal mine, a public utility area; however, it was not merely a synthesis of the Railway Disputes Act and the Act of 1900, but rather it added a significant principle: compulsory postponement of a strike or lockout during the investigations.

The period from 1925 to 1944 witnessed three significant developments, two of which crystalized in the wartime P.C. 1003 and became truly responsible in placing the Canadian labour-relations policy on a new and contemporary footing. First, following the amendment of the IDI Act, all provincial governments, except Prince Edward Island, passed similar legislation within the next seven years. Although this polarization did not last very long, the possibility of effective leadership by the Federal Government was evident and thus became a significant feature of this period. Second, the depression of the thirties, the acceptance of the under-consumptionist doctrine, and a spectacular change in the American public policy toward unions were manifested in the passage of the Wagner Act. Third, Canadian involvement in World War II gave the Federal Government emergency powers. In 1939, Order-in-Council, P.C. 3495, was passed which made it possible to extend the provision of the IDI Act to war

---

[14] A. W. R. Carrothers, *Collective Bargaining Law in Canada,* (Toronto: Butterworth's, 1965).

[15] Edith Larensten and Evelyn Woolner, "Fifty Years of Labour Legislation in Canada," in *The Labour Gazette,* Vol. 50, No. 9, (September 1950).

[16] Stuart Jamieson, *Industrial Relations in Canada,* (Ithaca, New York: Cornell University Press, 1957).

Table 6-2

THE DEVELOPMENT OF FEDERAL LEGISLATION ON LABOUR-MANAGEMENT RELATIONS

Year	Title	Foreign Precedents	Main Provisions
1872	Trade Union and Criminal Law Amendments Act	British Government passed identical law, Trade Unions Act, 1871.	Unions declared legal entities not subject to criminal conspiracy and strike damages.
1900	Conciliation Act	Patterned after the U.K. Conciliation Act, 1896.	Passed because of serious mining labour unrest in B.C. Authorized Minister of Labour to provide voluntary conciliation services as requested.
1903	The Railway Disputes Act	The union of arbitration boards, in settling Massachusetts Rail strike of 1877.	Parliament prompted to pass this legislation due to prolonged strike by CPR trackmen. Changed earlier policy of voluntarism into compulsion and carried three main provisions: three-man conciliation board with compulsory investigation powers; if parties consented, an arbitration board with no binding power; no restrictions on strike or lockout.
1906	The Conciliation and Labour Act	Patterned after British laws.	Proved inadequate and was replaced; technically it is considered in existence.
1907	The Industrial Dispute Investigation Act	Extension of Railway Dispute Act which was influenced by U.S. developments. Also accepted principle of conciliation from the Act of 1900.	Parliament passed Act after mining strike in Western Canada. Provided for: a one stage tripartite compulsory investigation; strikes and lockouts forbidden till completed investigation; applicable to mining, transport communication and public utilities and to other industries if both parties to a dispute agree.
1914	The War Measures Act	Influenced by U.S. measures.	Designed to secure industrial peace for facilitating war production.
1939	Order-in-Council (P.C. 3495)	Influenced by U.S. measures.	Provisions of IDA Act were applied to war production industries under legal authority of War Measures Act.
1944	Order-in-Council (P.C. 1003)	The Wagner Act of 1935	Introduced measures similar to those in Wagner Act; such as: worker's right to organize; proper criteria in determining bargaining agent; compulsory collective bargaining; establishment of labour relations boards. In addition to these, P.C. 1003 contained modified IDI Act provisions which included compulsory conciliations; no strike/lockout during investigation; compulsory arbitration during life of contract.
1948	The Industrial Relations and Dispute Investigation Act	The Wagner Act of 1935	Contained similar provisions as those in P.C. 1003, although their application, in terms of the Federal jurisdiction, became restricted in peace time.

production industries under the legal authority of the War Measures Act. What emerged from these factors was a public policy that incorporated the salient features of the IDI Act and the Wagner Act. To cope with the wartime production needs and the growing labour unrest, the Federal Government combined compulsory conciliation with compulsory collective bargaining under a new Order-in-Council, P.C. 1003. The Order borrowed provisions from the Wagner Act which included the workers' right to organize, the proper criteria in determining bargaining agent, compulsory collective bargaining and the establishment of labour relations boards. It also contained modified IDI Act provisions such as compulsory conciliation, no strike/lockout during investigation, and compulsory arbitration during the life of the contract.

There have been virtually no developments in the federal labour-relations law since the passage of P.C. 1003. With the end of hostilities in 1948, the Federal Government lost those emergency powers it acquired under the War Measures Act. Provisions of P.C. 1003 were, therefore, incorporated into the Industrial Relations and Dispute Investigations (IRDI) Act of 1948. Once again all the provinces, except Prince Edward Island, passed legislation patterned after the IRDI Act. British Columbia and Quebec, while retaining the main provisions of the IRDI Act, enacted the Industrial Conciliation and Arbitration Act and the Collective Agreements Act, respectively, to impose restrictions on unions somewhat similar to those contained in the American Taft-Hartley Act. The severity and hostility of the American public policy that was generated by the rash of postwar strikes was not otherwise paralled in Canada, perhaps because of the long history of government intervention in Canadian labour-relations policy. The effectiveness of the legal framework, which has changed its emphasis from the voluntary collective bargaining of the Conciliation Act of 1900 to the compulsory investigation and compulsory bargaining of the IRDI Act of 1948,[17] may be caused, in a limited sense, by the incidence of strikes and lockouts:

To the degree that the effects of Canadian legislation can be measured at all by strike statistics, the record seems to be one of mixed success and failure. Despite the elaborate machinery which most post war Canadian labour statutes provide for settling disputes, strikes and lockouts on the whole have increased greatly in size, frequency, and duration from the pre-war period.[18]

Federal — Provincial Jurisdiction

Sections 91 and 92 of the British North America Act (1867), as subsequently interpreted by the courts, have substantively determined the

---

[17] C. Brian Williams, "Notes on the Evaluation of Compulsory Conciliation in Canada," Vol. 19, No. 3, (July 1964), pp. 300-324.

[18] Stuart Jamieson, *Industrial Relations,* p. 114.

question of the distribution of power between the provincial governments and the Federal Government. However, these sections do not set forth the function of the two levels of government on labour-management relations, and legislation passed by the federal government has been tested periodically in the courts for constitutional validity. For example, the Industrial Disputes Investigation Act (IDI Act) of 1907 was made applicable to mining, transport communication and public utilities. Its jurisdiction over transport communication was questioned in Quebec, in 1911, in a dispute involving workers and the Montreal Street Railway Company, and the law was upheld. In an Ontario case, *Toronto Electric Commissioners vs. Snider,* in 1925, the Judicial Committee of the Privy Council declared that the federal law was infringing upon provincial rights and authority and should, therefore, be considered ultravires the Parliament of Canada. Federal jurisdiction in matters of labour relations became clearly defined and considerably limited in application after the Snider case. But, from this judicial circumscribing of Federal powers, one is not to infer that the provincial labour relations policy became unrecognizably different from the Federal policy after 1925 and that the development of a national system of industrial relations, formulated and sponsored by the Federal government over a period of half a century (from the passage of Trade Union and Criminal Law Amendments Act of 1873 to the Privy Council ruling on the IDI Act in 1925), came to a grinding halt. On the contrary, the Federal government promptly amended the IDI Act in the same year and defined its jurisdiction to cover all "undertakings within the legislative jurisdiction of the Parliament of Canada." [19] It also left the door open, through permissive clauses in the amended Act, for provincial legislatures to enact similar laws. The development of a national policy, particularly for those eighteen years during which the IDI Act remained constitutionally valid, continued at least for the next seven years, as all the provinces except Prince Edward Island had passed legislation comparable to the federal law by 1932.

Clearly, the question of federal jurisdiction is significant in the evolution of a national policy. The constitutional rights of the provinces being firmly established after the Snider case, the Federal Government could only strive toward building a national policy by legislating a model law. It did so by producing the amended IDI Act, and the divergence between federal and provincial policies that arose from the Federal Government's failure to introduce legal measures for the rights to associate and bargain collectively did not become pronounced as wartime exigencies resulted in two Orders-in-Council, P.C. 3495 and P.C. 1003, in 1939 and 1943 respectively, which extended federal jurisdiction to all war production industries. This factor plus the spirit of cooperation among the provinces helped to produce uniformity in the federal and provincial policies on labour relations. Federal jurisdiction, undoubtedly restricted in peace time, became more so by the Supreme Court ruling of 1950 and, in the past two decades, evidence of federal leadership in developing a national labour relations policy has not been forthcoming. Diverse provincial interests, lack of effective federal leadership, and its procedural inflexibility in the realms of conciliation and dispute settlement are responsible for reducing the degree of uniformity in federal-provincial policies. British Columbia, for instance, passed the Mediation Commissions Act, setting up a Mediation Commission which is permanent and independent and which may also become an arbitration tribunal in emergency cases. The new law replaces the old system of conciliation officers and *ad hoc* boards. Similarly, Ontario passed an Act that established a Labour-Management Arbitration Commission to facilitate grievance processing.

Power as a Negotiational Base

The Canadian collective bargaining process is based on the belief that conflict between labour and management can be resolved voluntarily through an interplay of the power, threat and counter-threat of the strike and lockout. In the case of an impasse, there is a provision for a third party intervention which may exogenously correct the power balance in individual conflict situations; however, the numerous cases in which settlement takes place without third party intervention or threat of social sanction is a happy commentary on the resilience and viability of the Canadian collective bargaining process. As Table 6-3 indicates, in certain years more than 60 per cent of the total agreements were achieved without a third party intervention. In the years when a lower percentage of cases were settled at the bargaining stage, the remainder were dispersed, without a specific trend, by the Conciliation Board, Post-Conciliation Bargaining, Arbitration and Post Strike Bargaining stages. One noticeable trend, however, is the proportionately higher percentage (nine out of fourteen years) of settlements at the Board level compared with the Conciliation Officer Stage. Nonetheless, this over-reliance and built-in expectation of the Board stage in the negotiating strategy may now decline because most provincial legislations (though not federal) require greater discretion in the use of the Board stage.

This section examines the contents of those collective agreements determined by the Stevens-Somers model. This cost-reward exchange nexus is largely contingent upon union-management attitudes, personality conflict situations and environmental constraints such as the Canadian economic performance, government intervention policy, and legislative requirement in setting up stages of conciliation. The inter-dependence of the personality with environmental variables is implicit in the discussion of expanding

[19] H. D. Woods and Sylvia Ostry, *Labour Policy and Labour Economics in Canada* (Toronto: Macmillan of Canada, 1967) p. 22. Subsequent Federal laws such as the recent Canada Labour Code of 1965 defines its applicability to employers and employees in works, undertakings or business connecting a province with any other province or with another country . . . The code also covers employment in those words, undertakings, or businesses which, although wholly within a province, have been declared by Parliament to be "for the general advantage of Canada or for the advantage of two or more of the provinces." *The Canada Labour (Standards) Code,* Queen's Printer and Controller of Stationery, (Ottawa, 1966).

Table 6-3

STAGE OF NEGOTIATIONS AT WHICH AGREEMENT WAS ACHIEVED[1]
(PERCENTAGE DISTRIBUTION OF EMPLOYEES AFFECTED) 1953-1966

Stage	1953	1954	1955	1956	1957	1958	1959	1960	1961	1962	1963	1964	1965	1966
Bargaining	61.6	38.7	62.5	52.1	62.8	30.6	50.3	67.4	32.7	38.2	64.9	27.7	41.7	38.1
Conciliation Officer	2.9	10.0	2.8	2.4	0.9	10.9	9.2	12.7	20.9	16.2	9.2	25.2	22.0	10.3
Conciliation Board	26.6	15.3	28.7	14.0	27.0	19.9	13.2	15.6	8.8	32.4	9.3	8.4	13.3	26.5
Post-Conciliation Bargaining	5.3	1.1	1.5	25.9	2.0	33.5	8.6	2.3	36.4	5.8	11.8	29.3	11.3	10.8
Arbitration	—	30.9	—	—	—	—	0.2	—	—	2.1	1.0	0.9	0.8	0.9
Post-Arbitration Bargaining	—	—	—	—	—	0.1	—	—	—	—	0.2	—	—	—
Strike	1.8	2.6	3.8	5.4	6.8	4.3	9.4	2.0	0.9	4.9	3.6	8.7	9.9	13.5
Post-Strike Bargaining	—	—	0.5	—	—	0.4	9.0	—	—	0.4	—	—	0.7	—
Not Recorded	1.9	1.3	0.2	0.2	0.4	0.2	—	0.3	0.3	—	—	—	0.3	—

[1] For negotiating units covering 500 or more employees, exclusive of Construction.
NOTE: Columns may not add up to 100 per cent due to rounding.
Source: Alton W. J. Craig and Harry J. Waisglass, "Collective Bargaining Perspectives", *Relations Industrielles/Industrial Relations*, Vol. 23 (1968) No. 4, page 584.

markets and management maximization — satisficing function and constitutes the background in analyzing a wide spectrum of provisions in collective agreements, such as wage increments, guaranteed annual income, wage parity, overtime, pension plan, technological change, subcontracting, vacations, paid holidays, paid sick leave, rest periods and other monetary and non-monetary provisions. The limitation of space will not permit discussion and analysis of these provisions separately and, they will be placed in three categories: wage provisions, fringe benefits and matters of industrial jurisprudence.[20] Their importance in union demands may be explained in our theoretical framework by a wider interpretation of the phenomenon of expanding markets which determines the need of a union to protect and improve its job territory. Why management resists in granting these union demands may be explained in terms of its satisfying function. What, indeed, is ultimately agreed upon and becomes embodied in the union-management contract is determined by their respective power in negotiational strategy.

One leading collective bargaining issue of the 1960's from each of the above three categories is selected in order to examine the rationale for its existence in union demands, its temporal cogency, and the nature of final settlement. The three issues are wage settlements, particularly the question of wage parity, paid vacations and technological change provisions.

WAGE SETTLEMENTS.   Unions use various arguments in negotiating wage demands through bargaining strategy. Management uses the other side of the same arguments in resisting the demands. The arguments include cost of living, production, employer ability to pay and wage comparisons with other industries or regions. For example, when unions ask for higher wages to cover an increased cost of living, management could argue that wage increments will lead to further increases in the cost of living with no real wage benefit to workers. Management produces counter-arguments and the settlement must lie in the delicate power play that goes on in the negotiating sessions and that eventually finds an equilibrium.

The Federal Department of Labour in Ottawa maintains a complete collection of any collective agreements signed in Canada (roughly 8,000). A supplement to the Labour Gazette, titled *Collective Bargaining Review,* is published monthly by the Department and analyzes those terms of settlement pertaining to negotiating units covering 500 or more employees, (excluding construction). The greatest attention in the analysis is given to wage settlements although other items, such as vacations, paid holidays, hours, overtime and group insurance plan are also reported.

In 1966, The Federal Department of Labour published a report entitled *Provisions in Major Collective Agreements in Canada.* It was a

---

[20] A more comprehensive classification of contract provisions, not used here because of space limitation, is: (1) relationship, (2) procedure, and (3) substance. See H. D. Woods and Sylvia Ostry, *Labour Policy and Labour Economics* (Toronto: Macmillan of Canada, 1967), pp. 12-13.

combination of two earlier reports that jointly covered 754,520 workers and examined the application of some twenty-five collective agreement provisions. Their major finding with regard to wage provisions was basically that very few agreements had provisions on general wage adjustment or reopening and that few agreements provided for guaranteed earnings.

Statistical exercise in computing monthly wage rate index numbers is straightforward. In Table 6-4, for instance, January 1965 is the base period, which equals 100. The average base rate in that month is calculated by weighting the wage rate in each of the 616 negotiating units by their respective number of workers. Index numbers for the subsequent months are calculated by dividing the average base rate for the desired month by the figures for January 1965, multiplied by 100. Thus, the March index number in durable goods is 6 per cent higher than the January base number.

Wage settlements for the five year period 1965-69 inclusive recorded in Table 6-4 show what are popularly called the costly or inflationary settlements of the last three years in which the highest negotiated wage increases in more than a decade are revealed. Worth noting are the non-commercial industries such as public administration, hospitals, education, welfare and community services which registered as much as 10.2 per cent increase in June 1967 over the previous year. A recent empirical study suggests that, although unions have been successful in obtaining high wage settlements, they are, in fact occasioned by the tight labour market situation rather than the union pressure and collective bargaining.[21]

The explanation of this unusual profile in negotiated wage settlements must run in terms of the union militancy permitted within the framework of governmental non-intervention policy. In 1965 and 1966, for instance, the largest percentages (9.9 and 13.5 per cent respectively) of agreements, during a period of fourteen years, were achieved at the strike stage as the longshoremen's settlement and the controversial Pearson formula became a landmark of the period. The protection and improvement of the job territory, which are intrinsic in union behaviour, assumes a militant fervour when environmental conditions appear favourable. Management satisfying function during this period was conditioned by two considerations that restricted management's aggressive posture, behaviour of labour cost per unit of output and the international competitive position of Canadian products. Although unit labour cost increased sharply because productivity was lagging behind wage increases, "it was still lower in 1967 than it was in 1960."[22] Canada's international competitive position was also not impaired because it had substantially improved due to a "decline in the exchange value of the Canadian dollar."[23] The factor that did contribute to a management hardline policy was, however, a 20 per cent drop in the corporate profits per unit of output between 1965 and 1967.

Wage Parity   A unique phenomenon in Canadian-American labour relations is the growth and stability of international unionism, explained in an earlier section in terms of labour, product and money market expansion. Once this relationship is established within a logical economic framework, it is not difficult to understand the union demand for wage parity which is based on an age-old precept, "equal pay for equal work." The UAW argues that automobile wages in Canada, for any given occupation, are 17 to 60 cents (or 7 to 20 per cent) lower than they are in the United States and wage differentials for skilled workers are even greater. According to a recent Task Force study, the wage gap was reduced after the 1964-65 settlements and the Canadian average hourly wage for a production worker in 1967 was only 10 per cent lower than his counterpart in the United States ($3.25 in the United States compared with $2.95 in Canada).[24]

Management resistance to these demands is implicit in its maximization function and is supported by a strong productivity gap argument which points out that wages are lower in Canada because productivity is lower almost in the same proportion. There is no immediate trend toward equalization in productivity either, because the Canadian supervisory personnel and, to a certain extent, the workers are less qualified than their counterparts in the United States. Furthermore, Canadian automobile plants provide rest periods that, according to the management estimate, amount to 6.75 per cent time loss. The United States-Canada Automobile Agreement of January 16, 1965, includes promises of rationalizing Canadian operations, which may equalize productivity between the two countries and thus pave the ground for wage parity; however, the "Big Three" automobile companies feel that the process of rationalization may take several years. The Economic Council of Canada, in its Third Annual Review, suggests that collective bargaining can achieve wage parity if a number of other factors are achieved, most important among them being productivity equalization. For the economy as a whole, income parity with the United States remains a much less attainable goal in the near future since, according to the Minister of Industry, Canadian productivity is 35 per cent lower than it is in the United States and is reflected in a 32 per cent lower earning level in this country.

FRINGE BENEFITS. If there were a hierarchy of preferences in union attitudes toward negotiated settlements, fringe benefits such as paid holidays, vacations, sick leave, health and unemployment insurance and pension plans would place very high. Featured prominently for the first time in union demands during the wage-freeze period of World War II, in the postwar years their growth in the United States has been almost three times as fast as the average hourly earnings. (Average hourly

---

[21] See S. M. A. Hameed, "Wage-Price Process in the Canadian Manufacturing: 1946-1963," *Journal of Economic Studies,* July 1968.

[22] Economic Council of Canada, *The Challenge of Growth and Change,* (Fifth Annual Report), September 1968, p. 187.

[23] *Ibid.,* p. 189.

[24] Norman Coates, *Collective Bargaining in the Automobile Manufacturing Industry,* A study commissioned by the Task Force on Labour Relations, October 1967.

Table 6-4

MONTHLY INDEX NUMBERS (JANUARY 1965=100) AND ANNUAL PERCENTAGE AND CENTS PER HOUR INCREASES IN BASE RATES UNDER MAJOR COLLECTIVE AGREEMENTS IN CANADA, MARCH 1965 TO JUNE, 1969*

| Year | Manufacturing | | | | | | | | | Commercial Industries Excluding Construction | | | Non-Commercial Industries** | | | All Industries Excluding Construction | | |
| | Durable Goods | | | Non-Durable Goods | | | Total Manufacturing | | | | | | | | | | | |
	Index Number	Year-Over-Year Increase %	¢	Index Number	Year-Over-Year Increase %	¢	Index Number	Year-Over-Year Increase %	¢	Index Number	Year-Over-Year Increase %	¢	Index Number	Year-Over-Year Increase %	¢	Index Number	Year-Over-Year Increase %	¢
1965																		
Mar.	100.6			100.3			100.5			100.4			100.9			100.5		
June	102.4			101.3			101.9			101.6			102.4			101.7		
Sep.	102.9			102.9			103.0			103.0			102.8			103.0		
Dec.	104.3			104.0			104.2			104.0			103.6			104.0		
1966																		
Mar.	104.7	4.0	8.7	105.7	5.4	10.0	105.1	4.6	9.3	105.0	4.5	8.7	104.8	3.9	7.0	105.0	4.5	8.6
June	106.3	3.9	8.5	107.0	5.6	10.5	106.7	4.7	9.5	106.6	4.9	9.6	105.8	3.3	6.0	106.6	4.8	9.2
Sep.	107.8	4.7	10.4	109.8	6.7	12.8	108.7	5.5	11.4	109.3	6.1	12.1	109.3	6.3	11.4	109.3	6.2	12.1
Dec.	108.8	4.3	9.7	111.7	7.4	14.4	110.1	5.7	11.9	110.7	6.4	12.7	111.2	7.4	13.5	110.8	6.5	12.8
1967																		
Mar.	110.7	5.7	12.9	112.7	6.6	13.0	111.6	6.1	12.9	113.1	7.8	15.6	115.3	10.0	18.4	113.4	8.0	15.9
June	111.9	5.3	12.0	114.2	6.7	13.4	113.0	5.9	12.6	114.4	7.3	14.8	116.6	10.2	19.0	114.6	7.5	15.2
Sep.	113.2	5.0	11.6	117.1	6.7	13.7	115.0	5.8	12.6	116.9	6.9	14.5	119.8	9.6	18.4	117.3	7.2	15.0
Dec.	114.3	5.1	11.8	118.1	5.7	11.9	116.0	5.4	11.8	118.5	6.9	14.5	120.9	8.6	16.9	118.6	7.0	14.8

Table 6-4 (cont'd.)

Year	Manufacturing									Commercial Industries Excluding Construction			Non-Commercial Industries**			All Industries Excluding Construction		
	Durable Goods			Non-Durable Goods			Total Manufacturing											
	Index Number	Year-Over-Year Increase %	¢	Index Number	Year-Over-Year Increase %	¢	Index Number	Year-Over-Year Increase %	¢	Index Number	Year-Over-Year Increase %	¢	Index Number	Year-Over-Year Increase %	¢	Index Number	Year-Over-Year Increase %	¢
1968																		
Mar.	116.0	4.8	11.4	119.0	5.7	11.9	117.4	5.3	11.7	119.6	5.7	12.4	122.8	6.6	13.3	120.0	5.8	12.5
June	119.1	6.4	15.4	121.1	6.1	12.9	120.2	6.4	14.4	121.7	6.4	14.0	124.3	6.6	13.5	121.9	6.4	13.9
Sep.	122.0	7.8	18.9	124.5	6.3	13.8	123.3	7.2	16.6	124.4	6.4	14.4	127.6	6.5	13.7	124.8	6.4	14.3
Dec.	123.0	7.6	18.6	125.9	6.6	14.6	124.4	7.3	16.8	126.0	6.5	14.8	129.8	7.4	15.8	126.4	6.6	14.9
1969																		
Jan.	124.1	8.3	20.4	126.6	7.0	15.4	125.4	7.8	18.2	127.9	7.7	17.4	131.3	8.1	17.3	128.2	7.6	17.2
Feb.	125.1	8.5	20.9	127.2	7.0	15.5	126.2	7.9	18.5	128.4	7.7	17.5	131.4	7.6	16.3	128.5	7.5	17.0
Mar.	125.5	8.2	20.4	127.5	7.1	15.7	126.6	7.8	18.3	128.9	7.8	17.8	131.7	7.2	15.5	129.0	7.5	17.1
Apr.	126.1	6.8	17.2	127.8	6.7	14.9	127.1	6.8	16.2	129.7	7.5	17.4	132.1	7.2	15.6	129.7	7.2	16.6
May	126.5	6.6	16.8	129.5	7.5	16.8	128.0	7.0	16.7	130.5	7.6	17.7	133.6	7.6	16.6	130.4	7.3	16.9
June	128.2	7.6	19.5	130.6	7.9	17.8	129.5	7.8	18.6	131.5	8.1	18.8	135.8	9.3	20.3	131.3	7.7	17.7

* The data are based on all "major collective agreements" covering 500 or more employees "in force" except those in the construction industry. The data refer to rates actually paid in the month specified. No adjustments have been made for retroactive wage increases. This corresponds to the procedure followed in preparing the general wage rate data issued by the Canada Department of Labour, and the average weekly and hourly earnings data published by the Dominion Bureau of Statistics.

** The Non-Commercial industries consists of public administration and defence; hospitals; education; welfare; religion and other community service C.C.C. and domestic service. Commercial industries consists of all industries except the non-commercial industries.

Source: Collective Bargaining Review, No. 6, (1969). Canada Department of Labour.

earnings in manufacturing increased by 107 per cent between 1947 and 1963, whereas fringe benefits during the same period increased by 335 per cent.)[25] In Canada, statistics on fringe benefits are not available for a comparable period, but from 1957 to 1965 the cost of payments required by law has increased from 2.6 to 3.2 per cent of the payroll in the manufacturing sector, and from 2.2 to 4.5 per cent in the non-manufacturing sector of the economy.[26]

Paid Vacations   Almost 100 per cent of the agreements studied by the Federal Department of Labour in 1966 provided for paid vacations. The survey reported that "within the various ranges of vacation benefits, the most frequent provisions were two weeks after one year, three weeks after ten years, four weeks after twenty years and five weeks after twenty-five years." [27] However, only 13 per cent of the agreements had provisions for extended vacations which include supplementary vacations, pre-retirement vacations, etc. A separate survey of the provisions of collective agreements that covered office employees in Canadian manufacturing industries was published in 1967. It appears that provisions for paid vacations for office employees, which also included journalists, editorial staff and draftsmen, are very similar to those reported above for the manufacturing industries as a whole.

Unions in Canada began to negotiate reductions in the standard work week quite early in the twentieth century; it was argued, then, that reduction was necessary to avoid sheer fatigue. But there were few effective settlements until the late 1930's when the union strategy was to obtain overtime by reducing the standard or normal work week in relation to average weekly hours paid for. "Another shift in bargaining strategy seems to have emerged more recently with the introduction of fringe benefits. Paid vacations, paid holidays and paid sick leave, which may be termed as hours paid for but not worked, were sought mainly as non-wage items during the wage-freeze of the World War II period. The trend toward longer paid absence has continued through the postwar period, especially since 1957."[28]

MATTERS OF INDUSTRIAL JURISPRUDENCE.   Collective agreements carry provisions not only for wages and fringe benefits, but also for a large number of non-monetary, procedural or regulatory issues. These issues are as important, if not more important, than the other two categories and include seniority and job rights, hiring, layoff and promotion procedures, retraining, work assignments, operating rules and disciplinary and grievance procedures (almost three-fourths of the space in a normal contract). Unions wish to democratize management by reducing their arbitrary, perhaps capricious, decision-making, in order to ensure that workers will receive uniform treatment in matters of promotion, layoff, vacation benefits and other privileges. Management, on the other hand, is interested in maintaining sufficient authority to conduct productive operations. This means management prerogative in setting production standards, determining work assignments, and retaining the right to discipline employees for violating company regulations.

COLLECTIVE AGREEMENT PROVISIONS FOR TECHNOLOGICAL CHANGE

Union and management responses to automation are varied and a large number of related provisions belong to the area of industrial jurisprudence, such as contractual arrangement against layoffs, freezing of specific deployment schedules, advance notice of change, consultation programme and work sharing. Unions, on broad social and philosophical grounds, argue that technological advances do not essentially benefit the whole society, since reduced costs are not revealed in lower prices for the consumers, but simply in increased profits. Automation brings a decline in union membership, increases professionalization and undermines local bargaining structure because as product markets tend to concentrate as larger firms alone can afford huge investment for introducing new technology, automation disrupts the balance of market power between union and management and has an adverse impact on union negotiation at the bargaining table. In order to combat the technological menaces, unions have thus evolved a threefold strategy: an obstructionist policy in which job security is a primary goal and is obtained through contractual provisions against layoffs, work sharing and some manner of guaranteed annual income; a transitional policy intended to mitigate the impact of change through retraining schemes, relocation allowances, plant-wide seniority, and advance notice; consultation programs; a compensation policy that recognizes what John R. Commons would call the worker's property right in the job, in that any sacrifice of this right must be compensated by severance pay, increasing supplementary unemployment benefits, protracted vacation pay, accumulated sick leave or pooled severance pay funds.

A comprehensive survey of negotiated settlements on technological change would show provisions similar to the ones outlined above. The Federal Department of Labour, for instance, produced a study of technological change provisions in major collective agreements, published in 1967.[29] It has used a similar, though less elaborate, classification of provisions as the one described above. The five major categories used in this study are advance notice, income maintenance, worker adaptation, employment sharing, and joint union-management procedure. Contrary to the public impression that there is an overwhelming union-management response to technological change in Canada, it appears that only 28 per

---

[25] Bevars D. Mabry, *Labour Relations and Collective Bargaining*, (New York: The Ronald Press Company, 1966), p. 88.

[26] S. M. A. Hameed, *"Employment Impact of Fringe Benefits and Overtime in Canadian Manufacturing Sector: 1957-1965."* (Mimeo.)

[27] *Revisions in Major Collective Agreements in Canada*, Canada Department of Labour, 1966, p. 1.

[28] See S. M. A. Hameed, *Hours of Work in Canada: Economic and Institutional Determinants*, A study commissioned by the Task Force on Labour Relations, 1968.

[29] David Ross, *Response to Technological Change*, Canada Department of Labour, 1967.

Figure 6-1

AGREEMENTS CONTAINING CERTAIN TECHNOLOGICAL CHANGE PROVISIONS
AS A PERCENTAGE OF ALL AGREEMENTS SURVEYED

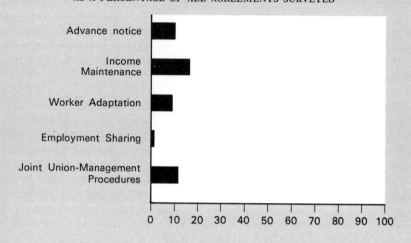

Figure 6-2

FREQUENCY OF MAJOR TECHNOLOGICAL CHANGE PROVISIONS AS A
PERCENTAGE OF ALL TECHNOLOGICAL CHANGE PROVISIONS

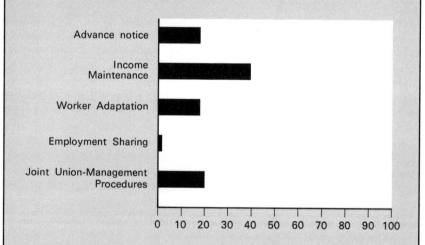

Source: Response to Technical Change, Canada Department of Labour, 1967.

cent or 133 agreements out of a total of 471 surveyed contained specific clauses on technological change. Figures 6-1 and 6-2 summarize the results of the Department of Labour survey. Of the total number of agreements, fifty-six or 12 per cent contained clauses on union-management consultation and negotiations, a development for which the Federal Department of Labour should be credited, as they maintain a Manpower Consultation Service which encourages setting up joint committees that may take appropriate steps before a final confrontation. The Manpower Consultation Service also suggests a joint union-management approach toward research and provides financial assistance for this purpose. The results of such committees in the United States have been encouraging in terms of setting up plant-wide employment reserves, subsidizing employees on shorter work-weeks, and providing a displacement differential to downgraded employees. Canadian railroad companies also signed an agreement with non-operating employees in 1962 which established a job security fund to which the employers contribute 1¢ per employee per hour worked. These funds are intended for retraining, transportation and similar purposes.

PROSPECTS OF COLLECTIVE BARGAINING

The primary functions of a theory are to provide an explanation for observed events and relationships, and to predict the occurences of as yet unobserved phenomena. The collective bargaining theory, as applied to an analysis of union growth, management resistance, the process of conflict resolution, and negotiated settlement was useful in establishing an "if-then" relationship between exploratory and dependent variables. The biggest test of our theory, however, is in establishing its generalized predictive power, beginning with an examination of the direction and magnitude of change in our independent variables (i.e. expansion of markets, management maximization-satisfying function, legal foundations of conflict resolution and power as a negotiational base) which are exogenously determined for our purpose. The period selected for projection is the 1970's.

Expansion of Markets

The concept of expanding markets can be operationalized into such quantifiable economic indicators as increase in G.N.P., volume of imports and exports, capital flows and rate of immigration. Projected estimates of these indicators to 1980 are not yet available but it is generally believed that in the opening year of this decade, the growth rate will be slower than it was in 1969. This is attributed to the anti-inflationary policy of the Federal Government which was particularly affected by the five per cent annual rate of inflation registered in the closing months of the 1960's. Economic forecasters, however, are optimistic about the remainder of the decade, predicting expansion in production and foreign trade. The economic outlook of the provinces is also healthy, suggesting that the decade ahead may be called "the soaring seventies."

Three implications of the foregoing economic forecast are relevant for the prediction of change in our two dependent variables, the degree of unionization and the structure of collective bargaining: a technological advance accompanied by a change in labour force structure; the growing size of the firm with internal organizational changes affecting white-collar worker and management interaction; a rise of multinational and multi-industrial operations called economic conglomerates.

Technological advances affect the labour force structure by requiring shifts in employment distribution among various sectors of the economy, by demanding higher skills and by changing the nature of job content. The net result is a phenomenal growth in the white-collar work force consisting of clerical, professional sales workers, and a growing proportion of women and professional workers (engineers, scientists and teachers), many of whom are in the public service or belong to essential services. This expanding trend is expected to continue into the 1970's with the number of white-collar workers far surpassing the number of blue-collar workers. This structural change in the labour force seems detrimental to the future growth of unionism, since, in the past, this portion of the labour force has been difficult to organize and unionism and its conventional appeals have not worked effectively. It is predicted, however, that as early craftsmen and industrial workers, menaced by the increasing competition due to expanding markets, found protection in unions, so will the white-collar group. Undoubtedly, the process of unionization will be enormously aided by a meaningful change in labour ideology, methods of organization, leadership image, protective legislation and demonstration of gains through collective bargaining.

Traditionally, white-collar workers have identified with management since their numbers were relatively smaller than the blue-collar employees and the nature of their duties brought them into frequent contact with management. Unionization and collective bargaining in these cirsumstances did not appear meaningful. But the impact of the expanding markets on the labour force and the organizational structure of the firm will both tend to siphon off the psychic benefits which the white-collar group earlier possessed. New recognition of the social and organizational downgrading of their status will come gradually, accompanied by an increasing realization of the menaces of the market and the need for protective organizations. Some evidence of this phenomenon may be found in the recent membership gains of the Canadian Union of Public Employees and Public Service Alliance of Canada. The impact of the white-collar segment of the work force on the organizational policies of the labour movement will be enormous and new strategies, if developed, will help to exploit the changing status perception of this group and thus accelerate the rate of unionization.

Historically, at each stage of market expansion, management grew stronger in order to cope with the forces of competition by keeping wage costs under control. Unions, in a parallel development, pushed their organizational frontiers to form provincial, regional, national and international bodies. In the 1970's, expanding markets will become instrumental in the growth of multinational corporations[30] which may be able to withstand prolonged strikes and not yield to union demands. Examples of such resistance are beginning to alarm union leaders: "The Proctor-Silex Co. at Picton, Ont., was able to sustain a ten month strike by the International Union of Electrical Radio and Machine Workers because it is part of a conglomerate that includes Smith-Corona, Singer and the Friden Corp."[31] As a counter measure, unions are beginning to consolidate their position through mergers, but the process is slow and at the present time there are only nine unions in Canada with a membership of over 50,000. According to I. W. Abel, International President of the Steelworkers, unions with a small membership cannot cope with multinational corporations. Although this is an alarming development for labour, it might bring a new organizational wave in the trade union movement, as unions begin to concentrate their power through mergers and through closer co-operation with unions in other European countries such as Portugal, Spain, Greece and Turkey.

There are indications that the structure of collective bargaining will also become increasingly centralized. Unions having the same jurisdiction, when encountered by a powerful employer, are beginning to consolidate power through coordinated bargaining:

The unions dealing with Canadian General Electric recently coordinated their bargaining activities for the first time with very good results. Unions affiliated to the CLC, having jurisdiction in the petro-chemical industry, established a Petro-Chemical Council back in 1967 and it is their plan to coordinate both their organizing and bargaining efforts in this country. There is also a co-ordinating Council of Performing Arts Union and a Canadian Council of Food Unions, established in 1968.[32]

Management Maximization — Satisficing Function

In order to predict management resistance to unions in the 1970's, we must know the direction and magnitude of change in our causal variables. Earlier it was determined that the principles of maximization and satisficing are the crux of the marginal and behavioral theories of the firm since they explain the management goal orientation that determines, for

---

[30] The U.S. government estimates that, on the basis of the current growth of conglomerates, 75 per cent of all business assets in the United States will be in the hands of only 200 companies by 1975, Ed Finn, "Unions and Conglomerates," *Canada Dimension*, Vol. 6, No. 5, (October-November 1969).

[31] *Ibid*, p. 13.

[32] John Fryer, "Future Trends in Collective Bargaining, *"Canadian Labour,* Vol. 14, No. 4, (April 1969).

our purposes, management attitudes toward unions and collective bargaining. Lack of empirical verification of these theories, leaves us with no better alternative than a series of deductions and some historical evidence of management behaviour in the past.

An examination of management behaviour *vis-a-vis* unions seems to suggest three important factors. First, the maximization principle has been, and will continue to be, an underlying force in determining management goals, values and attitudes. Second, the satisfying principle, at least up to the present time, has remained a deviation rather than a norm. Third, these two principles are not mutually exclusive.

Historically, management has resisted unions and protected managerial prerogatives on the basis of socially accepted property rights and their own concept of maximization. The withdrawal of Common Law support, the rise of the corporation and big business, economic prosperity and the rising level of profits tended to soften management attitudes and the maximization principle, at least in the large and complex business organizations, became submerged. What appeared on the surface was management concern, not so much for maximum profit gains, but for the attainment of other goals such as employee welfare, acceptance of unions, long-run survival and social acceptance of the business. Marginal and behavioural theories, demonstrate that the size of the firm is crucial in determining the role of maximization in a management resistance function, that the small business, as well as the giant conglomerates, are most likely to support the maximization principle and, therefore, a hard-line policy toward unions, and that an intermediary group may tend to satisfy, and consequently maintain, a soft and accommodating attitude.

The Canadian economy in the 1970's will produce a larger intermediary group through greater concentration, mergers and company takeovers. This process will enable management to fix target rates of return, accommodate union wage demands with little or no difficulty, and pass the burden of additional wage cost to the consumers. Economic forecasts of continuing prosperity with prospects of higher profits on one hand, and the increasing costs of complete shut down in automated plants on the other will make management keen to avoid industrial disputes. The goal of management will likely be to satisfy rather than to maximize. Unions attempting to organize and bargain with this intermediary group will find less resistance; smaller businesses and large multinational, multi-industrial corporations will be the areas of resistance.

Legal Foundations of Conflict Resolution

The Federal and provincial governments in Canada laid the foundations of conflict resolution toward the turn of this century by legislating a conciliatory procedure based on the principle of "voluntarism." The procedure soon changed its bias from voluntarism to compulsory conciliation during World War II when the principle of compulsory collective bargaining, borrowed from the American Wagner Act, became an additional feature of the governmental policy. These legal measures determined the nature, frequency and circumstances under which government will intervene in a labour-management conflict. Two significant factors that stand out in the historical survey of legislative evolution are the jurisdictional autonomy of the provinces to legislate their own labour laws and a tendency to experiment with the legal processes prevalent in other countries whenever federal leadership in legislating effective laws is felt inadequate. The federal-provincial background provided in earlier sections and the recent public concern about the inflationary nature of wage settlements and the rising incidence of strikes suggests some possibilities for future legislation.

The pattern of provincial borrowing from foreign labour-relations laws, (once from the United Kingdom and once from the United States), suggests possible recurrence if federal laws provide inadequate leadership. British Columbia has departed from the federal labour-relations policy, borrowing from Swedish law a Mediation Commission which has replaced the conciliation procedure. Although separate from the Department of Labour, this Commission makes recommendations that can become binding if the Provincial Cabinet feels it necessary. There is no compulsory postponement of the strike because the employees, irrespective of the Commission's hearing, may take a strike vote, give a written seventy-two hour notice to the employer, and stage a legal strike. Although not as drastic, the Nova Scotia Trade Union Act has introduced greater sanctions against illegal strikes and jurisdictional disputes. Quebec has set up an industrial court and Ontario has passed legislation to establish a Labour-Management Arbitration Commission. Prince Edward Island, Saskatchewan and Newfoundland have also passed legislation during September 1967 and August 1968.

There is nothing extraordinary about provinces legislating labour laws since they have the constitutional autonomy to do so. What is significant is a notable departure from the federal labour-management dispute settlement procedure. Three major provinces, Ontario, Quebec and British Columbia, have clearly indicated their preference for stricter legal control over industrial disputes. The changing pattern of legal measures in provincial conflict resolution predicts a probable amendment in the federal IRDI Act toward greater governmental intervention, introducing discretionary use of power when public interest is considered in jeopardy. The amendment may even follow the example of British Columbia in importing certain Swedish measures and in establishing an independent body with compulsory arbitration powers. By establishing the Prices and Incomes Commission, however, the Federal Government seems anxious to exhaust all the possible measures of moral suasion before adopting an austere legal policy.

Power as a Negotiational Base

Finally, the collective bargaining theory needs to predict the type of relationship and the outcome of negotiations that will be embodied in the collective agreements of the future. Both factors depend on the degree of expected change in the relative power positions of the protagonists. These power positions will be determined by: the rising wave of union militancy, the growth of multinational, multiindustrial corporations, and the greater government propensity to intervene.

The growth of union membership in Canada during the 1960's (42 per cent) may be mainly attributed to the white-collar breakthrough. These new entrants into the labour movement, having a different orientation and level of expectations, are militant and promise to continue that way as more and more unorganized groups become unionized. In a parallel development, it was shown that conglomerates and small businesses are becoming less vulnerable to union pressure through strike. Labour-management relations in the 1970's, consequently, are going to present a rugged pattern: union militancy matched by management hard-line. However, a strict government intervention policy, caused by a concern over inflation and the rising incidence of industrial disputes coupled with improved mediatory techniques, may keep the incidence of strikes at the pre-1964 average.

It has already been predicted that the structure of collective bargaining will tend toward increasing centralization and a larger number of settlements through co-ordinated bargaining. As the complexity and number of demands grows, placing greater strain and responsibility on the negotiators, the Canadian Labour Congress is already planning to use computers in analyzing relevant data and supplying this highly specialized information to the regional offices through an electronic network.

The tone and mood of labour and management in a negotiating session is greatly influenced by the perception of their respective power positions. If the constituents, and their perception of power, change in either or both the parties, a new 'hostility-cooperation' situation is created. Such changes will be numerous and each individual case will be affected differently. For example, where a conglomerate faces a small union, or vice versa, the outcome will tend to be in favour of the party with superior power.

In a decentralized bargaining situation, local unions draw up a list of demands that tend to emphasize matters of parochial interest. As the national or international unions begin to initiate bargaining with large corporations, however, issues of wider importance and concern will appear on the union demand list. With all reservations and conditions, given the changing spectrum of power and the accompanying trend toward centralized bargaining, negotiated settlements on shorter hours, increased paid vacation, guaranteed annual wages, wage parity in selected industries and Canada wide pension plans may be predicted. There is evidence that some unions have already bargained on a few of these issues: a thirty-two hour work week, comprising only four and one-half days, has been negotiated by the Photo Engravers' Union in Toronto; longer paid vacations have been adopted by Algoma, Stelco, Abitibi, Canadian International Paper and other large companies; guaranteed annual wage clauses may be found in the recent contracts signed by the limited Automobile Workers and the Pulp and Sulphite Workers.

CONCLUSION

Industrial relations, particularly collective bargaining, is an applied field requiring a pragmatic approach. Although conceptualizing and theorizing have been rejected by the policy-makers in favour of an intuitive insight acquired by long experience in the field, the scene is gradually changing: chance observations, scanty interviews and disjointed guesses are being substituted by theory-based research and systematic interpretations of data. The changing economic and social environment demands new policies and the restructuring of existing institutions. To meet the challenge of the revolution in technology and ideology, the legislators and the policy-makers need guidance from social science researchers. For example, there are and will be strains and dysfunctions in the collective bargaining relationship, and it is the responsibility of the researcher to identify their sources.

Manpower projections about the future growth of the labour movement in Canada indicate that union membership in the 1970's may decline as a proportion of the total labour force. Nonetheless, white-collar unionization of the skilled trades, professionals, and governmental and service workers will show positive gains. It is also expected that the average educational level of the union members will rise as the younger and better educated workers join the trade union movement. Carrying a different image of the changing goals, values and expectations in the new era, those younger workers now joining the unions are likely to create dissatisfaction and tension within the movement. The effectiveness of the strike as a bargaining weapon in satisfying the economic and social expectations of these younger workers remains undetermined. On the other hand, the change in management structure, organization and goals (maximization-satisfying) is introducing an additional strain in the Canadian society and the federal and provincial governments are keen to evolve adequate techniques for controlling industrial disputes that are adversely affecting the efficiency of the economy.

Where will this lead? — perhaps to political action by the unions or to an age of compulsory arbitration. The questions raised by the industrial relations system require serious consideration. Effective answers may be found if analysis is undertaken with regard for the rigour afforded by a theoretical framework.

7

ORGANIZED

LABOUR AND POLITICS

IN CANADA

Richard Ulric Miller

INTRODUCTION[1]

The appropriate political role of the trade union is viewed divergently by many non-communist labour movements. At one end of the continuum is the German Workers Confederation (DGB), a nonpolitical, neutral, economic organization. On the other end, are such unions as the Confederation of Mexican Workers (CTM), which are organizationally integrated into a political party as a functional unit and are expected to perform as the economic arm for party and government. Between the extremes, lie many patterns of elective, legislative or nonpartisan political action. In situations of political impartiality, sometimes referred to as "Gomperism," labour organizations refrain from aligning with any one party and instead "reward their friends and punish their enemies" without regard to party label.

The conflicting philosophies of union political action that collide in Canada makes it an interesting laboratory for the study of organized labour and politics.[2] The influence of tradition and example and a common political system push Canadian unions toward the British model of direct participation in politics through alliance with a labour party, while the hegemony in Canada of American based unions holding strong beliefs in nonpartisan political action exerts pressure in the opposite direction. The long history of unionism in Canada reveals a struggle between these opposing positions for dominance. Evidence that one side had finally gained ascendancy by 1961 seems to be indicated by the creation at that time of a new political organization, the New Democratic Party, to which Canadian unions pledged affiliation and active support.

The apparent clear-cut acceptance of elective or party political action invites our close scrutiny for several reasons.[3] First, the shift in political strategy suggests a resolution of the philosophical contradictions between Gomperism and elective political action. Is the change one of substance or merely appearance? In other words, how widely accepted, within labour ranks, is the new strategy and how deeply held are the convictions that it represents the appropriate role for trade unions in Canada? Second, if this is a real shift, what is the cause? Third, has the emphasis given to elective political action relegated to unimportance other forms of union political strategies involving such activities as legislative action (lobbying)? Finally, what is the future for labour in politics: further strengthening of party action, reversion to the non-partisan tactics of Gomperism or perhaps withdrawal completely from the political arena?

THE SEARCH FOR A POLITICAL STRATEGY: 1870-1932

Canadian labour's introduction to elective political action came in 1874 when the president of the Ottawa Trades Council, D. J. O'Donoghue, was elected to the provincial legislature.[4] This effort marked the beginning of a series of isolated attempts, primarily on the part of local trade councils, to place trade unionists in both federal and provincial legislatures. Despite the forays of the trade councils into politics, the national labour centre, the Trades and Labour Congress, remained aloof from direct political participation. While resolutions calling for independent political action were debated at various TLC conventions, the Congress limited the political pursuit of its goals to the submission of legislative demands to provincial and Federal governments and to lobbying through a parliamentary committee.[5]

---

[1] The author wishes to acknowledge the assistance he received from many individuals in the course of this study, but most particularly from Mr. George Home, Mr. John Fryer and Mr. John Harney. The author remains solely responsible for the interpretation and use of the material he received.

[2] For an extended discussion of trade union political action in Western Europe, see Everett M. Kassalow, *Trade Unions and Industrial Relations: an International Comparison* (New York: Random House, 1969), pp. 29-65.

[3] Elective political action was not unknown in Canadian labour circles before 1961. As will be discussed briefly, labour candidates were put forward as early as the 1870's and efforts made to form distinct labour parties or to affiliate with existing parties continued by individuals or groups within the labour movement through the era of the Cooperative Commonwealth Federation. See Gad Horowitz, *Canadian Labour in Politics* (Toronto: University of Toronto Press, 1968).

[4] Clifford A. Scotton, *Canadian Labour and Politics,* Canadian Labour Congress, pp. 4 and 5. See also H. A. Logan. *Trade Unions in Canada,* (Toronto: Macmillan Co. of Canada, 1948) p. 38.

[5] Around the turn of the century, the TLC employed John G. O'Donoghue, a son of Daniel, as a full-time "Parliamentary Solicitor" to represent labour's views to Parliament. *Cf.* Scotton, *Canadian Labour,* p. 8.

At the 1906 convention, a more positive step was taken in which encouragement was to be given to the formation of provincial labour parties.[6] There were to be no formal connections, however, between the parties and the labour movement and the TLC for its part would retain its role as the "legislative mouthpiece of organized labour . . . irrespective and independent of any body engaged in the effort to send representatives of the people to parliament and legislatures."[7] With the exception of a, brief departure, from 1917 to 1923, in which a dominion-wide labour party to which TLC unions would affiliate was advocated, this was the official Congress policy until 1956.[8] The TLC thereafter was to become "rigidly non-political" to the end of its days, according to one authority.[9] Whether for reasons of disillusionment with independent political action or for pressure from the United States based unions affiliated to the Congress, the adoption and repeated approval of the Gompersian policies of nonpartisan action symbolized defeat for proponents of a British style working class political action.[10]

Gomperist control of the Congress' political strategies was only partially successful, resulting in the reappearance from time to time of a movement for independent political action. For example, the advent of a business depression in 1913, coupled with the hostility of the traditional parties, forced the unions to look beyond economic sanctions and legislative activity for the attainment of their goals. Further impetus to direct political action was given by the enticing example of the British Labour Party. Bowing to the pressure, the TLC at its 1917 convention temporarily abandoned its 1906 declaration and reversed its stand.[11]

We, therefore, strongly recommend the organization of an Independent Labour Party for Canada upon the same lines as the British Labour Party has been organized, and giving recognition to organizations having similar objects as those affiliated with the British Labour Party.

While the resolution favoured a national party, the actual task of building the party was left to the provinces. It was not until 1921 that provincial party organizations had achieved a state considered sufficient to support a national party, the Canadian Labour Party.

Some success was achieved on the provincial level, notably in Ontario where a farmer-labour coalition controlled the government for several years, but results at the national level were disappointing. Of thirty candidates for parliament sponsored by CLP in 1921, only two were elected.[12] Disillusionment set in however, as an apparently irreversible procession of electoral defeats followed one upon the other. With diminished enthusiasm, the delegates to the 1923 TLC convention therefore offered little resistance to a demand to return to the 1906 declaration of political nonpartisanship.[13]

Although the TLC had withdrawn its support, the Canadian Labour Party continued to exist until 1927 but with little political significance. The provincial parties on the other hand, often operating in political obscurity, managed to survive the 1920's carrying with them a nucleus of ardent trade union political activists around which a new labour party could be formed. Strengthening this group was the presence in parliament of four independent labour members, most notable of whom was J. S. Woodsworth. In the 1930's, Woodsworth played an instrumental part in a renewed attempt to fashion a party ideologically in phase with the labour movement.

THE COOPERATIVE COMMONWEALTH FEDERATION: 1933-1961

The economic downturn in the early 1930's set in motion a number of diverse groups in Canada whose paths ultimately converged in Regina, Saskatchewan in 1933. The first of these groups, farmers drawn predominantly from the wheat-producing prairie provinces, had come together in a class conscious organization, the United Farmers of Canada, in 1926.[14] The second group, the League for Social Reconstruction, was established in 1931 by a group of university professors deeply influenced by England's Fabian Society. The final group drawn to Regina was the Socialist Party of Canada, whose strength lay primarily in British Columbia. At the suggestion of the UFC, a national conference was called to bring together "all groups who believed that capitalism should be overthrown, and that a new social order based on production for use and not for profit was needed."[15] Meeting in Calgary in 1932, the delegates to the conference agreed on the necessity for a new political party, to be called the Cooperative Commonwealth Federation. A founding convention for the CCF was set for July 1933 in Regina, at which time the programme and constitution were to be adopted.

The 1933 CCF convention produced what was in many respects a revolutionary document. The Regina Manifesto, as it was more commonly

[6] Horowitz, *Canadian Labour in Politics,* p. 60.

[7] *Ibid.* p. 427.

[8] At the 1923 TLC Convention, the Congress resolved that "labour political autonomy be left in the hands of the established political labour parties," and that the TLC "continue to act as the legislative mouthpiece for organized labour . . . independent of any political organization . . ." Logan, *Trade Unions,* p. 431.

[9] Horowitz, *Canadian Labour in Politics,* p. 61.

[10] *Ibid,* pp. 61 and 421. For contrasting interpretations, see Leslie E. Wisner, "The Trades and Labour Congress," *Canadian Labour,* April 1956, pp. 21-25; Eamon Park, "Labour's Political Diary," *Canadian Labour,* September 1961, pp. 212-22; Horowitz, pp. 62-63; and John Crispo, *International Unionism,* (Toronto: McGraw-Hill, 1967), pp. 244-45.

[11] Logan, *Trade Unions,* p. 430.

[12] Dean McHenry. *The Third Force in Canada,* (Berkeley: University of California Press, 1950), p. 22.

[13] Logan, *Trade Unions,* p. 431.

[14] S. M. Lipset, *Agrarian Socialism,* (Berkeley: University of California Press, 1950), p. 66.

[15] *Ibid.* p. 87. See also McHenry, *Third Force,* pp. 23-27 for a different interpretation of the founding of the CCF.

referred to, called for economic planning, socialization of banking and insurance, public ownership of utilities and basic industries, and socialized health services,[16] among other things. Without qualification, it was stated that "No CCF government will rest content until it has eradicated capitalism and put into operation the full program of socialized planning which will lead to the establishment in Canada of the Cooperative Commonwealth."[17]

The Canadian labour movement played a minor role in the early activities of the CCF. Although labour was indirectly represented in the party by those few members of parliament elected through the provincial labour parties, only one unionist of national stature, Aaron Mosher, President of the All Canadian Congress of Labour, had taken a direct part in the formation of CCF. Mosher's ACCL was a rival to the TLC, being composed mainly of the Canadian Brotherhood of Railway Employees.

Although the founding group of the CCF had envisaged a federal union of parties, trade unions and farmer organizations, the trade unions maintained a discreet distance.[18] Not until 1938 did the first union, United Mine Workers, District 26, affiliate with the party.[19] Barriers to affiliation, at least within the TLC, were raised by several groups: those unions following the traditional AFL policy of nonpartisanship; those unions under the influence of communist leaders who blocked affiliation with any but communist groups; and individuals who condemned CCF for its earlier association with A. R. Mosher." [20] This latter group, many of whom were in fact CCFers, accused the party of supporting dual unions and opposing international unionism. "Although Mosher and his organization never officially aligned themselves with the CCF, the damage was done as far as CCF-TLC relations were concerned.[21]

The farthest the TLC was willing to go was demonstrated in 1943 when a resolution was passed calling for a Trade Union Committee for Political Action. Additional resolutions were passed at succeeding conventions but implementation in the form of financial support and personnel was never provided.[22] Despite the rejection by the Congress itself of direct political participation, an undercurrent of sentiment favouring political activism carried many of the TCL's member unions into alliance with CCF. Jamieson estimates that nearly half the locals that eventually came to affiliate with CCF in Ontario, Saskatchewan, and Alberta were from the TLC.[23]

Added impetus to labour participation in CCF was provided in the late 1930's by a schism within the TLC. Succumbing to pressures emanating from the AFL, the TLC in 1939 expelled the locals of those international unions comprising the Congress of Industrial Organizations in the United States. The following year, the CIO locals combined with the old All Canadian Congress of Labour to produce a new national federation, the Canadian Congress of Labour.

Spearheaded by Ontario CCF trade unionists, a concerted effort to affiliate local unions with CCF was initiated in 1942. Some measure of success was quickly attained with both CCL and TLC unions in the province being induced to affiliate. When the returns were in from the

1943 Ontario election, in which CCF elected thirty-four legislators, nineteen from trade unions, the way was now paved for a retreat from political neutrality.

At its 1943 convention, the CCL confronted the issue squarely resolving that: [24]

Whereas in the opinion of this Congress, the policy and programme of the CCF more adequately expresses the views of organized labour than any other party:

Be it therefore resolved that this convention of the CCL endorse the CCF as the political arm of Labour in Canada, and recommend to all affiliated and chartered unions that they affiliate with the CCF.

For the remainder of its existence, CCL continued to endorse CCF, although not without opposition from some affiliated unions. Particularly hostile to the alliance were the United Electrical Workers, International Woodworkers of America, and the United Automobile Workers. Within these unions, communists holding leadership positions were agreeable to political action only if it involved the Communist Party's political organization, the Labour Progressive Party.[25]

The political activities of one final segment of organized labour in Canada, the Canadian and Catholic Confederation of Labour, requires brief mention. The CCCL, localized in Quebec, had been under the domination of the Catholic Church from its inception in 1921. Reflecting the policies of the Church, the CCCL as a body maintained a strong apolitical stance, declaring in its constitution that "no discussion of a political character shall be tolerated in a Congress of the Federation . . . Neither will it present nor support any political candidate, even though he be one of its members." [26]

Any affiliation or even cooperation with CCF was therefore ruled out. The CCF's consistent failure to achieve support for its candidates in Quebec was traceable in no small measure to these indirect barriers

---

[16] McHenry, *Third Force,* p. 28.

[17] *Ibid.* p. 29.

[18] Opposition within Moshers' own union, the CBRE, as well as bitterness between ACCL and TLC eventually forced Mosher to withdraw from the CCF and to prevent the affiliation of ACCL unions. Horowitz, *Canadian Labour,* p. 64.

[19] Dean McHenry, "The Impact of the CCF on Canadian Parties and Groups," *The Political Quarterly:* May 1949, p. 380.

[20] *Ibid.* p. 384.

[21] Horowitz, *Canadian Labour,* p. 64.

[22] Logan, *Trade Unions,* p. 437.

[23] Stuart Jamieson, *Industrial Relations in Canada,* (Toronto: Macmillan and Co. Ltd., 1957), p. 95.

[24] CCL. *Proceedings of the Fourth Annual Convention,* (1943), p. 54.

[25] Logan, pp. 556-557. See also Horowitz, pp. 85-130 for a detailed discussion of the communist attitude toward CCF during this period.

[26] Logan, p. 594.

interposed by the Church. Clerical opposition was also manifested directly, however, through open criticism of CCF, whose socialism was attacked as incompatible with Catholicism.[27]

THE CCF IN RETROSPECT

The CCF achieved its greatest political successes just after World War II. In 1944, it became the government party in Saskatchewan, a position it continued to hold until 1964. At various times, the CCF achieved the status of "official" opposition in British Columbia, Ontario, Nova Scotia and Manitoba.[28] As Table 7-1 shows, however, at the national level CCF achieved only mixed electoral success.

The CCF reached its pinnacle in the period between 1945 and 1949 when victory in four by-elections gave it a total of thirty-two members in parliament. However, the promise of active and widespread trade union support was proved illusory almost immediately. A peak of one hundred local unions, affiliating 50,000 members, was reached in 1944 and thereafter began to decline, eventually hitting a low of forty-four locals and 16,397 members in 1952;[29] moreover, those affiliations were concentrated in Nova Scotia and Ontario and consisted primarily of CCL unions (thirty-seven of the forty-four were from CCL).[30]

For various reasons, independent political action following the English model either held little attraction or, if it was attractive, it could not be implemented. The bulk of the Canadian labour movement continued to place its reliance on direct submissions to government, legislative lobbying and nonpartisan elective activity. Whether because of American influence and control, communist opposition, an alleged predilection of TLC leadership for the Liberals or further disillusionment with political action engendered by consistent electoral failures, the CCF did not become labour's parliamentary arm.[31] This does not imply, however, that the labour support CCF did receive was insignificant to the party. First, the main source of revenue for the party was the affiliated unions.[32] Second, a system of interlocking directorates between CCF and the CCL was established.[33]

Most of the officers who bridged the gap between the CCF and the unions entered the unions through the CCF rather than the other way about. The leaders who formed the nuclei of several of these unions were recruited from the CCF on the basis, among other things, of personal and ideological affinities.

Finally, though few in numbers, union affiliation with CCF came to represent a broad cross section of the Canadian labour movement, including miners, steelworkers, machinists, railway workers, printers, public service employees, packinghouse workers, upholsterers, office employees and construction workers. These particular union-CCF relationships, together with a continued attraction to direct political action on the part

Table 7-1

NUMBER OF SEATS WON IN NATIONAL ELECTIONS 1935-1958

	CCF	*Liberals*	*Conservatives*	*Social Credit*
1935	7	171	39	17
1940	8	178	39	10
1945	28	125	67	13
1949	13	190	42	10
1953	23	171	50	15
1957	25	103	110	19
1958	8	49	208	0

Source: 1935-1949: Dean McHenry, *The Third Force in Canada* (Berkeley: University of California Press, 1950) p. 135.
1953-1958: *Toronto Globe and Mail.*

of key trade union leaders, proved decisive in labour's ultimate decision to cooperate in the establishment of a new party.

THE NEW DEMOCRATIC PARTY

Origins

In 1956, efforts to merge the TLC and the CCL culminated in success and a single federation, the Canadian Labour Congress, was established. It had been expected that the main obstacle to union would be their antithetical political policies. The TLC leadership was personified by president Percy Bengough who hewed closely to the customary Gompersian approach. Support within the Congress' affiliated unions for more direct political action, perhaps in concert with CCF, was emerging but it continued to be ignored by the TLC executive. On the other hand, the

---

[27] David Lewis, "Socialism Across the Border: Canada's CCF," *Antioch Review:* Vol. 3, Winter 1943, p. 479. See also McHenry, *The Third Force,* pp. 131-133.

[28] C. A. Scotton, "A Brief History of the CCF," *Canadian Labour,* September 1961, p. 24.

[29] Horowitz, pp. 30-31. See also Eamon Park, "Labour's Political Diary," *Canadian Labour,* September 1961, p. 22, in which it is argued that the total number of union members affiliated with CCF never exceeded 20,000.

[30] *Ibid.*

[31] Even the CCL unions refrained from extending significant support, choosing rather to utilize the Centre's Political Action Committee as the political body through which they would work. See Horowitz on this point, pp. 82-84.

[32] Leo Zakuta. "Membership in a Becalmed Protest Movement," *Canadian Journal of Economics and Political Science:* Vol. 24, (May 1958), p. 198.

[33] *Ibid.* p. 197.

political activists within the CCL, fully cognizant of Bengough's opposition to labour alignment with a party, feared that the merger would result in the demise of PAC and, with it, years of effort to politicize and mobilize Canadian labour.[34]

CCL anxiety proved needless. Bengough resigned during the merger negotiations and was replaced by Claude Jodoin as president of the TLC. Jodoin was much more favourably disposed toward the CCF and toward the activism in politics that many on the CCL would undoubtedly propose for the combined labour centres.[35]

Harmony was further promoted by two compromise resolutions that directed the CLC to establish a Political Education Committee that would formulate political education programmes and would assist the affiliates in following suit. All affiliated unions and federations were urged to take an interest in political affairs, to continue the forms of political action and education carried on prior to the merger, and "to undertake such further activities as may in the future appear to be appropriate for achieving the basic objectives of the Congress."

Of greatest significance for the actual creation of a "new party" was the authorization of the Political Education Committee,[36]

under the guidance of the incoming Executive Council, to initiate discussions with free trade unions not affiliated with the Congress, with the principal farm organizations in Canada, with the Co-operative Commonwealth Federation or other political parties pledged to support the legislative programme of the CLC, excluding Communists or facist-dominated parties, and to explore and develop co-ordination of action in the legislative and political field.

In voting on the resolutions at the convention, only six delegates cast negative ballots. Supporting the resolutions were the Plumbers, Steelworkers, and Brotherhood of Railway Clerks. The single delegate who spoke in opposition was a member of the Textile Workers Union of America.[37]

A series of events followed in the wake of the CLC resolutions. At the national level, a Farmer-Labour Coordinating Council was set up to promote better understanding between those two groups and to explore coordinated action. Affirmation of the resolution was voted by the Manitoba Federation of Labour. The Toronto and District Labour Council, the Hamilton and District Labour Council, and the Ontario Federation of Labour not only accepted the CLC resolutions, but also endorsed the CCF.

Meanwhile, the CCF was being pushed irresistibly, if reluctantly, into the arms of organized labour. The 1957 federal election increased CCF Members of Parliament from twenty-three to twenty-five but left the Conservatives in control of a minority government. In the spring of the next year, a new election was called in which Prime Minister Diefenbaker requested the electorate to give him a majority government. The response was a landslide victory for the Conservatives, giving them a margin of 151 members over the combined strength of the other parties. While CCF representation in parliament had not been completely eliminated, as had that of the Social Credit Party, a mortal blow had nevertheless been struck. A number of national CCF leaders had lost their seats, leaving the party with virtually no representation in the West.[38]

THE 1958 RESOLUTIONS: The crisis that had befallen the CCF revolved around a question debated within the CLC since the 1956 convention. At issue was whether to give solid support to the CCF or to attempt to create a new party. The 1958 election results dictated the answer;[39] consequently, when the CLC convention convened in April, a declaration was approved commending the CCF for the contribution it had made to the welfare of the Canadian people and citing the need for "a broadly based people's political movement, which embraces the CCF, the Labour movement, farm organizations, professional people and other liberally minded persons interested in basic social reform. . . ." The executive committee was instructed to initiate discussion with CCF, farm organizations and "other like-minded individuals and groups" to formulate a constitution and a programme for a political "instrument" and then to report what had been accomplished to the next CLC convention.[40] It should be noted that Stanley Knowles, one of the CCF national officers who had lost his seat in parliament in the federal election, was elected by the convention to be an Executive Vice-President of the CLC, a position specially created for him.[41]

Three months after the CLC convention, the CCF held its own convention in Montreal. Responding to the CLC invitation, CCF authorized its national officers to enter into discussion with CLC, the Catholic federation, and "other like-minded groups and individuals," looking toward the establishment of a new party. The results of these discussions were to be reported to the next convention.[42] The extent to which CCF and CLC were already tied together is illustrated by the fact that the Chairman of the convention was Stanley Knowles, the Executive Vice President of CLC, who also held the position of English Speaking Vice President in CCF. Another unionist holding a CCF and a union position simultaneously was Morden Lazarus, member of the National Council

---

[34] Horowitz, pp. 162-164.

[35] Unknown to even some of his closest associates, Jodoin had once contemplated CCF membership in Quebec. Horowitz, p. 165.

[36] CLC. *Report of Proceedings,* First Convention, April 23-27, (1956), p. 49.

[37] *Labour Gazette,* June 1956, p. 647.

[38] Dennis H. Wrong, "Parties and Voting in Canada," *Political Science Quarterly:* Vol. 73, (September 1958), p. 408.

[39] Stanley Knowles, *The New Party,* (Toronto: McClelland and Stewart, 1961), p. 19.

[40] *Ibid.* p. 127. The Convention policy statement, suggesting that Labour and Social Democratic Parties elsewhere be studied as a guide for a new party, rejected an exclusive trade union party as having little chance.

[41] See *Canadian Labour,* May 1958, p. 3.

[42] "CCF Holds National Convention," *Canadian Labour,* September 1958, p. 23.

of CCF and Political Education Director for the Ontario Federation of Labour.

Following adoption of the resolutions at the two organizations' conventions, a joint committee, the National Committee for the New Party was established with ten representatives from each of the two organizations. Under the Chairmanship of Stanley Knowles, the Committee assumed the task of encouraging the widest possible discussion of the New Party, of the general principles which should be included in the constitution, and of the political programme it should seek.[43] To this end, discussion groups were held for members of both CCF and CLC affiliated unions. New Party clubs were established and a number of pamphlets were printed and distributed. The high point of the promotional activities came at the end of August 1959 when the National Committee convened a National Seminar on the New Party. In attendance were 131 CCF delegates, 122 unionists, twenty-nine farmers, and twenty-one business and professional persons.[44]

Many sections of organized labour in Canada, both CLC affiliates and non-affiliates, responded to the 1958 CLC and CCF resolutions. In the provinces, with the exception of Prince Edward Island, the federations endorsed the CLC stand on the New Party. The Newfoundland Federation rejected the new approach to political action at its 1958 convention but reversed its stand the next year.[45] The Ontario Federation of Labour initiated an "S.O.S." programme, Statement of Support, in order to get commitments of support from its affiliatees.[46] By January 1961, a "Statement of Support" had been obtained from 330 locals representing 150,000 members.[47] This was about one-third of the union members belonging to OFL-CLC affiliates. Review of the unions listed as signatories to the "S.O.S." includes nearly all industrial unions including Autoworkers, Steelworkers, Electrical Workers (IUE), Machinists, Textile Workers (TWUA), and Communications Workers (CWA). Prominent among the craft unions that signed were the Carpenters and the Plumbers from the Building trades, and the Printers (ITU) and Lithographers from printing. On the other hand, the majority of the construction unions were missing from the list, most notable of whom were the IBEW with sixty-six locals in Ontario alone. Also absent were most of the railway unions.

Outside of the CLC, the Canadian Confederation of Catholic Unions (CCCL) made constitutional changes with regard to political action. The CCCL's affiliates were given the right to adopt whatever attitude they thought appropriate in political matters, provided these matters did not run counter to the general interests of the CCCL.[48] This was interpreted by observers as providing leeway for CCCL affiliates to join a political party.[49]

Although momentum within the labour movement was building, two obstacles had to be overcome before the New Party could become a reality. First the activities persuant to the 1958 resolutions had not yet been accepted by CCF and CLC conventions nor had an agreement been made to proceed to a founding convention. Second, the founding convention itself would raise further issues between the groups and their mutual political goals. Agreement would have to be reached on party structure which would involve, among other problems, manner of affiliation, voting procedures and finances. The same was true for the new party's political programme.

THE 1960 RESOLUTIONS: The CLC's opportunity to decide the fate of the New Party came at its biennial convention in Montreal in April 1960. After over three hours of debate in which thirty-two spoke in favour of supporting the new party and only three against, the convention voted almost unanimously for a continuation of the joint discussions with CCF and for participation in a founding convention for the new party. The solitary negative reaction occurred when the entire IBEW delegation of forty-three members walked out of the convention hall just before the vote was taken, claiming it was adopting a position of neutrality.[50] IBEW hostility to the position on political action taken by the convention was manifested elsewhere. For example, when the Manitoba convention met in the following October, a resolution encouraging all affiliated locals to support the New Party was passed over the opposition of the IBEW which declared it would pull out if any federation money was spent for political action.[51]

The National Convention of the CCF met in Regina, Saskatchewan in August 1960. The city of the party's auspicious beginning, Regina was now to witness its passing from the national scene. As its final act, the convention instructed its National Council[52]

to continue participation in the National Committee for the New Party, in the preparations for the calling of a Founding Convention . . . and in the drafting of the proposed constitution and statement of program and principles for submission to the Founding Convention of the New Party.

Having been encouraged to proceed by the convention, the National Committee for the New Party announced a drive to establish a founding fund and also set the date for the Founding Convention in July 1961. Organized labour's portion of the New Party Founding Fund was set at

[43] "Report of the New Party Resolution Adopted at the 1958 Convention," *Canadian Labour,* April 1960, pp. 23-24.

[44] Gervase A. Cove. "Labour Shapes a Third Force in Canada," *American Federationist,* Vol. 67, (July 1960), p. 19.

[45] Ontario Federation of Labour-PAC, *Memo,* January 1960, n.p.

[46] *Ibid.*

[47] Ontario Federation of Labour-PAC, *Memo,* January-February, 1961, p. 4. Eventually 370 locals representing 170,000 members adopted the S.O.S.'s. Horowitz, p. 227.

[48] *Labour Gazette,* December 31, 1959, p. 1274.

[49] By way of historical note, the CCCL changed its name to Confederation of National Trade Unions (CNTU) at a special convention in 1960. The CNTU designation will be used hereafter in the paper.

[50] *Labour Gazette,* June 30, 1960, p. 559. Also see CLC *Proceedings of the Third Constitutional Convention,* April 25-29, 1960, pp. 34-48.

[51] *Labour Gazette,* November 30, 1960, p. 1132.

[52] Knowles, *The New Party,* p. 132.

$250,000 to be collected by March 31, 1961. The quota, however, was never filled; an eventual total of only $188,268 was collected.

A comparison of the list of unions contributing to the New Party Founding Fund for the province of Ontario with that for unions signing Statements of Support for the New Party is illuminating.[53] Standing conspicuously as the primary contributors are the industrial unions. Donations were not limited to these unions by any means, however, with financial support coming from forty-four different unions. Well represented also were unions from printing trades, railroads, clothing trades, and the building trades. A large number of these four groups had not signed the S.O.S. statements but apparently changed their positions on supporting the New Party. Unchanged in its position, however, was the IBEW. Only one of its sixty-six locals contributed to the fund; none had signed statements. Unfortunately, since only CLC affiliates were listed, the attitudes of the main independent unions could not be determined.

THE NEW PARTY FOUNDING CONVENTION: The Founding Convention represented the last obstacle to the fulfillment of the hopes of many unionists for obtaining their own "instrument" for political action. Of the 1,771 delegates encamped in Ottawa for the convention, 659 were from organized labour.[54] Chairman of the convention was Stanley Knowles, Executive Vice President of CLC and former CCF Member of Parliament.

The four main groups participating in the convention were organized labour, the CCF, a delegation of 400 from Quebec, and New Party Clubs. The farmers who had been the mainstay in the early years of the CCF and whose support was sought, remained aloof. One observer attributed this to the Western farmers' suspicions that the CLC would dominate the New Party; therefore the farmers stayed away.[55]

Almost immediately a fight broke out between two groups contesting for leadership of the Party. T. C. Douglas, premier of Saskatchewan and a moderate, was opposed by Hazen Argue, parliamentary leader of CCF who was supported by the old guard socialists. Douglas won, receiving 1,291 votes to Argue's 380.[56] Other areas of difficulty that arose in the course of the convention were the name of the party and the emphasis to be placed on bi-culturalism. After hours of deliberation, the name "New Democratic Party" was accepted. In the latter case, the delegates from Quebec finally prevailed upon the convention to accept the word "federal" as a substitute for "national" in all party documents. This change in wording symbolized for the French Canadians their right to an equal position in the party.[57]

The Structure of NDP

The CCF-labour relationship had foundered, at least in part, on the issue of trade union affiliation. The first wave of labour organization enrollment raised for many CCFers the spectre of union domination. The fears were exacerbated as the fortunes of the party waned after 1945 and individual memberships declined. Thus, the terms by which trade unions were to affiliate provincially and federally were engineered to retain control of conventions by the constituency organizations.[58] The result was not only to cool labour's ardour for CCF but also to provide the Communists with a convenient issue of "taxation without representation" to impede party affiliations.

The structure by which labour would participate in any party was an issue that was carried over into the NDP. That the conflict remains unresolved was demonstrated anew at the 1969 Federal convention when delegates from two British Columbia ridings introduced a resolution to eliminate affiliated membership status. If adopted this move would have required trade unionists to either drop out of the party or acquire individual membership. The resolution was rejected but the issue clearly remains.[59]

Other foci of disagreement also merit brief mention. The organizational chart that follows contains referent points to the discussion of NDP-trade union structure.

MEMBERSHIP: Membership in the party can be either individual or affiliated.[60] If individual, the applicant joins through the party organized in his province. Affiliated membership, on the other hand, is open to "trade unions, farm groups, cooperatives, women's organizations, and other groups and organizations ... abiding by the constitution and principles of the Party." Applications are accepted from all levels of unions or other qualifying organizations on the local, national or international level. In those cases where the organization has membership in more than one province, the Federal Party has jurisdiction; otherwise, the organizations must affiliate with its provincial party.

The CLC itself, has maintained a policy of non-affiliation. Using the example of the British Trade Union Congress and the Labour Party, the CLC chooses a separate course by which it can continue to make submissions directly to governmental bodies without regard to party.

At the October 1969 Convention in Winnipeg, the party membership was estimated to be approximately 350,000, of which slightly over

---

[53] See CFL*PAC, *Memo,* March-April 1961 and July-August for complete enumeration of unions contributing to the fund up to June 1961.

[54] James P. Mutchmor, "Canada's New Party," *Christian Century,* September 20, 1961, p. 1104. Horowitz, using figures derived from Fred Schindler, "The Development of the New Democratic Party" (M. A. Thesis, University of Toronto, 1961), states at one point that union representation was 631 of 1802 total delegates (p. 226) and at another point, the union delegation was stated to be 530, (p. 233).

[55] *New York Times,* August 1, 1961, 11:5.

[56] Argue left the party and joined the Liberals soon after claiming it had become "a tool of a small labor clique."

[57] Mutchmor, "Canada's New Party," p. 1103. See also "Three Views of the New Party Convention," *Canadian Forum,* September 1961, p. 124.

[58] See Horowitz, pp. 78-84.

[59] *Toronto Globe and Mail,* October 30, 1969.

[60] NDP, *Federal Constitution,* Article II.

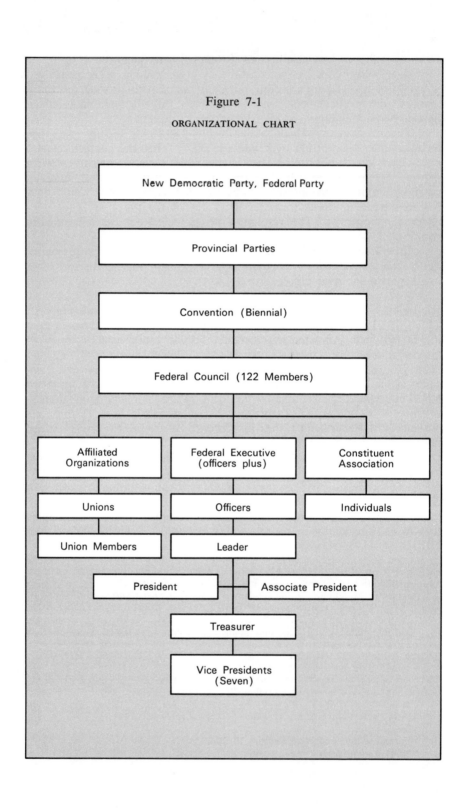

Figure 7-1

ORGANIZATIONAL CHART

New Democratic Party, Federal Party

Provincial Parties

Convention (Biennial)

Federal Council (122 Members)

Affiliated Organizations

Federal Executive (officers plus)

Constituent Association

Unions

Officers

Individuals

Union Members

Leader

President

Associate President

Treasurer

Vice Presidents (Seven)

Table 7-2

NDP—UNION AFFILIATIONS AS A PROPORTION OF TOTAL UNION MEMBERSHIP
AS OF JANUARY 1 OF EACH YEAR 1963-1968 (THOUSANDS)

	Total Union Membership (a)	*NDP Affiliated Union Members (b)*	*Per Cent of Total*
1963	1,449	200	13.8
1964	1,493	218	14.6
1965	1,589	216	13.6
1966	1,736	200	7.4
1967	1,921	247	12.9
1968	2,010	261	13.0

Source: (a) *Labour Organizations in Canada.* (Queen's Printer, Ottawa, 1969), p. xii.
   (b) *Canadian Labour,* March 1967, p. 28 for years 1963-1967 and CLC, Political Education Department for 1968.

250,000 were from some 800 affiliated local unions.[61] A review of the affiliation statistics shows that this form of membership is very highly concentrated, geographically and among a few unions. At the conclusion of 1968, a single province, Ontario, accounted for 80 per cent of affiliated membership and three unions, Steelworkers (82,004), Autoworkers (70,406), and Canadian Food and Allied Workers (22,325) accounted for 68 per cent.[62] Conspicuously absent are the building trade unions, independent unions such as the Teamsters, and the railroad brotherhoods.

At its peak in 1944, CCF enrolled an estimated 50,000 trade unionists, approximately 7 per cent of the total union membership of that year. Although the NDP doubled this at its inception, as Table 7-2 shows, it quickly reached its zenith. Since 1964 union affiliations have barely kept pace with the growth of union membership. Efforts to increase union affiliation to 300,000 by 1968 fell far short of the mark and a long range goal of 500,000 affiliated union members seems likewise unattainable. Explanations for the difficulty in obtaining affiliated union members are not hard to find. For example, many observers have pointed to the barriers raised by the international parent bodies. In this regard, constitutional bars may prohibit the endorsation of candidates or parties, or even the discussion of political issues at union meetings.[63]

[61] *Toronto Globe and Mail,* October 30, 1969. As of January 1, 1969, 764 locals had affiliated 255,928 members.
[62] Political Education Department, Canadian Labour Congress.
[63] John Crispo, *International Unionism,* p. 248.

It is questionable, however, whether the main impediment to union affiliation is the parent union. Internationals such as the Sheetmetal Workers and Locomotive Engineers, which have maintained an intransigent stand against political action, constitute a very tiny minority.[64] Constitutional restraints have either been modified or ignored by both international and Canadian sections. Organizational devices have been developed in different unions to skirt the policies of the parent union without openly contravening them. Typical here are such groups as the Canadian Machinists Political League, the Active Ballot Clubs of the Retail Clerks International, and the Provincial Legislative Improvement Committee formed by the Ontario Provincial Council of Carpenters. PLICO was established to provide financial support and other aid to "the party which endorses and works for the legislative program of the Carpenters, Ontario Federation of Labour, and the CLC."[65] Carpenters' locals vote to affiliate with PLICO and pay a per capita fee of 50 cents per year. The NDP is not mentioned but there is little doubt to which party the aid would be extended.

Rather than being the fault of the international, therefore, the chief obstacle to union affiliation seems to be the Canadian members themselves. Among many leaders, the Gomper's tradition continues to be very strong and may be maintained even in the face of pressure from the international to become active politically.[66] The rank-and-file worker, unlike his European counterpart, seems to feel no strong class consciousness that can be fulfilled through active support of NDP. Preferences for Liberal and PC candidates still hold sway, but the Canadian worker clings fiercely to his sense of individual identity in opposition to perceived attempts to tell him how and for whom to vote. Whether this characteristic is subject to change, at least among the urban "working class," will be considered in a later section of the essay.

CONVENTIONS: The NDP convention meets once every two years and is considered the supreme governing body of the party. Six groups are represented at the convention on the following basis:[67]
1. *Federal Council.* All members.
2. *Federal Constituency Associations.* Permitted one delegate for the first 50 members, one for each of the next 50 members up to 200 members, and then one delegate for each 100 members thereafter.
3. *Affiliated Groups.* One delegate for each 1,000 members or fraction thereof.
4. *Central Bodies.*
    a. City Centrals — one delegate.
    b. National Centrals — two delegates.
    c. Provincial Centrals — two delegates.
5. *Federal Party Caucus.* All members.
6. *Young New Democrats.*
    a. Federal Executive — all members.
    b. Provincial Young People's Section — two delegates.
    c. Youth Clubs — one delegate for 50 members or less, one delegate 50-200 members, and one delegate for each additional 100 members.

The procedure by which delegates were to be selected for federal conventions was of special concern to all participants in the founding of NDP for reasons already indicated. In this case the British labour party — TUC model was deemed inappropriate and an effort was made to avoid bloc voting by affiliated unions. As a consequence, proportionate representation was accorded only to local unions. In addition, the scale of representation permitted the constituency associations is so much greater than that for the affiliated unions, the balance of control rests with the former group. Using the 1969 Federal Convention to illustrate, organized labour was able to muster only 218 delegates of the 900 at the Convention.[68]

It should not be overlooked, however, that since many trade-unionists hold individual memberships, constituency associations are frequently represented by trade unionists. Thus, while they may not be able to dominate any single convention, the unions are still capable of exercising a potent influence over the directions of deliberations and the character of decisions.

OFFICERS: The NDP Constitution provides for the election of the following officers: a leader who acts as leader of the party in Parliament; a President and an Associate President, one of whom must be English speaking and the other French speaking; seven Vice-Presidents; and a Treasurer.[69]

Although the party leadership has been filled since founding by a non-trade unionist, T. C. Douglas, the labour groups have held each of the other offices from time to time. Eamon Park from the Steelworkers, one time head of the CCL Political Action Committee, has filled nearly all federal offices. The Associate President was held initially by Gerard Picard of the CNTU. At the 1969 Federal Convention, Roland Morin of the Autoworkers was elected to the post of Associate President and Mary Eady, former editor of the *Packinghouse Worker,* became Treasurer of the federal party. The number of trade unionists holding vice-presidencies, NDP staff positions and other such positions is evidence of the interlocking nature of the administration of the NDP and the Canadian labour movement.

FEDERAL COUNCIL: The Federal Council of the NDP meets twice a year. It is called by the Executive and functions as the governing body of the party between conventions.[70] The Federal Council brings together the

---

[64] *Ibid.* p. 250.

[65] *Canadian Labour,* September 1967, p. 43.

[66] Horowitz cites the case of the International Brotherhood of Electrical Workers whose Canadian sections have resisted any affiliation with NDP despite a rebuke from the international president. *Canadian Labour in Politics,* pp. 238-39.

[67] NDP, *Federal Constitution.* Article IV. pp. 6-7.

[68] *Toronto Globe and Mail,* October 30, 1969.

[69] NDP, *Federal Constitution.* Article VI.

[70] *Ibid.* Article VII.

officers, representatives of the convention, of parliament and of the provincial parties, and the Young New Democrats. In addition, the 1969 Federal Convention enlarged the Council's membership from 110 to include one representative each from the twelve unions having the largest number of affiliated party members. The twelve unions selected at that time were: Autoworkers; Retail, Wholesale, and Department Store Union; Machinists; Rubber Workers; Amalgamated Clothing Workers; Canadian Food and Allied Workers; Textile Workers (TWUA); Canadian Union of Public Employees; Woodworkers; Glass and Ceramic Workers; and Canadian Brotherhood of Railway, Transport, and General Workers.[71]

The formal granting of representation rights on federal party units is a significant step away from past practice. Although these trade union representatives are only twelve of 122, they symbolize nevertheless, the affiliated unions' right to be directly represented.[72] Moreover, this modification was made at the same time that the resolution to dispense with affiliated membership was rejected.

Until 1969, union participation on such bodies as the Federal Council was accomplished by alloting to labour the privilege of running candidates for one-third of the vacancies to be filled. The allotment grew out of the fact that labour was one of the three groups, along with CCF and "other liberal minded people," actually participating in the founding of the party.[73] The uncertainty of this proposition was demonstrated at the 1967 Federal Convention when unions sought election of seven candidates for twenty vacancies on the Federal Council but were able to elect only six. The trade unions are now to be guaranteed at least twelve positions openly labeled "for labour only."

Provision for the allocation of positions on provincial councils directly to affiliated unions was an accomplished fact prior to the 1969 federal change. The Ontario Provincial Party has provided representation to trade unions for some time on its Provincial Council; participation is at the rate of "one member from each national or international union with paid up affiliated membership of two thousand or more in Ontario."[74] According to 1969 CLC statistics, this would give places on the council to nearly the same unions now admitted to the Federal Council.

THE EXECUTIVE: The executive is the real seat of power in the NDP. Composed of the officers plus other members elected from and by the Council, it runs the Party between meetings of the Council.[75] Although labour has been consistently well represented on this body, reaching half of its total at various times over the years, attempts to limit representation of trade unionists on NDP executive councils have been consciously undertaken by the CLC. A formal policy was established, for example, that precluded any member of the Congress' executive group from holding simultaneously an equivalent position in the Federal party. The policy has informally been extended to include staff members and non-executive board officers at the federal level.[76]

Thus, non-trade unionists within the NDP are not alone in their desires to make their party's connections with organized labour less obvious. There are several reasons for this. First, the trade unionists have sought to protect their independence of action, looking toward the day when an NDP government is elected. The relationship between the British Labour Party and the TUC has served in this regard as a point of reference. Second, the desire has existed from the beginning to project the image of a broadly based party, drawing upon all groups in society, not merely labour. At various times allegations of union "bossism" have been leveled against the NDP to the detriment of campaigns to attract farmers and independent middle class voters.

Finally, it should not be overlooked that the NDPers within the Canadian Labour Congress are a minority, and a small one at that. Of the slightly more than 2 million organized workers in Canada, only about 250,000 or 12.5 per cent are affiliated with NDP. This is an influential minority but nevertheless one with constraints on its ability to act on behalf of labour with the NDP. Indicative of this fact was the disinclination of the CLC even to endorse NDP prior to 1967.[77]

PROVINCIAL PARTIES: Article X of the NDP Constitution provides that each province shall have a party "fully autonomous as to its constitution and program" so long as those are not in conflict with the federal party's principles and constitution. The machinery for provincial parties exists in most cases but the extent of electoral success as well as trade union participation varies enormously. Clifford Scotton, Federal Secretary of the NDP, acknowledged in 1969 that "the picture east of Ontario is pretty bleak. In Quebec and the Atlantic provinces — with the exceptions of major industrial centers such as Montreal, Moncton, Cape Breton, and Halifax — the NDP has never succeeded in building strong organizations."[78] Some success, however, has been achieved in Ontario, Saskatchewan, Manitoba and British Columbia. In Quebec, embarrassingly large sums of money have produced neither federal M.P.'s nor even a provincial party.[79] To the extent that a provincial party existed in Quebec, it was argued that this could only be said of the Island of Montreal.[80] As Table 7-3 shows, organized labour has refrained almost completely from participating in the party.

[71] *Canadian Labour,* November, 1969.
[72] The informal arrangements, i.e. dependence upon unionists holding NDP offices, were considered unsatisfactory and the need for separate representation long felt necessary. Interview with CLC officers, November 23, 1967.
[73] *Ibid.*
[74] New Democratic Party of Ontario, *Constitution* (as amended 1966), p. 16.
[75] NDP, *Federal Constitution* Article VIII.
[76] Interview with Mr. George Home, Director, Political Education Department, CLC, November 20, 1967.
[77] *Ibid.*
[78] Clifford A. Scotton, "Prospects for the NDP," *Canadian Labour,* November 1969, p. 25.
[79] *Ibid.*
[80] Blair Fraser, "The La Pierre Generation: Can it Make the NDP Win?" *Maclean's,* October 1967, p. 96.

Table 7-3 reveals several interesting facts about the NDP-trade union relationship. First, success in affiliating union members in proportion to total provincial union members is greatest in Ontario and weakest in Quebec. If union support is considered vital to NDP electoral success, then it seems clear that Quebec is a case in point. Closer inspection, however, reveals that the level of union affiliations is low in the prairies where the provincial parties have done quite well, in contrast to the Atlantic provinces, where despite the relatively higher rate of affiliation electoral failure has been conspicuous. Even in Ontario, where union strength is greatest, NDP was able to do no better than third through the 1960's. Clearly, union support through affiliation is important but it is not the controlling factor in provincial elections.

Apart from questions of union affiliation at the provincial level, the bonds of the NDP-labour relationship emerge in other ways. In Alberta, British Columbia and Ontario, trade unionists have been put forward as candidates and, on at least one occasion, union approval was required before the party itself could endorse a candidate.[81]

YOUNG NEW DEMOCRATS' SECTION: The last unit of the party, the YND Section, is also autonomous. It has a three level structure: Federal; Provincial; and local youth clubs.

Finances

Like many political counterparts, the NDP suffers from inadequate financing. Large deficits have been incurred not only as a result of provincial and federal campaigning but also from day to day party administration.[82] In a continuing battle against insolvency expenses have been pared in numerous ways and efforts to obtain more members and to expand donations have been increased. According to Desmond Morton, the problem of money is paralyzing the party, practically and psychologically.[83]

In a very real sense, we are losing opportunities everyday. At a time when the party's stock was at an all time high, we were without a Director of Organization and shortly after, we were without a Research Director. We have as a Federal Secretary, the best publicist ever to serve the Canadian labour movement, yet he is left without the funds to publish a single pamphlet.

Impoverishment and its psychological impact produced a "continued and wearing bickering" between those provinces supplying the bulk of the federal office's income (Ontario and Saskatchewan) and those providing "little or nothing" as well as between the trade unionist and the constituency associations.[84]

Income derived from trade union sources represents a very large proportion of the revenues received by the party at all levels. Union affiliation fees were estimated to supply approximately $85-95,000 for the federal budget, a sum nearly equal to that obtained elsewhere.[85] In

Table 7-3

MEMBERSHIP BY UNION AND NDP AFFILIATION, 1967

	Union Membership	*Affiliated with NDP*	*Per cent*
Atlantic	120,707	17,157	14.2
Quebec	569,430	9,936	1.7
Ontario	721,581	198,882	27.6
Prairies	198,151	9,275	4.7
British Columbia	240,228	19,157	8.0
Canada	1,920,647	254,407	13.2

Source: Union Membership: Department of Labour, *Labour Gazette,* February 1968, p. 94. Affiliated membership: Political Education Department, CLC.

Ontario in 1967, through affiliation fees and organization funds, labour contributed $141,000 of the $346,000 received by the party.[86] Unions further contributed nearly 60 per cent of the monies collected for the provincial elections of that year.[87] Consequently, the opposition to ending affiliated membership is not difficult to fathom. As one party official observed, concerning the attempt to establish only individual memberships, "If you want to commit suicide this is one of the ways of making a start at it."[88]

One of the mechanisms by which labour money is funneled into elective political action is the Committee on Political Education. Money

---

[81] See "A Loss," *The New Democrat* (Ontario), November 1968, p. 2 in which a member of the Hamilton West Riding Association expressed objections to a resolution passed by the Hamilton Labour Council requiring its endorsation of a candidate for municipal elections as precedent for action by the Hamilton and Area Council of the NDP.

[82] For example, the 1967 provincial election in Ontario left that party indebted in the amount of $88,777. *Globe and Mail,* November 13, 1967. For the same provincial party it was anticipated that an operating deficit of $15,000 would be incurred in 1969. See *The New Democrat,* April 1969, p. 4. The 1968 federal election created a debt of $100,000. *Macleans,* October 1969.

[83] Desmond Morton, "NDP and Victory," *New Democratic News,* November 1967, p. 8.

[84] *Ibid.*

[85] *Globe and Mail,* October 30, 1969.

[86] *The New Democrat,* December 1967, pp. 4 and 5.

[87] *Ibid.* The party is not quite as fortunate in other provinces where union affiliations are negligible or as in British Columbia and Prince Edward Island where legislation precludes the use of union dues money for political action.

[88] *Globe and Mail,* October 30, 1969.

collected by COPE is placed in a trust fund administered by union leaders headed by the Executive Vice-president of the CLC, William Dodge. COPE apparently has been successful in raising funds in the United States from the parent international unions at the same time that contributions were being received from their Canadian locals. Canadian labour leaders justify using United States union money on the basis that "since contributions to COPE in the United States come from the dues dollars of union members, including those in Canada, a share of funds contributed for political activities should be allocated to COPE in Canada." [89]

Sole reliance on financial contributions as a measure of trade union support of the NDP would grossly underestimate its true value. Labour unions have supplied manpower for elections as well as for daily administrative activities. In the 1965 federal election, Ontario unions provided fifty-five full-time workers. Two years later, an estimated seventy full-time workers were supplied for the provincial election alone.[90] In addition, permanent organizers, part-time party workers and general office facilities have been made available.[91]

Yet, despite Canadian labour's support for the NDP, it seems unable to please any of the sections of the party and it is subjected to attacks from the political opposition. On the one hand, the continuing fear of union domination is raised by one NDP group while another group simultaneously argues that labour is too little involved. In the latter case one NDP official stated that if organized labour in Canada gave one-tenth of the money to the New Democratic Party with which it is affiliated as the United States labour movement gives to the party with which it is not affiliated, the NDP would soon come to power in Canada.[92] Critics of the NDP have accused the NDP of being in the pocket of the United States unions, calling for legislation to make illegal union contributions for political action.[93]

Labour and the NDP Programme

CCF socialists, referring to the Regina Manifesto of 1933, sought to include in the initial party platform a pledge to support government ownership and control of industry. Trade union delegates resisted, however, declaring that the purpose of the founding convention was not to create a socialist party but rather "a broadly based people's democratic party of the left." [94] The CLC view prevailed.

Public ownership, as a consequence, was placed far down the priority list. In its place emphasis was given to economic planning through a National Investment Board to control investment, a guaranteed Full Employment Act, subsidized job retraining and relocation, and planned quotas for imports and exports. Expansion of public ownership would be directed toward the operation of utilities and resource development, the elimination of monopoly power concentrations and "the operation of major enterprises immediately and directly affecting the entire nation."[95] In the area of social welfare, the Party programme called for free education, a National Housing Authority, a comprehensive and social security programme, and a federal labour code.[96]

A second point of contention between CCF and CLC delegates was the issue of national defense, particularly Canadian membership in the North Atlantic Treaty Organization. The socialist view of withdrawal from NATO and Canadian neutrality was rejected by union delegates who argued that "neutralism in today's international situation makes not a particle more sense than does neutralism in a trade union situation."[97] As a compromise, it was agreed that withdrawal of Canadian forces would be necessary only in the event that NATO received nuclear weapons. In addition, it was recommended that NATO's policies and objectives be reappraised and its economic and social activities expanded.[98] Finally, the party programme established at the first convention demanded immediate termination of the North American Air Defense (NORAD) agreements and rejected the storing of nuclear weapons on Canadian soil.[99]

The activists of the party in its early years were drawn largely from the CCF and the CCL-CIO unions. They shared common outlook and experiences, and favoured moderate, reformist policies. To the chagrin of vintage CCFers, any reference to socialism was carefully avoided and a conscious effort was undertaken to move the NDP rightward.[100]

In 1965, an element of younger activist members, lacking either trade union or CCF traditions, began to emerge as a third force in the party. Self proclaimed as "radical pragmatists," their central goal was electoral success, to produce an NDP government and at the earliest possible moment. The thrust of this group was to project a youthful image that would be attractive to voters as well as to sharpen further the modern fiscal and monetary tools that had obviated the need for the socialism of the 1930's.

The "young Turks" introduced divisive elements which began to divide the NDP into factions along unaccustomed lines. Generational

---

[89] Wilfred List, "U.S. Union Money Aids NDP Coffers for Campaign Use," *Globe and Mail*, April 25, 1968.

[90] *Globe and Mail*, November 13, 1967. More than half of these workers came from the Steelworkers (23) and the Autoworkers (15).

[91] Opposition to supplying "too much" manpower has come from some sections of labour who fear the trade unions' own organizing and bargaining activities will be impaired.

[92] This statement is attributed to David Lewis in a speech to five hundred delegates of a Political Education Committee meeting. See *Canadian Labour*, December 1968, p. 33.

[93] See, for example, the editorial of *Toronto Daily Star*, April 19, 1967 and articles in the *Globe and Mail*, April 15, 1964 and the *Hamilton Spectator*, July 18, 1966.

[94] *New York Times*, August 2, 1961.

[95] See NDP, *The Federal Program of the New Democratic Party*, 1961, pp. 3-6.

[96] *Ibid.* pp. 15-20.

[97] Claude Jodoin, "Obligations of Collective Security," *Free Labour World*, June 1961, p. 243.

[98] NDP, *Program*, pp. 26-28.

[99] *Ibid.*

[100] One delegate to the 1963 Federal NDP convention lamented, "We've become mature. We're not mad at anyone now. So what? Perhaps these is nothing new about us. If they continue stiffling the minority, then we won't be democratic. After that there won't be a party." *New York Times*, August 11, 1963.

conflict became manifest, a left-right polarization materialized and an anti-American note sounded.[101] In the latter case, the American involvement in Viet Nam was strongly denounced and a programme to achieve economic independence from the United States was proposed.[102]

While the trade unions continued as a restraining force on party platform and policies, the solidarity of labour began to fracture. The unions were beset by conflicts as youthful staff members rallied to the new group. Senior labour men, desirous of ending the party's long standing elective failures, embraced the pragmatists' viewpoint with enthusiasm. For other unionists, however, the repudiation of democratic socialist doctrine placed in question all the efforts expended since 1933. Principles were to be cast aside for political expediency in an exercise of self-interest. Moreover, the injection of anti-Americanism as a party issue left many trade unionists to confront an uneasy dilemma. They were members of American international unions as well as NDP members. How could the party decry Canadian economic dependence on the United States and simultaneously justify international unionism. The leaders of Canadian national unions such as the Canadian Brotherhood of Railway, Transport and General Workers Union prevented the question from being glossed over.

The 1968 election of the Liberal government headed by Pierre-Elliot Trudeau cast into doubt the strategy of pragmatism and from it, apparently, stemmed the rightward evolution of NDP. As it had in the previous CCF-NDP programmes, the Liberal party successfully exploited the symbols of youth, vigour, moderation, and Canadian independence which were to be the key to the NDP's future.[103]

As the 1970's opened a new political posture seemed to be in the making for the NDP. The latent strains of Canadian nationalism were being amplified but not in conjunction with pragmatism. Socialism was rediscovered by a still more youthful party contingent, pressing for recognition. Led by Professor Melville Watkins, the core of Canada's economic problems was identified as the American based multinational corporation.[104]

For socialists, the multinational corporation represents all the evils of uncontrolled corporate power without even the slight saving grace of perhaps sharing a sense of national self interest. Of course, for socialists, economic independence is not sought to bolster the status and power of the elite. Instead, it is because we believe that corporate priorities are not necessarily Canadian priorities. It is because key decisions about our future are not being taken by or on behalf of Canadians . . ." [105]

In a debate with Rene Levesque in February 1969, John Harney of the Ontario NDP concluded: "We want Canada to continue and we want it to be socialist. What we must realize is that it can only continue *by being socialist.*" [106]

Emerging in full force at the 1969 Federal Convention, the self-styled "Wafflites" left their full imprint on the party. Resolutions on public ownership, foreign investment, and withdrawal from NATO, customarily rejected at past conventions, were accepted. Calls to the United States to withdraw from Viet Nam and to Canada to abstain from the Organization of American States because of American domination were approved. Only a floor fight caused deletion of a section in a resolution encouraging Canadian support of Latin American liberation movements.[107] Although the principal document of the new left in the NDP, the so-called "Watkins Manifesto," was rejected, it nevertheless received substantial support from the delegates.

A new coalition now appears to have grown out of the 1969 Federal convention with the Watkins group on the left, the "radical pragmatists" in the center and the bulk of the trade unions on the right. Structural changes increased labour's direct participation in the party machinery but admitted the Wafflites as well.[108] The issues of nationalism versus continentalism and radical politics versus moderation squarely confront the coalition. Whether the trade unions can continue to participate in the face of the dilemmas that these issues pose remains to be answered.

LABOUR AND THE OTHER PARTIES

Canadian labour has by no means restricted its favours to a single party such as the NDP. On the contrary, both trade union leaders and rank-and-file members have frequently aligned themselves with the Liberals, the Progressive Conservatives, and any number of minor parties. While this support has generally fallen short of direct union affiliation, participation

---

[101] The nomination of a party stalwart for party President was thwarted at the last minute and a member of the "radical pragmatists," James Renwick, elected in his place.

[102] Toronto *Globe and Mail,* July 16, 1965 and July 7, 1967.

[103] In the face of a threat from the CCF in 1945, the Liberal party under Mackenzie King moved center-left, adopting for its programme many policies advocated by CCF. ". . . King's swing to the left had defeated CCF's bid for major party status. The CCF success was much smaller than it had expected. The success was actually a defeat, a disappointing shock from which socialism in Canada has not yet recovered." Horowitz, *Canadian Labour in Politics,* p. 38.

[104] See, for example, Melville Watkins, "The Multi-National Corporation in Canada," *Our Generation,* Vol. 6, No. 4, (Spring-June 1969), pp. 97-102.

[105] Desmond Morton, *Socialism Canada Seventies,* Toronto-New Democratic Party of Ontario, 1969, p. 6, 22.

[106] Quoted from John Harney, "No Socialism, No Canada," *New Democrat,* April 1969 in *Ibid. p. 23.* Italics in the original.

[107] *Globe and Mail,* October 31, 1969. See also "Symposium on the NDP Convention," *Canadian Dimension,* December-January 1969-70, pp. 5-9; and the *New Democrat,* November-December, 1969.

[108] As previously noted, the Federal Council was enlarged to include representation from the twelve largest unions. Further, Watkins was elected one of the seven vice-presidents and several supporters obtained seats on the Federal Council.

on an individual basis has been open and widespread.[109] Eugene Forsey notes, for example, that the Toronto TLC was split for many years between PC and Liberal adherents. The political division was such that during meetings each group gathered on its own side of the union hall.[110]

In part, TLC policies of non-partisanship paradoxically played a role in creating bonds between particular officers and parties.

In cultivating friendly relations with government, some TLC leaders naturally became involved in the political party which formed the government ... The government of British Columbia was a Liberal-dominated coalition: R. K. Gervin was a Liberal. The governments of Ontario and New Brunswick were Conservative: A. F. MacArthur and James Whitebone were Conservatives.[111]

These informal associations insured the government's attention to labour matters and also were a source of small amounts of patronage.

The Liberal party in particular has attracted labour support, even in the face of CCF and NDP appeals for support. In a 1958 survey of trade union leaders, Porter found that 26 per cent of officers from independent unions favoured the Liberals and 12 per cent of their counterparts in the TLC did likewise.[112] The peak of TLC leadership support for the Liberal party came during the 1945 federal election. In a move that has been characterized as "cautious and hesitant," the Trades and Labour Congress endorsed the party.[113] ". . . this step was taken under exceptional circumstances. It was unprecedented, and it was never repeated." [114]

Even more so than the labour officialdom, the rank-and-file member or worker seems to prefer the Liberal party. As Table 7-4 indicates, both union and non-union worker vote almost twice as heavily for Liberal candidates in federal elections as for those of the NDP. Despite its efforts over the years NDP could still only count on one of every four labour votes cast while its centre right opposition was garnering approximately every other vote. As the NDP openly admitted, "the workers still favour Liberals." [115]

A continuing trade union attraction for the Liberal party is indicated in other ways. In Quebec, the CNTU has unofficially aligned itself, at least federally, with this party.[116] A Liberal-labour coalition was created in Windsor, Ontario in 1944 under the impetus of a Communist dominated faction of the UAW which sought to unseat the Conservative provincial government of George Drew.[117] In more recent years a move to merge NDP in Ontario with the Liberal party was apparently considered by certain groups within the labour movement of that province.[118] It was reported that officers of the United Steelworkers initiated the discussions, and although the Federal leaders of the NDP denied any knowledge of the talks, some individuals in the provincial party felt that only through a merger of NDP and Liberals could the Conservatives be unseated.[119]

The PC, on the other hand, has not generally enjoyed labour support. Porter found that only 9 per cent of the TLC leadership in 1958 favoured PC; a relatively larger number of independent leaders, 16 per cent, but

Table 7-4

COMPARISON OF FEDERAL ELECTION RESULTS 1963 AND 1968 (PERCENT)

	Liberals		*P-C*		*NDP*		*Other*	
	1963	*1968*	*1963*	*1968*	*1963*	*1968*	*1963*	*1968*
Union	38	46	28	21	21	28	13	5
Non-union	43	47	34	32	11	14	12	7

Source: The New Democrat, July-August 1968, p. 3.

none of the former CCL officers,[120] supported the Progressive Conservative party. In contrast to labour's elite, the general trade union membership supports PC somewhat more heavily in elections, to the extent of 21 per cent. The proportion of unorganized workers supporting this party in 1968 was 32 per cent, doubling the number of votes given to NDP. (See Table 7-4.)

Canadian labour, unionized or not, clearly does not identify its fortunes with the party that purports to speak for labour. It is of no little irony for NDP that labour gives greater support, at least in recent federal elections, to the Conservatives. Waning union affiliations to NDP and lack of financial support should not, therefore, be surprising. The concluding section of this article will return to this point to see whether labour's attitude toward the NDP is undergoing a change. First, however, the special case of Quebec must be considered.

LABOUR AND POLITICS IN QUEBEC

It is tempting to observe that labour party political action in Quebec has been a resounding failure. Evidence to support this conclusion appears

[109] It was reported recently that a local of the Canadian Union of Public Employees affiliated with the Liberal party.
[110] Interview with Eugene Forsey, November 23, 1967.
[111] Horowitz, pp. 181-82.
[112] John Porter, *The Vertical Mosaic,* (Toronto: University of Toronto Press, 1965), p. 350.
[113] Horowitz, p. 182.
[114] *Ibid.*
[115] Modern Lazarus, "Union Vote Edges to NDP But The Workers Still Favor Liberals," *The New Democrat,* July-August, 1968, p. 3.
[116] See essay by F. Isbester in this volume.
[117] For a detailed discussion of this see Horowitz, pp. 108-113.
[118] Toronto *Globe and Mail,* December 23, 1963.
[119] *Ibid.*
[120] Porter, *The Vertical Mosaic,* p. 350.

from a variety of sources: in early 1970, the NDP was unrepresented in the provincial legislature; in the 1968 federal election, no NDP candidates from Quebec ridings were elected; only 9,500 of the more than one-half million union members of Quebec were affiliated with NDP at the close of the 1960's; and a survey commissioned by the NDP indicated that in 1968 only 9 per cent of Canada's French speaking population supported the party at the polls in contrast to 22 per cent for the Conservatives and 53 per cent for the Liberals.[121]

The electoral failures of the New Democrats in Quebec are not recent. Its predecessor, the Social Democratic Party (CCF), received little support from either the general population, polling only 1 per cent of the vote in 1956, for example, or from organized labour. Instead, the trade union political strategy in Quebec has historically followed a classical Gompersian, non-partisan approach. Particular leaders might associate as individuals with various parties but no formal links between union and party could be created. Labour worked with the governing party, limiting its political activity to the presentation of submissions, briefs and reports as these seemed appropriate.

The circumstances that have dictated a union non-partisan approach are not difficult to uncover. First, the industrialization of Quebec received a slow start, gathering impetus only when the Liberal government of L. A. Taschereau came to power in the 1920's.[122] Prior to this time the province's population was predominantly rural and agricultural. The Taschereau economic programme, by attracting large infusions of foreign investment had achieved the transformation sought by the Liberals when they gave way to the Union Nationale in 1936. Industrial employment significantly exceeded that of agriculture and an internal migration had urbanized the general population.

While accelerating industrial development, the pre-World War II provincial governments retarded union growth. To ensure that investors would find a hospitable climate in Quebec, wages and taxes were kept low and legislative support for collective bargaining was avoided. Unionized workers counted, consequently, for only 9 per cent of the non-agricultural labour force in 1935 and lacked the militancy then becoming characteristic in other provinces.[123]

Organized labour's position was further weakened by the existence of two labour centres that were hostile to each other's interests: the church-dominated Canadian Catholic Confederation of Labour, and the United States International's Trades and Labour Congress. Internecine strife was exacerbated even more by the appearance of a third trade union group, the C.I.O.-affiliated CCL. Unable to develop a solid front, the three groups were played off against each other with great facility by the Union Nationale governments of Maurice Duplessis. Duplessis, for example, maintained good relations with the CCCL at the expense of the other two centres until about 1950. The suppression, however, of CCCL strikes at Asbestos (1949) and Louisville (1952) by Union Nationale ruptured the old association and the Catholic Confederation withdrew support from Duplessis. The loss of the CCCL was not greatly missed by Union Nationale which then turned to the TLC. Thus, "although the TLC was officially neutral in politics, in most elections between 1944 and 1956 the Union Nationale could depend upon the open support of a number of the leaders of its affiliated unions, some of whom held high posts in the Congress." [124]

Although the split between TLC and CCL unions has long since been healed, the division between the former Catholic unions, now the Confederation of National Trade Unions, and those belonging to the CLC remains. Recent efforts to close this breach through unification have failed and each is now devoting considerable resources to raiding the other's jurisdictions. [125]

The reluctance of the labour movement in Quebec to become politically active was not only forced by disunity but also was a matter of philosophical choice. The TLC was politically conservative, resting contentedly on its informal association with the government party. The CCL was few in numbers (representing only about 20 per cent of the Quebec labour movement) and was doubly stigmatized by its identification with the CCF and with certain Communist trade unionists. Mere organizational survival in the face of a hostile provincial government and rival labour groups dominated its energies until the merger with TLC.

The Catholic Confederation does not present a contrasting picture in terms of political action. The CCCL for many of its years was controlled by the Catholic hierarchy "whose main concern was not so much to strengthen the bargaining position of the French-Canadian worker as to protect him from the secularizing influence of the international (American) unions . . ." [126] The Church also opposed the CCF for its promotion of the class struggle and "its materialistic conception of the social order." [127]

Clerical influence, however, was not the only pressure governing the political approach of the CCCL in its early years. Such leaders as M. Alfred Charpentier, president until 1946, openly espoused a non-partisan philosophy. Charpentier argued that the centre should never act as an adversary to government but on the contrary must be a collaborator, regardless of party. Party affiliation was excluded, leaving the CCCL with a political role limited to acting as a governmental watchdog and to presenting legislative submissions. Whatever it did politically, the centre was to respect the individual liberties of its members. [128]

In 1946, the Catholic confederation gradually began to abandon its apolitical posture. Educational committees to orient the membership politically and a programme to publicize the confederation's legislative demands provincially were initiated. Most important, however, the CCCL

---

[121] *New Democrat,* (Ontario), July-August 1968, p. 3.
[122] Herbert F. Quinn, *Union Nationale: A Study in Quebec Nationalism,* (Toronto: University of Toronto Press, 1963), pp. 29-36.
[123] *Ibid.* p. 86.
[124] *Ibid.* p. 122.
[125] See essay by F. Isbester in this volume.
[126] Quinn, *Union Nationale,* p. 41.
[127] *Ibid.* p. 56.
[128] Guy Lortie, "Evolution de l'action politique de la CSN," *Relations Industrielles,* Vol. 22, No. 4, pp. 535-538.

intervened directly in the 1952 elections, identifying a number of candidates as "friends" and at least five (four Union Nationale and one Liberal) as "enemies" of the Confederation.

In each succeeding election, despite a significant amount of dissent within its ranks, the Catholic centre increased its political activism. Moreover, it continued to modify its organizational structure to facilitate these activities. Important in this respect was a constitutional amendment in 1959 empowering CCCL affiliates to adopt whatever political attitudes thought suitable, provided these did not run counter to the general interests of the centre. It was widely speculated at the time that this change would enable councils, federations, and other affiliates to join the New Party then being created.[129] An official delegation headed by Picard went to the Winnipeg founding convention of NDP and two of the CCCL's affiliates, the labour councils in Montreal and Shawinigan, officially extended their support to the New Party.[130]

While the visible signs pointed to an impending union of NDP, CLC, and CCCL, the relationship foundered because of renewed inter-union rivalry. A proposed merger of CLC and the newly renamed CNTU was rejected and with it went the latter's support for the NDP. In addition, a new CNTU president, Jean Marchand informally drew his labour centre into the orbit of the Liberal party. Under Marchand, the CNTU moved away from partisan political action. The centre reaffirmed its independence of all political parties, but continued to place heavy reliance on legislative submissions. In addition, the precedent of direct non-partisan action established by Picard in 1952 was carried out more fully in the 1962 election. The Creditistes of Real Caouette were identified as a danger to society, especially to labour, and an intensive effort was launched to prevent their election.[131] Moreover, any remaining doubt as to the right of the president of the CNTU to denounce or to endorse a particular political party was removed at the confederation's fortieth convention. Specifically, an amendment to the constitution authorized the Confederal Board to indicate its preference for a political party and empowered the President and General Secretary "to make public statements of a political nature on behalf of the CNTU, after consulting the political action central committee and within the framework of the decisions taken by the Confederal Board.[132]

The vehicles for the fulfillment of an autonomous but active political programme also crystallized at this time. A central political action committee was created which in turn fathered like committees at the municipal and regional levels. In a manner somewhat reminiscent of the political action committees of the old CCL, the CNTU was now prepared to bring mass pressure to bear in support of its demands or friends and against its enemies.

The QFL reflects a similar disinclination to stray very far politically from its traditional non-partisan, passive role. Although it supplied workers and financial support for the 1968 federal election, the CLC affiliate argued that there were not sufficient funds to engage in political action on a continuing basis.[133] And although the General Secretary of the QFL in 1969, Gérard Rancourt, was a strong supporter of NDP his affiliates were not. Of about 280,000 members in 1969, only 9,500 were affiliated to NDP.

Table 7-5

UNION LOCALS AFFILIATED TO NDP: JANUARY 1, 1969

Union	Number of Locals	Number of Affiliated Members
UAW	1	534
CBRT	6	3,391
IUE	1	186
CFAW	31	2,867
USWA	13	2,534
Total	52	9,512

Source: CLC, Political Education Department.

The few locals affiliated were predominantly industrial unions located around Montreal: autoworkers (UAW); Railway, Transport and General Workers; electrical workers (IUE); Canadian Food and Allied Workers (CFAW); and Steelworkers (USWA). (See Table 7-5.)

As long as the organizational and ideological disunity of labour continues in Quebec, it seems probable that Gomperistic political practices will be the Quebecois norm. With the membership susceptible to the lures of Social Credit, Union Nationale and Liberals, and the officialdom itself not agreed on an ideological rationale for a "labour" party, there are, therefore, few political options open beyond non-partisan elective action and legislative lobbying.

TRADE UNION POLITICAL ACTION IN CANADA:
SOME CONCLUDING OBSERVATIONS

In tracing the historical development of English trade unionism in their classical work *Industrial Democracy,* the Webbs perceived a continuing evolution in the methods that labour employs to achieve its objectives. Mutual insurance and collective bargaining were believed to be merely way-stations leading eventually to political action. "Whether for good or evil, it appears inevitable that the growing participation of the wage

---

[129] "Thirty-eighth Annual CCCL Convention," *Labour Gazette,* December 31, 1959, p. 1274.
[130] Lortie, "Evolution," p. 551.
[131] See *ibid.* on this point, p. 553.
[132] *Labour Gazette,* December 1962, p. 1372.
[133] Hélène David, "Outils syndicaux et pouvoir ouvrier," *Socialisme 68: Revue du Socialisme International et Quebecois,* 1969, p. 8.

earners in political life and the rising influence of their organizations must necessarily bring about an increasing use of the Method of Legal Enactment."[134] In Great Britain, the creation of the Labour Party and its rise to power have certainly borne out this prediction. Are the Webbs' assumptions, however, equally applicable to Canada? Does the emergence of the New Democratic Party and its direct support by Canadian Labour demonstrate the fulfillment of the Canadian parallel? The concluding observations of this essay are directed to and return briefly to the issues raised in the initial pages.

First, it is clear that political action remains of lesser importance to collective bargaining as a trade union method in Canada. Despite the publicity given to CLC endorsement of NDP and to affiliation by Congress members, the economic weapons of strikes, boycotts, and picketing used to support direct negotiations with employers occupy centre stage. The structure of both trade unionism and collective bargaining as well as the mentality of labour's leadership are geared to little else.

Second, political action is, nevertheless, a supplemental method of great importance. This is not a recent development but rather one with historical antecedents stretching back to the earliest days of labour organizations in Canada. One must differentiate, however, between several gradations in political action: non-partisan legislative action; non-partisan elective action; and partisan elective action. In non-partisan legislative action, the trade unions submit briefs on various issues to particular governmental agencies and reinforce the briefs by individually or collectively lobbying the members of parliament. Particular labour leaders frequently will establish close informal links with government parties, accepting patronage in exchange for cooperation with government programmes. This form of political action has been and continues to be predominant by a substantial margin over the other two approaches. For example, each year in January, February or March, the provincial and federal federations traditionally offer their views on such topics as wages, employment, medical care, insurance and housing to their respective governments. In order to present union views as forcefully as possible, a Labour Lobby was organized in recent years in which union members visit their legislatures en masse to confront MP's or MLA's directly with union demands.

Non-partisan elective action, however, also has an established place among Canadian labour's political arsenal. Direct intervention in elections is the norm but it is limited to endorsement of particular candidates regarded as friendly or hostile. The trade union maintains its independence from all parties, distributing its favours without regard to political label. The CNTU has now arrived at this point after an evolution that carried it from apoliticalism to legislative action.

Although partisan elective action, which involves direct affiliation with a particular party identified as "labour's party," has had a long history in Canada, it has assumed any importance only since 1940. The CCL's alignment with CCF at that time initiated a significant shift in political action that culminated in the merged federation's participation in NDP. Since 1961, the CLC and a number of its affiliates have strongly supported the

NDP as the political arm of organized labour, striving to establish in the minds of Canadian workers the same association that the British Labour Party holds for its English counterparts. The results of recent elections as well as the record of union affiliations indicate that this has not succeeded. Apart from Manitoba, no provincial NDP governments exist and in some provinces no party exists. Workers, unionized or not, continue to favour the Liberals federally and a variety of other parties provincially. To the enduring grief of NDP, Quebec, an essential province for national political success is the apotheosis of the non-partisan, legislative political approach.

SOCIAL CHANGE AND LABOUR'S POLITICAL ACTIVITIES

Many facets of contemporary life in Canada are being radically transformed. It is probable that any one major change or all taken together could shift the emphasis away from collective bargaining to political action and could strengthen direct partisan elective action in place of the traditional Gompersian approaches. For example, the continuing urbanization of the population has apparently institutionalized the NDP, giving it a solid base among many city dwellers. Increasing union support has strengthened NDP's urban base financially and numerically and given it a jumping off point to provincial and federal governmental power.[135]

Other trends in the labour force and union membership which give evidence of the displacement of blue-collar workers and the emergence of white-collar, professional and governmental employment tend to offset the effects of urbanization. Government employees, if not legally precluded from political action, may still feel that adverse political activities that pit them against a government party are inappropriate. The fact that 50 per cent of CNTU's membership is in the public employment sector undoubtedly has had a dampening affect on the Centre's enthusiasm for partisan elective action.

The middle-class oriented, white-collar and professional workers are not prone to radical politics, at least in North America, and lacking a class mentality are predisposed to an independent political posture, frequently swinging back and forth between parties as issues and candidates change. This phenomenon would also impede the forging of union or "professional association" bonds with any particular "labour party" and the discarding of legislatively oriented activities. Analysis of recent federal elections seems to refute the contention that a working class mentality is developing very strongly among even the so-called "working class." As

---

[134] Sidney and Beatrice Webb, *Industrial Democracy,* (New York: A. M. Kelley, 1965).

[135] See Wallace Gagne and Peter Regenstreif, "Some Aspects of New Democratic Urban Support in 1965," *Canadian Journal of Economics and Political Science,* November 1967, pp. 529-550.

Table 7-6

FEDERAL ELECTION RESULTS BY INCOME LEVELS AND OCCUPATIONS: 1963-1968
PERCENTAGE

	Liberals		*Conservatives*		*NDP*		*Others*	
	1963	*1968*	*1963*	*1968*	*1963*	*1968*	*1963*	*1968*
Income Levels								
Upper	46	50	34	30	9	16	11	4
Middle	42	47	31	28	15	19	12	6
Lower	30	38	37	27	13	19	20	16
Occupation								
Executives	49	51	30	34	9	11	12	4
White-Collar	51	55	27	28	12	13	12	4
Labour	38	46	29	24	17	23	9	4
Farm	33	36	49	45	8	15	10	4

Source: The New Democrat, July-August, 1968, p. 3.

Table 7-6 demonstrates, whether considered by occupation or income level, the groups which would presumably constitute the support for class politics do not view themselves as such. More lower income groups vote Conservative than NDP, although a shift to the NDP is occurring from Conservative and Liberal ranks. Those occupations encompassed by the term "labour" supported NDP more strongly in 1968 than 1963, but again this was true of their support for the Liberals.

Changes in union structure could also affect labour's political weapons. Amalgamation of craft unions into industrial unions or industrial unions into general labour organizations might generate a course of political action different from the present situation.[136] Although this may be true, the Canadian union movement is not changing its structure very rapidly. This is a product of normal institutional lag but it is also largely a result of the predominance of United States international unions. Mergers cannot take place without the parent union's approval, which likely will not be forthcoming if the need for merger is not as strong in the United States.[137]

Organizational structure in which constitutional barriers to political action exist, or the Canadian locals lack autonomy, also act as constraints. This has typified the craft unions to a larger extent than their industrial union counterparts.

The international character of Canadian unionism itself is an obstacle to partisan action. Federal or provincial parties which emphasize nationalism place the Canadian labour movement in a paradoxical position that can be rhetorically obscured but cannot be resolved. Until union structure is modified — that is, until the unions are "Canadianized," Gompersian political action will have to be the norm.

There are many issues and trends of which the political impact for labour remains to be discovered: the "radicalization" of NDP; the receptiveness of the other parties, particularly the Liberals, to new programmes of reform and welfare; the "status" of Quebec; economic and political relations with the United States. In the future, a picture of labour and politics emerges, in the absence of a national or international calamity, not too different from the contemporary position; that is, resort to legislative action merely to supplement collective bargaining; little real enthusiasm for party action; and, consequently, only partial fulfillment of a Canadian parallel to the Webbs' hypothesis of union political action.

[136] See Adolf Sturmthal, "Economic Development and the Labour Movement," in A. M. Ross (ed.), *Industrial Relations and Economic Development,* (London: Macmillan Co., 1966), pp. 165-181.

[137] John L. Fryer, "Labour's Changing Role," *Canadian Labour,* June 1968, pp. 15-17, 71-72.

8

QUEBEC LABOUR
IN PERSPECTIVE
1949-1969

Fraser Isbester

When Marcel Pépin succeeded Jean Marchand, in 1965, as President of
the Confederation of National Trade Unions, he turned immediately to
the basic issues of wages, hours and working conditions. Marchand's legacy
was a modern business union: tough, self seeking, ideologically uncommitted, and poised to adapt itself to whatever the political and economic
future might bring.

As 1965's future evolved into the reality of 1970, it brought Pépin:
two changes in the provincial government (from Liberal to Union Nationale and back to Liberal); a change in the Quebec Labour Code; an up-
surge of "grass roots" unrest which, while not exclusively confined to
Quebec's labour unions, has been distinguished in Quebec by a high degree
of violence and threats of violence; a revivified rival central labour body
in the Quebec federation of Labour (CLC); an undeniable tendency of
press, public and many union members to identify the CNTU with the
separatist elements in Quebec's political mix; and finally, and most important, a high and sustained pace of industrial growth, partially pur-
chased with a spiralling rate of inflation — a spiral that has done little
to reduce Quebec's high regional unemployment rates and a provincial
unemployment rate that has chronically exceeded the national rate.

For professional Quebec-watchers, the month to month adjustments
of the CNTU and its President to changing economic, social and political
circumstances has been one of the most fascinating aspects of the past
five years. No single institution in Quebec is more essential for a comprehension of the "quiet revolution" and its progress than the CNTU.

Although Quebec's unions initiated and remain central to the quiet
revolution, they are by no means in control today. They are no longer

initiating change; instead, they are borne along by the currents of change. Quebec has followed the classic pattern of revolutionary movements, whether "quiet" or "noisy." By 1961, it was clear that Quebec was undergoing a bourgeois revolution in which the alliance of the working people and the newly emergent middle class had gained for each its immediate goal but had left the future indeterminate. Events in Quebec are proving once more (if more proof were needed) that pragmatic self-interest is the outstanding characteristic of groups of "committed" working men whose livelihood stems from a general acceptance of "the logic of industrialism."

As ever, Quebec is different; while its unions, in common with unions in the rest of Canada, may be narrowly pragmatic, the milieu in which they have sought their ends and the resultant method, has been at variance from the Canadian pattern. Quebec's unions have worked as much by political as by economic means. Understanding the present state of union-management relations in the province thus requires some explanation of recent Quebec labour history.

Quebec's unions in 1970 showed an improvement in the balanced strength between those affiliated to the Canadian Labour Congress (CLC) and those affiliated to the Confederation of National Trade Unions (CNTU).[1] This balance, of relatively recent duration, may be traced to the change in economic circumstances and the social shift that so markedly affected the people of Quebec and their institutions during World War II. However, the public reaction to internal divisions within the CNTU and the political reactions of a radical element in 1970 may weaken the relative position of the CNTU.

The CNTU was originally a confederation of Catholic unions, most of which were conceived, organized, subsidized and given direction by the Catholic Church in Quebec.[2] In their beginnings, their primary motive was non-economic preservation of the cultural integrity of French Canada. In contrast the CLC inherited a long tradition of trade unionism and its member unions have always had the improvement of the wages, hours of work, and working condition of their members as their major goal. No long-term goal could be enunciated for the CLC or any of its affiliates. Of the two, the CLC unions are much older.

Between 1827 and 1900, the idea of trade unionism and its mani-festation in the trade unions themselves migrated from the south and took root in Quebec's soil.[3] This was the period of Canada's preparation for the

---

[1] According to the figures available in November 1970, Quebec had about 606,000 labour unionists of whom 207,000 were members of locals of unions affiliated to the CNTU.

[2] For a good, concise account of the development of the Catholic unions during their first fifty years, see Samuel H. Barnes, "The Evolution of Christian Trade Unions in Quebec" in Aranka Kovacs ed., *Readings in Canadian Labour,* (Toronto: McGraw-Hill, 1961).

[3] The most recent, and certainly the most exhaustive study, of this early period of trade union growth is contained in Eugene Forsey's essay, "Insights into Labour History," *Industrial Relations,* Vol. 20, No. 3, pp. 445-465.

great leap to industrial maturity, and labour, no less than capital and management, was subject to many exogenous influences. It was not until 1907 that the Catholic Church in Quebec conceived a coordinated policy to consciously encourage the organization and expansion of Catholic unions.[4] These unions and their inspiration were largely "home grown" — a response to the universal and seemingly inevitable effect of industrialization upon a traditional society.

By 1921, the Catholic unions had been united in a Confederation, known then as the Federation of Catholic Workers of Canada or FCWC, with a membership representing about one-third of the total number of organized workers in Quebec. Like its affiliated unions, the Confederation was church dominated and remained so until 1946. The Confederation represented one more piece in the complex interrelationship of church, land, culture and language that has historically differentiated Quebec. After 1929, it was identified in English as the Confederation of Canadian Catholic Labour (CCCL).

THE RISE OF LAY LEADERS IN THE CNTU

World War II transformed these exclusively Catholic unions into lay-led business unions with outlook and behaviour similar to their rival unions. The change was swift and was accompanied by a number of unusually prolonged and sometimes violent strikes.

The most celebrated of these, the Asbestos workers' strike of 1949, is generally conceded to have a dual significance. It marked the maturation of the Catholic unions, and it also signaled the sea-change that has come to be known as Quebec's "quiet revolution." Jean C. Falardeau says the strike will be celebrated in history as a "quasi-revolution." [5] Father Jacques Cousineau, writing while the strike was still in progress, predicted it would live as ". . . one of the most important events in the social history of French Canada." [6] Samuel H. Barnes wrote: "This strike has taken on symbolic significance as the time when the Canadian and Catholic Confederation of Labour became of age, when it proved its independence, its courage, its new aggressiveness, and its willingness to oppose authority." [7] But Frank R. Scott and Stuart Jamieson attach the most importance to the strike. For each of them it is the critical turning point in the social history of postwar Quebec.[8]

Time has made it increasingly clear that Scott and Jamieson were correct in isolating the Asbestos strike as the critical moment. But, as Trudeau observes:

It was the date which was the determinant and not the place, nor the particular industry; chance could well have dictated that the strike break out in another location than Asbestos.[9]

The CCCL and its new leaders were ready for this highly significant strike. As Jean Marchand, then secretary-general, remarked years later,

"The strike was good; it was necessary; it is always necessary, every so often, for people to suffer together and to win once more their rights." [10] For Marchand, the strike was an exercise in union solidarity, but for all of Quebec the strike struck the first blow against the old order: it was a blow for nationalism.

Of seven months duration, the strike terminated at one-thirty in the afternoon of July 1, 1950. [11] Many, such as Trudeau, have claimed that the eventual settlement was a triumph for labour. In the absolute sense this was not true. The price paid for the material satisfactions guaranteed in the new contract was too great. In the psychic sense, however, the strike was a victory. Not only did Catholic labour fight and win, but it gained the support of the rest of organized labour. It mobilized the sympathy of the French Canadian intellectual community and it put the church in a position that demanded support of the strike. What had been a dreary, overly long, excessively subdued quarrel between labour and management in the asbestos fields came to represent instead the economic and social transformation of all French Canada. Suddenly, the province was galvanized. In retrospect, it seems that only the English Canadians were unaffected and remained aloof from the strike.

For the church, the decision to support the strikers was a Rubicon. The church in Quebec was now unavoidably committed to a new approach in industrial relations. The collective "Pastoral Letter of the Bishops of the Civil Province of Quebec," which was published in February 1950, was a clarification of this stand. [12] This document laid down a broad general scheme for the relationship of labour, church, state and management. In addition, it clearly outlined the duties and responsibilities of union chaplains. The Bishops, in effect, gave official recognition to what had already

---

[4] It should be noted that the Quebec Church first overtly participated in the affairs of organized labour in 1900, that the first Catholic unions were formed by 1901 and that prior to each May Day celebration, an effort was made by some of the Bishops to prepare and take part in the proceedings.

[5] Pierre Trudeau, *La grève de l'Amiante,* (Montreal: University of Montreal, 1955), p. 11. By permission *Editions du Jour,* Montreal.

[6] Jacques Cousineau, S. J., "La grève de l'Amiante," *Relations,* No. 103, (June 1949), p. 146.

[7] Samuel H. Barnes, "The Evolution of Christian Trade Unions in Quebec," in Aranka Kovacs, ed., *Readings in Canadian Labour* (Toronto: McGraw-Hill, 1961), p. 63.

[8] F. R. Scott in Trudeau, (ed.) *La grève,* p. ix and S. Jamieson, "Labour Unity in Quebec" in Mason Wade (ed.) *Canadian Dualism* (Toronto: Universities of Toronto and Laval Presses, 1960), p. 299.

[9] Trudeau, "La grève," p. 81.

[10] Radio Canada Interview, September 1965.

[11] The short account is based on the writer's M.A. thesis, "Another Look at the Asbestos Workers' Strike of 1949," (Dept. of History, Bishops' University, 1963). Other accounts include Trudeau, "La grève"; Jacqueline Sirois, "Asbestos Strike," *Montreal Standard,* May 28, 1949; "The Facts on the Asbestos Strike," *Engign,* May 28, 1949.

[12] Extract from "Le problème ouvrier en regard de la doctrine sociale de l'Eglise." Lettre pastorale collective des Evêques de la province civile de Québec, Les Editions Bellarmin, Montréal, 1950.

become fact: the chaplain in the union had lost his temporal power and authority, becoming no more than a religious figurehead.

As such he is neither leader, director, business agent nor propagandist. In the beginning there was need for the chaplain of these organizations to go now and then beyond his normal functions. Unionism today no longer requires this unusual action. The chaplain must take upon himself the noble function of educator. It rests with him to stimulate and encourage in times of trial, but above all to fill the minds with the wonderful social doctrine of the Church . . .[13]

Had the Church, therefore, renounced the idea of leading the Catholic union? The answer is a qualified yes. A closer examination of the facts leading up to the Pastoral Letter suggests that throughout its life the Catholic Workers' Federation was a weak instrument, financially, numerically, and administratively. Such success as it enjoyed was largely a result of the devotion of French Canadians to their faith, and the close relationship between church and state in Quebec.

From long before the reign of Maurice Duplessis, the church had worked to create and sustain good relations with each provincial government. Although it secured all of the advantageous industrial relations legislation under Liberal administrations, it worked to maintain the CCCL in a favoured status during the Duplessis years. By 1949, however, the relationship between Duplessis and the CCCL was breaking up and neither religion nor the law could hold it together. In 1949, by showing its open hostility to labour, the government also lost much of the confidence of the public.[14] The Church was thus left in an uncomfortably ambivalent position and the Asbestos strike forced its leaders to make a decision.

The strike, its inconclusive settlement and the subsequent publication of the Bishops' Pastoral Letter had another, more general effect. The spell of Maurice Duplessis — *le chef* — seemed at last to have been broken and gradually the soft voice of reform became a clamour, strident and imperative. Duplessis' National Union Party won one more election, in 1956. In 1960, leaderless, with no programme and little policy, weighted down with the guilt of numberless corrupted politicians at every level of political organization from poll to cabinet, the once invincible machine of Duplessis was vanquished by the provincial Liberal party.

It is impossible to point to a particular event, the strike, or a particular act, the Bishops' Letter, as the initiator of change. It is fair to suggest that the former unleashed the social will to change and the latter gave change a formal status. The Bishops' Letter was really the capstone, not the foundation, of a new structure of Catholic social thought in Quebec. The strike was a manifestation of the impact of improving communications technology, the rapid development of mineral and hydraulic (resources of the North) and the integration of Quebec's extensive primary production industry with its more recently developed secondary manufacturing industry.

The social discontent evident in Quebec in 1949 was composed of an analysis of economic growth, urbanization, deterioration of traditional attitudes and the viability of traditional leadership and policies, especially economic liberalism, and an awareness of greener pastures.

Among the groups that found common cause in the defeat of the Duplessis government, most prominent were the unions. In moving into the political sphere as adversaries of the government, the unions faced several problems: the probable hardening of government attitude to unions in its interpretation of the law or in the introduction of new legislation; the choice of a party — Liberal, Social Credit, or CCF; the inevitable alliances with diverse "nationalist" organizations, splinter parties of the "reform " genus, revolutionaries and intellectuals; and, most importantly, affiliation of all the Quebec unions into a single labour central.

THE EBB AND FLOW OF THE UNIFICATION MOVEMENT

Paradoxically, it was the government's repressive labour policy that most facilitated unification. In successfully opposing an attempt to alter substantially the labour law of the province,[15] and in the stand of the CCCL in Asbestos, all of Quebec's unions had rediscovered the wisdom of *e pluribus unum*. The "black eye" that the government had received as a result of its intervention in Asbestos did nothing to change Duplessis' attitude. Further clashes between strikers and police were certain.

The most serious of these battles took place during a strike in the small textile town of Louiseville. The strike followed the Asbestos pattern. It was declared illegal; it dragged on until the strikers, economically on the point of ruin, exploded in a short destructive outburst of physical violence; the provincial police intervened; the *Riot Act* was read; police violence, arbitrary arrests, illegal detentions and all the other tactics of suppression were called into play.[16] Labour's reaction was extreme. Meetings of the CCCL Executive were held to discuss the possibility of a general strike in support of the Louiseville workers. For a time it seemed as though this would surely take place.[17] Although it did not, the possibility of such an event hastened a favourable conclusion to the strike. It was the only time in the history of the province that a central labour organization had put forward the idea of a general strike.

As in the case of the Asbestos strike, the CCL and Trades Labour Congress (TLC) joined with the CCCL to form a united labour front

---

[13] *Ibid.,* p. 74.

[14] See Gérard Picard, Radio Broadcast, May 13, 1949 (mimeo), Library, New York State School of Industrial and Labour Relations, Union Files.

[15] See *Bulletin des Relations Industrielles,* Vol. 4, No. 7, (March 1949), pp. 68-69; *Le Travail,* Vol. 35, No. 12, (February 1949), p. 1, *Laborer and Learning,* February 1949, *Montreal Star,* February 3, 1949.

[16] J. P. Lefèbvre, "Louiseville," J. P. Lefèvbre, *et. al., En Grève,* (Montreal: Editions du Jour, 1963), pp. 131-177; *Montreal Star,* December 12, 1952; *Montreal Gazette,* December 12, December 17, 1952; *Le Devoir,* December 12, 1952.

[17] *Montreal Star,* December 12, 1952.

in defence of the Louiseville strikers. Not only did the international unions contribute expressions of solidarity, but they also provided the funds and the food necessary to support a continuation of the strike.

The policy of collaboration between the CCCL and the CCL was to continue and to be strengthened in the years to come. The same cannot be said of the relations between the CCCL and the TLC. By 1954, the solemn pledges of union solidarity and the uncompromising opposition to the Union Nationale were forgotten by the TLC. This is not too surprising. The TLC had never been noted for its radicalism and, if during the late 1930's and early 1940's it had seemed to swing leftward the TLC had slipped back into its conservative mold, with the return of prosperity and with the expulsion of its communist members. After the Asbestos strike, Duplessis was quick to seek a crack in the labour front. He found it, easily, in the TLC. By September 1950, only two months after the Asbestos strike, the annual convention of the Quebec Federation of Labour (TLC) was resounding to the praise heaped on Mr. Duplessis, his Minister of Labour, Mr. Antonio Barette, and the Union Nationale.[18] From that moment, the cooperative spirit built up by the Asbestos strike began a gradual deterioration. The three national centres cooperated briefly in both the 1952 CCCL strike of the retail clerks at Dupuis Frères, a large Montreal department store, and in the Louiseville strike later the same year; nevertheless, in June of 1952, the Quebec Federation of Labour (TLC), in convention, adopted a resolution denouncing the "revolutionary mentality" of the Catholic, national unions.[19] By 1954, the TLC was on the same friendly basis with the government as had once been the prerogative of the CCCL. When the CCL and the CCCL invited the TLC to join them in a march on Quebec to protest the repressive nature of new labour legislation, the TLC refused.[20] The break was thus complete.

Reginald Boisvert, in his contribution to Trudeau's *Grève de l'amiante*, concludes wryly:

> ... *We have seen in these events the total reversal of positions in the relations between the CCCL and the TLC ... Thus, while before 1949, the TLC (which forms the Provincial Federation of Labour or QFL) freely accused the CCCL of collusion with employers and the government, while the CCCL generally charged the TLC of (sic) communism, the situation today is completely the opposite. It is the QFL which accuses the CCCL of revolutionary leanings and the CCCL which accuses the QFL of collusion with employers and government.*[21]

Although the TLC, like the AFL, was officially neutral in politics, the Union Nationale could depend on the open support of a good number of its affiliated unions. As a reward for this collaboration, the TLC unions probably received preferential treatment from the government in jurisdictional disputes with the other two central bodies.[22]

The foregoing is not to suggest that the CCCL and CCL stood in solid opposition to the Duplessis government. Their individual solidarity was riddled by defection and internal disputes, so much so indeed, that to protect itself from a possibly lethal split the CCCL, after a bitterly opposed entry into provincial politics in 1952, voted to remain aloof from the 1956 election, refusing to endorse any particular candidate or any party.[23]

Shortly after the 1956 election, the Union Nationale began to find it increasingly difficult to play one union off against another and to get trade union leaders to support the party openly. The most important reason for this new development was the national merger of the TLC and the CCL in 1956 to form the Canadian Labour Congress. Provincially, the affiliated unions of these two bodies were merged in the Quebec Federation of Labour, and negotiations were begun to bring the Catholic unions into the new body.

In its demand for social legislation and in its criticism of the government's labour policies, the new Quebec Federation of Labour (QFL) showed a militancy that had not characterized its activities for many years. This was primarily the result of the infusion of "new blood" from the traditionally more agressive CCL unions. Although there may have been an element of disillusionment in the attitude of former trade union supporters of the Union Nationale, the most important single factor in turning the QFL into a bitter foe of Duplessis and the Union Nationale was the Murdochville Strike of 1957. This strike, which broke out in a small company mining town deep in the interior of the Gaspé peninsula, was to be the most serious industrial conflict that the province had seen since the Asbestos strike of 1949.[24]

The dispute was between the Gaspé Copper Mines Ltd. and the United Steelworkers of America (CLC), but from its earliest moments the strike had the solid support of the entire Quebec trade union movement. It lasted over a year. In the summer of 1957, sporadic acts of violence gave way to a serious outbreak between strikers and strikebreakers, occasioned by a "march" on Murdochville.

As a result of this violence, Duplessis was bombarded by telegrams demanding intervention. He acquiesced, arranging a temporary settlement that was satisfactory to the strikers. The dilatory way in which the

[18] *Montreal Star,* September 28, 1949.

[19] *Montreal Star,* June 17, 1952.

[20] *Montreal Gazette,* June 14, 1954.

[21] Reginald Boisvert, "La grève et le mouvement ouvrier", in Trudeau, ed., "La grève," pp. 367-368.

[22] See, for example, "Accusations leveled against QFL," *Montreal Gazette,* September 28, 1954.

[23] For an account of the debates leading to this decision, see Fernand Dansereau, "Gérard Picard et Jean Marchand interviennent en faveur d'une action politique plus pousée," *Le Devoir,* September 24, 1954.

[24] Roger Chartier, "Murdochville: les faits," *Relations Industrielles,* Vol. 12, No. 4, (October 1957), pp. 374-381; Emile Gosselin, "La marche sur Murdochville," same journal, pp. 382-383; André Raynaud, "La marche sur Quebec," same journal, pp. 383-384; *Montreal Gazette,* May 24, August 20, August 27, 1957; *Montreal Star,* August 20, August 23, 1957; "Murdochville: derniere piece au dossier," *Relations Industrielles,* Vol. 13, No. 2, (April 1958), p. 232.

Table 8-1

WAGES INDEXES, 1950-1964 (BASE, 1949)

Year	Canada	Ontario	Quebec
1950	104.9	105.0	97.0
1951	116.5	116.5	115.0
1952	126.7	127.0	125.4
1953	133.9	134.4	132.8
1954	137.4	138.3	137.3
1955	142.1	143.2	142.3
1956	150.0	150.7	150.1
1957	158.1	159.0	158.2
1958	163.9	165.0	164.3
1959	171.0	172.2	171.3
1960	176.5	177.4	177.2
1961	181.8	182.9	183.3
1962	187.5	188.5	189.7
1963	194.2	195.1	196.7
1964	201.8	202.7	205.1
1965	211.8	212.8	215.1
1966	224.2	224.1	230.2
1967	239.4	238.6	245.6
1968	255.8	255.9	262.0

Source: Calculated from figures provided by Dominion Bureau of Statistics: *Annual Review of Employment and Payrolls, 1951-1965*, Catalogue No. 72-201 (Ottawa: Queen's Printer, 1966); *Review of Employment and Average Weekly Wages and Salaries, 1957-67*, Catalogue No. 72-201 (Ottawa: Queen's Printer, 1969); *Review of Employment and Average Weekly Wages and Salaries, 1966-68*, Catalogue No. 72-201 (Ottawa: Queen's Printer, 1970).

provincial government responded to the Murdochville situation, however, together with the government's consistent refusal to modernize its labour and social legislation was enough to arouse the antagonism of the Quebec Federation of Labour (CLC). Together with the now deep-rooted opposition of the CCCL to the Union Nationale administration, this meant that at the next provincial election the government would face a labour movement more solidly united in opposition than it had ever been before. When the inevitable defeat came for the Union Nationale in June of 1960, the labour movement found itself in the unfamiliar role of kingmaker. Strangely, the merger of the CLC and the CCCL was not a byproduct, and the failure of Quebec's unions to undertake a *de jure* merger when they presented, *de facto,* a united public front is the root of the present labour antagonism in the province.

In Quebec, as in the rest of North America, the long period of

Table 8-2

UNION MEMBERSHIP AND NUMBER OF LOCALS

Year	CCCL		TLC		CCL	
	Members	*Locals*	*Members*	*Locals*	*Members*	*Locals*
1950	80,089	424	459,068	2,865	301,729	1,175
1951	86,184	440	470,926	2,982	312,532	1,231
1952	89,013	457	522,965	3,169	330,778	1,337
1953	104,486	451	558,722	3,318	352,538	1,414
1954	100,312	454	596,004	3,471	360,782	1,424
1955	99,801	445	600,791	3,598	361,271	1,532
1956	101,000	432				
1957	99,372	411			*CLC*	
1958	104,255	449			1,030,000	5,238
1959	97,092	459			1,070,129	5,404
1960	101,942	477			1,144,120	5,518
					1,153,756	5,605
	CNTU				1,122,831	5,606
1961	98,457	472			1,070,837	5,650
1962	102,186	483			1,049,145	5,652
1963	110,577	541			1,079,909	5,696
1964	121,540	623			1,106,020	5,818
1965	150,053	694			1,585,947	6,922
1966	188,401	787			1,282,039	5,905
1967	197,787	859			1,450,619	6,873
1968	201,292	1,030			1,571,514	7,312
1969	207,983	984			1,588,651	7,384

Source: Department of Labour, *Labour Organizations in Canada,* 1950 + (Ottawa: Queen's Printer, 1950-1969).

economic expansion that began in 1939 had not reached its peak in 1965. Excepting the recession of 1957, the 1950's brought exceptional prosperity to the province. Perhaps a case may be made to support the allegation that the Union Nationale "sold out" the province by allowing the exploitation of its resources by foreign capital and foreign managements. If so, it is not substantiated in the wages of labour; labour unquestionably participated in the general prosperity of the period. (See Table 8-1.)

Furthermore, the new-found vigour of the Catholic, national unions carried them to membership heights that gave them a proportionately greater percentage of the total organized labour force in Quebec than they had ever enjoyed previously. (See Table 8-2.)

The leaders of the CCCL had never been enthusiastic proponents of a merger of the three national centres. The first merger proposal in 1953 was the result of resolutions approved at conventions of both the TLC and the CCL, advocating new approaches to unity.[25] Together, the two "neutral" labour bodies formed a "Labour Unity Committee," [26] which in March 1955 reached agreement on a "Statement of Principles" to "... govern the merger of the two Congresses." Two months later, on June 9, 1955, the merger was announced. Both the TLC convention in June and the CCL convention in October unanimously approved the agreement.[27] In April 1956, the founding convention of the Congress was held in Toronto, Ontario. In addition to ratifying minor changes in the proposed constitution, the convention approved proposals to seek the affiliation of the CCCL.[28]

The CCCL was not aware of these developments. They were discussed during the conventions of 1953, 1954 and 1955. At the latter meeting, not only was the merger issue the subject of the General President's report, but it was the principal consideration of the convention.

Jean Marchand made the position of the CCCL executive clear.

Organic labour unity is not an absolute value to which all other values must be subjected, and the CCCL must not forget its origin, its past and its ideology in exchange for amalgamation with the international unions.

. . .

In place of organic labour unity, what is needed is a formula which would respect the characteristics of each group but which would be of a nature to satisfy the labour world's instinct of solidarity.[29]

One year later Marchand made the position of the CCCL even clearer:

We find ourselves faced by this dilemma: if we maintain the status quo, we are doomed to union inefficiency. The problem exists on the economic and social levels, and at these levels we suffer from a congenital defect, since our present structure does not allow us to cover the economic field that we should cover, especially since the advent of large scale basic industry.

Nevertheless, we must maintain as many of the CCCL's characteristics as we can since they have been at the base of the Confederation's value and dynamism.[30]

In February 1957, the Quebec Federation of the CCL and the TLC merged. As virtually its first piece of business, the new Quebec Federation of Labour in a unanimous vote passed a resolution that urged the executive of the CLC to find an affiliation formula that would facilitate the merger of the CCCL with the CLC.

At the thirty-sixth Convention of the CCCL, held in September 1957 at Quebec City, the delegates voted for labour unity in principal, but with certain reservations. In effect, the membership seemed to favour affiliation with the CLC on the national level but wished little redefinition of their status at the provincial level. This was not likely to appeal to some of the CLC affiliated unions.[31]

The 1959 convention was widely expected to be the "unity convention." Such was not the case. "The fact is," Jean Marchand said, "that back in 1955 the principle of affiliation was adopted by the CCCL convention provided that the CCCL could keep its 'integrity' and its freedom to expand."[32] Autonomous expansion, he said, was a stumbling block and the two parties had not found a mutually satisfying formula.[33]

In contrast to previous years, the debate was uninspired and desultory. Ex-president Picard injected a brief note of urgency with a speech in which he pressed for prompt unification and settlement of any jurisdictional disputes as they might subsequently arise. He pointed out that his own union, the National Metal Trades Federation, had already formed a joint policy committee with the United Steelworkers of America. Picard's remarks were strongly seconded by Ted Payne, who alleged that labour unity was essential to negotiate favourable contracts with the large companies, such as the Aluminum Company of Canada, which controlled the basic industries of Quebec.[34]

By 1960, affiliation was practically a dead issue. At the 1960 convention, Jean Marchand reported:

The Canadian Labour Congress would have no objection to granting the Canadian and Catholic Confederation of Labour the status of a national union on condition its affiliated unions have the right to negotiate for mergers with our syndicates and federations. If the CCCL accepts this condition there is no doubt that, strictly speaking, it will no longer have the status of a national union within the meaning of the Constitution of the CLC.[35]

Discussion of the committee's report was brief. The convention voted its adoption and resolved once more to continue affiliation talks. In a special convention held the following year, the subject of affiliation was never raised. As one former union officer remarked, "I can't recall any direct reference made to that possibility during the Convention. Moreover, I do not feel that the present CNTU leaders are very sorry about the present state of affairs . . . they were content to approve the establishment of a joint committee for the purpose of studying a 'code of ethics' which would govern the relationship between the two organizations."[36]

What caused this situation? Why should affiliation, so much the central issue of one convention after another, have completely dropped out

[25] TLC, *Proceedings, 68th Convention*, 1953, pp. 355-360, and CCL, *Proceedings, 13th Convention*, 1953, pp. 35-37.

[26] *CCL Proceedings, 14th Convention*, 1954, Resolution 33-4.

[27] *CCCL Proceedings, 15th Convention*, 1955, p. 78 and TCL *Proceedings, 70th Convention*, 1955, p. 307.

[28] *CLC, Proceedings, 1st Convention*, 1956, pp. 94-97.

[29] *Labour Gazette*, Vol. 55, No. 11, (November 1955), p. 1266.

[30] *Labour Gazette*, Vol. 56, No. 11, (November 1956), pp. 1389-1390.

[31] CCCL, *Procès verbal*, 36th Convention, 1957, p. 253.

[32] *Ibid.*, p. 218.

[33] *Ibid.*, "Report of the Labour Unity Committee," p. 104.

[34] *Ibid.*, p. 211.

[35] *Labour Gazette*, Vol. 60, No. 12, (December 1960), p. 1270.

[36] From an interview with a CNTU officer, November 1966.

of sight by 1961? No single answer is adequate but the question deserves study because it illuminates the transformation that had overtaken the Catholic, national unions during the preceding fifteen years.

The urge to merge first arose as a spontaneous reaction to the co-operative anti-government campaign that began in 1948. Weakened temporarily by the subsequent defection of the TLC from the united front, it eventually gave rise to the merger talks between the TLC and the CCL in 1955 and 1956. The idea was infectious. A combination of the three national centres was naturally both frightening and attractive to the CCCL. It is not surprising, therefore, that it became a central issue at its convention in 1955. Moreover, the clearly demonstrated weakness of the CCCL in one strike after another between 1949 and 1955 did not jibe with the new militancy with which its leadership imbued the organization. Merger with the stronger centres was thus made more attractive.

Yet, to the extent that the new leadership had defined its conception of the role of the CCCL in Quebec, the idea of merger seemed somewhat anomalous. In identifying the "new" CCCL with the "new" nationalism of Laurendeau and others, an organic tie to the international-union-dominated CLC seemed to be at least an ambiguous step, if not downright contradictory. Thus, one explains Marchand's attempt from 1955 onward to reap the benefits of both merger and independence as not only an indication of the weakness of the CCCL, but also of the absence of a long-term set of goals, and the absence of a policy based on the post-war conception of the Catholic, national unions. It may also be that Marchand, knowing exactly what he wanted for the unions, did not feel himself, sufficiently strong during the 1950's to insist upon his personal preference for continued independence. In guiding the nine member unity committee of the CCCL, therefore, he may have given sufficient support to the idea of unification to maintain his following in the unity bloc but been so adamant in his demand for an explicit definition of the CCCL's post-merger status as to effectively block the negotiations.

What of Picard's role? Though it was he who first generated and exemplified the revised militancy of the postwar CCCL, it seems from his earliest pronouncements on the subject that a merger was for him "too much, too fast." *Relations,* that former bastion of clerical conservatism, as recently as 1953 congratulated Picard for taking a strong stand in his speech to the annual convention. Invoking the memory of Henri Bourassa, the great French Canadian nationalist, and Alfred Charpentier, Picard's predecessor, the Jesuit journal urged the CCCL and its leadership to follow Mr. Picard's "instinct of independence." [37] Earlier in the same year, in commenting upon the CCCL's membership reaching the 100,000 mark, *Relations* said: "It has proved that confessional unionism is a normal thing in a Catholic country, and it ought, consequently, to stay that way." [38] As events later proved, both *Relations* and Mr. Picard were not irrevocably committed to an anti-merger policy.

In 1957, after his convention speech on affiliation, Picard declared an unequivocal "I'm for it." [39] His decision to retire from the presidency and to seek election to the federal parliament in a Montreal riding, coupled with the ominous implications of a proposed joint steelworkers-metal-workers bargaining committee, were probably enough in the final instance to put Picard on the side of the merger faction. *Relations,* in a series of articles by Father Jacques Cousineau, cautiously endorsed this stand.[40]

Why, in spite of all this, the CCCL failed to unite with the other central labour bodies is readily understandable, yet how the merger failed is not so clear. Apparently, it was the simple act of procrastination, that finished the merger move. With the passage of time, the interest of the general membership waned, the ardour of the active advocates of merger cooled and the threat of break-away unions became progressively weaker.[41] Most of all, the gradual emergence of a policy and the crystallization of the new image of the Catholic, national unions in the minds of the public and the general membership seemed to give the lie to the logic employed to justify unification.

ORGANIZATIONAL REFORMS

It was an exciting time to live in Quebec. After years of almost total and unquestioning obedience to Duplessis, the spirit of rebellion was abroad in the land. Institutions that had long been acknowledged the acme of reaction were now crying out with increasing fervour for the reform of the social and economic foundations of Quebec society. At the centre of this increasingly populous bloc of reformers and reform insti-tutions stood the CCCL, already deeply involved in the task of reforming its own structure and philosophy. Jean Marchand observed in an interview: "The province exploded with the death of Duplessis. Before he died the only ones to oppose him openly were *Le Devoir, Cité Libre,* and the Confederation of Catholic Workers of Canada." [42] Concurrently, the CCCL, under the direction of its ubiquitous Secretary General had begun a pro-gramme of internal reform and centralization.

[37] "Pour un syndicalisme nation," *Relations,* No. 156, (December 1953), p. 331.
[38] "Fête du travail et unité syndicate," *Relations,* No. 153, (September, 1953), pp. 229-230.
[39] *Labour Gazette,* Vol. 57, No. 11, (November 1967), p. 1443.
[40] Jacques Cousineau, "Que fera la CTCC?" "Lucidité et paix a la CTCC" and "Garder a la CTCC son âme," *Relations,* No. 213, (September, 1958), pp. 231-233; No. 215 (November 1958), pp. 294-295, and No. 225, (September 1959), pp. 227-230.
[41] This was not to suggest that it was entirely an empty threat. In 1955, when a long strike of the pulp and paper workers in the mills of the St. Maurice Valley failed to produce results, the International Union of Pulp, Sulphite and Paper Mill Workers supplanted the Catholic unions in mills having a total employment of over 3,000 in five communities. For three years in a row, 1958, 1959 and 1960, the Catholic, national unions actually suffered a decline in membership in spite of a reasonably successful organizing drive. Nineteen-sixty alone saw the defection of thirty-six locals with almost 2,000 members. *Labour Gazette,* Vol. 60, No. 12, (December 1960), p. 1271.
[42] H. B. Myers, *The Quebec Revolution,* (Montreal: Harvest House, 1963), p. 18.

As early as 1955, it had been suggested that any form of merger with the international unions would automatically imply internal reforms in the CCCL. Consequently, it is not surprising that the Executive submitted a resolution to the thirty-fifth convention in 1956 asking for approval in principle of structural reforms which would make the administration of the CCCL more efficient and would thus reduce its operating costs. At the thirty-sixth Convention, in 1956, the Executive was accordingly instructed to appoint a committee "whose duty it will be to draft ... one or more constitutions clearly defining the rights, duties, obligations and privileges of the new modified organizations or bodies." [43] The "reform principles" mentioned in the resolution suggested a reorganization of the CCCL into six occupational divisions from its present fifteen federations. The occupational groups were to preserve their autonomy with respect to professional affairs but their administration was to be centralized. Likewise, City Central and Regional Councils would maintain their legislative authority in regional or municipal matters but, except for certain special services, they would be administered centrally. The per capita tax would be increased and it would be collected and administered through the central organization. This would permit the CCL to assume the additional administrative load associated with the proposed centralization and expansion of services.

Not everyone was happy with this suggestion, but the following year, such was the enthusiasm for and interest in the labour unity debate that the committee's report, which was substantially the same as the recommendations of the previous year, was approved with scarcely a murmur of dissent.[44] The convention also adopted, with very little debate, a motion to strengthen the centrally controlled defence fund by means of payroll deductions pro-rated according to each member's annual salary. This move was expected to bring in an additional $600,000 per year.[45]

Centralization of the unions was thus assured, and at the 1958 convention, outgoing President Gérard Picard, strongly supported by Marchand, pushed through a resolution authorizing the CCCL secretariat to consult the Episcopate of the province of Quebec concerning the continued confessional nature of the CCCL. The retiring president urged that the word "Catholic" be dropped from the Confederation's title as it was misleading and no longer accurate. A report was promised for the next convention,[46] and in 1959, by a vote of 480 to 20, the convention adopted a resolution put forward by Jean Marchand which established non-confessional unionism, in principle if not its particulars.[47]

During the 1959 Convention, it was also decided that, in the interest of economy and following the example of the CLC, the CCCL should hold future conventions biennially.[48] The next convention, however, was to be held in 1960 and it became a milestone in the development of the Confederation. The convention approved a change of name and became La Confédération des Syndicats Nationaux (CSN) or the Confederation of National Trade Unions (CNTU). To go with the new name, the Confederation shook off the last vestiges of clerical control by adopting a new statement of principles that set forth the basic outline of the Church's social doctrine without specifically explaining its origin.

Jean Marchand had emerged victorious, the architect of an independent, non denominational confederation of national trade unions. There remained only one final move and it was not long in coming. In March 1961, Roger Mathieu, the president, resigned, claiming ". . . the tasks to be accomplished in the immediate future require the presence of someone having another preparation than my own." The following day Jean Marchand was elected president of the Confederation by the Executive Committee.[49]

This essay will return to a more complete analysis of the reformation that Marchand accomplished, but of more immediate concern is the impact of this reformation on the unification movement. The reformation eliminated all possibility of merger. Observers at every convention from 1955 to 1958 reported a large bloc of uncommitted delegates. Unsure of the merits and disabilities implicit in the merger issue, they sought an opinion. The extent of this ambivalence may be seen in the apparent contradiction between the spirited near-unanimity expressed in debate and the closeness of the vote on the merger issue in 1957. Even so, the merger faction won the vote. Why then did it lose out in the end? It lost because the gradual metamorphosis that took place in the structure, aims and outlook of the Catholic, national unions gave the undecided bloc, for the first time in many years, a recognizable framework within which to judge the merger issue. Through Jean Marchand's oratory and the changes which he and Picard affected, the membership began to see the outlines of a possible future for the CNTU as an independent and influential labour body. The death of Duplessis in 1959 and the "explosion" of nationalism that followed this event gave Marchand's vision a perspective that could not help but be appreciated by every French Canadian. From that moment, all talk of merger was wasted breath.

There were, of course, subsidiary reasons for the ultimate failure of the affiliation forces. Certainly, the most important was the possibility of a split, but one might also mention the opposition of many priests, some of whom published a pamphlet arguing strongly against all of the proposed reforms in the CCCL.[50] The by no means always cooperative attitude of the CLC, which was unwilling or unable to give much ground on the key issue of dual unions, was also an obstacle according to Mr. Marchand.[51]

Yet these were minor problems, easily overcome. The merger issue was not defeated by them. In fact, the merger issue was never defeated;

[43] *Labour Gazette,* Vol. 56, No. 11, (November 1956), p. 1393.
[44] CCCL, *Procès verbal,* 36th Convention, 1957, pp. 218-233; *Labour Gazette,* Vol. 57, No. 12, (December 1957), pp. 1447-1448.
[45] *Ibid.,* p. 1448.
[46] *Labour Gazette,* Vol. 58, No. 12, (December 1958), pp. 1366 and 1368.
[47] *Labour Gazette,* Vol. 59, No. 12, (December 1959), p. 1272.
[48] Resolution 68, CCCL, *Procès verbal,* 38th Convention, 1959, p. 267.
[49] *Labour Gazette,* Vol. 61, No. 4, (April 1961), p. 335.
[50] *Labour Gazette,* Vol. 59, No. 12, (December 1959), p. 1273.
[51] *Labour Gazette,* Vol. 59, No. 12, (December 1959), p. 1273.

it simply disappeared, drowned in the renascent nationalism that buoyed the hopes of the Confederation's postwar executive for continued independence. One French-speaking union officer who recently move from Montreal to Ottawa, remarked:

"I used to be all in favour of the merger. It seemed to be pointless and self-defeating to have the labour movement divided along such arbitrary lines. When I came to live outside of Quebec, I learned how little real awareness English Canada has of the French language and culture. After a few years you can't help being assimilated in this environment. Now, although I no longer belong to the CNTU, I wish them well. I hope they never affiliate. They are too vital a safeguard of the interests of French Canada." [52]

Near the end of his life, Mr. Duplessis' adversaries were forcing him to take the defensive; in a year or two, they might have overcome him. Nevertheless, it is doubtful whether the forces of change in Quebec had ever reached the degree of urgency that one may describe as revolutionary. The revolution may have been coming but few could feel it. Indeed, it is a measure of strength of the Union Nationale that the death of Duplessis did not leave it leaderless. With remarkably few dislocations, Mr. Paul Sauvé was able to assume the role of *le chef,* pressing forward immediately with a programme of reform. He entered into negotiations with the federal government over the long-contended issue of federal aid to the universities. He revoked Bill 34, a flagrantly pro-government, Duplessis amendment to the *Election Act.* The almost forgotten art of debating was re-introduced into the legislature. Public works were no longer denied to any constituency simply because it had voted against the government. The *Labour Relations Act* was revised in favour of the unions. Even Sauvé's political enemies found little to tax him with and it seemed as if incipient revolution might give way to orderly evolution under the continued aegis of the Union Nationale. But Paul Sauvé died four short months after the death of Duplessis. The party disintegrated and the psychological impact of Sauvé's attempted reformation served only to spread the revolutionary movement, giving it, for the first time, a province-wide basis.

It was at this time that Quebec's unions, especially the CNTU, became so important. In effect, the CLC fired the first shot with the Radio Canada producers' strike of 1959 and in the subsequent withdrawal of the Quebec locals of the Canadian Conference of Authors and Artists (CLC) from the parent union. The process of division along linguistic lines spread rapidly and Quebec nationalism was again a political force to be reckoned with. It was a new nationalism, however, which recognized the implications of industrialization and changing technology for the economy and for society.

The leading role of the CNTU is evident in the special convention of September 1961, Jean Marchand's first convention as President. In addition to the extensive structural alterations that were approved, other resolutions also indicated the considerable extent to which the CNTU had accepted the idea of centralized planning and had become an integral part of the Liberal party reform machinery. The convention also demonstrated the enormous vitality with which the Confederation had become endowed.

Debate on structural reforms took more than two days and resulted in constructive and badly needed changes. Over the years, a frequently voiced complaint at conventions had been that the quality of services, such as the technical assistance or the education programmes, given to locals of CNTU unions often varied from one federation to another, and from one central council to another, depending on the size of membership. The major aim of the structural reforms adopted in 1961 was to overcome this defect by providing assistance of a uniform quality to all local unions. Such reforms required greater centralization and, as a result, a CNTU branch office, fully financed by the CNTU, was to be established in each community then having a central council. This branch office would assume all of the functions previously performed by the council in the field of education and organization. Through another reform, the CNTU secretariat was delegated the power to decide the "minimum membership" that a federation had to have before undertaking to provide technical assistance to its local unions. If the federation's membership was below the minimum, all assistance to local unions would automatically be given by the CNTU through its branch offices. Provision was also made for the standardization of the constitution of the CNTU locals so as to achieve, first, an effective control of financial records of local unions by the CNTU treasurer, second, the protection of individual members against criminal or undemocratic practices by local leadership, and third, organization of union meetings, elections and other administrative matters according to standard procedures.

One of the main objectives of the reform was to amalgamate the existing sixteen federations into six federations that would group employees by economic sectors as follows: Federation of Building, Wood and Furniture Workers, Federation of Metal, Chemical Products and Mine Workers; Federation of Pulp, Wood, Paper, Printing and Editing, Cardboard Box and Paper Products Workers; Federation of Municipal Corporations and School Boards, Hospital and Public Service Employees; Federation of Trade, Office, and Service Employees, Barbers and Hairdressers. By 1965, thirteen federations remained, but the reorganization of central union services at the regional level was well advanced through the intermediary of the sixteen affiliated central labour councils.[53] The Convention of 1961 also adopted a number of regulations making disaffiliation more difficult for a union, a central council or a federation.[54]

In economic matters, the CNTU seemed to move very close to the New Democratic Party platform without formally approving it. No doubt the influence of Gérard Picard was still extensive in doctrinal matters, but

---

[52] Interview with a former CNTU official.

[53] Department of Labour, *Labour Organization in Canada* (Ottawa: Queen's Printer, 1966), p. 84.

[54] CNTU, *Procès verbal,* Convention Special, 1961; *Labour Gazette,* Vol. 62, No. 1, (January 1962), pp. 35-36.

there was a new respect for Michel Chartrand, leader of the New Democratic Party in Quebec, who, attending conventions as a fraternal delegate, had for years been virtually shunned by members and Executive alike.[55] A debate on unemployment gave rise to a spate of ideas and opinions on state intervention, nationalization, and socialism, the preaching of which had previously been the doubtful prerogative of the radicals and intellectuals within the CNTU. In 1961, the ideas were obviously accepted and supported by the vast majority of the rank and file.[56] There are four possible reasons for this leftward shift in the orientation of the Confederation. First, it had been consciously encouraged by the Executive committee under the three presidencies of Picard, Mathieu and Marchand. Thus, *Le Travail,* the union's bi-monthly publication, edited by Gérard Pelletier who was at that time an outspoken socialist, had been waging a long-term campaign to educate its readers on the subject of socialism. Second, Pope John XXIII's encyclical, *Mater et Magistra,* seemed, in the words of Marchand, to be ". . . confirmation of certain points of view we have been upholding." [57] The encyclical dealt at some length with the idea of socialization, which it defined as the "progressive multiplication of relations in common life." It expressed the Church's concern for the progressive alienation of the working man from the ownership of the productive enterprises and, in effect, gave the Church's approval to certain measures such as social security, government intervention in private enterprise, socialization of certain vital facilities and worker participation in ownership and management.[58] During the special convention of 1961, much was made of this document and the happy coincidence of its pronouncement with the fortieth birthday of the CNTU. Jean Marchand stressed its liberating aspects: ". . . (it) should protect us, at least for a while, from the attacks of the social conservatives." [59]

The third reason for the increased interest in socialism was undoubtedly the auspicious beginning made by the New Democratic Party. Labour unions across the country were endorsing a resolution that urged labour unions and local councils to help in building an effective political organization.[60] A possible fourth reason was the current vogue for *la planification,* the result of the drive by Quebec's new Liberal government to modernize all aspects of public administration and to impose some order on the economic growth of the province. This word had caught the imagination, if not the comprehension, of most French Canadians.

Although the tenor of that convention may have been socialistic, the delegates left no doubt that the CNTU was a supporter of the Liberal party. René Levesque, a key figure in the Radio Canada strike and now Quebec's Minister of Natural Resources, was a guest, speaking on the urgency of retraining and on the imperative of continuing government-CNTU collaboration.[61] His statement was extravagantly applauded by the delegates and he was effusively welcomed by the executive. Subsequently, the 1961 federal election gave Marchand the opportunity to emphasize the Liberal party connection and, in addition, to speak out strongly against the growing force of French Canadian nationalism. This marked a major break with the leftist political inclination that the CNTU leadership had inherited from Gérard Picard. Yet it is not necessarily true that Marchand was any less convinced of the efficacy of some of the techniques of socialism. The key to the meaning of the CNTU's political attitude under Marchand lies in a resolution that was passed endorsing Marchand's election-time stand. It is nothing less than an endorsement of American style political opportunism — Gomperism — and a repudiation of the principle that was being so actively promoted among the CLC affiliated unions — organic and financial ties to the socialist party at the federal and provincial level.[62]

Marchand could not help but be aware that in the political field, the CNTU leadership had gone one way while the rank and file had gone another.[63] As for separatism, it was Marchand's opinion that the anti-English feelings were developed exclusively in educated circles and that no hint of it could be found in the working class.[64] Furthermore, the Church, which still retained some influence in the unions, was now urging labour to take more responsibility in the economic and political life of the community.

In 1964, in his report to the biennial convention, the President made a moderate plea for objective, serious, patient study of the problems involved in economic planning rather than one-sided advocacy of *la planification*.[65] This was in marked contrast to previous conventions where planning was a magic word and where fraternal delegates from European organizations spoke as though they had been asked to publicly commend the various kinds of economic planning in Western Europe. Mr. Roger Bonety, Chief Liaison Officer between the French Confederation of Christian Workers and the Commissariat au Plan, followed Marchand to the rostrum. He warned the CNTU delegates that all was not well with economic planning in France and that planning the economy required a new training, greater knowledge, new technical skills and a new brand of vigour.[66]

---

[55] This is a personal observation but one which is shared by other observers at the CNTU conventions as well as by members of the executive and by general members who were interviewed.

[56] Again, a personal observation.

[57] Pope John XXIII, *Mater et Magistra*, (Montreal: Palm Press, 1961).

[58] *Ibid.*

[59] *Labour Gazette*, Vol. 62, No. 1, (January 1962), p. 34.

[60] *Ibid.*, p. 31.

[61] *Labour Gazette*, Vol. 62, No. 1, (January 1962), p. 31.

[62] CNTU, *Procès verbal*, 40th Convention, 1962.

[63] As witness the strong labour support of Social Credit at the polls, June 18, 1962 in spite of Marchand's television, radio and newspaper appeals to the contrary.

[64] Interview with Mr. Marchand, Radio Canada, September 1965.

[65] CNTU, *Procès verbal*, 41st Convention, 1964.

[66] It should also be noted that the CNTU had hired in 1963 a new economic advisor, Mr. Bernard Solasse, a former French labour official, who, prior to joining the CNTU permanent secretariat, was in charge of economic studies and education in the French Confederation of Christian Workers. I am told that Mr. Solasse, during education sessions, had advised a number of CNTU members that 'the Canadian "open economy" cannot be subjected to the same kind of economic planning as the French economy; that while it may be possible to derive some inspiration from the principles of French planning, the French techniques cannot be abruptly imported into Canada.'

Flowing from the Marchand and Bonety speeches and the instructional work of Mr. Bernard Solasse and members of the Education Department of the CNTU, there was a growing realization on the part of the rank and file delegates that a labour congress without highly competent and specialized technical advisors could not survive in the increasingly complex industrial urban society of Quebec. This marked a major change in the orientation of the CNTU, an organization that traditionally had been close to its rank and file. The realization found concrete expression in the recommendations put forward and adopted by the Convention in 1964. Among these recommendations, bearing on the educational and technical needs of the labour movement were: that the educational sessions in economics be increased at all levels of the Confederation under the auspices of the newly established Office of Economic Training; that the recently established Office of Industrial Engineering undertake the training of local technicians in the field of time-study and job evaluation; that two new educational specialists be added to the permanent staff of the Education Department.[67]

The Convention was marked by an unusually business-like attitude, not only in the matter of economic planning but also in all of its deliberations. Underlying this calm less polemical behaviour were three major influences. First, the atmosphere of political uncertainty engendered on the one hand by a series of debilitating minority federal governments, and, on the other hand, by recent violent manifestations of provincial separatism, hung depressingly over the delegates. Second, the increasing numerical strength of the unions — a 40 per cent gain since the gloomy days of the Asbestos and Louiseville strikes — probably contributed to a greater sense of self-assurance and maturity. Third, it is also likely that the general and unbroken trend of improvement in the province's economic situation generated a moderating influence.

In general, it might be concluded that the CNTU had passed through the crisis of political maturation and reached a serene, slightly left-of-centre, but essentially self-interested, independent adulthood. It has proved itself to be a vital and forceful organization, willing and able to adapt to changing conditions What then of the drive for labour unity? By the time of the special convention of 1961 the movement for merger was moribund and the specter of renewed union rivalries was discernible.

RAIDING RETURNS

In a discussion of the CNTU's new image, President Marchand explained in 1962:

I have been asked if the wish expressed in my report to extend CNTU activities on a nationwide basis could be interpreted as a challenge to the Canadian Labour Congress and a declaration of war against international unions. This was not my intention. I said that the CNTU must

*be expanded according to the most appropriate and most efficient formula,
that is to say, affiliation to the CLC or the achievement of labour unity
according to any means agreed upon by the parties could very well be that
'most appropriate formula'. Mass union raiding does not seem to me any
more possible than it is desirable for either party.*[68]

In 1964, however, mainly at the insistence of the unions, the provincial
government passed a new labour law[69] that incorporated the former
Professional Syndicates Act, the *Industrial Relations Act* and a number of
lesser acts and by-laws to form Title One of a new and comprehensive
labour code for the province.

Based on the American federal legislation, Title One is an exceptionally liberal law, extending full union privileges to all employees below
the status of foreman and excepting only policemen and firemen. The
CNTU quickly entered the new organizing territories thus opened up —
hospital employees, provincial and municipal government employees,
nurses and teachers. The effect of this rapid expansion, similar in kind,
if not in degree, to that of the CIO in the United States in 1936, was to
draw new members from other unorganized sectors such as office and
clerical workers, and from those already organized by the internationals.
The organizing rivalry thus unleashed was soon the basis of renewed
raiding, a situation that was further aggravated when, in the summer
of 1964, the CLC accused the CNTU of practicing segregation on religious
and nationalist ground.[70] At the CNTU convention in September of that
year, Marchand returned the compliment. Among the CNTU president's
more moderate remarks was a statement to the effect that when the
country is already deeply divided, the CLC president had shown great
irresponsibility in unjustly accusing the CNTU of racism.[71] Furthermore,
Marchand stressed, if the CNTU can be charged with discrimination
because the majority of its members are French Canadian, then surely,
using the same logic, the CLC is also discriminatory.[72]

---

[67] CNTU, *Procès verbal,* 41st Convention, 1964, Resolution No. 9, p. 5 and Res.
62-66, p. 17 of inserted list of resolutions and decisions following p. 408.

[68] *Labour Gazette,* Vol. 62, No. 1, (January 1962), p. 37.

[69] 12-13 Elizabeth II, c. 45, 1964.

[70] *Canadian Labour,* Vol. 9, No. 7-8, (July-August 1964), p. 25. See also:
"Labour Cannibals" (editorial), *Canadian Transport,* Vol. 50, No. 5, (March
1, 1964), p. 2, and "La CSN sabôte le syndicalisme industriel" (Statement
by Roger Provost, President, QFL), *Canadian Labour,* Vol. 9, No. 10, (October
1968), p. 49.

[71] This remark echoes to some degree the reaction of the Royal Commission on
Bilingualism and Biculturalism to the English-Canadian attitude to the French-
Canadians. Jean Marchand was at this time an alternate chairman of this
commission and according to his own and others' remarks he was shocked
at the total indifference to French Canada and its problems which was uni-
versally exhibited at Commission hearings west of the lakehead. One is
tempted to conclude that there was indeed, perhaps unconsciously, an element
of cultural defensiveness in the aggressive organizing drive which Marchand
unleashed in 1963.

[72] *Labour Gazette,* Vol. 65, No. 1, (January 1965), p. 30.

Marchand's contention was accurate. Unlike the days of the Asbestos strike, the CNTU was now able to provide a high quality service to its members. It had the resources and seemed more willing to commit them than were the AFL affiliated bodies. This fact, and not nationalism, lay behind the drawing power of the CNTU.[73] For the first time since its founding the CNTU grew more rapidly than the CLC.

Not everyone in the CNTU was happy with this situation though this was scant comfort to Mr. Jodoin or to the President of the Quebec Federation of Labour, Mr. Laberge. The aggressive organizing campaign brought the administrative and financial resources of the CNTU near the breaking point and highlighted two particular problems. The first was lack of provincial aid in the administration of an overly ambitious union education and assistance programme. The dual result was failure to achieve the goals of the programme and financial difficulties. A second major problem, which was the result of a prematurely rapid expansion, was the lack of trained, responsible leaders at the local union level. This led to inefficient administration and, in a few cases, to corrupt practices. It also contributed to the rash of wildcat strikes, slowdowns and walkouts that plagued industrial relations in Quebec, beginning in 1965.

The problem of allocating resources so as to ease this strain was primarily the responsibility of Marcel Pépin, who from 1962 to 1965 was the secretary general of the union. As an administrator Pépin was superb — one of the little known "new men of power." Marchand, the visionary, initiator of change, drew the attention of the press and the sympathy of the public. Pépin, the administrator, remained a unionist, sharing the pragmatic, short-term outlook of those with whom he worked. One columnist summed up the difference between the two men in terms of their respective attitudes to labour conflict and radical trends in the CNTU.

Marchand in his later days as President tended to put the brakes on militancy. Pépin however says: "It is not our job to snuff out grass roots initiatives. We must rather encourage and support them." He does not worry about securing public acceptance of union actions.[74]

When Marchand left the presidency to win election as a Federal Member of Parliament in the Liberal party, Pépin brought to the presidency a narrower view of the CNTU's role and scope in Quebec. The immediate consequence was a growth in the ideological committment of member unions and a pressure for the re-establishment of local autonomy. This corresponded fairly closely to Pépin's own thinking about "grass roots initiatives" and it probably conformed to some of his own responses to the problems of centralization. Consequently, although he could profess a belief in political action, he was not obliged to commit the CNTU. Instead, the unions and union locals were free to commit themselves or not, as they wished, to the labour-oriented political parties. Pépin was able to neglect long-term reforms and concentrate on the development of more effective bargaining for short-term goals.

THE CNTU, THE QFL AND QUEBEC NATIONALISM — 1965-69

Pépin's focus on the immediate needs of labour can be easily justified. In 1969, a mere 27 per cent of Quebec's labour force was organized. Sixty-nine per cent of the blue-collar manufacturing labour force, 80 per cent of the miners, 41 per cent of the hospital employees, 32 per cent of other employees in the public sector, 29 per cent of service employees, 19 per cent of retail store employees and 6 per cent of the clerical workers in the area of finance banking and insurance were organized. Although wages have increased more in Quebec than in Canada as a whole, the average Quebec industrial wage, in absolute terms, is less than the national average. Within the province itself, the industrial wage earners have a higher average per capita income than employees in the public or service sectors. Unemployment, always of serious proportions, was, in 1970, at 6.9 per cent, substantially above the national average of 5.0. It would be fair to generalize that more than any other region of North America, Quebec continues to be haunted by the spectre of hard times that was the heritage of the 1930's.

However necessary and justifiable this pressure for immediate improvement of the work conditions in Quebec, Marchand's carefully crafted, centralized CNTU was being subjected to strong centrifugal pressures as a result. Ultimately, this led to a disintegration of the solid front in the area of collective bargaining goals and strategies. In retrospect, the decentralization that was formalized in the biennial Congress of 1968 was foreseeable and not necessarily inimical to the long-term goals established in the earlier years.

The CNTU's major problem, and the major problem for the QFL as well, has been the accommodation of the emergent public service unions. Formed under new and untested legislation, comprised of persons unused to unions and the negotiating process, the CNTU's task, in the early stages of organizing the public sector, was relatively simple and best conducted centrally. Each area of public employment was organized separately and the gains in one area became the basis for more effective organization and gains in another area. The right to organize, was won first by the hospitals in 1964, followed by the provincial civil service, 1965 and 1966, then Hydro Quebec engineers and construction workers 1966, then civil service professional employees, 1966, and teachers, 1967.

---

[73] I have been told repeatedly that the determining factor in switching is the quality of service. An active union member who left a CLC affiliated union in Montreal to join the CNTU in 1964 put it this way to me. "Those guys from the international really neglected us. We used to see them once a year, when the contract was expiring. They would quickly sign a new contract and then quickly take a plane back to the States. Then, all year grievances and problems kept piling up and nobody did anything about them. With the CNTU, at least the guys stay here."

[74] Evelyn Dumas, *Montreal Star,* January 30, 1969.

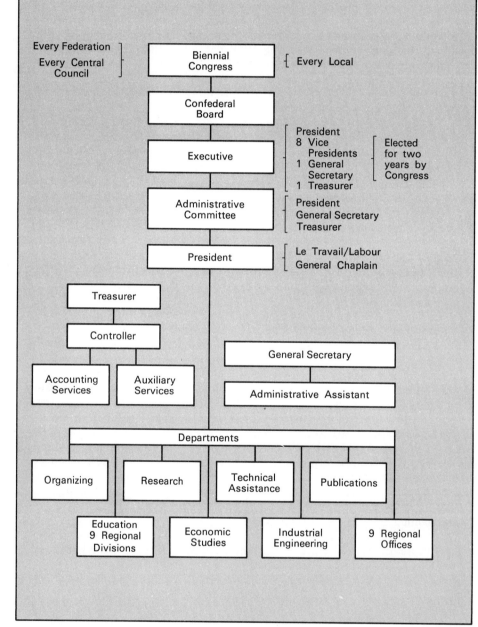

Figure 8-1

STRUCTURE OF THE CNTU

Throughout this period, the unions had an additional advantage — the lack of a coherent government policy on salaries. Seemingly, the Labour Code of 1964 was enacted without thought to its great implications. The Lesage government, faced with crisis situations region by region and area by area, had no opportunity to reflect on policy or guidelines; it simply reacted. The change of government in mid-1966 also changed the labour relations policy. In the fall of 1966, the government introduced wage guidelines, allegedly to put a ceiling on local school board expenditures. The teachers, by early 1967 had made clear their intention to have a greater increase than the budget guidelines. A strike ensued. Special legislation (Bill 25) put the teachers back in their classrooms and fixed regional salary schedules for one year. For the first time since 1964, the unions had lost a round.

Pépin and his secretary general, Robert Sauvé, were not slow to recognize the implications. Sauvé argued cogently for an integration of the bargaining strategies of the new organization. Only centralization and a united front by all of Quebec's unions could overcome the determined stand of a strong government, he contended. In his pragmatic fashion, Marcel Pépin set about creating this united front in the summer of 1967. Two groups presented problems. The Q.F.L. with 25,000 members in the public sector and the Association of French Catholic Teachers (Corporation des Enseignants du Québec) with an equal membership both asked for a no-raiding pact as a prior condition to their joining the CNTU in a common front in public service bargaining. Two years later, the organizations were no closer to agreement. As Evelyn Dumas, writing in the *Montreal Star* concluded of these talks, about the only thing that they had accomplished was improvement in communication and understanding between the various groups.[75]

Meanwhile, even within the CNTU, the attempt at uniting the various public service unions was breaking down and leading to some degree of factionalism. Then, in November 1967, Robert Sauvé resigned his post as secretary general.[76] In effect, Sauvé challenged the CNTU. He disclaimed the "centralize or die" epithet that had been attached to him, but argued for a strong federal organization with central policy determined and adhered to by member unions.

He was replaced by Raymond Parent who, largely because of the challenge implicit in Sauvé's resignation, was able, with Pépin, to unite the leadership of the CNTU unions around a policy of reform. In essence, the CNTU returned to its pre-1961 structure, to a decentralized organization in which responsibility for organization, education and collective bargaining reverted to the unions and the Confederation provided some special services such as research and special studies, communications and publications. The Confederation remained the voice of the CNTU on matters of public policy. (See Figure 8-1.)

Events move quickly and sometimes more quickly in Quebec than

[75] *Ibid.*

elsewhere. The rise of Quebec nationalism in the period from 1966 to 1970, coupled with the autonomy created by the organizational changes of the CNTU, has led to an identification of member unions with the nationalist or separatist organizations. Initially, this identification could be useful as an organizing device but ultimately it is extremely dangerous. If the effect of increasing nationalism is negative, some of the blame will be attached in the public mind to the CNTU. If Parti Quebecois grows in strength, its ties are to the lower levels of union leadership. To date, Mr. Pépin has maintained an independent political stance. He tends to think of problems and their resolution at local or union level and that is the stratum of union organization that is now so heavily politicized. The Confederal Bureau of the CNTU no longer influences the course of the quiet revolution. Rather, it reacts to external change communicated to it principally through its affiliated unions and locals.

The future of unionism in Quebec today is uncertain. The Quebec Federation of Labour, now quite as politically active as the CNTU and acting with increased autonomy, may be led into the organizational ambit of the CNTU. If it is not, one can only conclude that the future holds continued debilitating inter-union conflict and that the effectiveness of unions in the face of a strong, determined government will probably deteriorate.

[76] See "Text of Letter of Resignation of Robert Sauvé," *Le Travail,* Vol. 43, (December, 1947), p. 21.